28 CHINESE

RUBELL FAMILY COLLECTION

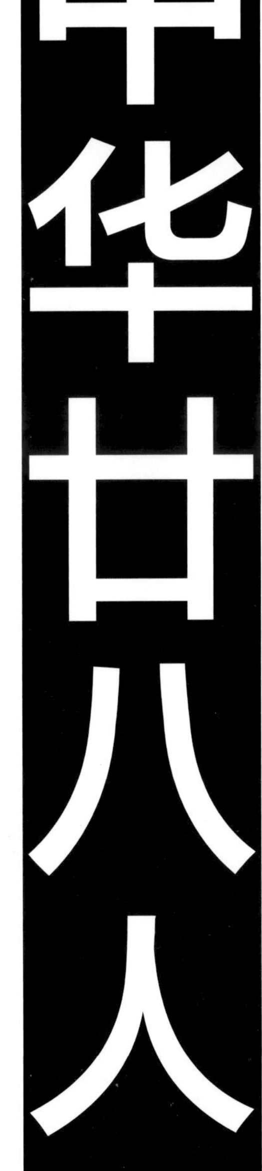

This catalog is published on the occasion of the exhibition
28 Chinese
at the Rubell Family Collection/
Contemporary Arts Foundation, Miami, FL
December 4th, 2013 through August 1st, 2014

Publication and Exhibition
Editor and Director of the Rubell Family Collection: Juan Roselione-Valadez
Design & Photography: Chi Lam
Chief Translator and Researcher: Judy Yi Zhou
Translators: Lidu Yi, Chi Lam, Ruben de Bie, Aaron Gu, Ina Yinan Li, Yijun Mao, Jin Yue Li
Proofreading and Editing: Cara Despain, Laura Randall, Judy Yi Zhou
Collection Manager: William Vargas
Foundation Education Manager: Cara Despain
Registrar: Laura Randall
Associate Registrar: Matthew Snitzer
Archivist: Anita Sharma
Installation Technician: Leyden Ayure
Assistant Technician: Sonia Alvarez
Press Officer: Tanya Selvaratnam
Foundation Intern: Noel Kassewitz

ISBN: 978-0-9911770-0-4

Library of Congress Control Number: 2013954532

Printed by Rex Three, Sunrise, FL

Typeface: Trade Gothic, Heiti, Helvetica

Rubell Family Collection
Contemporary Arts Foundation
95 NW 29th Street
Miami, Florida 33127
United States of America
info@rfc.museum
www.rfc.museum

Cover: Liu Wei, *Truth Dimension No. 2* (detail), 2012, oil on canvas, 87 1/8 x 70 2/8 in. (222 x 180 cm), acquired in 2012

出版此场刊是为了艺术展
中华廿八人
于卢贝尔家族收藏/当代艺术基金会
美国佛罗里达州迈阿密
二零一三年十二月四日到二零一四年八月一日

出版和展览
卢贝尔家族收藏的编辑和主任: Juan Roselione-Valadez
设计与摄影: 林志坚
首席翻译与研究员: 周易
翻译: Lidu Yi, 林志坚, Ruben de Bie, 顾泱, 李一楠, 毛怡君, Jin Yue Li
校对和编辑: Cara Despain, Laura Randall, 周易
收藏馆经理: William Vargas
基金会教育部经理: Cara Despain
登记员: Laura Randall
助理登记员: Matthew Snitzer
档案保管员: Anita Sharma
安装技术员: Leyden Ayure
助理安装技术员: Sonia Alvarez
新闻发布员: Tanya Selvaratnam
基金会实习生: Noel Kassewitz

ISBN: 978-0-9911770-0-4

Library of Congress Control Number: 2013954532

Printed by Rex Three, Sunrise, FL

Typeface: Trade Gothic, Heiti, Helvetica

Rubell Family Collection
Contemporary Arts Foundation
95 NW 29th Street
Miami, Florida 33127
United States of America
info@rfc.museum
www.rfc.museum

封面: 刘韡, 《真实维度 No. 2》(截面), 2012, 布面油画, 87 1/8 x 70 2/8 寸 (222 x 180 厘米), 收藏于 2012

Mera, Don, and Jason Rubell in conversation with Juan Roselione-Valadez, Director of the Rubell Family Collection/Contemporary Arts Foundation

September 2013

Juan: Last September you made another intense visit to China where you visited 42 studios in just over one week. This was your fourth trip there in the last four years and you've conducted 100 studio visits in the course of five trips. Many of these artists you're visiting are not well known outside of, or inside of, China. These trips have culminated in our exhibition. It seems to be of particular interest to you, to have the ability to engage with the artists you may collect and exhibit and to be privy to their process. Why is the artist's studio so alluring to you? What is your fascination with them? Why is it so important for you to witness the artistic practice and progress?

Mera: It's completely inside of our practice as collectors; there is something essential in the experience that we get visiting the studio. Now, what should be said in advance is that we don't visit the studio to avoid the gallery. We always acquire artwork via a gallery. It's interesting because in China the gallery has been slow in coming around to representing artists, or the artist has been slow in recognizing the gallery's role. But that's happening less now because they understand the function of a gallery and how important it is. For us, because the artist is so new and oftentimes they haven't even had a solo exhibition—though they may have been part of a group exhibition—the studio represents entering the inner, inner sanctum of the artist's practice and life. It's a very sacred place; it's where we see—it's a comfort zone that the artist has that we cannot take for granted. We always feel like someone is letting us into a very intimate experience about who they are, why they make the work, and it gives us a real opportunity for us to engage, but also to feel and experience and learn to trust the artist, and think about whether this artist's work should be in our collection.

Don: Even the very best of the young artists do not come out fully formed and it's very important for us to visit the studio, to speak to the artist, to understand the ambition of the artist, the vision of the artist, and to look at the work in an unedited

梅拉，多恩和杰森·卢贝尔与卢贝尔家族收藏／当代艺术基金会主任Juan Roselione-Valadez 对话

2013年9月

Juan: 去年九月你们再一次到访中国的时候，在一周内就拜访了上达42名艺术家的工作室，行程相当紧张。在过去四年内的五次旅程中，你们一共拜访了超过一百多名艺术家的工作室，当中很多是甚至在中国都不很有名的小众艺术家。这些旅行和经历都在我们这次的展览中得到了淋漓尽致的展现。看起来你们似乎很享受与各位艺术家交流融入的的过程。为什么你们对艺术工作室如此之感兴趣？是什么让你们这么着迷？为什么你们觉得参与进艺术家创作的过程如此重要呢？

梅拉： 这完全是我们收藏家的本能，拜访各个艺术工作室对我们是非常关键的。这里需要澄清的是，拜访艺术工作室并不是为了躲避画廊，我们一直都还是通过与画廊来购买作品的。因为在中国，画廊和艺术家没有很好的对接，导致了一些画廊不能及时联系到艺术家展示优秀的作品，或者有时艺术家没有清楚地认识到画廊所扮演的角色。但现在这个情况正在一点点好转因为越来越多的艺术家意识到了与画廊合作的重要性。对我们来说，正是因为很多新兴艺术家即使参与过一些集体的展览，但还没有办过自己的个人展，所以拜访他们的工作室代表着能更深入地了解他们艺术创作与生活的一个机会。工作室是一个神圣的地方－－我们不应认为拜访艺术家的舒适区是理所当然的事情。我们总觉得拜访他们的工作室就像是被他们邀请到了他们最私密的空间，让我们真实的看到他们是什么样的人和他们创作艺术的初衷。这给了我们很好的机会去参与其中但与此同时也是一个彼此建立信任的过程，这些都让我们更好地决定是否要把他们的作品纳入我们的收藏。

多恩： 即便是最优秀的年轻艺术家也没有完全羽翼丰满，所以对我们而言，拜访他们的工作室是非常重要的，因为给我们机会与他们对话，了解他们的创作初衷、抱负和视野，观赏未经修饰的作品，并了解这些艺术家的真实潜力。

Juan: 艺术家的性格，人生经历或行为举止是否会影响你对他们作品的看法呢？ 尤其在中国这样一个有着完全不同文化背景的国家。

多恩： 在某种程度上来说或许会有一些，但是我认为很少，因为最终他们的作品呈现的就是他们

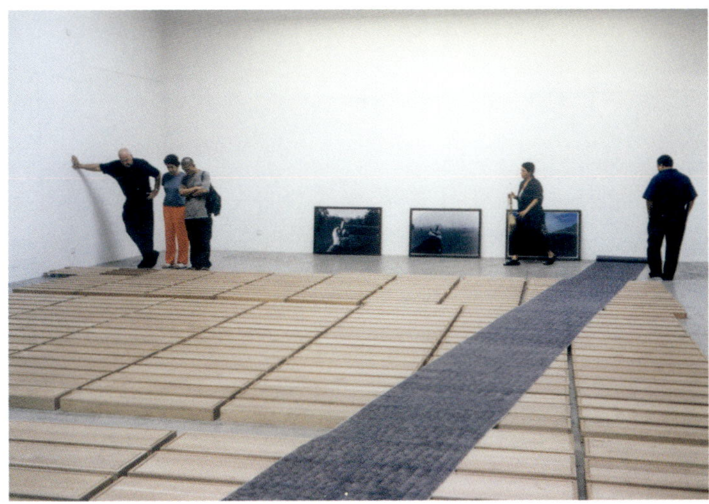

Don and Jennifer Rubell, Zhang Huan, Mera Rubell with Ai Weiwei in his studio, Beijing, Sept 2001
多恩和珍妮弗·卢贝尔, 张洹, 梅拉·卢贝尔以及艾未未在他的工作室, 北京, 2001年9月

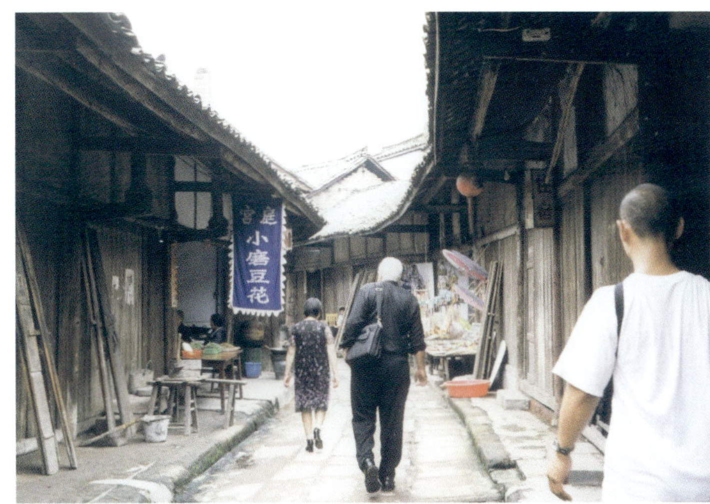

Don Rubell and Zhang Huan, Beijing, Sept 2001
多恩·卢贝尔和张洹, 北京, 2001年9月

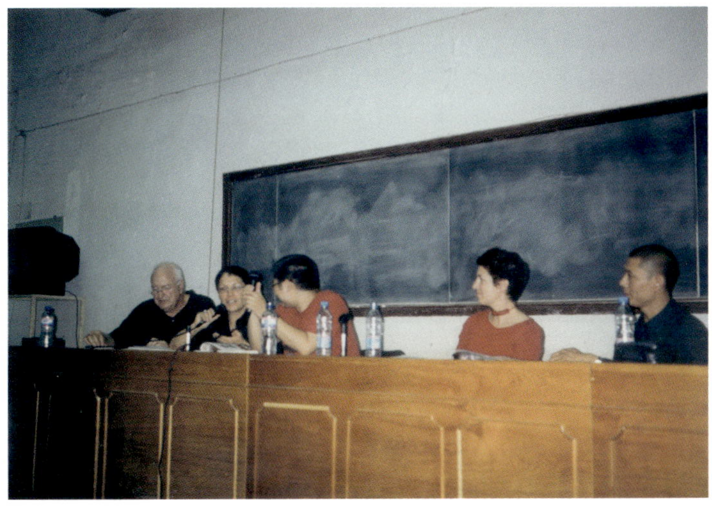

Don, Mera and Jennifer Rubell with Zhang Huan at Xi'an Academy of Fine Arts, Xi'an, Sept 2001
多恩, 梅拉和珍妮弗·卢贝尔以及张洹在西安美术学院, 西安, 2001年9月

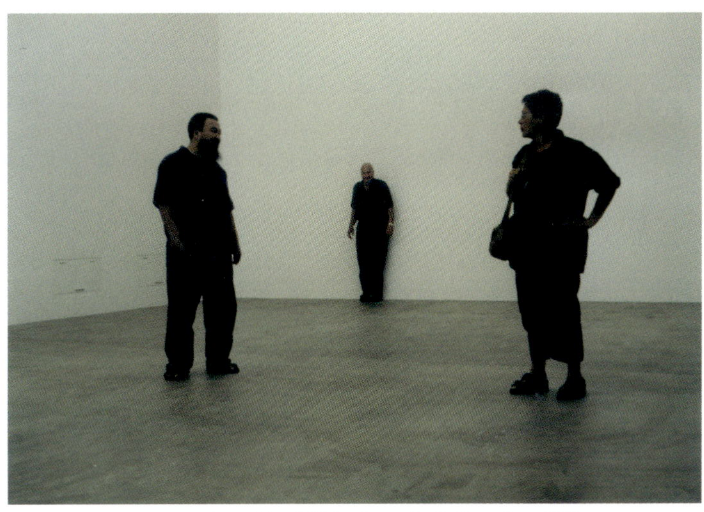

Ai Weiwei, Don and Mera Rubell in Ai Weiwei's studio, Beijing, Sept 2001
艾未未, 多恩和梅拉·卢贝尔以在艾未未的工作室, 北京, 2001年9月

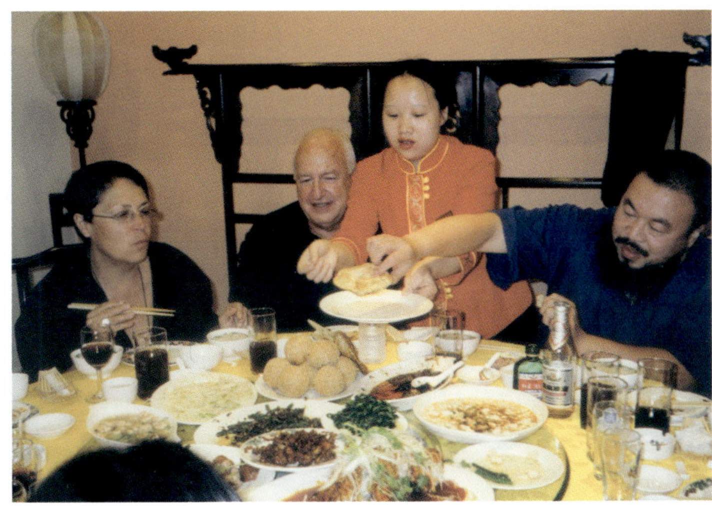

Mera and Don Rubell with Ai WeiWei, Beijing, Sept 2001
梅拉和多恩·卢贝尔以及艾未未, 北京, 2001年9月

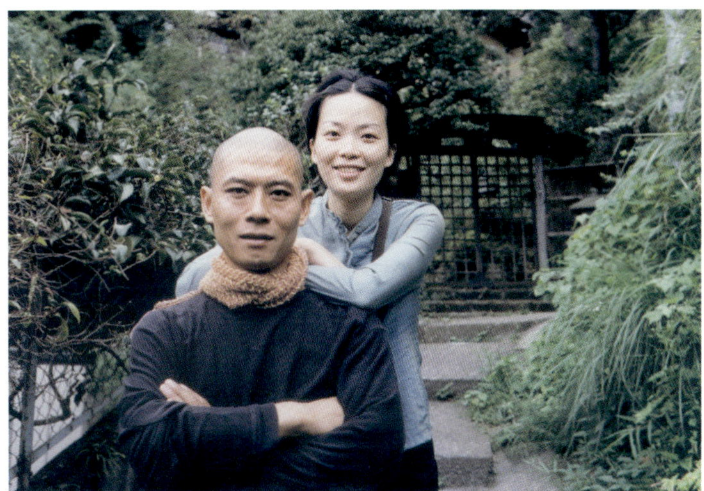

Zhang Huan and Hu Junjun, Beijing, Sept 2001
张洹和吴军军, 北京, 2001年9月

form, to understand where the possibility of the artist exists.

Juan: Does the artist's persona, life experience or demeanor affect your view of their artwork, perhaps especially so in a foreign country such as China?

Don: Only in a partial sense. It's only a small portion. Ultimately the artist's work speaks for the artist. Sometimes it's easier to understand the artwork by seeing the persona, but this is not the definition of the artist, the definition of the artist is his or her work.

Jason: In order for us to collect Chinese art I think it was essential to have the studio interactions. To understand a new art language and culture, the personal and physical interaction with the artists was essential. The nuances of China wouldn't have become apparent through visits to contemporary Chinese exhibitions in Chelsea galleries. In fact, for many years prior to engaging in this project we simply dismissed Chinese art—we didn't put forth the effort and energy into a thorough exploration of the contemporary scene. It was vital to this project that we were able to touch, smell, hear, feel and taste something about China itself.

Mera: I think it's very important to realize that, at the end of the day, it is the artwork as Don just stated. However, we can't forget the moment we encounter the artist. The moment that we encounter the artist, there is often very little work available. What you are seeing is the beginning, and what we've enjoyed for the last 50 years—the essence of what we really, really love is to engage with a prediction, with a sense of what the artist can become. And based on the limited work that a young artist has in a studio, we need all the information we can get. But, at the end of the day, like Don said, it is all in the work, the work has to speak for itself.

Juan: As Jason mentioned, Chinese art had been a blind spot for you. Why did it recently come to the forefront of your research?

Jason: China as a place or even as a concept is a topic with which the West is totally obsessed. We're bombarded with a glut of products produced in China and hear constantly about its global economic ambitions and its pivotal role in the 21st Century, so it's fascinating to delve into a young art scene and see how that art reflects a country's ambitions,

真实的自己。有些时候与一个艺术家见面会帮助我更好的理解他／她的作品，但个性不会变成一个艺术家身份的定义，只有他／她的作品才能诠释一个艺术家。

杰森：　我们对中国的了解实在是少之又少。为了使我们更好地收集中国艺术，与艺术工作室的交流不可或缺。与艺术家们的直接接触对我们了解一种新的艺术语言和文化而言非常关键。中国社会的复杂与微妙是纽约Chelsea画廊里的当代中国艺术展很难呈现的。事实上，这个项目开始之前我们一直对中国艺术没有很高的重视 – 我们没有拿出足够多的精力和心思去真正的探索和感受。所以对这个项目来说，真正的去用各种感官体会中国当代的艺术气息是十分关键的。

梅拉：　　我认为，最重要的还是象Don刚刚提到的——艺术作品本身。但是我们至今不能忘记刚与艺术家见面的时刻。一开头，这些艺术家往往只有很少量的作品可以展示给我们看。你所看到的是一个开端，　而我们过去50年来最享受的，最热爱的，是对艺术家发展和未来的一种预言与展望。基于年轻艺术家在工作室里的作品很有限，我们需要获取尽可能多的信息去了解他们的艺术。可最后归根结底，就像Don所说的那样，没有比作品本身更好的方式让我们可以去了解艺术家了。

Juan：　就像Jason刚刚提到的，中国的当代艺术曾经对你们来说是一个盲点，那为什么近期它能够进入你们感兴趣的视野范围内呢？

杰森：　中国是西方社会十分着迷的一个地方，或者说是一个概念。我们被大量中国制造的产品包围着，它飞速的经济增长已经使它成为了二十一世纪举足轻重的成员。所以对我们来说，深入研究这个国家逐步成熟的艺术氛围如何反映整个国家的大环境是很有意思的。当然了，了解中西方当代艺术之间的联系也很有趣。

Juan：　请具体说说你是如何筛选出这一百个工作室的好吗？我记得当时Don有很多手写的名单经常被大家讨论和修改。

多恩：　我们是通过多方面来作出决定的。首先最重要的是我们与一些艺术馆馆长的对话。其中对我们最有帮助的应该是田霏宇先生（Phil Tinari）. 之后就是我们对《艺术界》和《艺术》这两个刊物的反复阅读。经过对各路资源的对照，我们可以得到一个最初的名单。之后我们与一些画廊取得了联系，听听他们的想法。Lu　Jie在这方面很有用，给我们足够的信息，就像上了一堂中国当

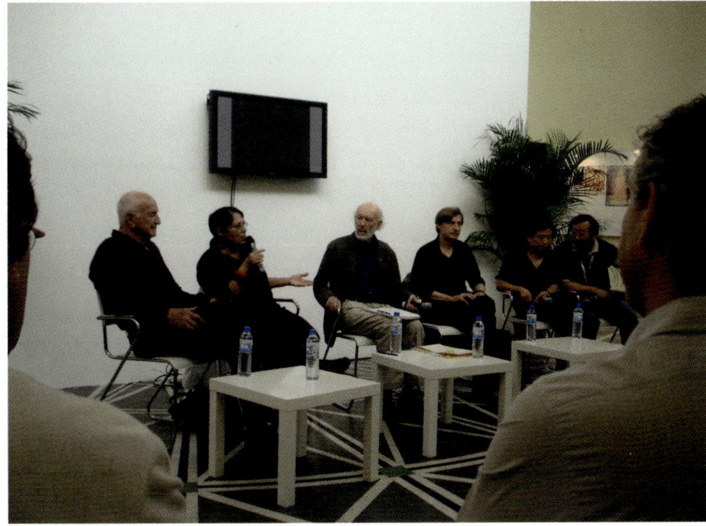

Don and Mera Rubell, Nick Waterlow, Jerome Sans, Zhang Zikang and Jin Hua at ShContemporary, Shanghai, Sept 2008
多恩和梅拉·卢贝尔, Nick Waterlow, Jerome Sans, Zhang Zikang 以及 Jin Hua 在上海当代艺术博览会, 上海, 2008年9月

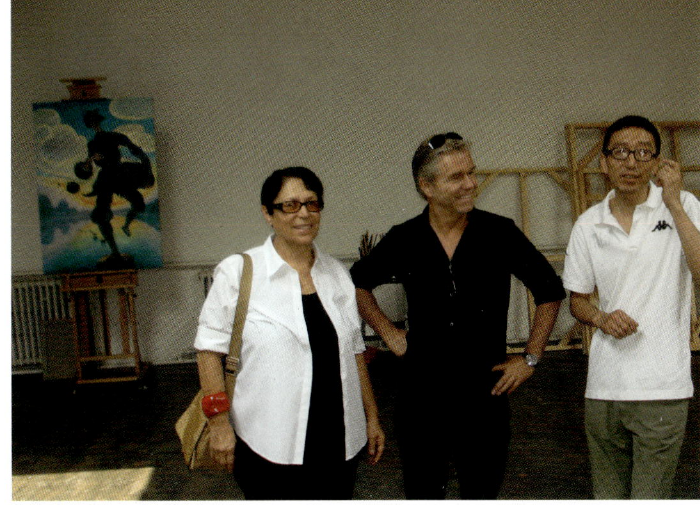

Mera Rubell, Urs Meile, and Wang Xingwei in his studio, Beijing, Sept 2008
梅拉·卢贝尔, Urs Meile, 以及王兴伟在他的工作室, 北京, 2008年9月

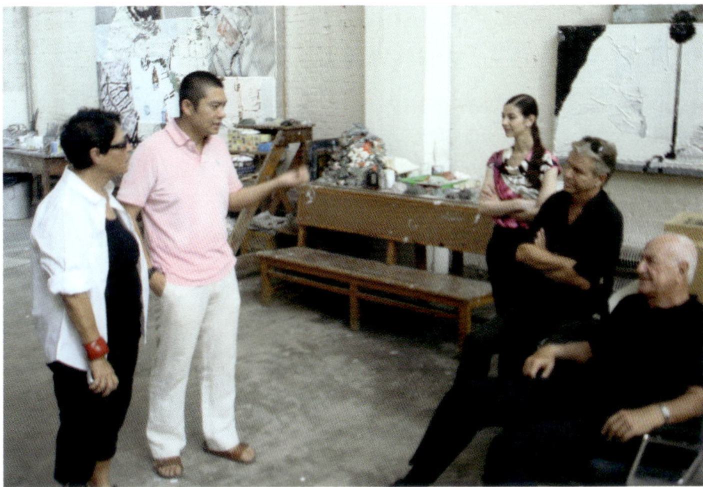

Mera Rubell, Li Songsong, Nataline Colonnello, Urs Meile and Don Rubell in Li Songsong's studio, Beijing, Jan 2011
梅拉·卢贝尔, 李松松, Nataline Colonnello, Urs Meile 以及多恩·卢贝尔在李松松的工作室, 北京, 2011年1月

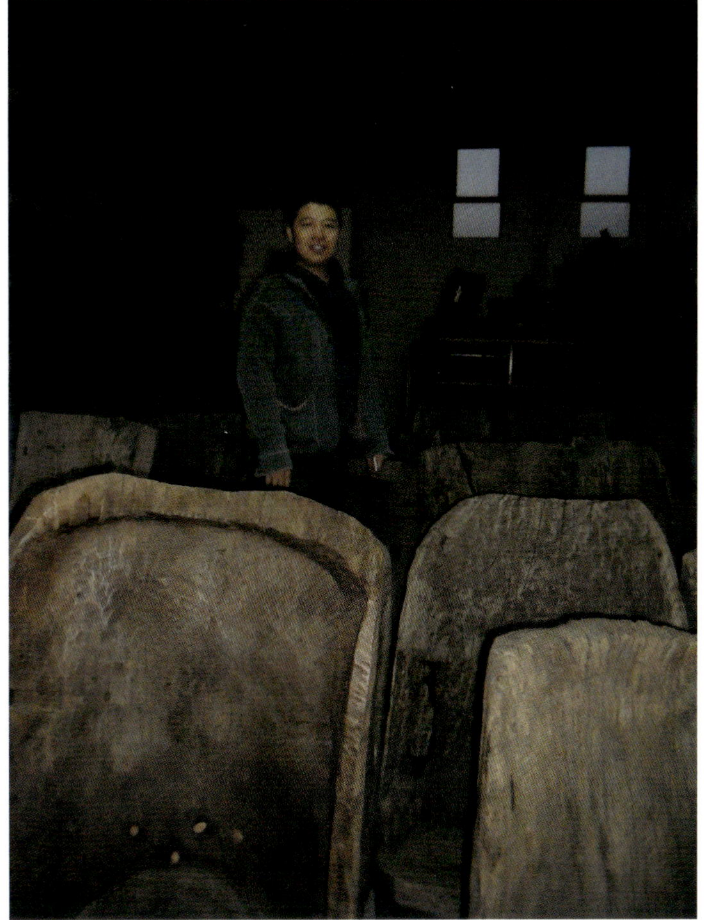

He Xiangyu in his studio, Beijing, Jan 2011
何翔宇在他的工作室, 北京, 2011年1月

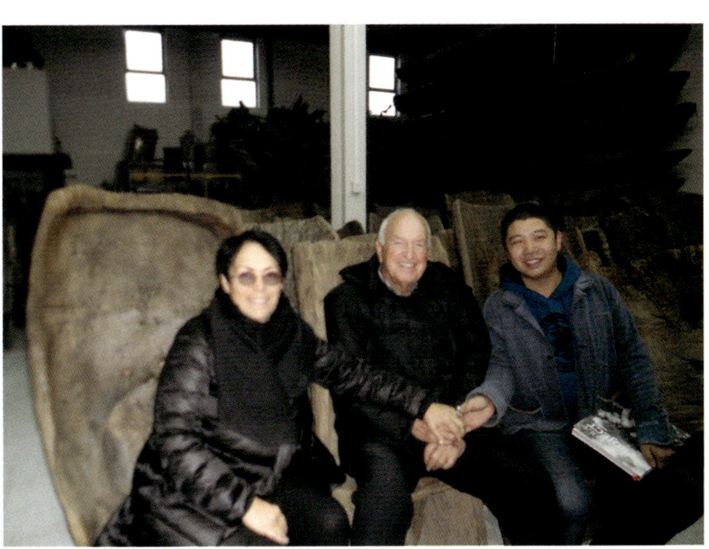

Mera and Don Rubell with He Xiangyu in his studio, Beijing, Jan 2011
梅拉和多恩·卢贝尔以及何翔宇在他的工作室, 北京, 2011年1月

issues and desires. It's also intriguing to see how Chinese art relates to Western contemporary art.

Juan: Please elaborate on how you winnowed your list down to 100 studios. I recall Don's many handwritten lists which were constantly being discussed and revised.

Don: The decision was based on several different methods. First and foremost were the conversations we had with several curators throughout the years, most notably Phil Tinari in Beijing. Adding to this was our complete rereading of the journals *Leap* and *Yishu*. We carefully cross-referenced these sources to give us some basic lists to work from. Then we met with the various gallerists and sought out their input. Particularly useful in this regard was Lu Jie, who kindly offered up what amounted to a course on the history of contemporary art in China and Urs Miele and his team, who provided us with an analysis of their perception of the young art scene in China. We also spent extensive time with Pearl Lam, Leng Lin, David Tung, Lorenz Helbling, Tian Yuan, and Natalie Sun among others. Only after all this preparation and countless visits to museum exhibitions were we prepared to begin visiting artists' studios.

Mera: I have to highlight Pearl Lam's friendship and generosity which was instrumental in us realizing this challenging project.

Don: I should add that the original lists were constantly being added to by the recommendations of the artists whose studios we visited, for artists still remain the greatest sources of understanding about art. I should also add that these 28 artists could have been joined by several others but weren't because of certain circumstances—most importantly the absence or unavailability of key works at the time we visited their studios.

None of this would have been possible without the incredible logistical support of Xiaoming Zhang and Luluc Huang, who were absolutely instrumental in arranging the studio visits. These required trains, planes and vans and impossible-to-meet schedules, but somehow every planned visit was achieved, although some days extended to 18 hours and endless cups of green tea.

Juan: In a recent exhibition of ours, *How Soon Now*, the women artists far outnumbered the men. This

代艺术史课一般；还有麦勒（Urs　Meile）和他的团队，给我们提供了他们对中国年轻艺术家的深入解析。除此之外我们还与 Pearl Lam, Leng Lin, David Tung, Lorenz Helbling, Tian Yuan, and Natalie Sun 等等有密切合作。只有在做好如此充足的准备和多次拜访博物馆展览后我们才动身去拜访各个艺术工作室的。

梅拉： 我要特别指出Pearl Lam 对我们的友谊和慷慨，促进了我们实现这个具有挑战性的项目。

多恩： 这里我想特别提一下，有些我们去拜访过的艺术家们也会给我们推荐一些其他值得去的艺术家工作室，因为他们毕竟是最了解艺术的人。还有就是原本还有更多人能加入这28位艺术家的行列，但由于种种原因，尤其是当时我们拜访的时候没有呈现重要作品，他们遗憾未能参与进来。

当然了，如果没有 Xiaoming Zhang 和 Luluc Huang为我们安排如此详细的工作室参观日程，这一切都是很难实现的。一路上需要火车、飞机、火车，行程紧的看似难以实现，但最后即使有时一天下来会有18个小时，加无数杯绿茶提神，我们还是令人咋舌的把名单上的工作室一个不漏的参观完了。

Juan: 在我们最近的一场展览——《How Soon Now》中，女艺术家的人数远远超过男艺术家。而在本场展览中仅有两名女艺术家，这是为什么？

多恩： 在所有调查研究之后，我们仅能找到少数几位女艺术家。如果我们考虑到在中国的许多艺术院校中的学生大多为女性的话，这个结果尤其令人惊讶。我怀疑如果我们在十年后再办一场类似的展览，情况将十分不同。如果我们看看四十年前美国的情形，就能发现类似当今中国这样令人沮丧的境况。

Juan: 你当年首次接触到当代艺术就是以一种拜访艺术工作室的形式进行的。那是六十年代的事了，当时并不是计划好的艺术工作室拜访，而是当你们在街上散步的时候自然发生的－你们碰巧看到了艺术家将曼哈顿的一些店面改成艺术工作室和展览区。

梅拉： 在六十年代，Don还在医学院就学，而我在哈莱姆区的"启蒙计划"教书；的确，在他学习的间隙，我们常在周边散步很久。当时，房地产市场非常差，经济也很糟糕，所以艺术家们实际上还能租到价格低廉的工作室。在纽约的街道

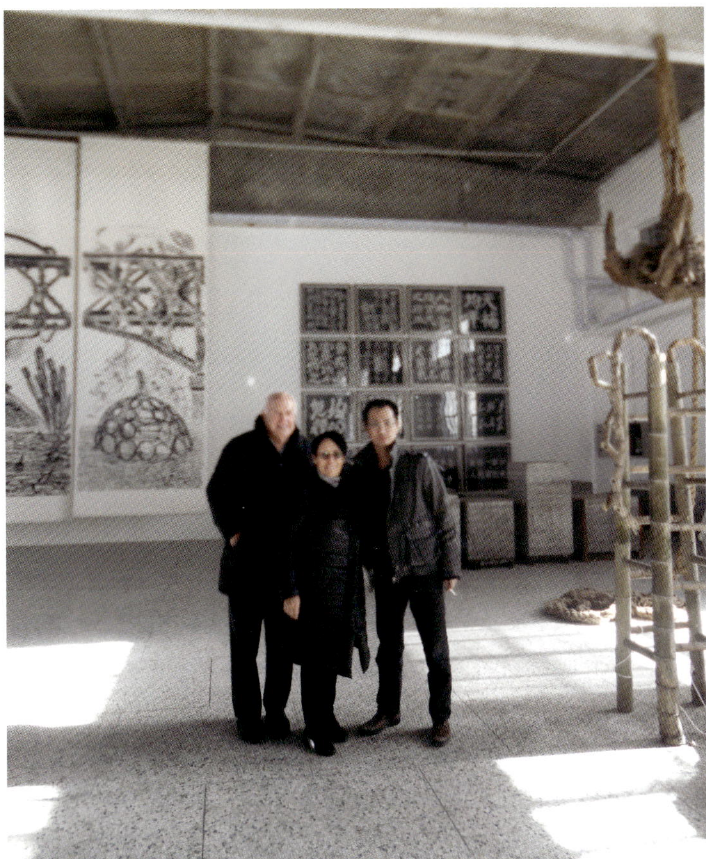

Don and Mera Rubell with Qiu Zhijie in his studio, Beijing, Jan 2011
多恩和梅拉·卢贝尔以及邱志杰在他的工作室，北京，2011年1月

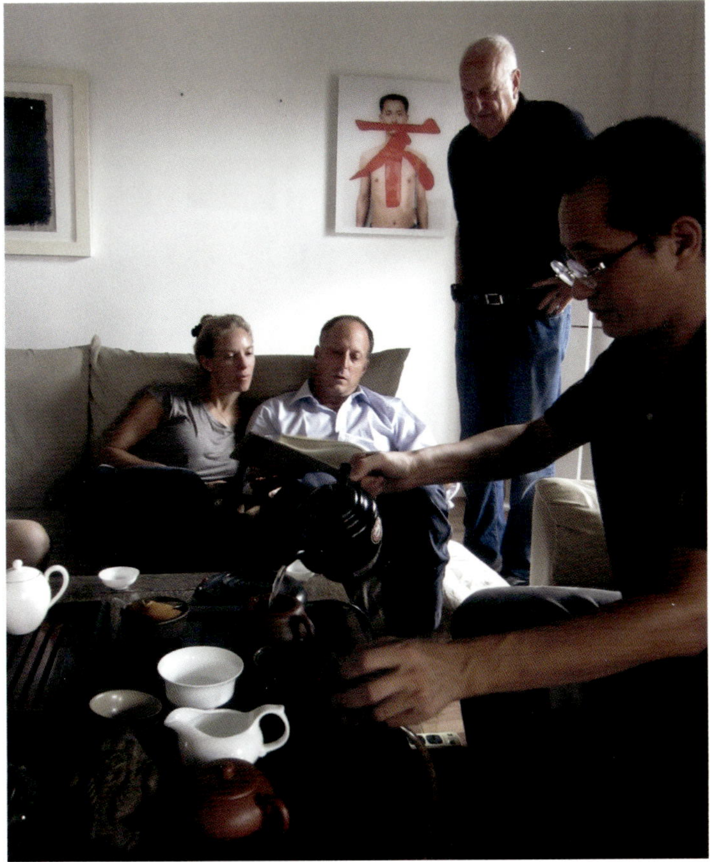

Michelle, Jason and Don Rubell with Qiu Zhijie in his studio, Beijing, Aug 2011
米歇尔，杰森和多恩·卢贝尔以及邱志杰在他的工作室，北京，2012年8月

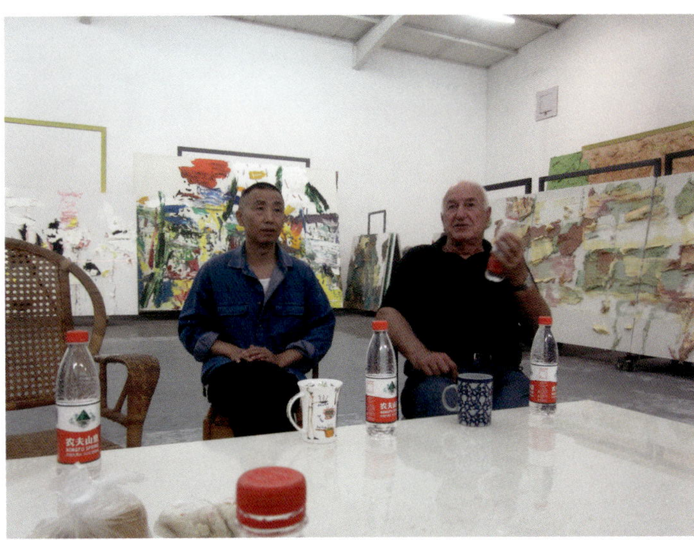

Zhu Jinshi and Don Rubell in Zhu Jinshi's studio, Beijing, Aug 2011
朱金石和多恩·卢贝尔在朱金石他工作室，北京，2011年8月

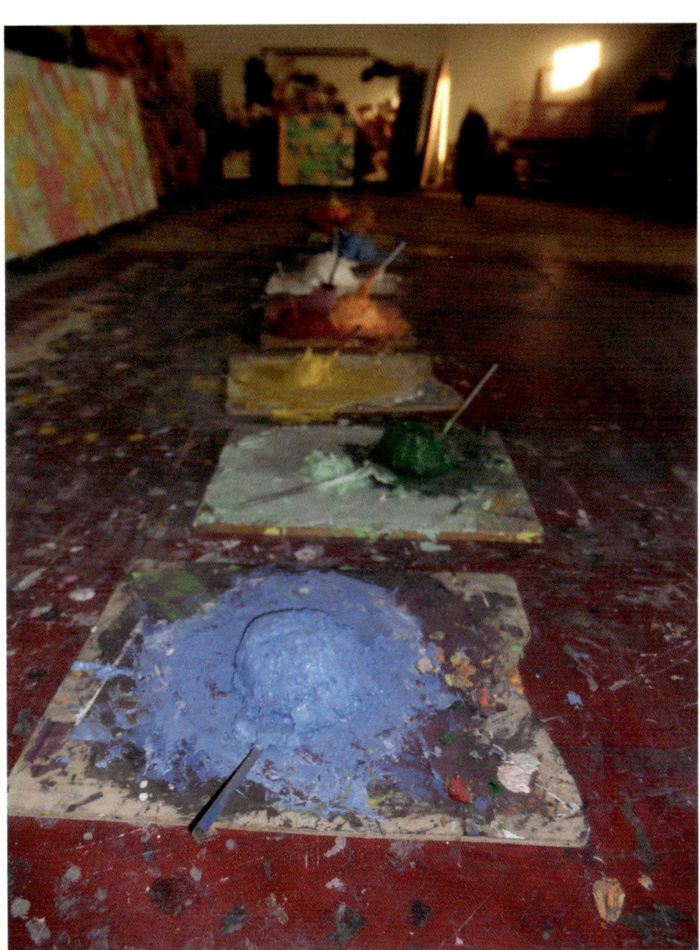

Zhu Jinshi's studio, Beijing, Aug 2011
朱金石工作室，北京，2011年8月

exhibition has only two women artists. Why is this?

Don: After all the research, we were not able to find more than a handful of female artists. This was particularly surprising if we consider that in many of the art schools in China, women represent the majority of the art students. I suspect that if we were to do a similar exhibition 10 years from now we would find a different situation. If we look at the situation in the United States 40 years ago, we would have found a similarly dismal situation to the one in China today.

Juan: Your very first engagement with contemporary art was in the form of a studio visit. Not a planned studio visit, but one that happened organically as you walked down the street in the 1960's and artists were repurposing Manhattan storefronts as studios and exhibition spaces.

Mera: In the 1960's, Don was in medical school and I was teaching in the Head Start Program in Harlem, and yes, in his breaks from his studies, we would take long walks in our neighborhood. At the time, real estate was so bad, and the economy was so bad, that artists could actually rent very inexpensive studios. So we encountered an entire universe walking into storefronts on New York City streets. We discovered brilliant people living their lives as artists, and we were just so grateful that they let us in.

Juan: So in some ways nothing has changed with your practice.

Mera: It's true, yes.

Juan: Do you think you're relating something in yourself to the artist's persona?

Mera: I guess it's like going out and finding friends in the world. You know, you can always find friends that think like you, act like you, look like you and eat like you. You can have a very comfortable life by having people around you that mirror you, what you think, what you believe and what you want to do. For us, the dynamic of our life has been to really engage with people that almost always challenge what we think, or what we do or what we eat. I'd never had seahorse soup before, you know, that's a challenge, or been asked how I feel about donkey meat. It shakes you into a different reality and we feel very privileged that that is the case.

上走着走着会走进各个店面，我们就这样闯入了另一个宇宙。在那里，我们发现了非常聪明的人们，过着艺术家的生活，我们当时非常感激他们接纳了我们。

Juan: 所以从某种程度上来说你们［寻找艺术］的方式没有任何改变。

梅拉: 是的，的确如此。

Juan: 你认为你有将自己的一些东西带到艺术家的个性中去吗？

梅拉: 我想这就像在全世界交朋友一样。要知道，你总是能找到与你思考、行事、长相以及饮食习惯类似的朋友。你基本上可以找到一群和你拥有相同想法、信念以及愿景的人们，你们在一起可以过着非常舒适的生活。对于我们来说，生活的动力则是真正地深入那些总是挑战我们的想法、所做或食物的人们。我以前从未尝过海马汤，你知道那可是个挑战，或者被问起驴肉的味道如何。它将你带入一个不同的现实世界，我们真的极度幸运，能拥有这样的生活我们真的感到很荣幸。

多恩: 你可以把艺术家的个性看作是甜点，而［他们的］艺术品则是主餐，个性增加了艺术家成功的可能性，但没有好的作品，个性不能发挥任何作用。

Juan: 你如何看待你们与你们所拜访的艺术家之间的关系？你们是否感觉到，可能刚开始时，艺术家会把你当作局外人 – 那是怎样的？观察人们对你们的利用价值或对你们［的拜访］感到心有余悸与否de心态转变是非常有意思的。你有没有注意到过这些极端？

梅拉: 我想收藏家绝大部分时候处在一个某种程度上尴尬的位置。因为人们对于收藏家有许多陈见。这个人是来做交易的，你知道吧？他们认为你来到工作室就是进行交易的；一切都是买卖。我想起初——他们会把我们想像成十分挑剔的人，是带着批评和意见来的。而且。。。就像是在逛街购物一样的去购买艺术。

Juan: 你是否会认为许多人不喜欢拜访工作室，无论他们是否是收藏家？

梅拉: 我想这需要时间；如何拜访艺术工作室是需要很长一段时间去学习的。艺术工作室并不是一个购物的地方。如果你纯粹是想购买艺术品，我想你最好还是只去画廊算了。一次艺术工

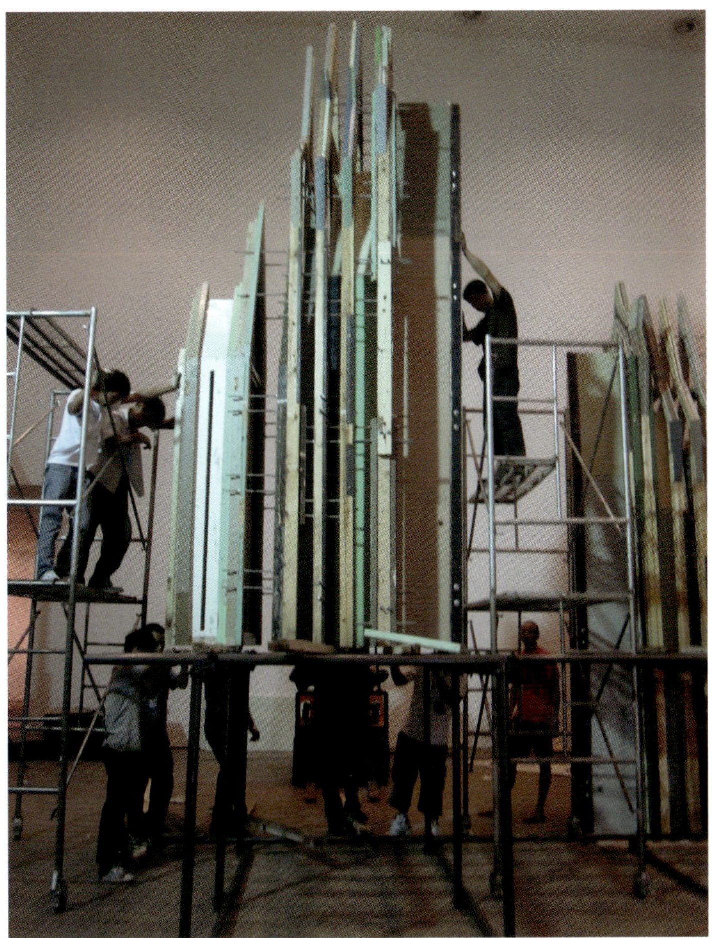

Liu Wei installation at Today Art Museum, Beijing, Aug 2011
刘韡的工作室，北京，2011年8月

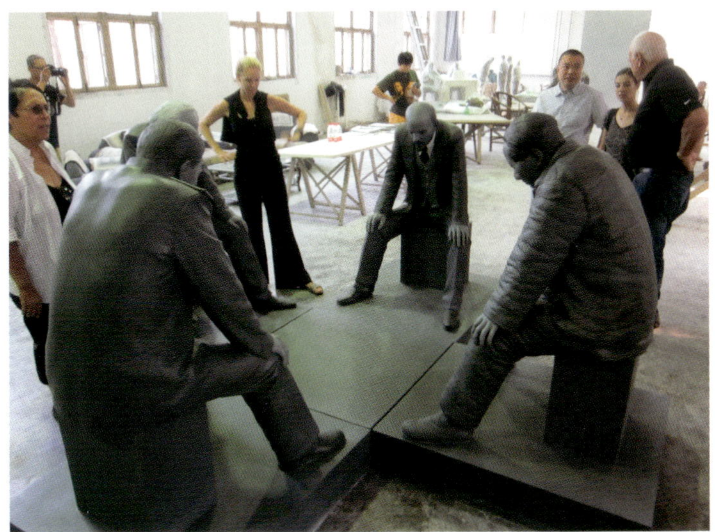

Mera and Michelle Rubell, Li Zhanyang, Nataline Colonnello and Don Rubell in Li Zhanyang's studio, Beijing, Aug, 2011
梅拉和米歇尔·卢贝尔，李占洋，Nataline Colonnello 以及多恩·卢贝尔在李占洋的工作室，北京，2011年8月

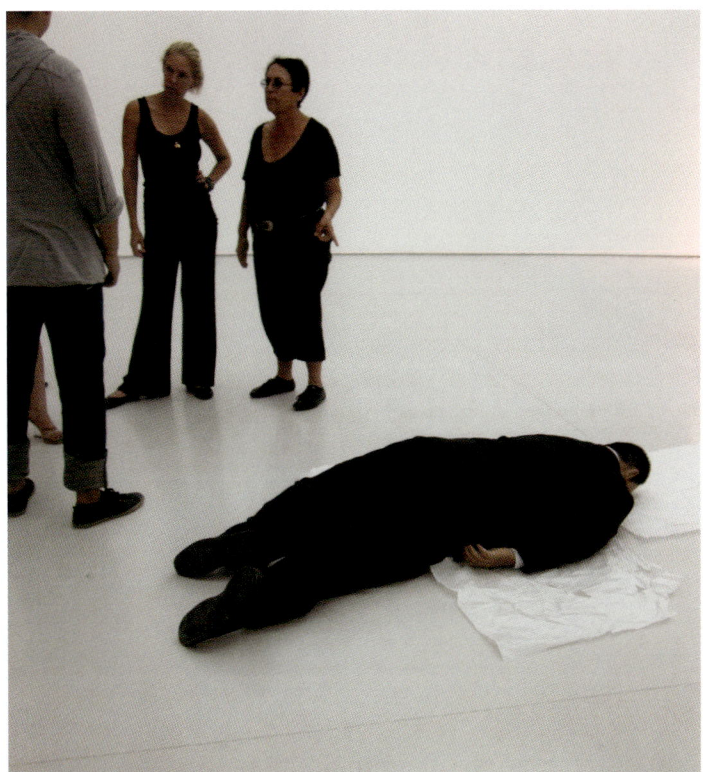

Michelle and Mera Rubell with He Xiangyu's sculpture at White Space Beijing, Beijing, Aug, 2011
米歇尔和梅拉·卢贝尔与何翔宇的雕塑在何翔宇的工作室，北京，2011年8月

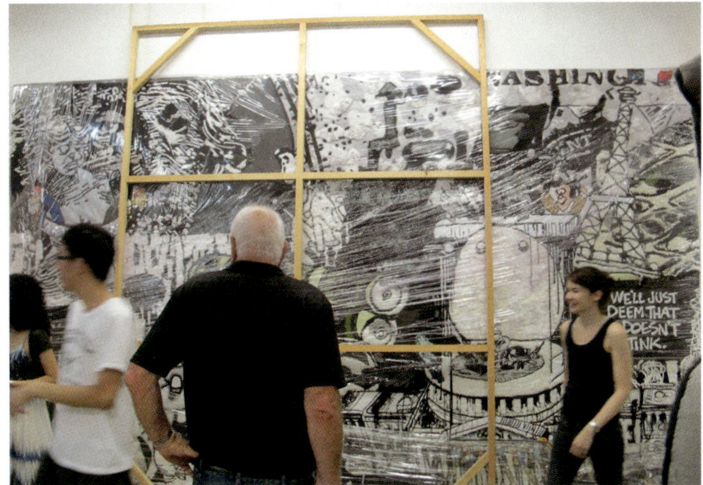

Xu Zhen and Don Rubell in Xu Zhen's studio, Shanghai, Aug 2011
徐震和多恩·卢贝尔在徐震的工作室，上海，2011年8月

Don: The persona, if you will, of the artist is the dessert, the artwork is the entrée, and the persona adds to the possibility of success of an artist, but absent good work, the persona won't do any good.

Juan: How do you perceive your relationship to the artist you're visiting? Do you feel like the artist relates to you as the other, perhaps initially, and what is that like? It can be interesting to perceive that shift when people feel they do or do not have something to gain from you or that they should or should not be intimidated by you. Do you ever notice this polarity?

Mera: I think that for the most part the collector is in some ways, in an embarrassing position because there are a lot of stereotypes connected with the role of the collector. It's usually the person who is transactional, you know? They think that you are going to come into the studio to make a transaction; it's about deal making. I also think that initially— they expect us to be critical, to come with criticism.

Juan: Would you say a lot of people, artists and collectors alike, don't feel comfortable with studio visits?

Mera: I think it takes time; it takes a long time to learn how to do a studio visit. And the studio is not a place for shopping. If you want to go shopping for art, I think you should stick to the gallery. A studio visit is more about an intimate interaction with the artist. And what do I mean by intimate? You're basically going into someone's real private space; it's almost like entering someone's brain. They're really opening up their brain, their heart, their life, because artwork that is good, is open— is open for all kinds of conversation, is open for questions. You enter a space that…some artists we visited in China literally had a space what, 12 by 16 feet? And that encompassed the kitchen with a hole in the ground for a bathroom. They're living very, very modestly and so I think that they're apprehensive about being judged—as anybody would. When someone is coming to your house it's always standard to apologize about not having time to make the bed. We're always nervous about people coming into our house. You can imagine if you're nervous about someone coming into your house because your bed is not made and they may not like your cooking or whatever, you could imagine how an artist feels when you are coming

作室拜访更像一场与艺术家的亲密互动。什么叫亲密？你基本上是在进入一个人最真实的私密空间；甚至就像走入了一个人的大脑里一样。他们真正地敞开他们的大脑、心扉、生活，因为好的艺术品是敞开的——向所有的对话、问题敞开。当你走进一个空间…我们在中国拜访的有些艺术家真的只有一块十二英尺乘以十六英尺大小的空间，包括了厨房以及地板上的一个洞作为厕所，他们的生活十分节俭。所以我觉得他们很担心被人评价—就像任何人一样。当某人来到你家，你总是会道歉没有时间铺床。我们总是对别人来到我们家而感到紧张。比如说，家里还不够干净。我们会为给客人做饭而感到紧张，因为…所以你可以想象得到，就连当人们来你家做客时你都会因为床没铺好、他们不喜欢你做的饭菜或其他什么事而感到紧张的话，那作为一名艺术家，当你走进他工作室时，他她会有怎样的感觉，不仅因为你在审视他们的私生活、生活方式与社会经济状况，同时你还在评判他们的想法、食物、家庭或价值观。你在做一个重大审判，他们认为最终你将通过买或不买他们的作品来给予你的评分。所以我们的是一种完全不同的体验。我们从不为了购买艺术品而拜访艺术工作室，我们几乎不在艺术工作室买艺术品，这种情况很罕见。

谈到我们在中国拜访的一百间艺术工作室，每位艺术家都知道我们是去看望他们的；这是一个互动。但愿，在我们的每一次互动中，都不只是我们在评估他们。这是一个有关他们和我们的真实对话—我们去其它工作室与参观别的艺术品、收藏品的一些经历。这是一场有关艺术的真实对话；也是一场有关中国的对话。这是当你跟一个初次见面的人讲话后感觉还可以继续谈下去的一种对话。这才真正地打开了对话之门。

多恩： 在艺术界有很多不同的角色。但总的来讲，收藏家的角色是最明确的了，因为他们只有一个职责，就是收集艺术品。有的评论家着重于艺术本身，而有的评论家则侧重于宏观概念。但是由于收藏家只有收集这一个角色，当他们造访工作室时，归根结底，他们对这个工作室的真实感受最终将体现于他们是否购买此艺术品。只有在少数非常幸运的情形下，他们可以越过本职并与艺术家建立起真正的友谊。尽管在从不购买任何艺术品的情形下，与艺术家建立长期的友谊也许并不现实，但你还是可以在短时间的工作室参观中与艺术家展开有趣的对话。因为很多时候，那并不是购买艺术品的时机。

Juan: 就你而言，收藏家好像并不需要做到面面俱到，但是在你的基金会中，你承担了策展人、理事、教育家等多重角色…

in, not only are you judging their personal life—the way they live, their socio-economic situation—but you're judging what they think and what they eat, and what their family is like, or what their values are. You're making a huge judgment and they expect that at the end of it you're going to give them some sort of grade by buying or not buying their work. So ours is a whole different experience. We never go to the studio to buy art, it's very rare that we buy art in the studio. It's very rare.

Regarding the studios we visited in China, every artist knew that we were coming to meet them; it was an interaction. *Hopefully*, in every interaction we had, it was not just about us evaluating them. It was a real conversation about them and us— our experience with going to other studios, our experience with looking at other art, the collections. It was a real conversation about art; it was a conversation about China. It was a kind of conversation you have with a person you meet for the first time where you feel, you know what,—we could have another. This really opens the door to a dialog.

Don: There are many different roles in the art world. And in many respects, the collector's role is clearest because they have only one function, and that's to collect the art. There are critics that describe the art, describe the general terms, but ultimately since the collector has really only this one role, when the collector visits a studio in the ultimate sense, his true feelings about the studio will manifest themselves whether he eventually buys the work or doesn't buy the work. In certain very fortunate circumstances, one can transcend that and develop a real relationship with the artist. Is it possible to have this relationship with the artist without ever purchasing the art, in the long term, probably not. But in the short term of a studio visit you can have very interesting dialogue because many times, it isn't the moment to buy or not buy art.

Juan: You speak about collectors as though they're not multifaceted, but via your foundation you're assuming the role of a curator, of a trustee, of an educator…

Don: You have all those roles, but ultimately it's about purchasing the art, and expressing your true feelings about the art that's produced by the artist by either purchasing the art or not purchasing the art.

多恩： 虽然有这么多的职称，但归根结底，就是购买艺术品，并且通过是否购买艺术品来表达你对此作品的真实感受。

杰森： 我想我们在扩展对收藏家的定义。在当代艺术基金会中我们承担着策展人、出版人与教育家的身份。我们的公共使命使我们的角色早已超越了单纯的艺术品收集者。有时候，我们的多重角色对于艺术界成熟的机构来说可能有些混乱，但是我们很享受从老套角色中解放出来的自由。

Juan: 你在造访工作室中所体验过的最黑暗的经历是什么？

多恩： 最近有一次在中国，体会到了艺术和生活的差距。我们走进艺术工作室看到那里家徒四壁。离开后我们才知道这位艺术家已经被关了一个月，那天刚刚被放出来。很明显，对他来说，他有比我们的造访更重要的事情去操心。

梅拉： 是的，当时情况真的很特殊。我们走进他家，他的工作室，然后他请我们在桌子前坐下。那是个方形的桌子，然后基本上，我们都面面相觑，对发生的事情一无所知。我们通过翻译跟他说："你有什么（艺术品）可以展示给我们看么？"他既非咄咄逼人也非不懂礼貌，只是好像心不在焉。就好像他本来很欢迎我们来，但是当我们来了却又变了想法一般。我们当时想肯定是发生了什么事情。我们感觉到他好像刚经历过感情创伤，很可能在我们进来之前刚刚发生。我们知道我们进入（房间）时正赶上那位艺术家受创伤的时候。所以我们觉得我们唯一能说的就是："我们很高兴能拜访你，见到你非常开心，不过如果你现在状态不好，我们可以重新约，但我们不想给你添麻烦"。当时非常的…不过还好，我想他挺感激我们察觉到了他的状况。他当时简直什么话都说不出口。之后，我们听说他有道歉，他说他刚从监狱里被放出来，原本以为对话交流不会有什么问题，而且还很期待和我们交谈，但他当时并不知道那天早上他必须还要重新接受察看。（我们到的时候，）他才刚从一个缓刑会议回来。真的是太惊心动魄了。

多恩： 不过总的来说我们从来没有未受邀请就造访工作室。由于艺术家有邀请我们，我们来的时候他们不太可能特别不友好。

Juan: 你们收集了很多被看作叛逆或不羁的艺术作品。你认为艺术如何反映了人类存在中令人不安的一面？为什么这一点很重要？甚至，它是否重要？

Jason: I think we push the boundaries of the definition of the collector. In the Contemporary Arts Foundation we take on the position of curator, publisher and educator. The idea that we are merely an accumulator of objects has definitely changed for us through our public mission. At times our multifaceted roles can be confusing to established organizations inside the art world. These freedoms from stereotyped roles are amazingly liberating for us.

Juan: What is the darkest experience you've had during a studio visit?

Don: There was a recent experience in China that brings out the difference between art and life. We walked into the studio and the artist had absolutely nothing there. We found out after leaving that this artist had just been jailed for a month and he had just gotten out that day. It was very clear that there were bigger issues for him than our studio visit.

Mera: Yes, that was really something because we walked into his home, his studio, and he sat us down at the table. It was a square table, and basically, we looked at each other, and we didn't know what was up. Through an interpreter, we said, "Do you have anything to show us?" And he wasn't aggressive or disrespectful; it was like he was in a zone. Like he had been open to having us come, but as soon as we came he felt otherwise. We thought something had happened. It could have happened right before we walked in. We knew we entered at an emotionally traumatic moment for the artist. And we felt like the best thing we could say is "We are happy to visit you, happy to meet you, but if you feel like this isn't the right moment, we can reschedule, but we don't have to burden you with our visit." And it was very… well, I think he appreciated that we were sensitive to his condition. He literally couldn't communicate about anything. And afterwards we heard that he apologized, he said he was recently released from jail and he thought he'd be open to an interaction. He was looking forward to meeting us but he literally had just returned from a probation meeting. That was intense.

Don: But in general we never visit a studio uninvited. Since the artist has invited us, it's not very likely that they will be too antagonistic when we do show up.

杰森： 这点是最重要的。对的，它是最重要的。所有优秀的流芳百世的艺术都是这样的。是它创造了主题，那些永恒的流传千古的主题，至少，它们在缔造它们的那个时代里是恒久且充满意义的。这就是当代艺术的定义，也就是为什么有些艺术品拥有持久的吸引力而有些却昙花一现。

梅拉： 你可以根据你的想法随意涂抹。人类的想法是共通的…

Juan： 你们的收藏跨越几代艺术家，通常当审视一个年轻艺术家时，你会注意其与早期艺术家之间的关系。比如，Nate Lowman曾和Michael St. John一起学习并深受其还有Richard Prince以及Cady Noland的影响。他们三位都出现在了你的收藏中。关于中国，你可能对大部分教授不太熟悉，并且你的收藏中也没有很多早期艺术家。中国艺术家也许会受西方艺术家影响，但是他们更多地是借鉴一些你们也许并不了解的艺术家和文化。这是否在你们与中国工作室创作的艺术品的接触与理解上造成困难？

多恩： 一开始，对中国当代艺术史的了解匮乏确实造成了巨大的障碍。Lu Jie在其中给予了我们很大帮助。她对一些主要的历史性展览以及参展艺术家进行了简要讲解，我们还拿到了许多重要展览的展册及关于艺术家们的个人专著。其中很大一部分艺术家我们已经比较熟悉了，因为在过去20年中，他们的作品经常出现在西方的展览中。但是其中一些最具有影响力的艺术家还从来没有在西方展出过。另外，2001年起的新一代艺术家与我们之前在西方所看到的一代（中国）艺术家们有很大不同。大多早期艺术家的作品好像专供出口品，而我们发现这代年轻艺术家却更加关注个体特性，从旧生活到飞速发展的生活方式的转变，以及工业化生产对其生活的冲击。他们急切地渴望通过他们的艺术捕捉到曾被文化大革命抹杀的历史的延续性.

Juan: You've acquired many artworks that some would deem transgressive. How do you think art reflects the disturbing facets of our existence and why is that important? Or is it important?

Jason: It's the most important. That's it; it's the most important. That's what all good or lasting art does. It creates the subjects, the subjects that are lasting and permanent, or at least significant at the time in which it is made. That's the definition of contemporary art. And that's why some art has lasting power and some does not.

Juan: Your collection now has several generations of artists and oftentimes you draw from these earlier generations when considering a younger artist. For example, Nate Lowman studied with Michael St. John and cites him as well as Richard Prince and Cady Noland as influences, all three of whom are in your collection. In China, you weren't familiar with the majority of the professors, and the earlier generations weren't in the collection. Chinese artists may count Western artists as influences but they're also drawing heavily from artists and a culture unfamiliar to you. Did this make your engagement with and understanding of the artwork in Chinese studios more difficult?

Don: Initially, this lack of familiarity with the contemporary Chinese art history seemed an insurmountable obstacle. Lu Jie was particularly helpful in aiding us in navigating these waters. By briefing us on the major historical exhibitions, as well as the artists who contributed to them, we were able to obtain many of the key exhibition catalogs as well as monographs about the individual artists. Many of these artists were familiar to us through their presence in western exhibitions over the last 20 years, but some of the most influential never made it to the West. Also, this new generation, since 2001, has been quite different than the generation we have seen in the West. While many of the early generation seemed made for export we came to understand that this younger generation is much more focused on individual identity, the transformation from the old ways to a rapidly changing lifestyle and the impact of industrialization on their lives. They are very anxious to capture in their art the continuity of their history which had been obliterated during the Cultural Revolution.

Ai Weiwei 艾未未

Born in 1957, Beijing, China
Lives and works in Beijing, China

一九五七年生於中国北京
居住和工作於中国北京

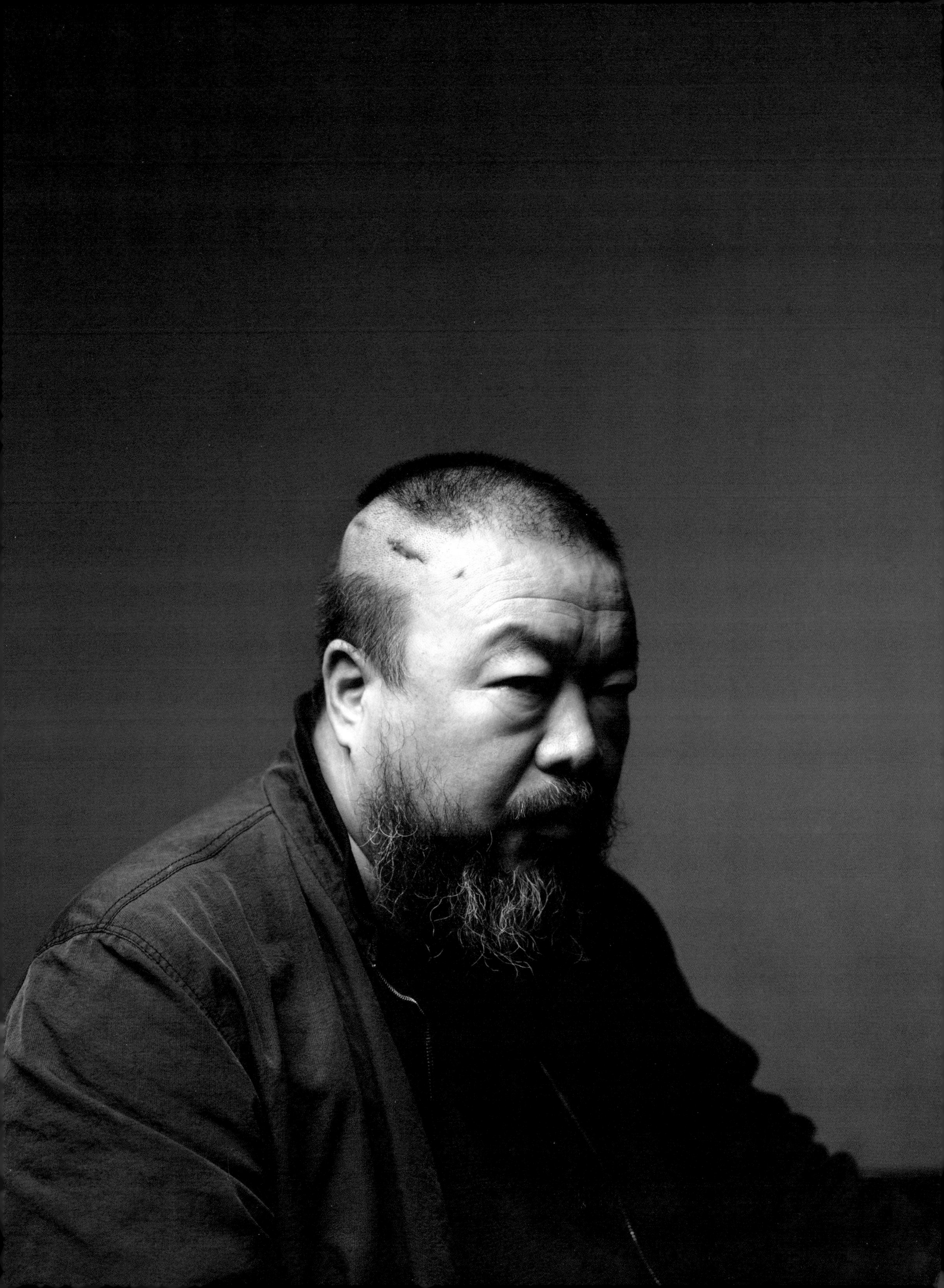

The idea originates from a visit to Kunming, Yunnan, where Pu'er tea is a famous product. The tea leaves are often compressed into blocks called bingcha (tea cakes) for easy transportation along ancient routes on horseback and would travel to faraway places such as Tibet. As a play on the age-old tradition, a whole ton of tea was pressed into a cube to look like a minimalist sculpture. The work provides a different vantage point to what is ingrained in Chinese history and customs.

- Ai Weiwei Studio

这个主意来自一次去云南昆明的旅行，那里特产普洱茶。为了方便携带，茶叶常常被压缩成一块块的茶饼，驮在马背上，沿着茶马古道被带到遥远的地方，比如西藏。为了重新演绎这种古老传统，我把整整一吨茶压成了一个方块，看起来像一个极简主义雕塑。这个作品提供了一种不同的角度去审视烙印在中国历史与习俗里的一些文化。

- 艾未未工作室

Ai Weiwei, *Ton of Tea*, 2005, Pu'er tea leaves from Yunnan Province with wooden base, 39 3/8 x 39 3/8 x 39 3/8 in. (100 x 100 x 100 cm), acquired in 2008

艾未未，《一吨茶》，2005，一吨压缩云南普洱茶叶，木底座，39 3/8 x 39 3/8 x 39 3/8 寸 (100 x 100 x 100 厘米)，收藏于 2008

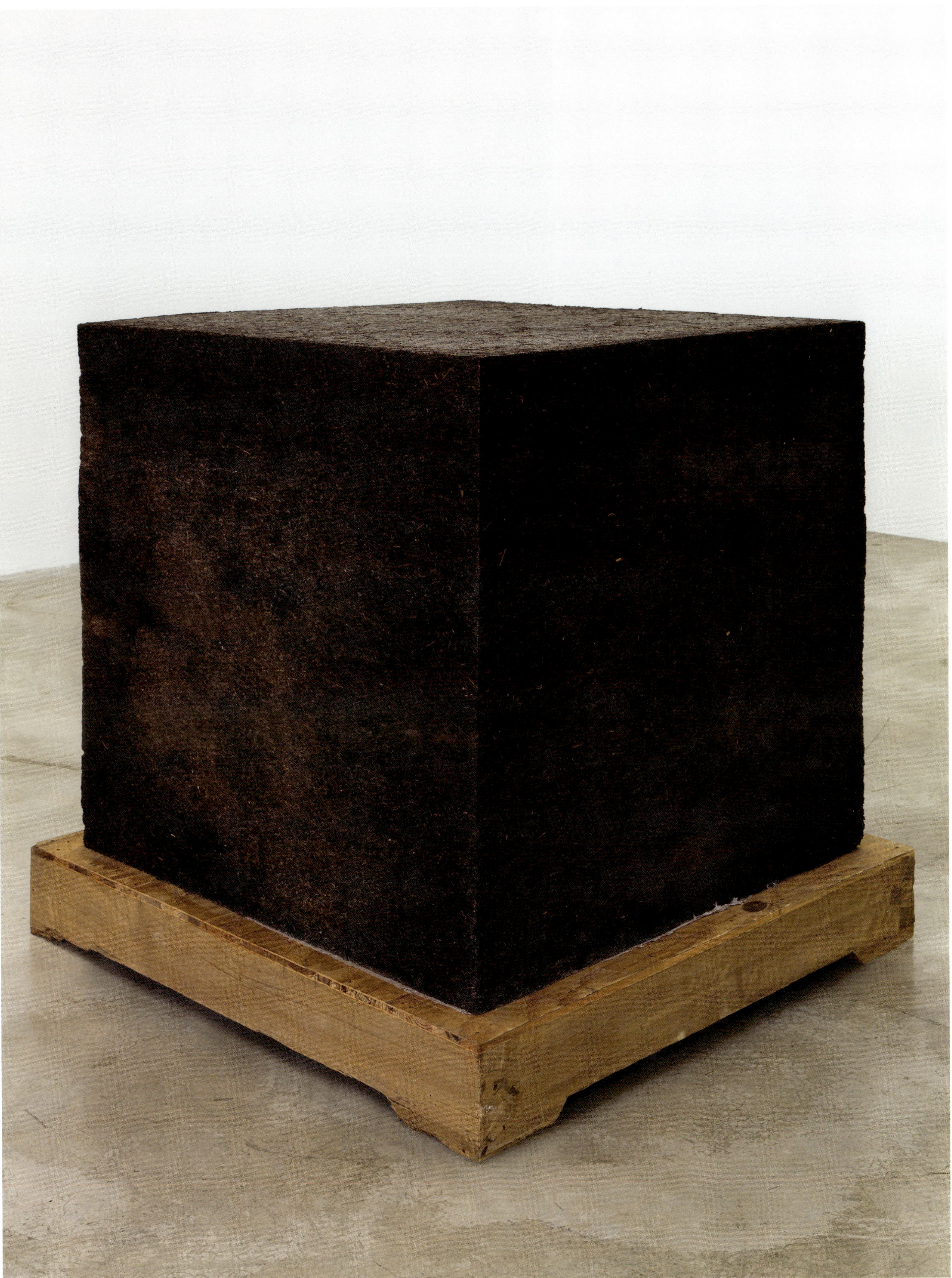

Antique tables from China are made with clear, logical principles of proportion and structure, taking careful consideration of the type of wood that is used. With traditional joinery techniques, no nails were used in building the furniture. Not only does it reflect the craftsmen's profound understanding of aesthetics and materials, these objects are also status symbols in Chinese culture. In constructing *Table with Two Legs*, Ai Weiwei intervened and reconstructed the original structure, purposely without leaving any traces. By destroying the original form and function, the work challenges our perception and becomes some sort of mysterious object.

- Ai Weiwei Studio

充分考虑到了木料的质地，中国古董桌子的制作具有清晰且符合逻辑的比例与结构。根据传统的木匠工艺，制作家具无需使用任何钉子。这不仅反映出工匠对美学和材料的透彻了解，也从而体现这些物品在中国文化中的地位象征。在制作两条腿的桌子时，艾未未不留一丝痕迹地介入并重组了［桌子］原来的构造。这件作品摧毁了桌子原本的形状与功能，从而变成了一个神秘的物品，挑战我们的感知。

- 艾未未工作室

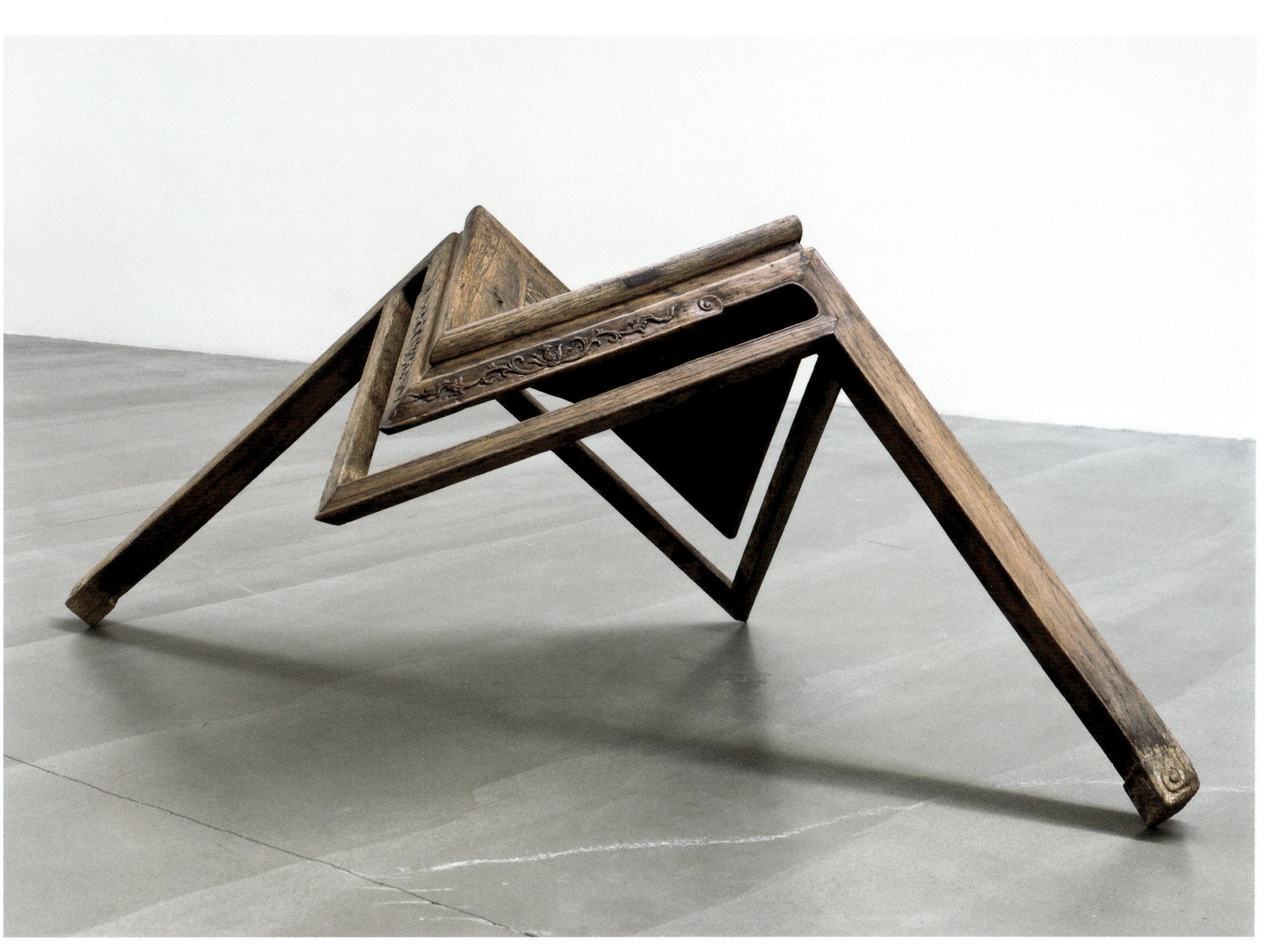

Chen Wei 陈维

Born in 1980, Zhejiang, China
Lives and works in Beijing, China

一九八零年生於中国浙江
居住和工作於中国北京

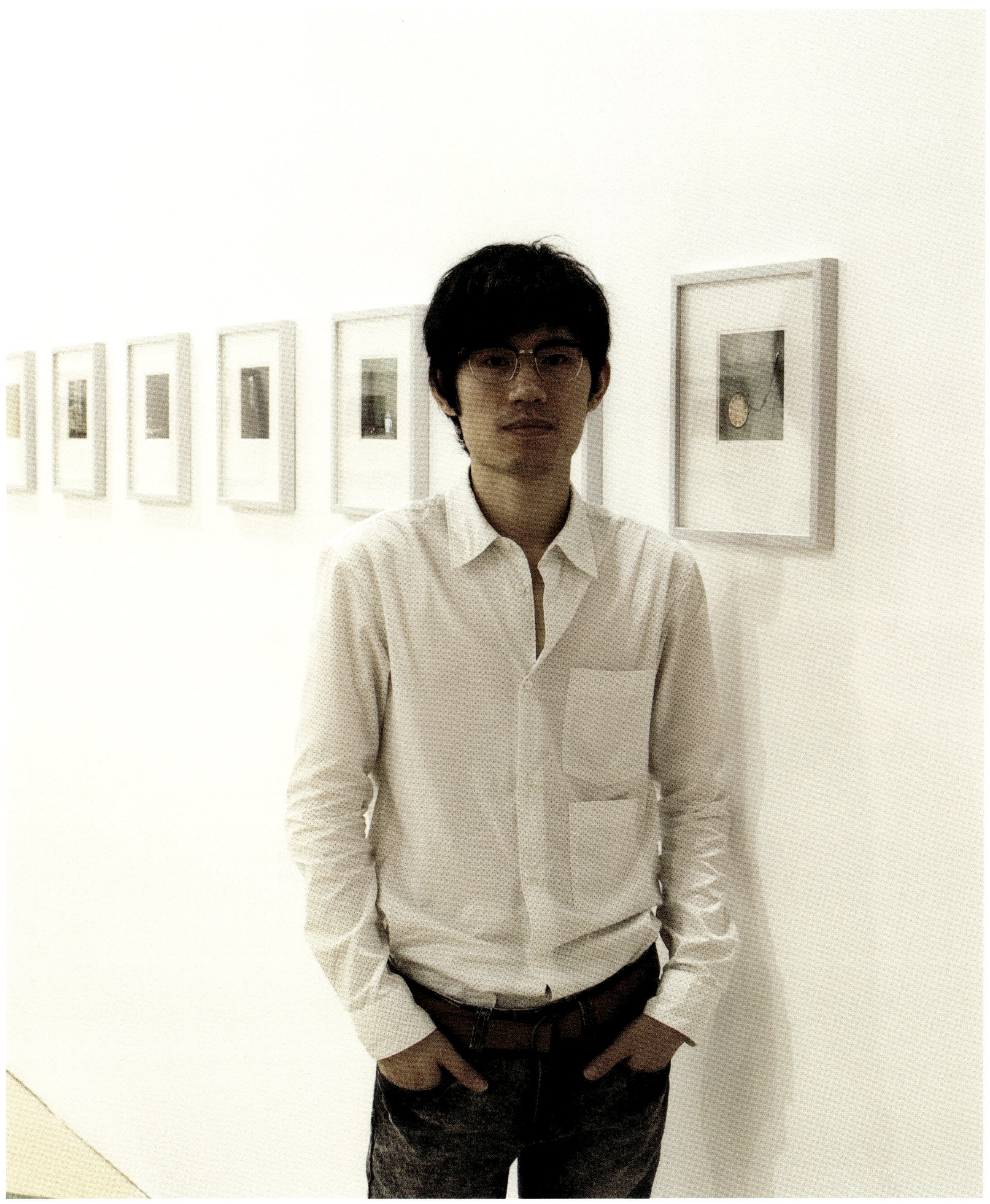

A small piece of news, a short story, a magazine, poster or a television commercial, or again another artwork, perhaps it is just a kind of situation... They all could become clues to my work and they are all essential to my daily life.

My early work consisted of shooting character performances in outdoor scenes, a similar process to acting without a stage or something even similar to documentations of performance art. These works were all concerned with performances of people in urban environments. Their performances are silent, boring, neurotic or even distorted.

Afterwards, I turned my attention to work indoors and to comparatively closed spaces. Notwithstanding the change in environment, the people within the scenes perform as characters and there continues to exist a similar expression of absurdity and suspense.

At that time, I started studying what kinds of environments and objects provide this sentiment of nervousness and absurdity, or the kinds of mechanical spectacles inhabiting our space. Slowly, the human figure started to disappear within my photographs and so did the narrative components—the scene and objects occupying it became the central concern. I construct these different scenes in my studio, assembling and organizing the objects together. As such, the scene and the objects inhabiting it constitute the narrating tools themselves. Through this process, I hope to face some taboo issues and attempt to express existing contradictions.

Therefore, most of my work is completed in the studio by building a scene and collecting objects. After arranging the scene's objects and their relationship with one another, as well as finding their proper place, light settings are adjusted and shooting is completed. From there, I rinse the negatives and scan them to adjust some details and finally print, frame and display.

The majority of my work is photography based. I also do a few installation works.

- Chen Wei

一则小小的新闻，或者小说的片段，杂志，海报，或者一段电视广告，或者另外一件作品，或者只是一种状态…它们都有可能成为我作品的线索，也都是我日常生活中不可或缺的。

我的早期作品拍摄的是人物在户外场景中的表演，它们有点像舞台表演，只不过我将户外的现有场景作为舞台，也有点像行为表演的摄影记录。它们都是关于人物在都市之中的表演，他们的表演是静默的，无聊的，神经质的，甚至是扭曲的。

之后，我将注意力转向了室内，相对封闭的空间，人物仍然在场景中如同表演者般存在，仍然有那么多荒诞的如同悬念般的事件存在。

这时候我开始关注是什么样的环境承载了这些荒诞而神经质的事物，是什么样的机制使得那些奇观被我们随处可见。然后人物便从作品中慢慢隐退，原有的故事性被削弱，物件与场景本身成了主角。我会在工作室重建这些来自于生活中的场景，我也会重新整理并组合这些物件，使得物件与场景本身的语言足以构成叙事的功能。我希望通过这样的工作，能使得我自己去正视一些被一再回避的问题，也试图令一些隐含的矛盾和多重的关系能够被显现出来。

所以，目前我的摄影作品大部分也是在工作室里完成，通过搭建场景，搜集物件，然后再处理好这些场景的物件的关系，安置好它们，再进行灯光的设置和拍摄，之后需要冲洗底片，接着再将底片扫描到电脑，再进行一些细节上的处理和修饰，最后打印成照片，装框，展出。

我的基本工作以摄影为主，另外也会做一些装置作品。

- 陈维

24
Chen Wei, *Unnamed Room No. 2*, 2006, archival inkjet print, Ed. 3/8, 59 x 43 1/4 in. (150 x 110 cm), acquired in 2011
陈维，《没有命名的房间 No. 2》, 2006, 收藏用喷墨打印, 版本 3/8, 59 x 43 1/4 寸 (150 x 110 厘米), 收藏于 2011

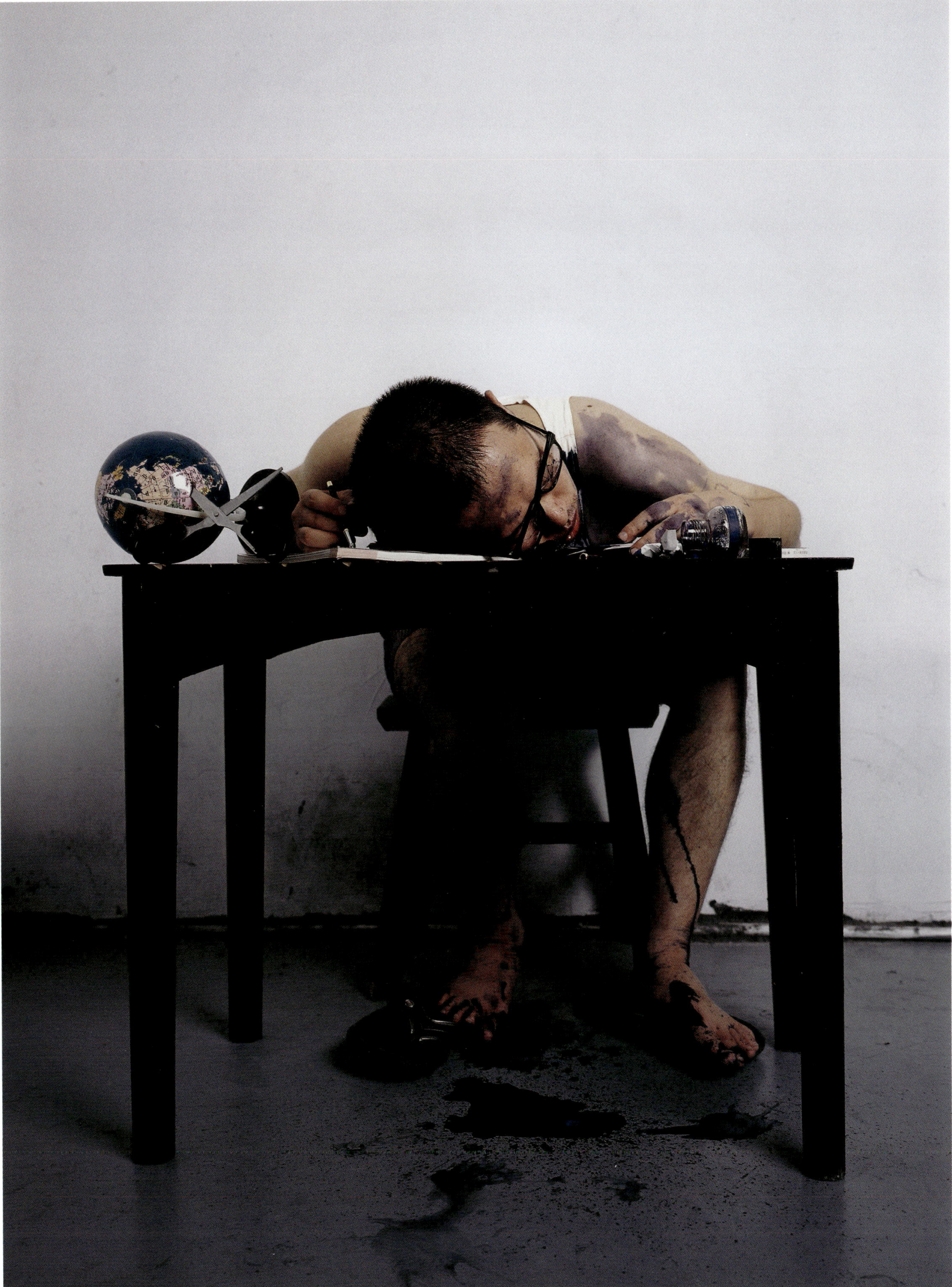

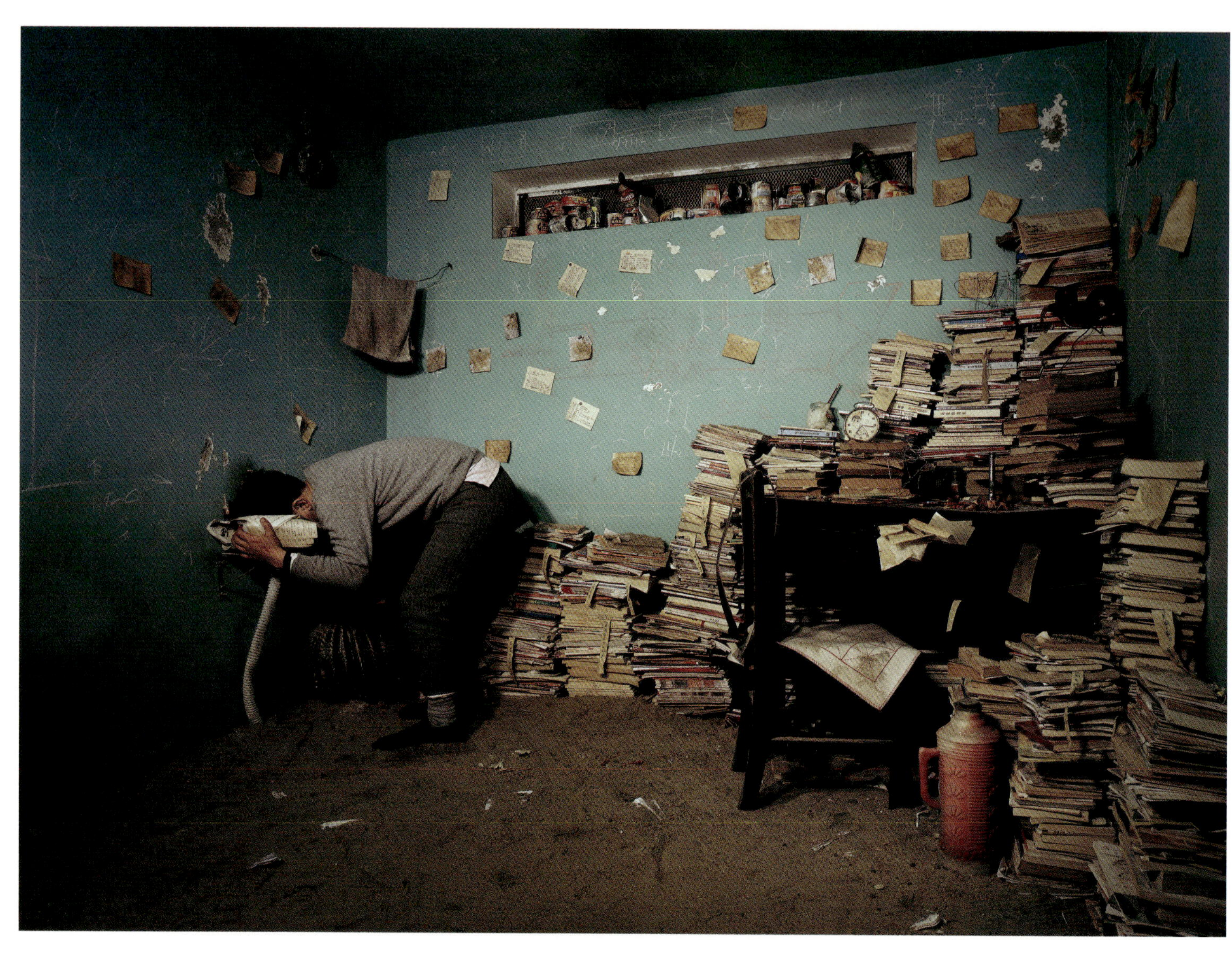

Chen Wei, *Sand and Nobody No. 1*, 2007, archival inkjet print, Ed. 3/6, 47 1/2 x 63 in. (120 x 160 cm), acquired in 2011
陈维，《沙子与没有人 No. 1》，2007，收藏用喷墨打印，版本 3/6，47 1/2 x 63 寸 (120 x 160 厘米)，收藏于 2011

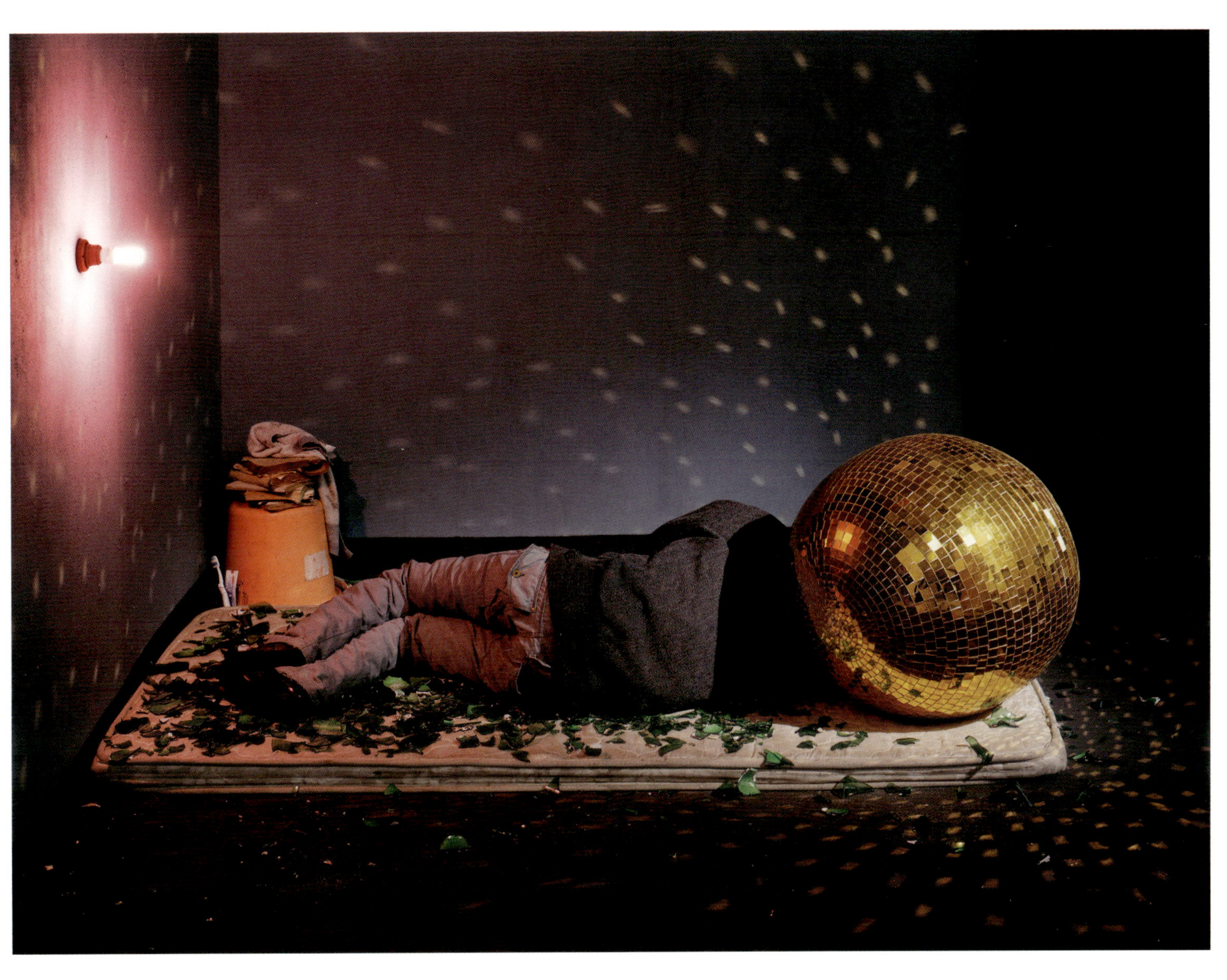

Chen Wei, *The Stars in The Night Sky Are Innumerable*, 2010, archival inkjet print, Ed. 2/6, 39 1/2 x 51 in. (100 x 130 cm), acquired in 2011
陈维，《数不尽的星空》，2010, 收藏用喷墨打印, 版本 2/6, 39 1/2 x 51 寸 (100 x 130 厘米), 收藏于 2011

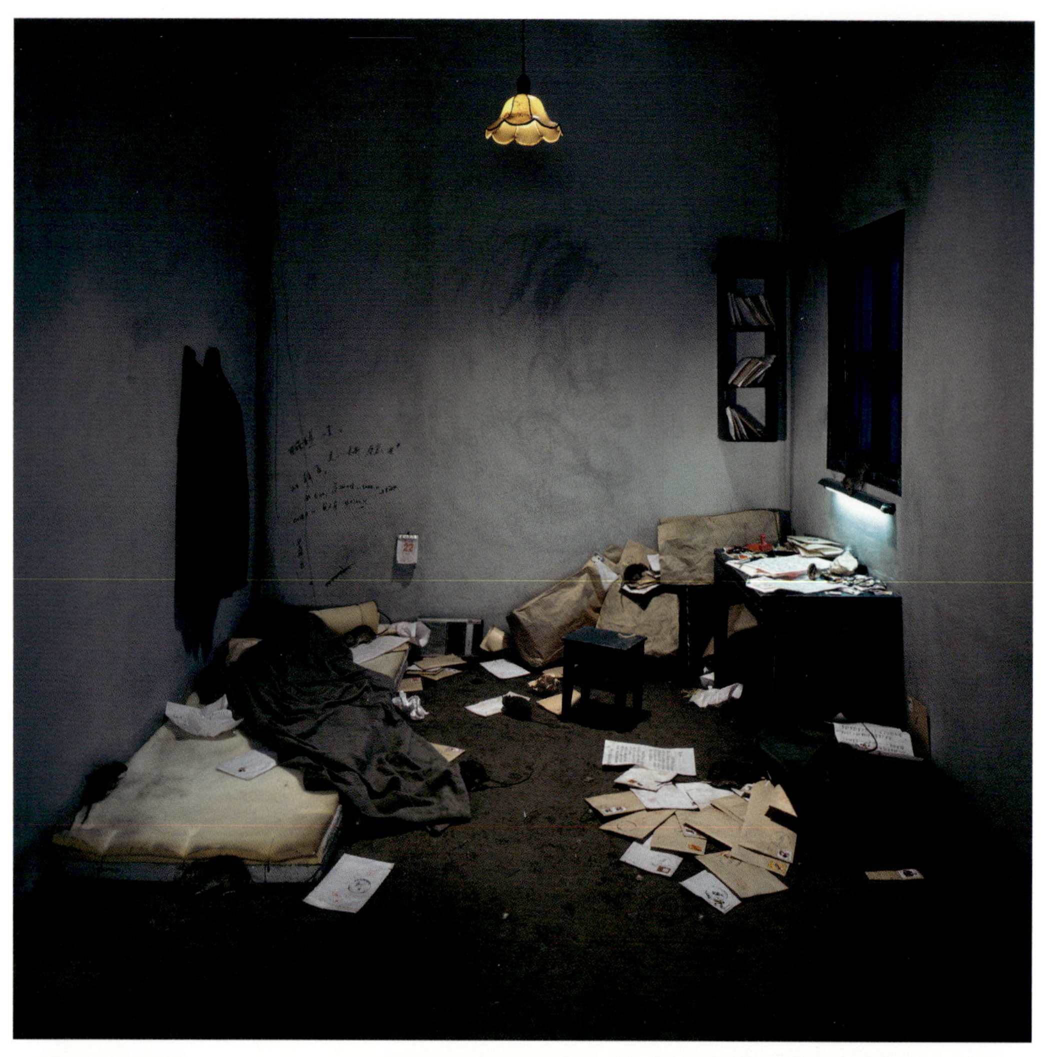

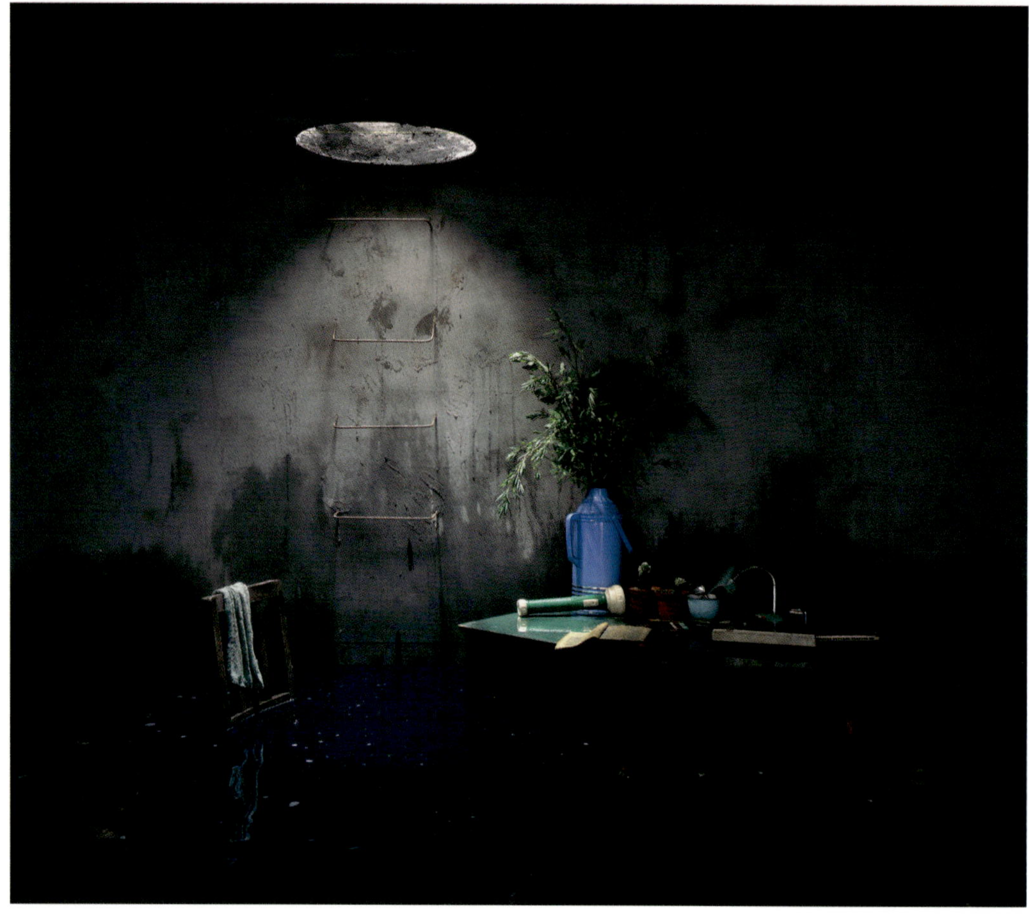

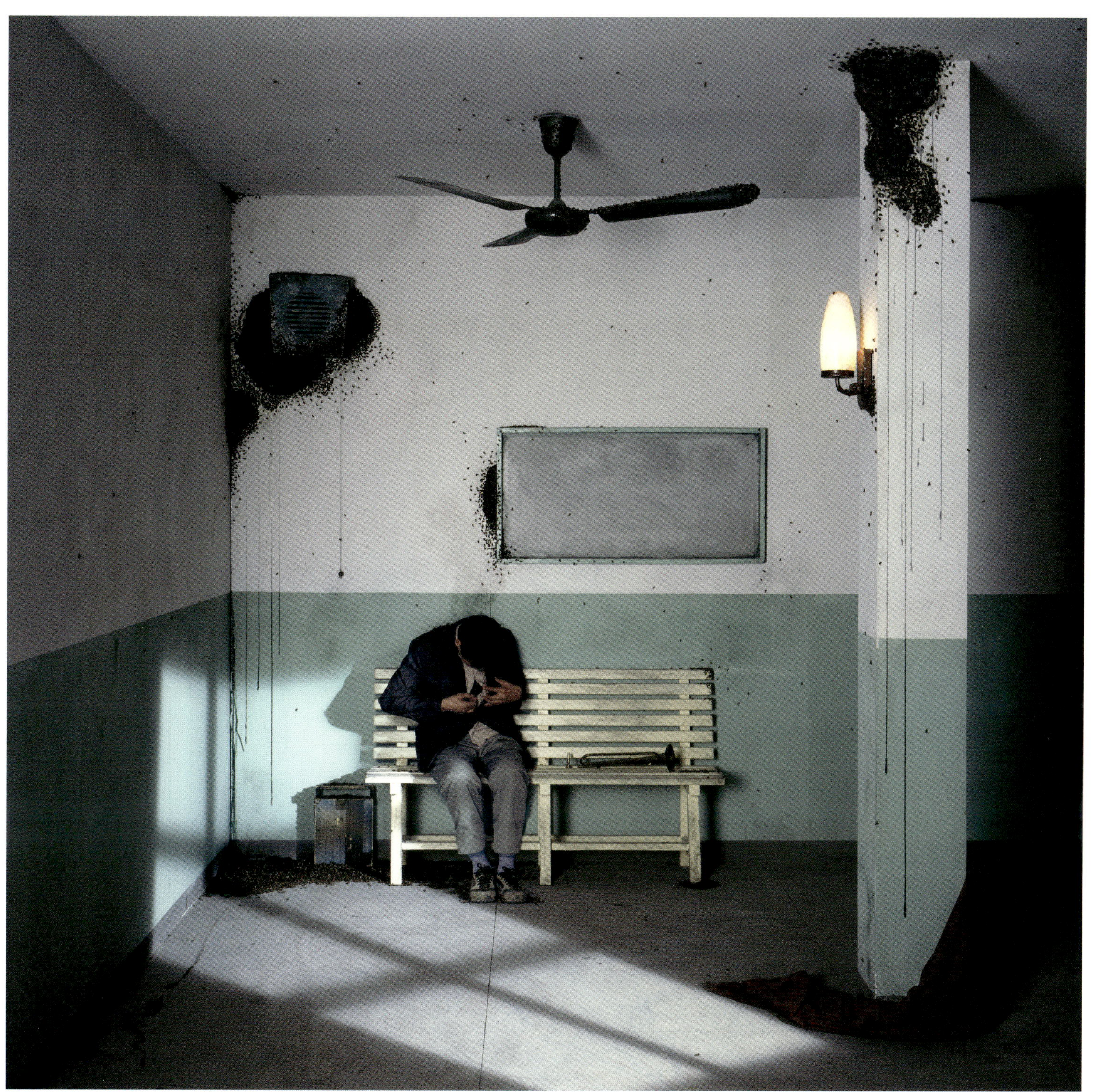

Chen Wei, *A Rat's Post Office*, 2008, archival inkjet print, Ed. 4/6, 59 x 59 in. (150 x 150 cm), acquired in 2011
陈维，《鼠的邮局》，2008，收藏用噴墨打印，版本 4/6，59 x 59 寸 (150 x 150 厘米)，收藏于 2011

Chen Wei, *Blue Ink*, 2009, archival inkjet print, Ed. 6/6, 67 x 59 in. (170 x 150 cm), acquired in 2011
陈维，《蓝墨水》，2009，收藏用噴墨打印，版本 6/6，67 x 59 寸 (170 x 150 厘米)，收藏于 2011

Chen Wei, *Honey in The Broadcast*, 2008, archival inkjet print, Ed. 4/6, 59 x 59 in. (150 x 150 cm), acquired in 2011
陈维，《广播中的蜜》，2008，收藏用噴墨打印，版本 4/6，59 x 59 寸 (150 x 150 厘米)，收藏于 2011

Chen Zhou 陈轴

Born in 1987, Zhejiang, China
Lives and works in Beijing, China

一九八七年生於中国浙江
居住和工作於中国北京

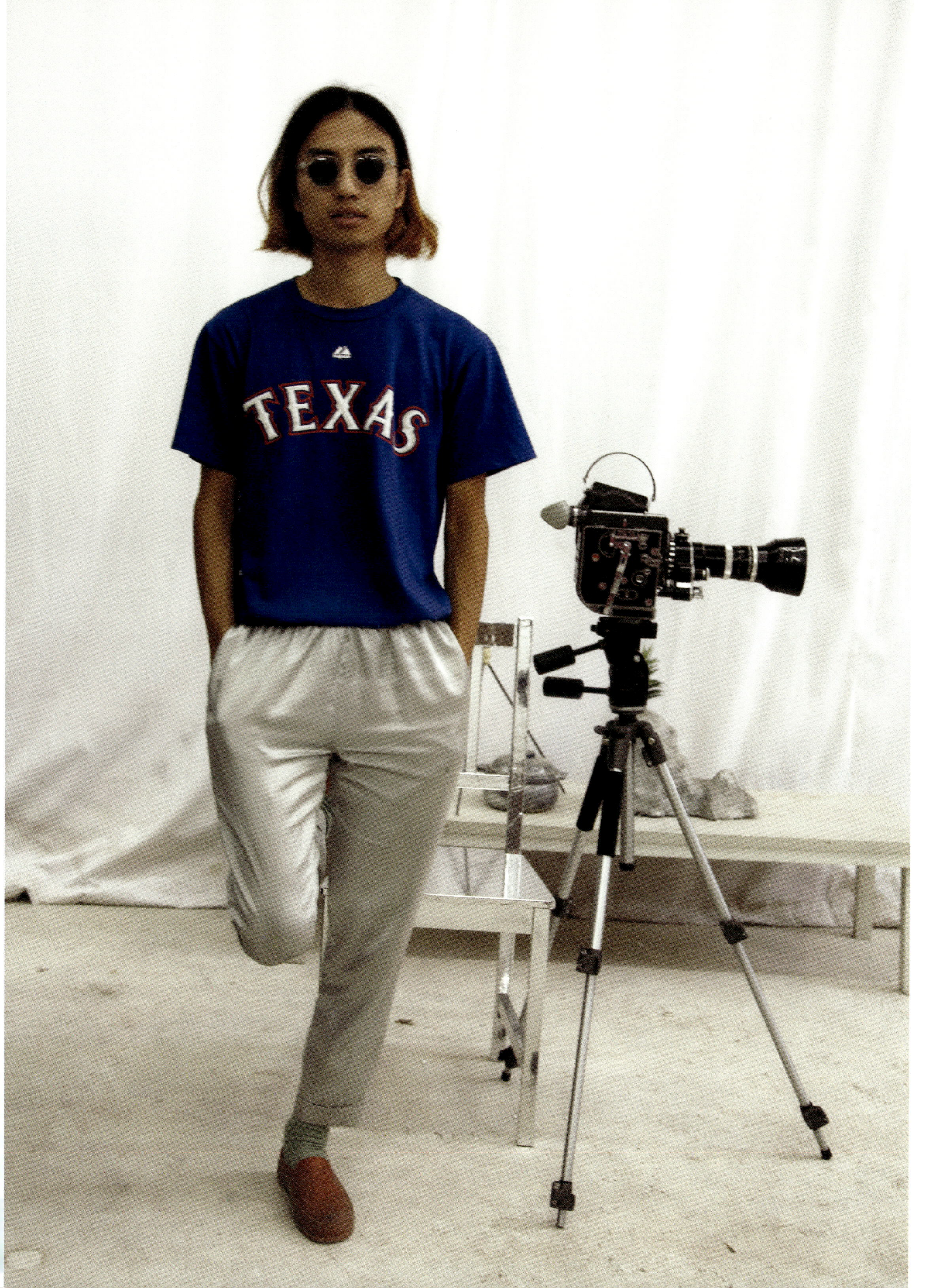

Spanking the Maid II is a long-form script I adapted from Robert Coover's novel *Spanking the Maid*. It is divided into four chapters: "Top Tier Conference," "Fitness Program," "The Master and the Maid," and "Koro." *Spanking the Maid II* is the second chapter—"Fitness Program." The four chapters in the movie make up a circular system of power/violence. "Top Tier Conference" describes something similar to the "Pittsburgh Conference," where elites make a rulebook for national muscle-training programs. "Fitness Program" is about the violence of media, showing the broadcasted media production of the national muscle-training rulebook. "The Master and the Maid" is the main part of the movie, which describes the tranquil and quiet daily life of the master and the maid, without sex or violence. But buried underneath the surface between them there is a hidden violence and an inner lust. In this part of the movie, the master works out his muscles, and he is also a novelist (whom I imaged to be the novelist Robert Coover). He is writing the novel *Spanking the Maid*. This leads to the fourth part of the movie, "Koro," which is in fact the plot of the master's novel. This part is about the imaginary power/violence dynamic. In this novel written by the master there is also a planter and a maid. The planter punishes the maid's mistakes in various ways including spanking her. But what is different from the original [Robert Coover's] novel is that this planter gets a weird disease called Koro, which causes the patient to suddenly have a fear of death because he feels that his penis has shrunken or curled into his stomach. This is a psychological disease. This imaginary planter is a psychological projection of both the master in the third part of the movie "The Master and the Maid," and one of the participating elite in the first part of the movie "Top Tier Conference." This completes the circular system of power/violence. The script was completed in 2012 and so far the second part of the movie has been shot.

\- Chen Zhou

《打女佣的屁股II》是我根据　　　罗伯特·库佛（Robert　Coover）的原著小说（Spanking the　maid）改编的一个长片剧本，一共分为四个章节：［顶层会议］，［健身节目］，［雇主与女佣］，［缩阳症（Koro）］。《打女佣的屁股II》便是其中第二个章节–［健身节目］。
全片四个章节组成了一个权力／暴力的循环体系，［顶层会议］描写的一个类似彼德伯格会议，高层精英在制定一套全民肌肉训练法则。［健身节目］是关于媒体的暴力，也是全名肌肉训练法则的一个媒体传播的产品。［雇主与女佣］是全片的主体，描写雇主和女佣没有任何性与暴力的平静的日常生活。但在他们之间存在着一种潜在的，内心的暴力和色情。在这部分中，雇主锻炼肌肉，也是一个小说家（是我虚构的小说家Robert　Coover）他正在写一部小说，那部小说便是《打女佣的屁股》。因此带出全片的第四部分［缩阳症（Koro）］也就是雇主写的小说情节，这部分是虚构的权力／暴力，同样的在这个小说情节中有一个庄园主和女仆，庄园主会用各种手段惩罚女仆的失责（打屁股），但与原著小说不同的是，这个庄园主得了一种怪病叫缩阳症，缩阳症指患者突然间自感阴茎缩小或缩入腹中而产生极度的死亡恐惧。这是一种精神性的心理疾病。这个虚构的庄园主正是第三部分［雇主与女佣］那个雇主的心理投射，也同时是第一部分［顶层会议］中的一个参会精英。这便完整的链接了一个权力／暴力的循环体系。这个剧本是2012年完成的，至今已完成第二部分的拍摄。

\- 陈轴

Chen Zhou, *Spanking the Maid II*, 2012, HD film (color, sound), Ed. 2/4, duration: 13 min., acquired in 2012
陈轴，《打女佣的屁股 II》，2012, 高清数码电影 (彩色, 有声), 版本 2/4, 片长 13 分钟, 收藏于 2012

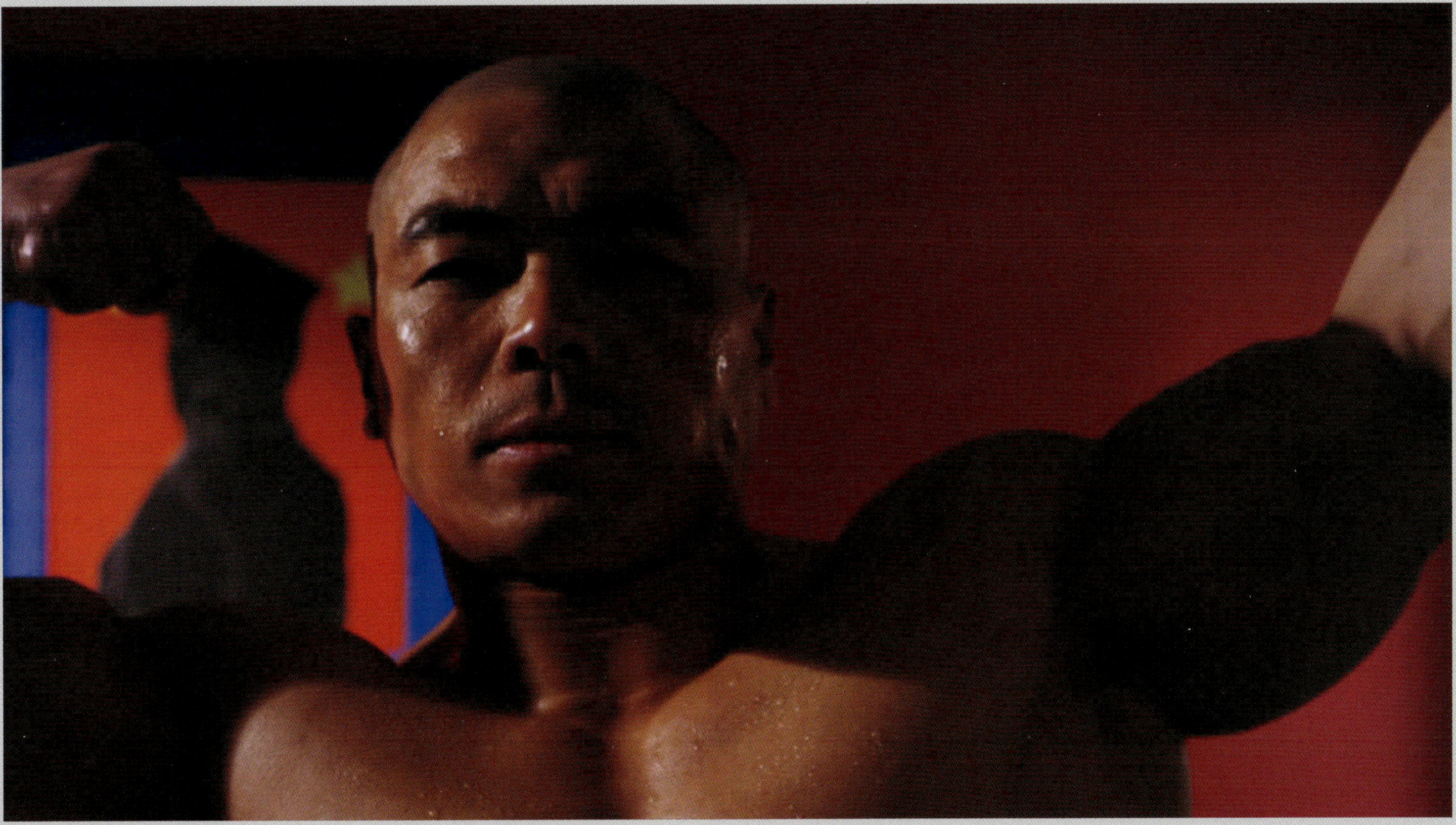

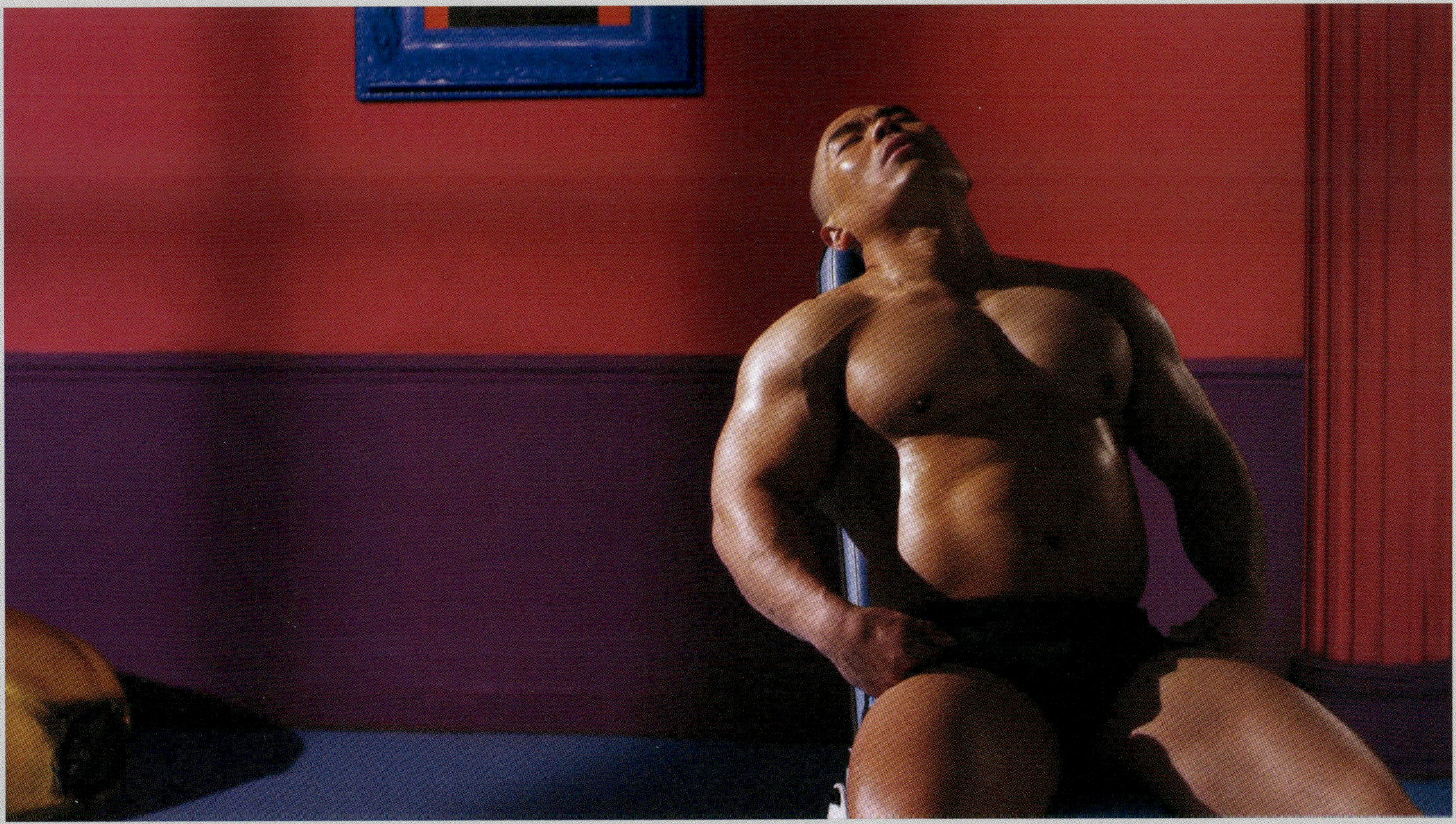

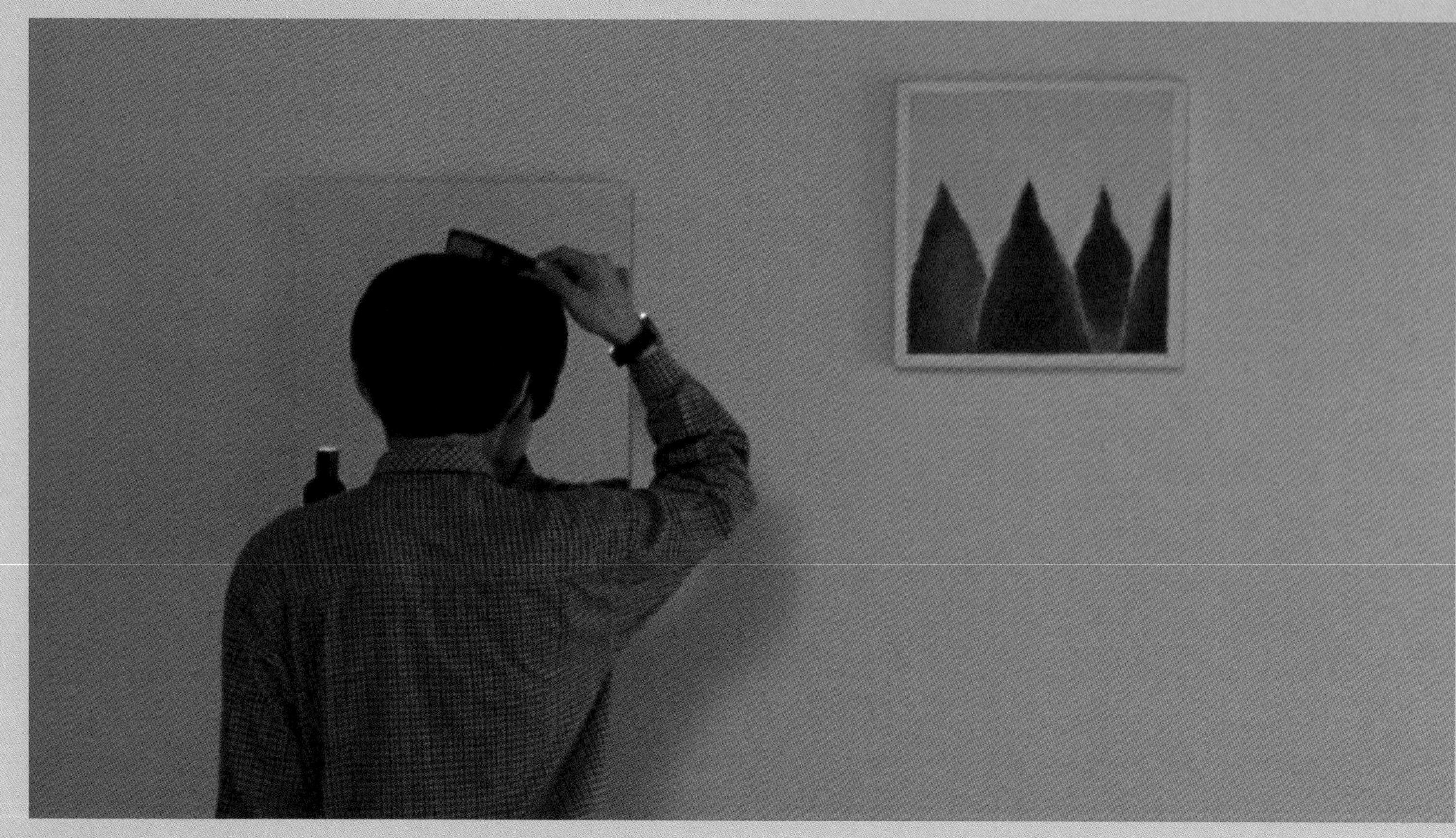

Morning! originated from food. I once spent 8 yuan on a very small piece of German bread and I still haven't forgotten the memory of eating it for the first time. It felt like an aromatic white cloud, and every time I think back that aroma lingers around me. I relied on that feeling to finish shooting *Morning!*.

- Chen Zhou

《早！》最先来自于食物，我曾经花了8块钱买了一个很小的德国面包，我至今都无法忘记第一次吃它的记忆。那种感觉像是一股白色的香味，当我想起的时候香味就会萦绕在我身边，我凭着那种感觉完成了《早！》的拍摄。

- 陈轴

Chen Zhou, *Morning!*, 2011, 16mm film transferred to HD Beta (color, sound), Ed. 1/4, duration: 13 min. 12 sec., acquired in 2012
陈轴，《早！》，2011，16 mm 电影转高清 (彩色, 有声)，版本 1/4，片长 13 分钟 12 秒，收藏于 2012

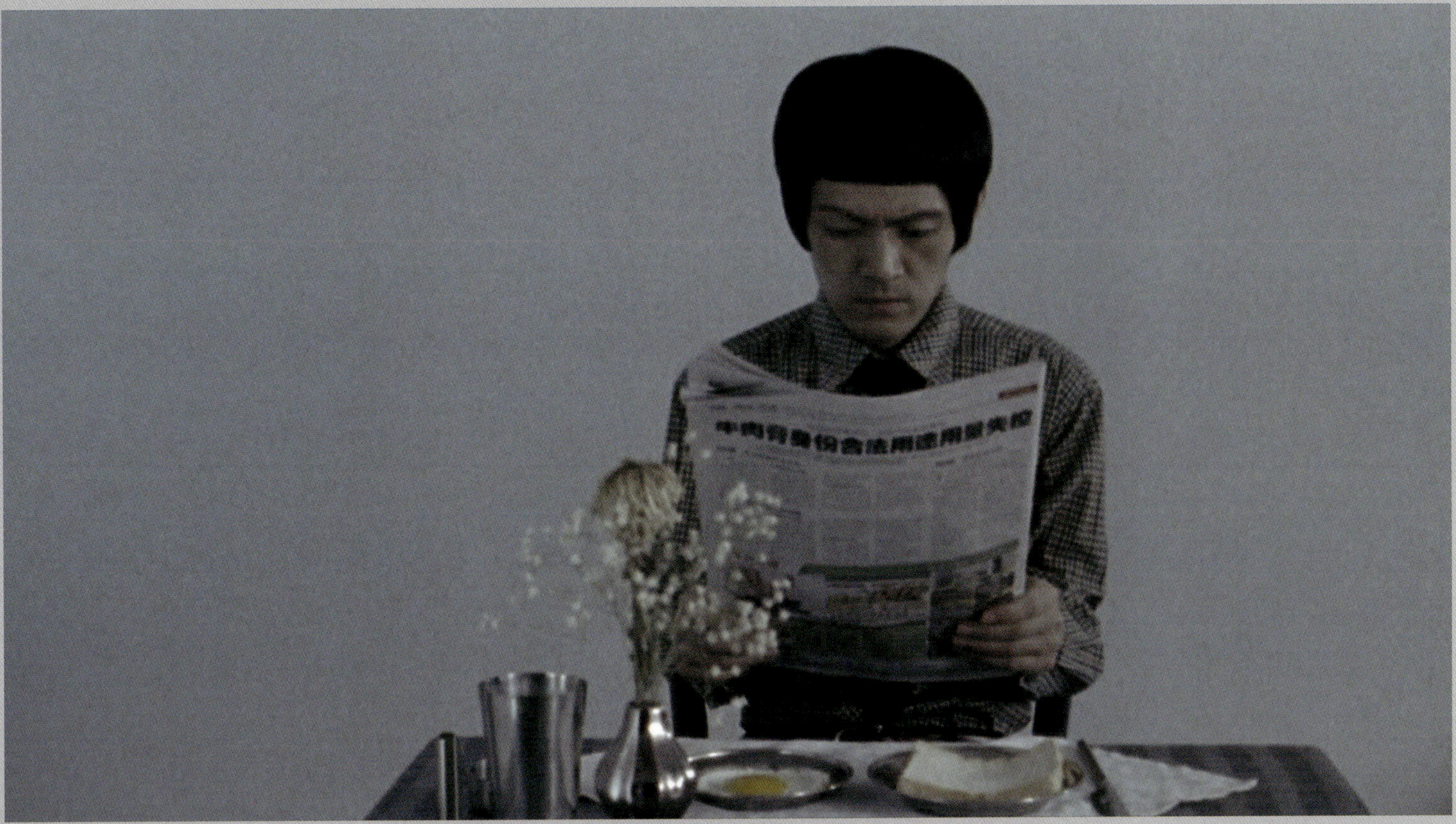

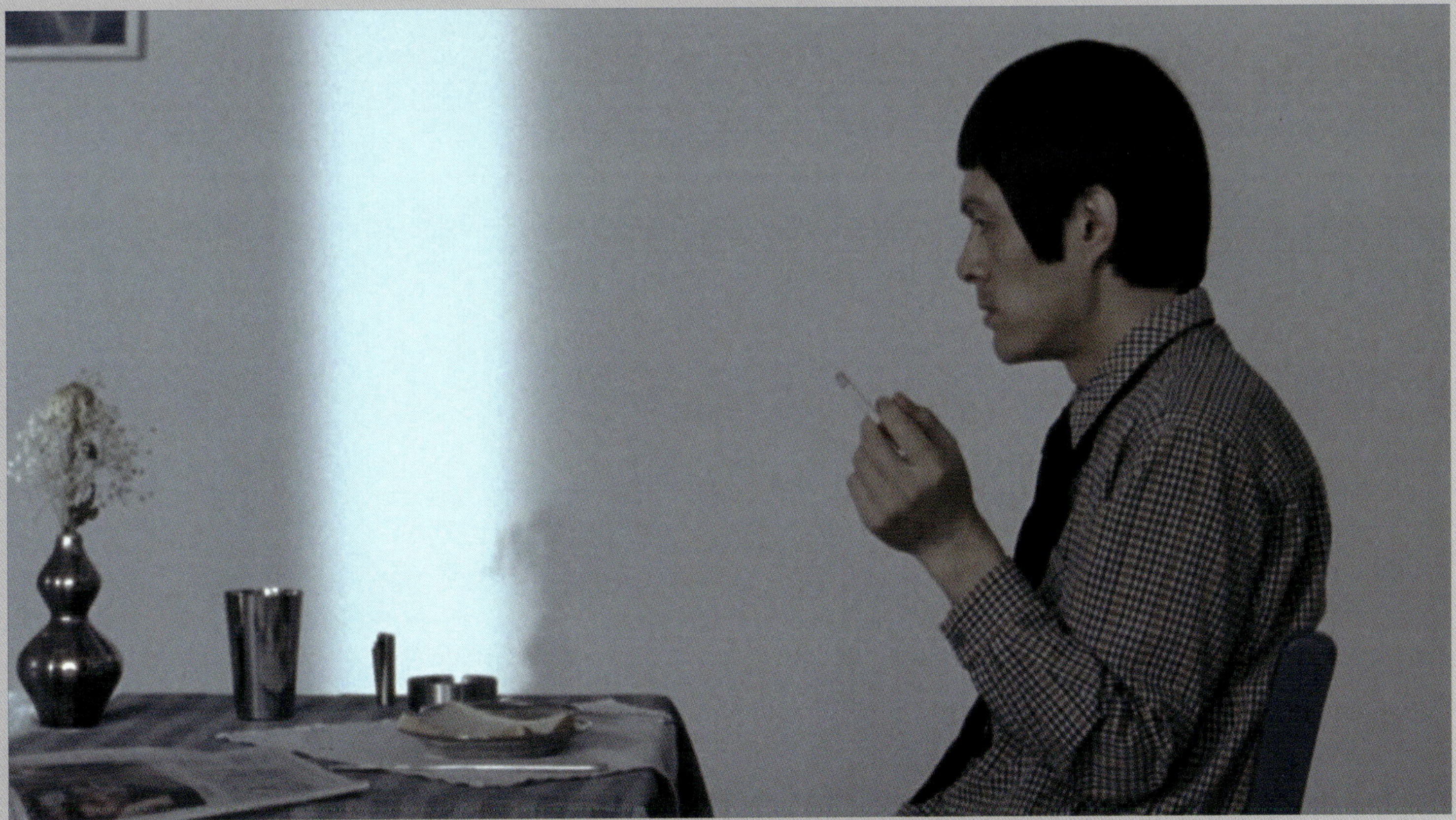

Fang Lu 方璐

Born in 1981, Guangdong, China
Lives and works in Beijing, China

一九八一年生於中国广东
居住和工作於中国北京

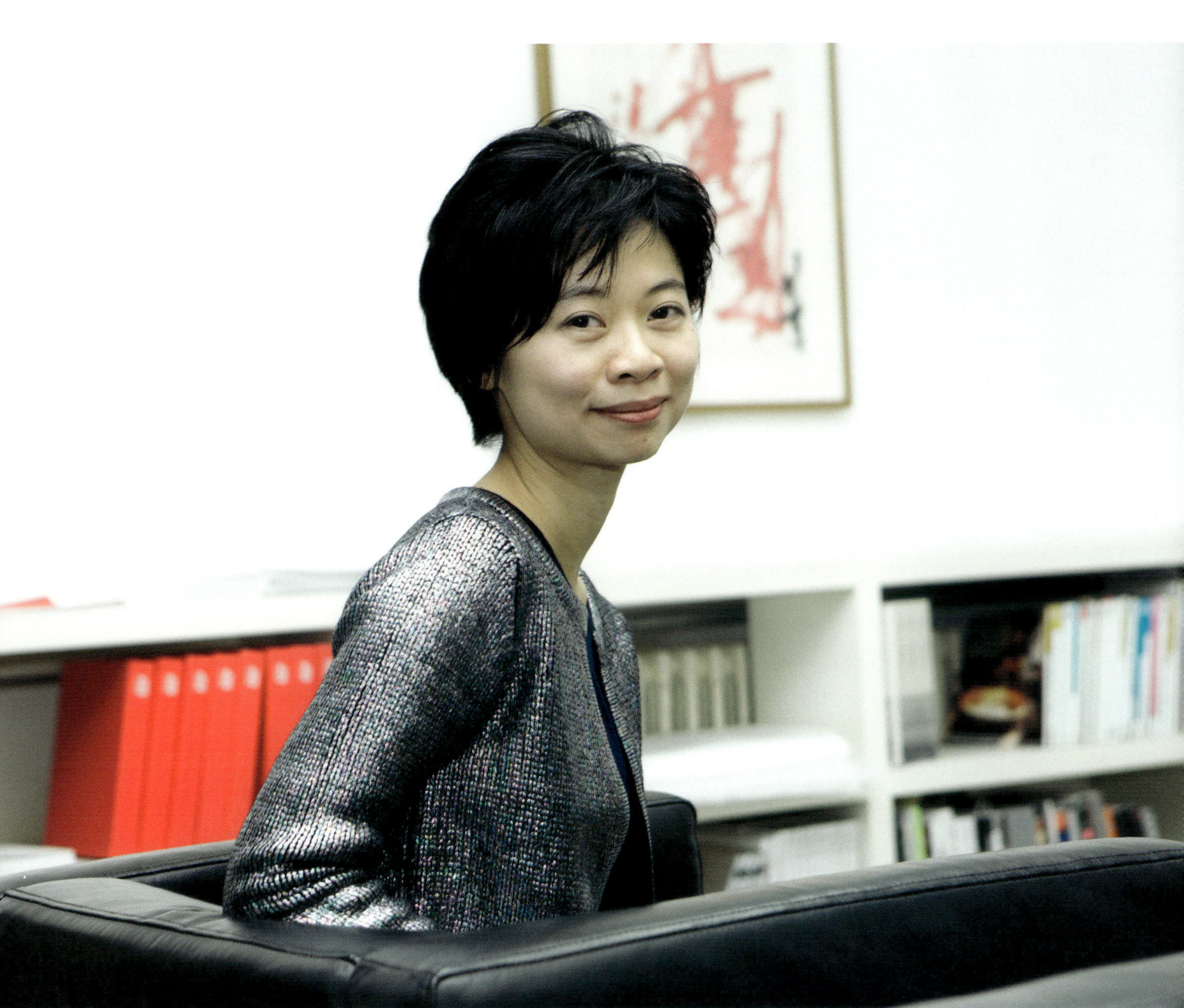

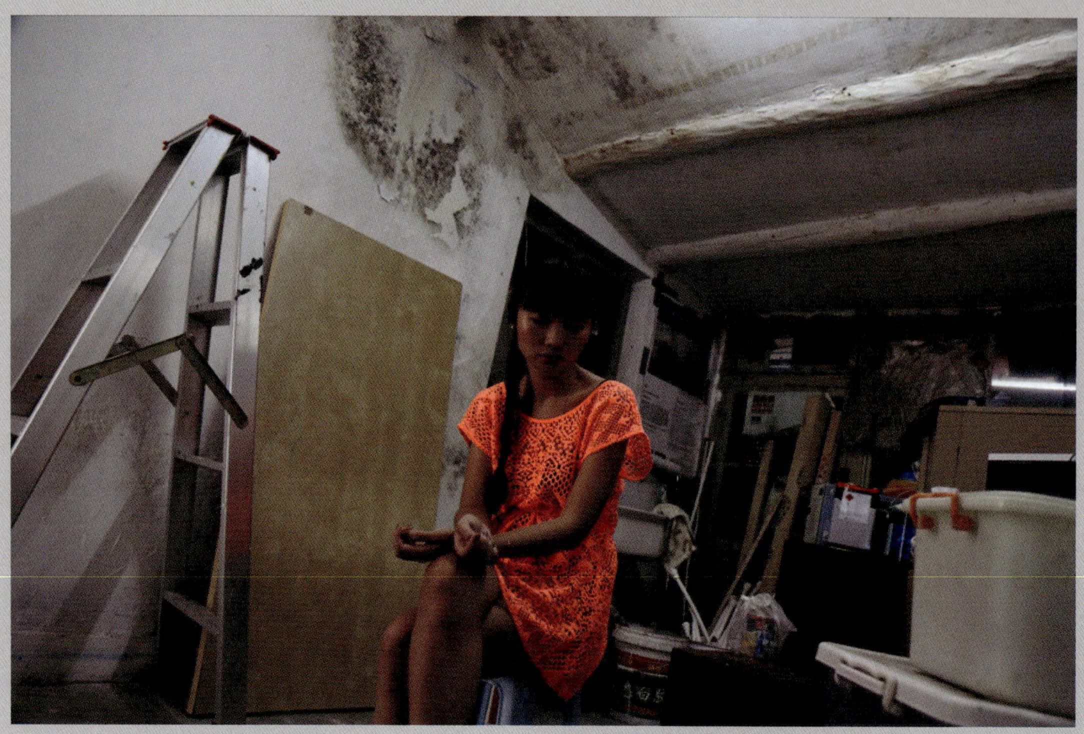

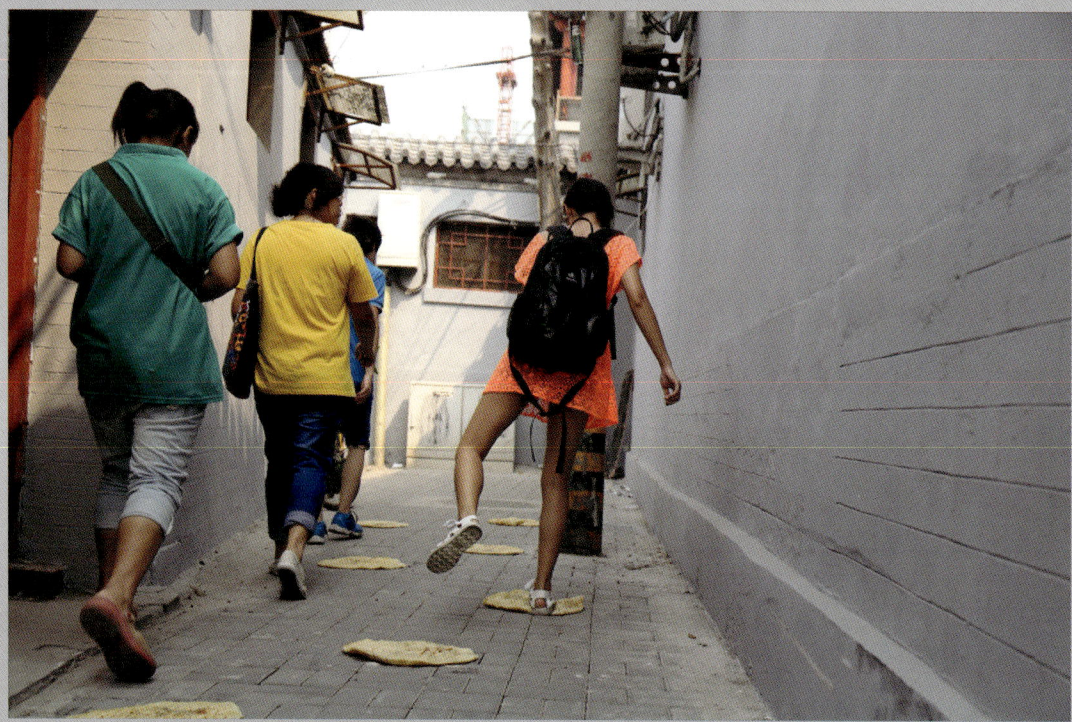

The street is "her" living room, the hutong (alley) "her" studio. Wandering in the streets and alleys, "she" buys groceries like an ordinary woman who is living her daily life, but afterwards, she destroys, uses and creates these goods in peculiar ways, just like an artist redesigning an object. The title "Lovers are Artists" comes from a chapter of Roland Barthes' *A Lover's Discourse: Fragments*, pointing to the different ways people who are in love can be in touch with our world, just like the ways artists perceive the world.

- Fang Lu

Fang Lu, *Lovers Are Artists (Part One)*, 2012, four-channel video (color, silent), Ed.1/5, performer: Guan Xiao, photography: Hai Li, project produced by Arrow Factory (Beijing), No. 1, duration: 5 min. 14 sec., No. 2, duration: 2 min. 30 sec., No. 3, duration: 6 min. 36 sec., No. 4, duration: 3 min. 35 sec., acquired in 2012

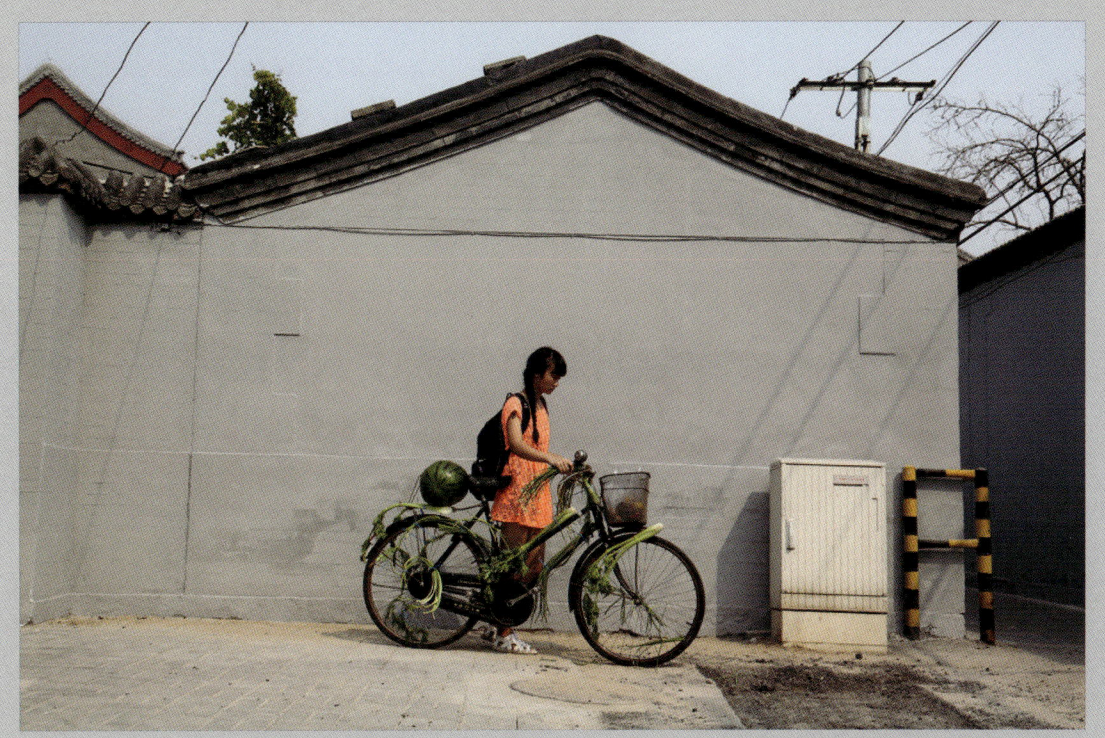

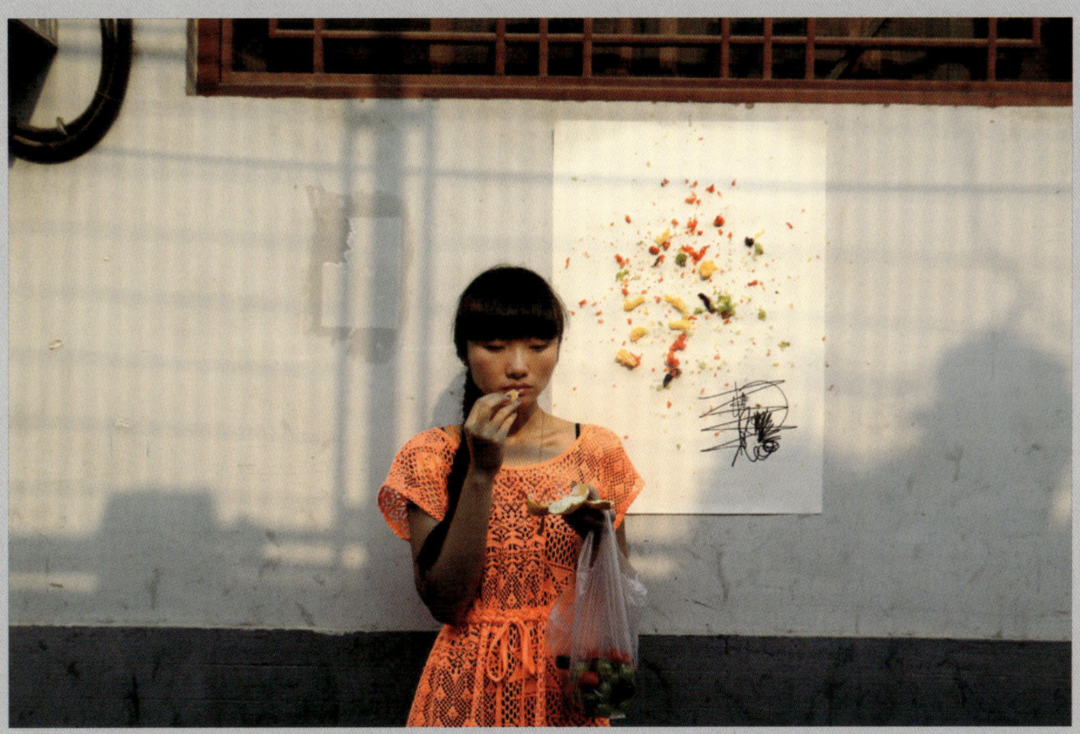

街道是"她"的客厅，胡同是"她"的工作室。游走于大街小巷，"她"像日常生活中的女性一般购买胡同里出售的蔬菜和食品，但之后又像艺术家改造物品一般把这些物体破坏、用奇特的方式来使用和创造。"恋爱的人就是艺术家"题目来自罗兰巴特《恋人絮语》中的一个章节，指处于恋爱状态中的人能够用不同的方式来感知我们的世界，就如同艺术家对世界的感知。

- 方璐

方璐，《恋爱的人就是艺术家 – 第一部》，2012，四频录像装置 (彩色，无声)，版本 1/5，表演者：关小，摄影：海蠡，生产：于箭厂空间，频道一：5 分 14 秒，频道二：2 分 30 秒，频道三：6 分 36 秒，频道四：3 分 35 秒，收藏于 2012

He Xiangyu 何翔宇

Born in 1986, Liaoning, China
Lives and works in Beijing, China

一九八六年生於中國辽宁
居住和工作於中國北京

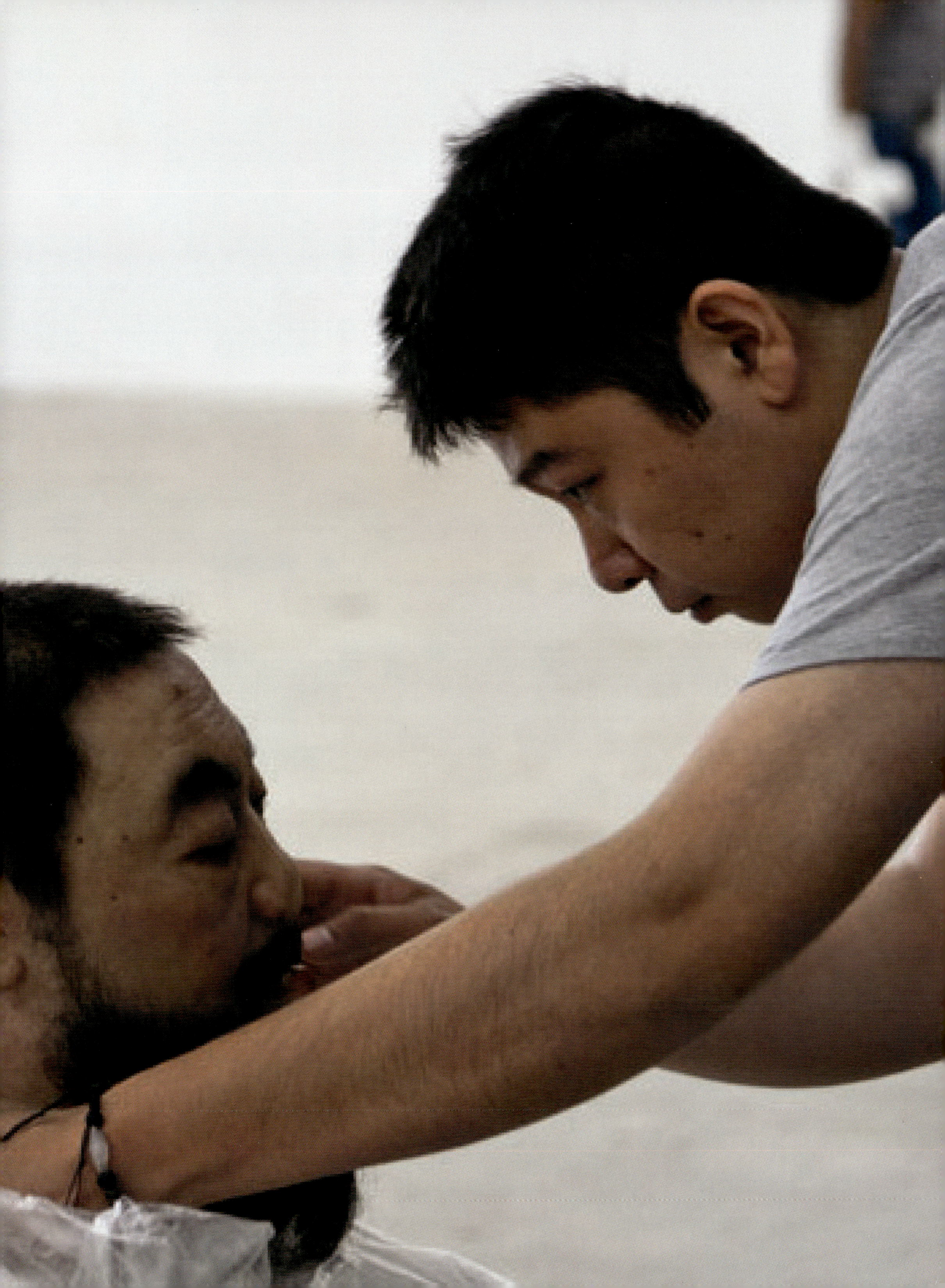

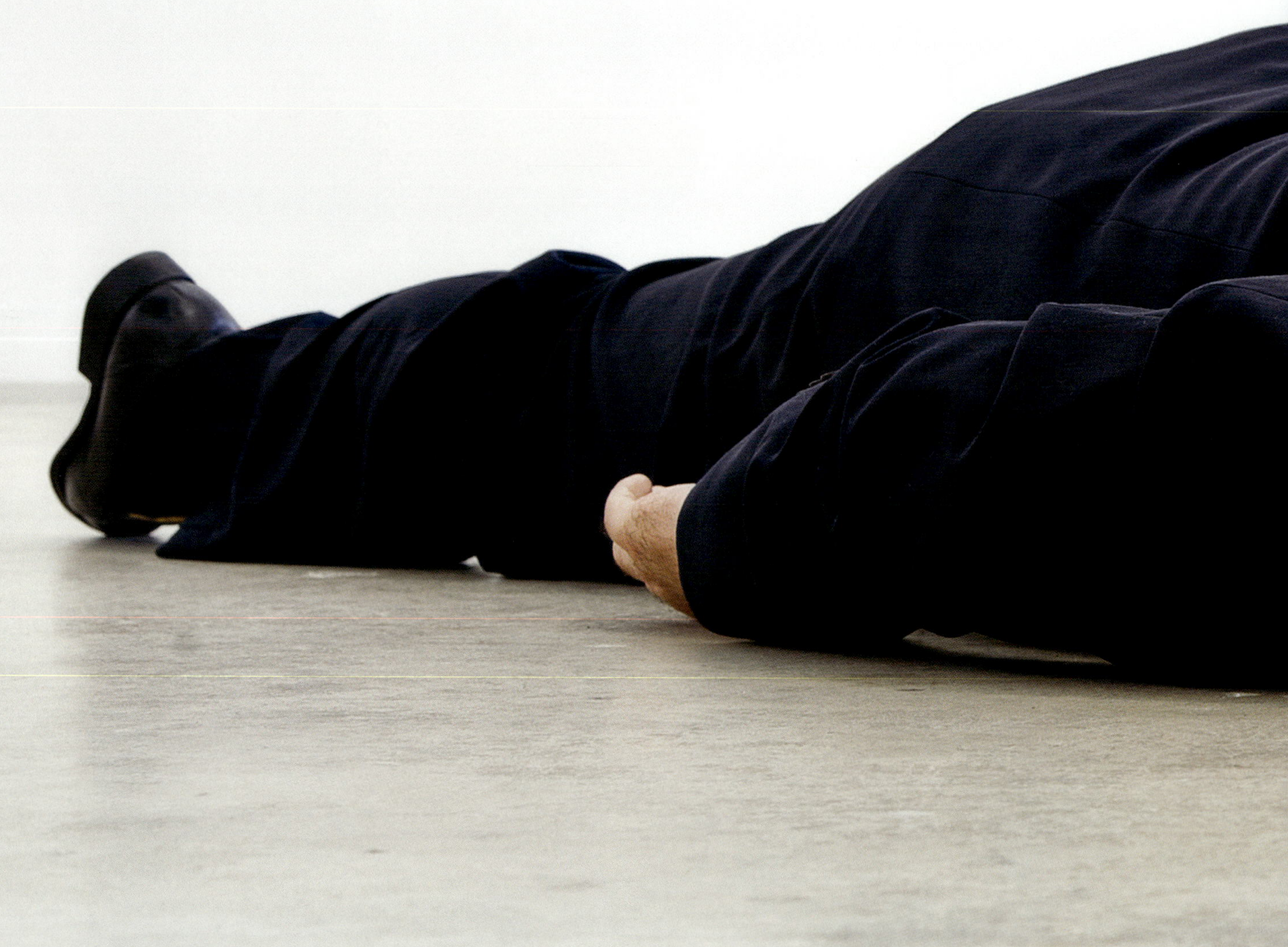

I was inspired by the Ai Weiwei tax evasion case and used fiberglass to make a sculpture of him. In the piece Ai Weiwei wears the suit worn by People's Representatives during People's Congress meetings and lies on the ground facing down. It at once alludes to his entrapped position and his status as an idol. It also reflects an individual's actions as well as the essential connection and speculative relation between fate and the power structure.

- He Xiangyu

He Xiangyu, *The Death of Marat*, 2011, fiberglass, silicone, fabric, human hair and leather, Ed. 1/3, 13 x 80 1/2 x 33 1/2 in. (33 x 205 x 85 cm), acquired in 2011

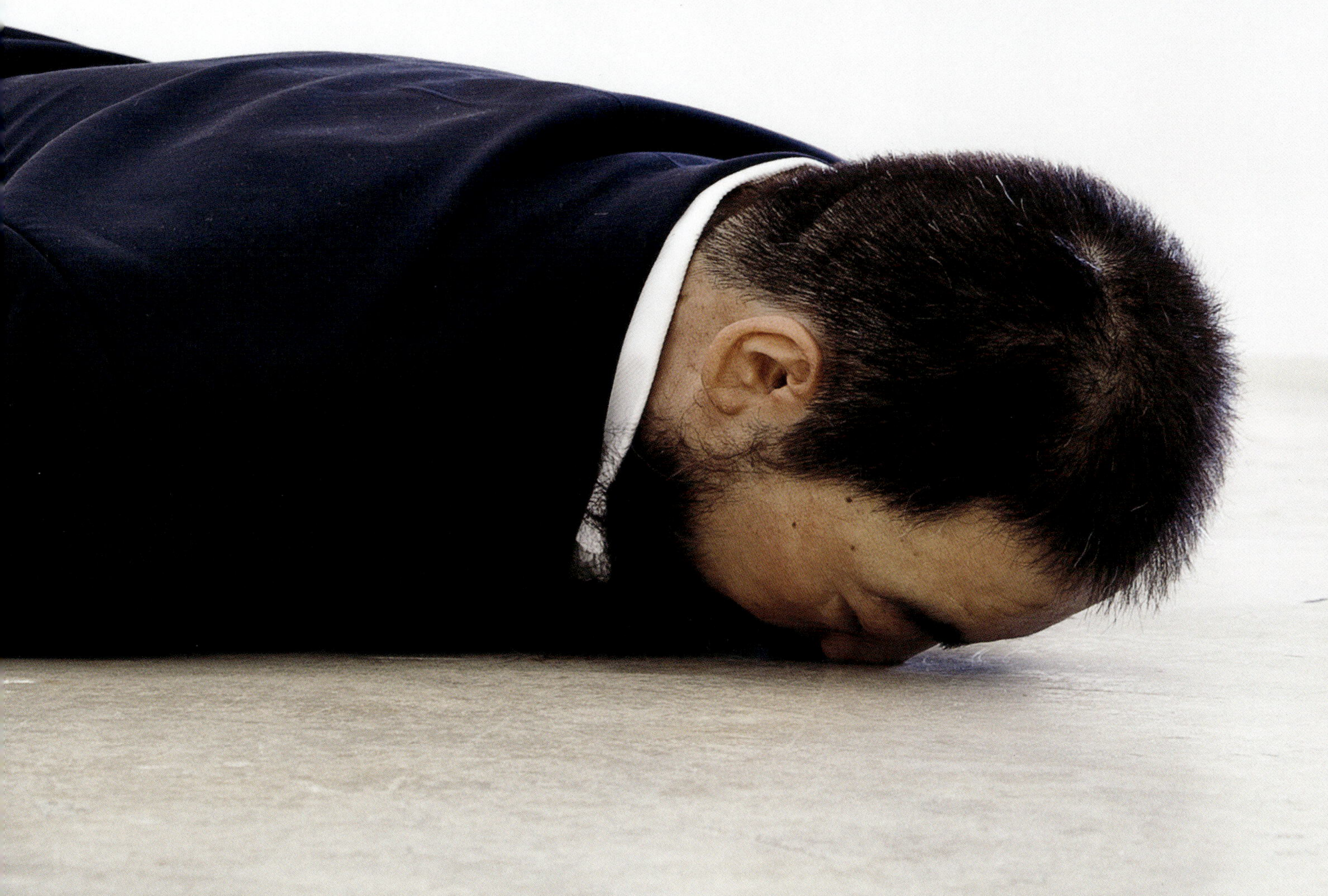

《马拉之死》，我受"艾未未偷税事件"的启发，用硅胶制作了一件艾未未的塑像，作品中的艾未未身穿中国人大开会时代表的衣着伏地倒下，既影射了艾未未当时身陷囹圄的境遇以及他的偶像地位，同时也在反思个体行动以及命运与权力系统之间的生命联系与思辨关系。

- 何翔宇

何翔宇，《马拉之死》，2011，玻璃纤维，二氧化硅，头发和皮革，版本 1/3, 13 x 80 1/2 x 33 1/2 寸 (33 x 205 x 85 厘米), 收藏于 2011

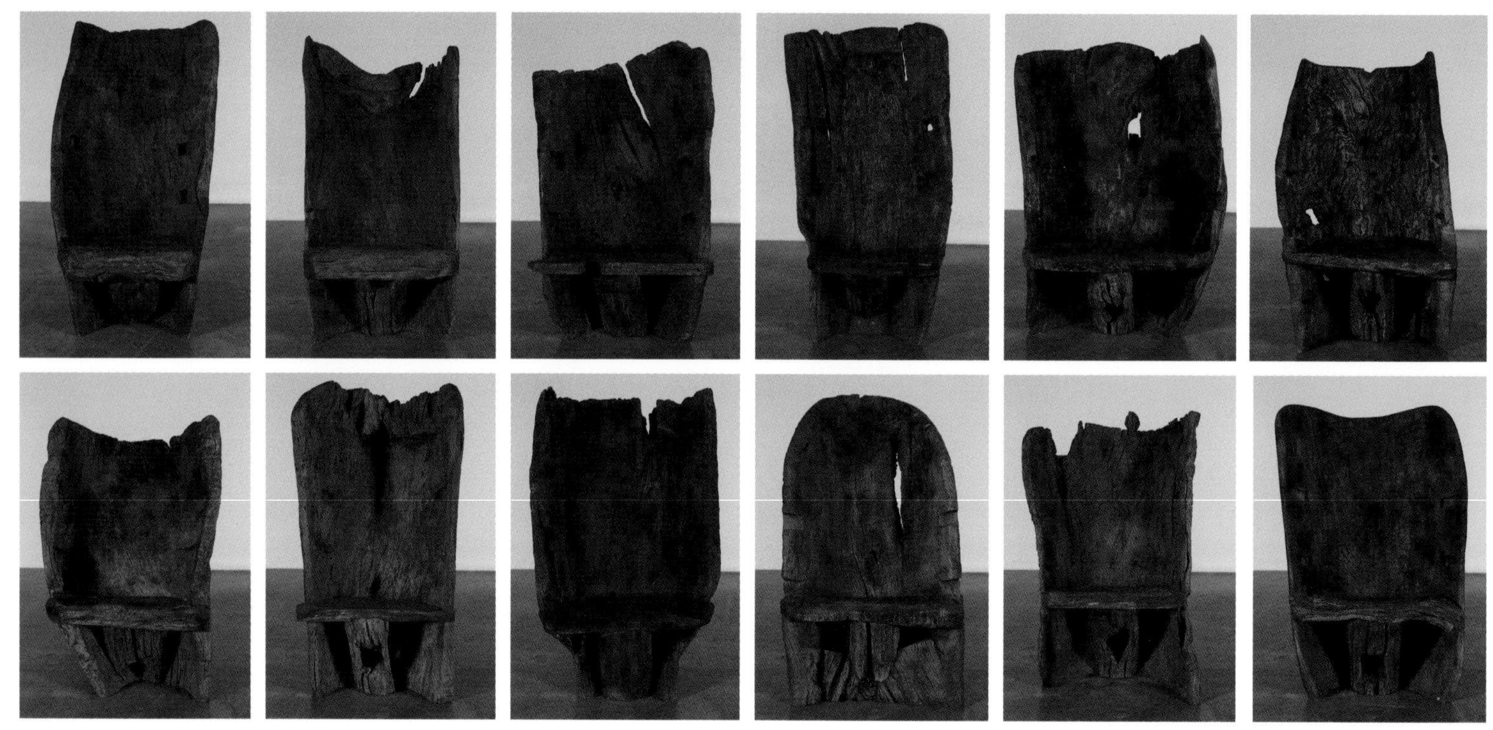

I collected a lot of abandoned wooden drainage pipes from Yunnan province, and then broke them down and rebuilt them into over 100 chairs. Even though each chair looks different, every single one shows the poignancy and vicissitudes of the passage of time.

Different individuals, the same destination. The group of empty chairs evoke an ambiguous yet tenacious sense of collective fatalism. Hence, I produced a four chapter dance piece, respectively titled "tristesse", "agony", "despair" and "rebirth". The dance recounts the story of men who were born among the group of empty chairs; they amuse and fall in love with one another, until one day they realize they can no longer leave the chairs—leaving would cost them their lives.

- He Xiangyu

我搜集了大量已被云南山民弃用的古老的原木水渠，并将其拆卸重组成一百余把椅子，椅子虽各具形象，但每把都显现出苦涩沧桑的岁月感——

不同的个体，相同的归宿，空荡的椅群营造出一种暧昧且难以摆脱的集体性的宿命感，因此我编排了一个以"悲伤"、"痛苦"、"绝望"、"重生"4个章节为主题的舞蹈剧，剧目讲述了人从空荡的椅群里出生，相互嬉戏，相互爱恋，直到一天发现他们不能离开椅子，如果离开将会死去－－－

- 何翔宇

He Xiangyu, *The Man on the Chair*, 2008-2009, wood (13 unique works), each: 44 3/8 x 27 x 35 1/2 in. (113 x 68 x 89 cm), acquired in 2011
何翔宇，《椅子上的人》，2008-2009，木材（十三件作品），每张: 44 3/8 x 27 x 35 1/2 in. (113 x 68 x 89 cm)，收藏于 2011

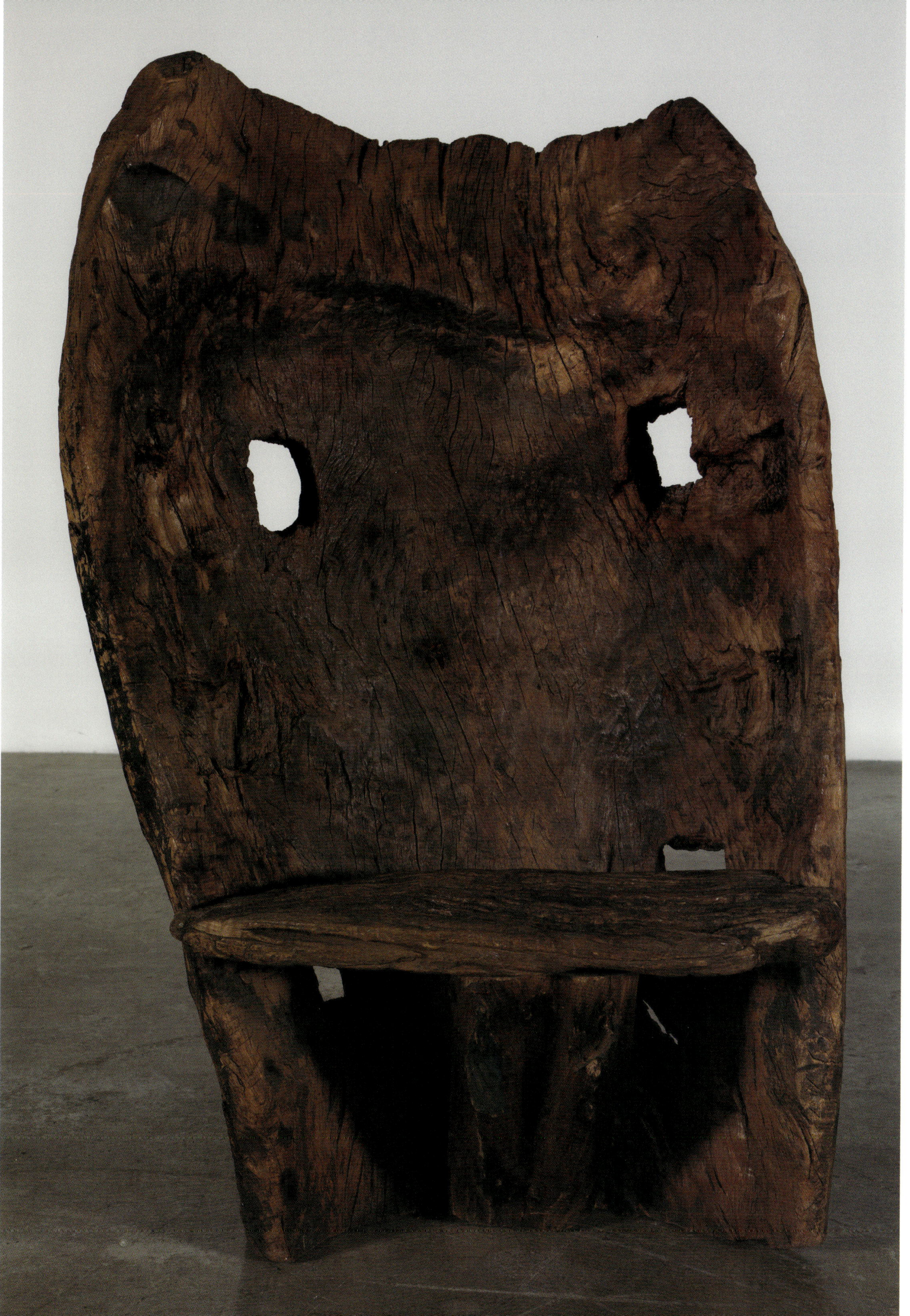

Cola Project ran from the beginning of 2009 to the end of 2011. In the beginning, it was only a ton (1000 liters) of Coca-Cola I purchased from a big supermarket. Then I started working in a simple "kitchen" built in the studio, while at the same time I also drew a large amount of drafts and carried out many different relevant experiments. At the end of 2009 I decided to move the worksite to the city of Dandong in Liaoning Province (where China borders with North Korea), and hired 10 industrial workers to build about a dozen or so 150 x 120 cm iron woks and a simple rain-proof shelter, and also purchased over 10 tons of wood to start the core work of the *Cola Project*. Over a period of a year and a half, we worked relentlessly. The 10 workers worked a total of over 6000 hours, boiled up 127 tons of Coca Cola, and extracted over 40 cubic meters of Coca Cola residuum. What "happily surprised" me at the same time was, during the process of "extraction", the police, fire, border patrol, and environmental protection departments all came to investigate me and collect evidence, and I also paid some fines.

- He Xiangyu

"可口可乐计划" 2009年初 – – 2011年底，开始只是在大型超市购买了1吨可口可乐，然后工作在工作室搭建的简易"厨房"开始，同时绘制了大量草图并做了很多不同的相关试验。2009年底，决定将工作地点转移至辽宁省丹东市（中国相邻朝鲜边境的城市），并雇佣10名普通工人搭建10于口150X120CM的铁锅和简易防雨棚，同时购买了10几吨木材开始了可乐计划的核心工作，1年半连续不停的作业，10个工人工作6000多小时，煮了127吨可口可乐，所"萃取"的可口可乐残渣有40多立方，同时令我"惊喜"的是在"萃取"过程中，公安、消防、边防、环境保护等不同部门全部前来对我的行为进行调查和取证，并缴纳了部分罚款。

- 何翔宇

He Xiangyu, *Cola Project- Extraction*, 2009, 10 wooden boxes with empty Coca-Cola bottles tagged with time, 178 x 93 1/8 x 12.5 in (452 x 236.5 x 32 cm), acquired in 2011
何翔宇，《可乐计划-萃取》，2009，10个木箱和有时间标签的可口可乐空瓶，178 x 93 1/8 x 12.5 寸 (452 x 236.5 x 32 厘米)，收藏于 2011

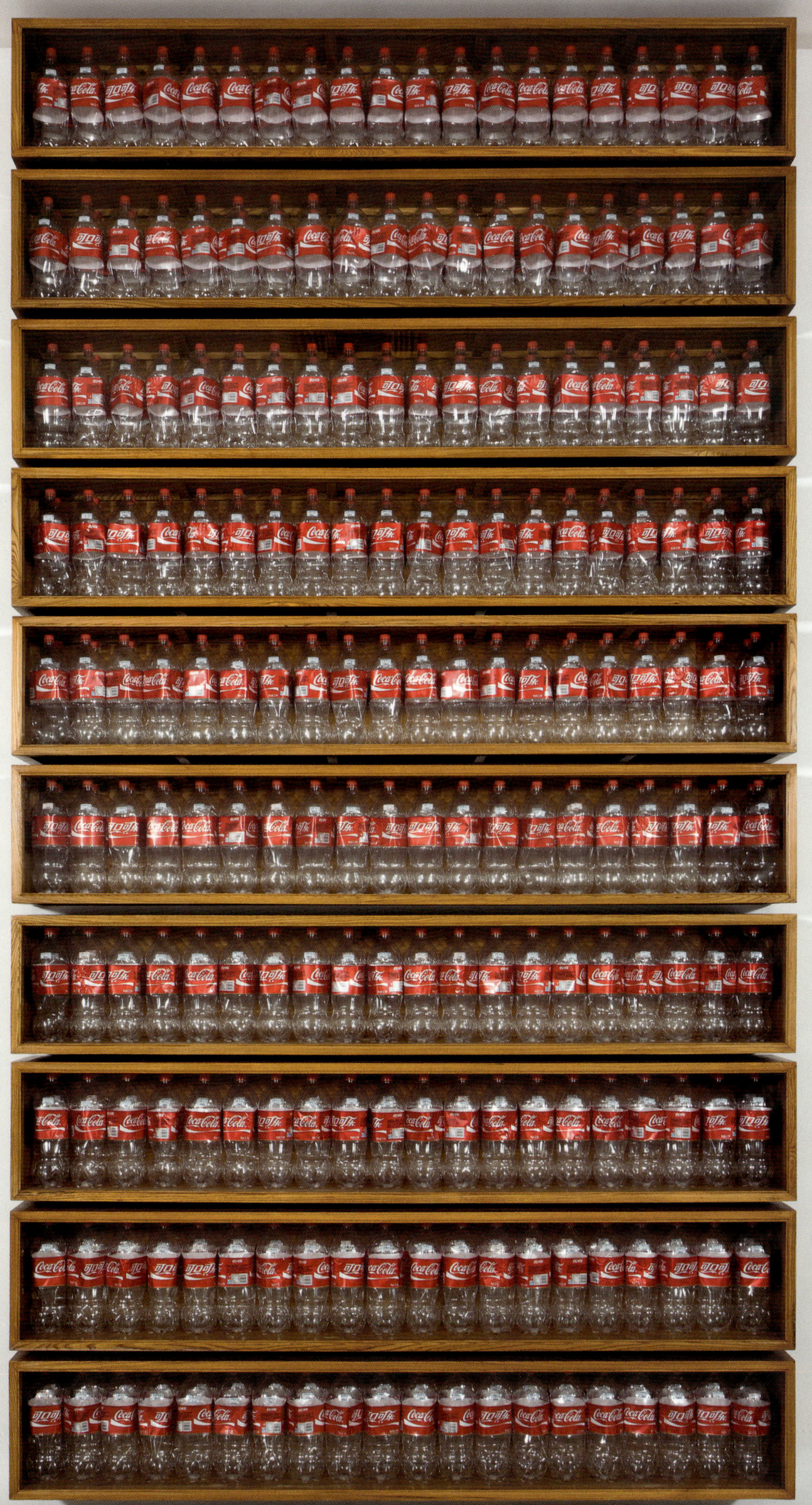

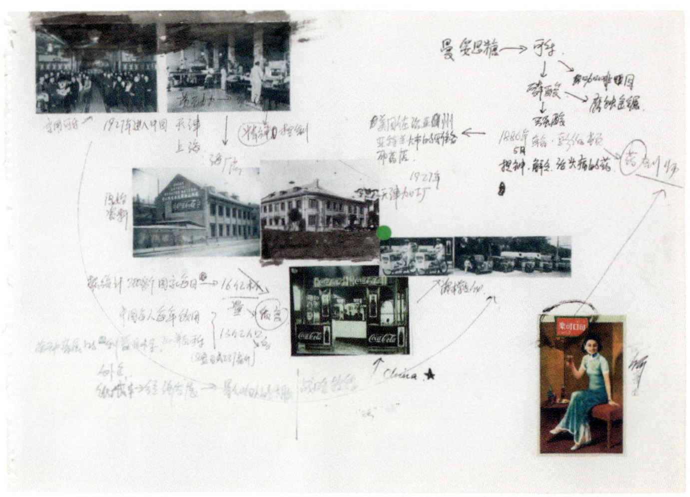 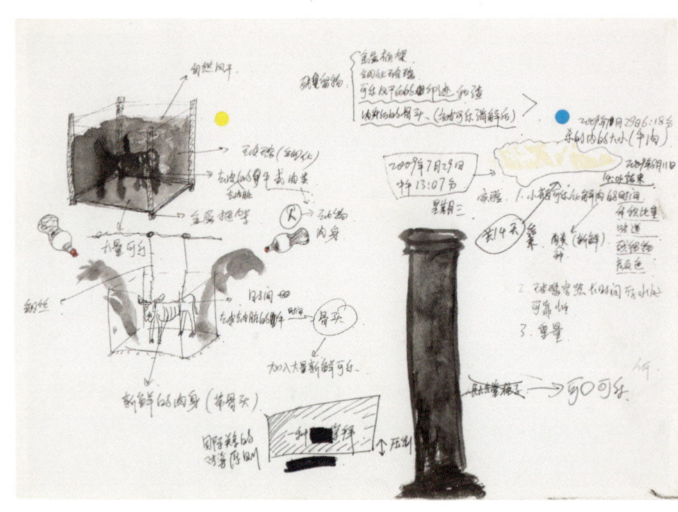

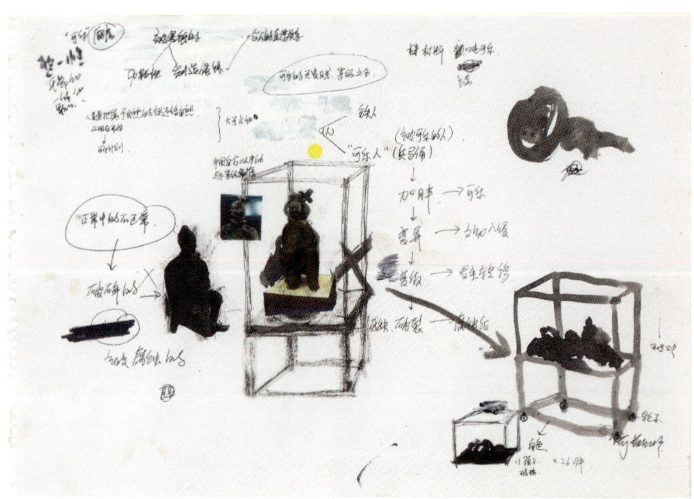 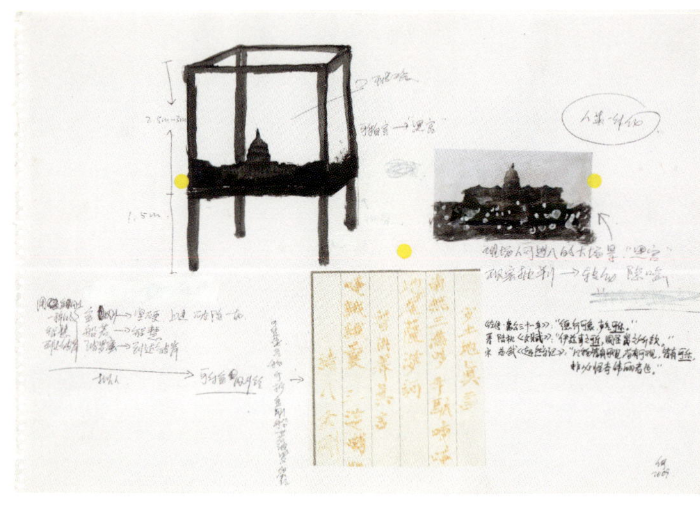

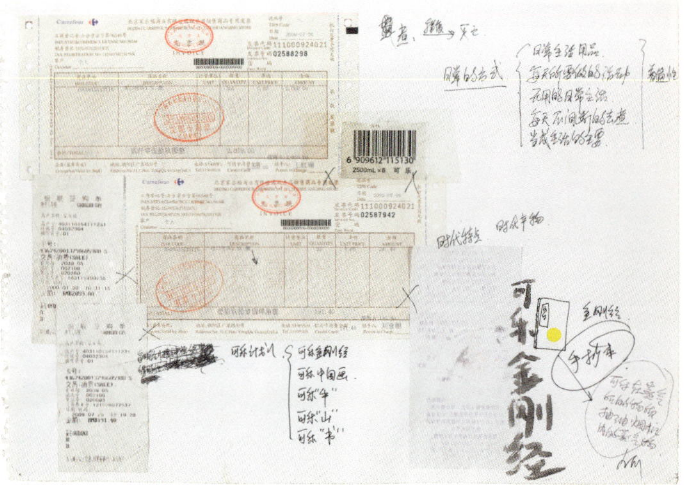 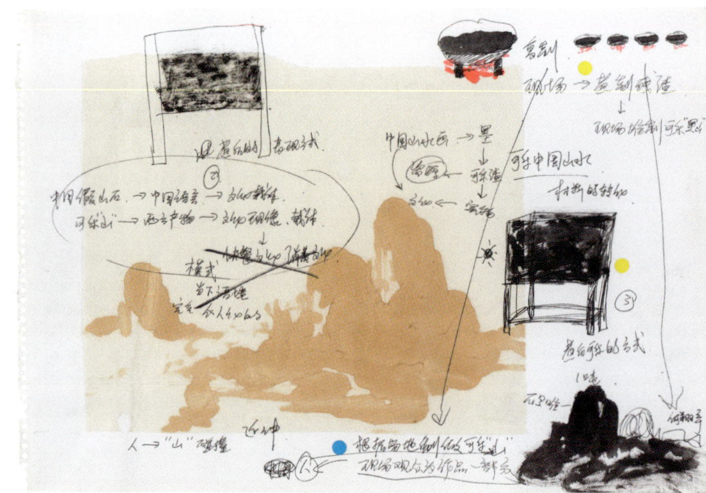

He Xiangyu, *Cola Project - 8 Sketches*, 2010, ink, watercolor, barcodes, printed invoices and photographs on paper, each: 16 x 20 7/8 in. (40.5 x 53 cm), acquired in 2011

何翔宇，《可乐计划 - 8 草稿》，2010，墨，水彩，条形码，复印发票和照片，每幅: 16 x 20 7/8 寸 (40.5 x 53 厘米)，收藏于 2011

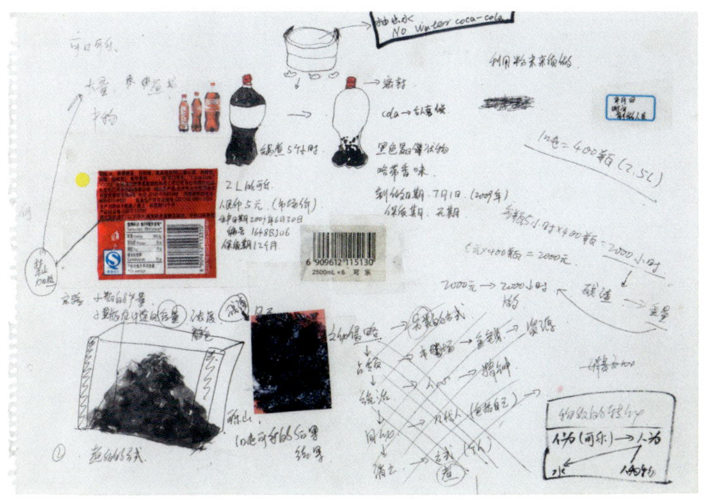
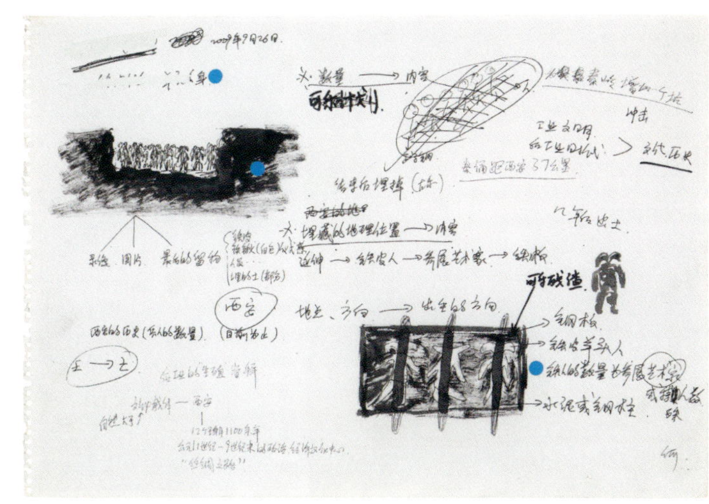

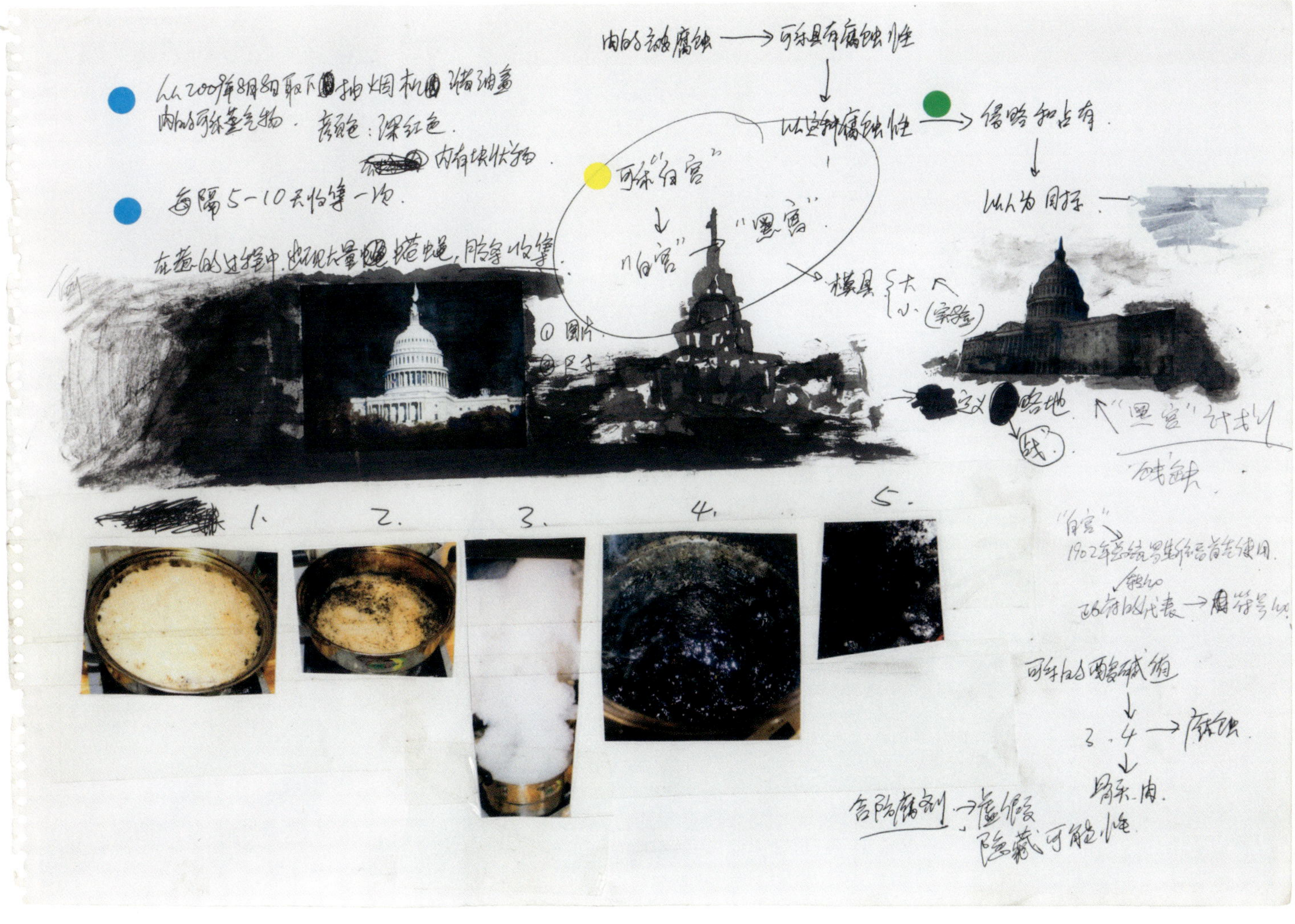

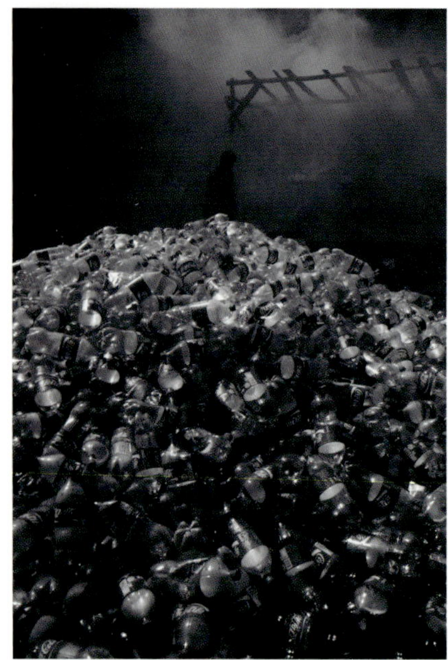
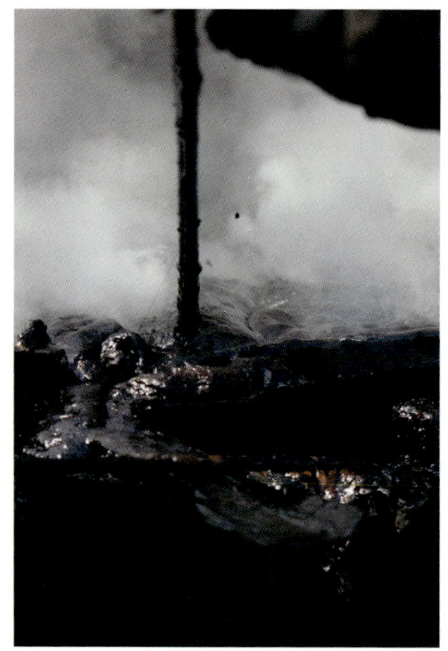
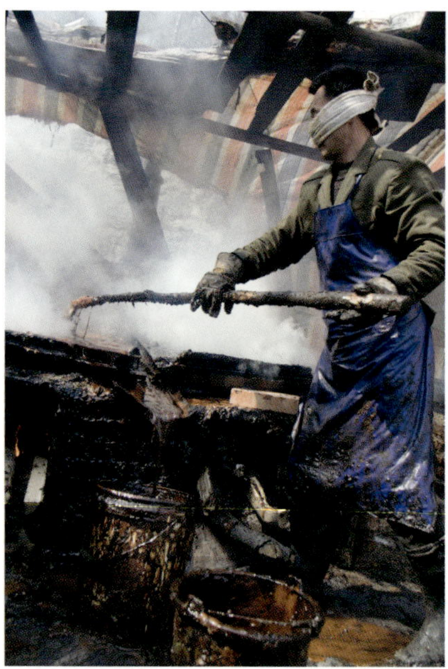
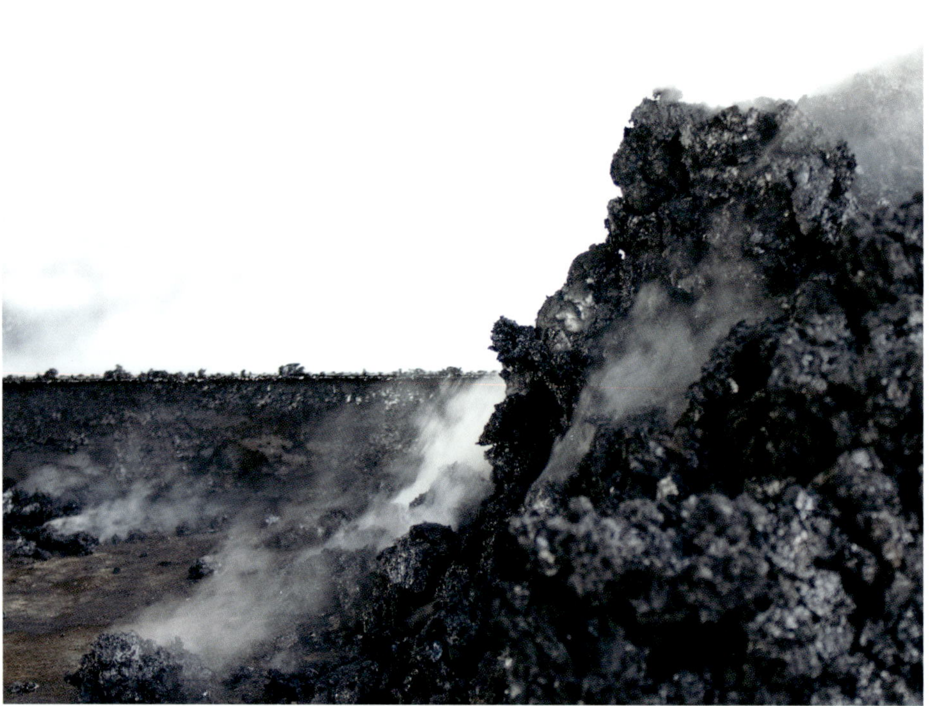
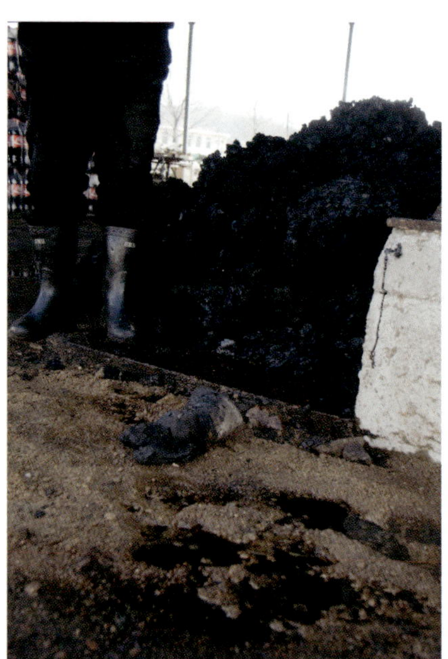
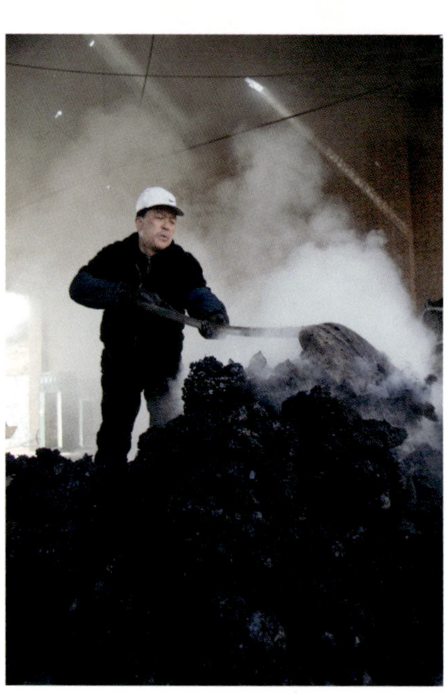

He Xiangyu, *Cola Project - Extraction Documentation*, 2010, C-print, Ed. 1/3 (11 works), each: 17 3/4 x 12 5/8 in. (45 x 32 cm), acquired in 2011
何翔宇，《可乐计划-萃取记录》, 2010, C-打印, 版本 1/3 (共11幅), 每幅: 17 3/4 x 12 5/8 寸 (45 x 32 厘米), 收藏于 2011

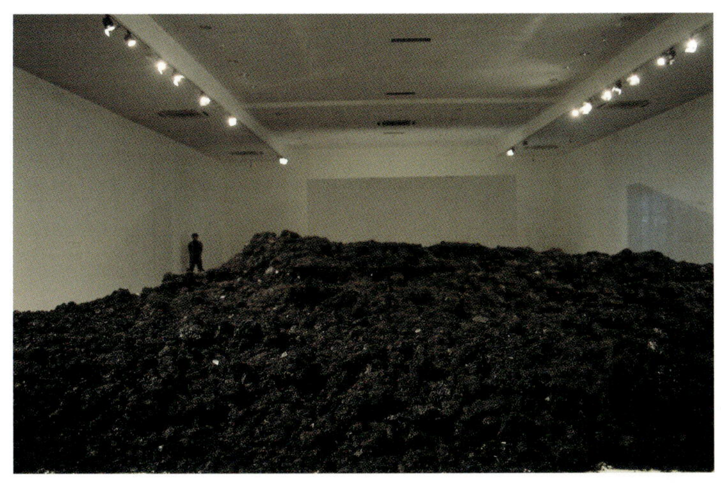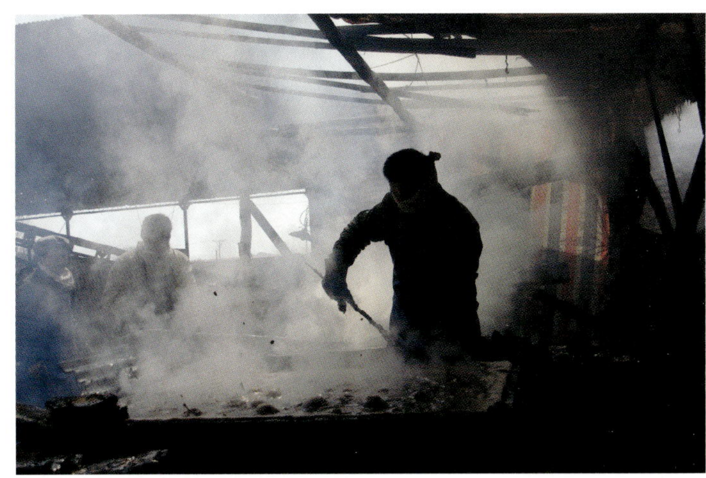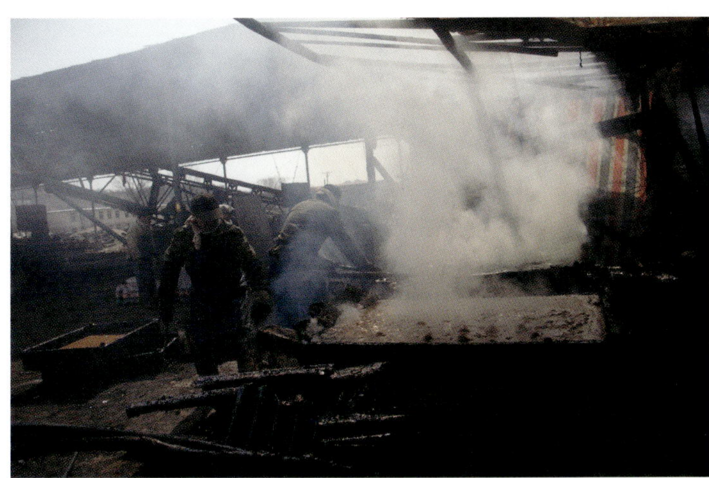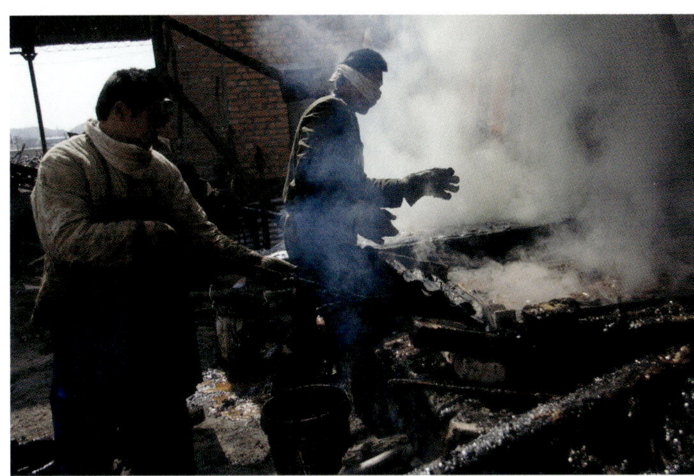

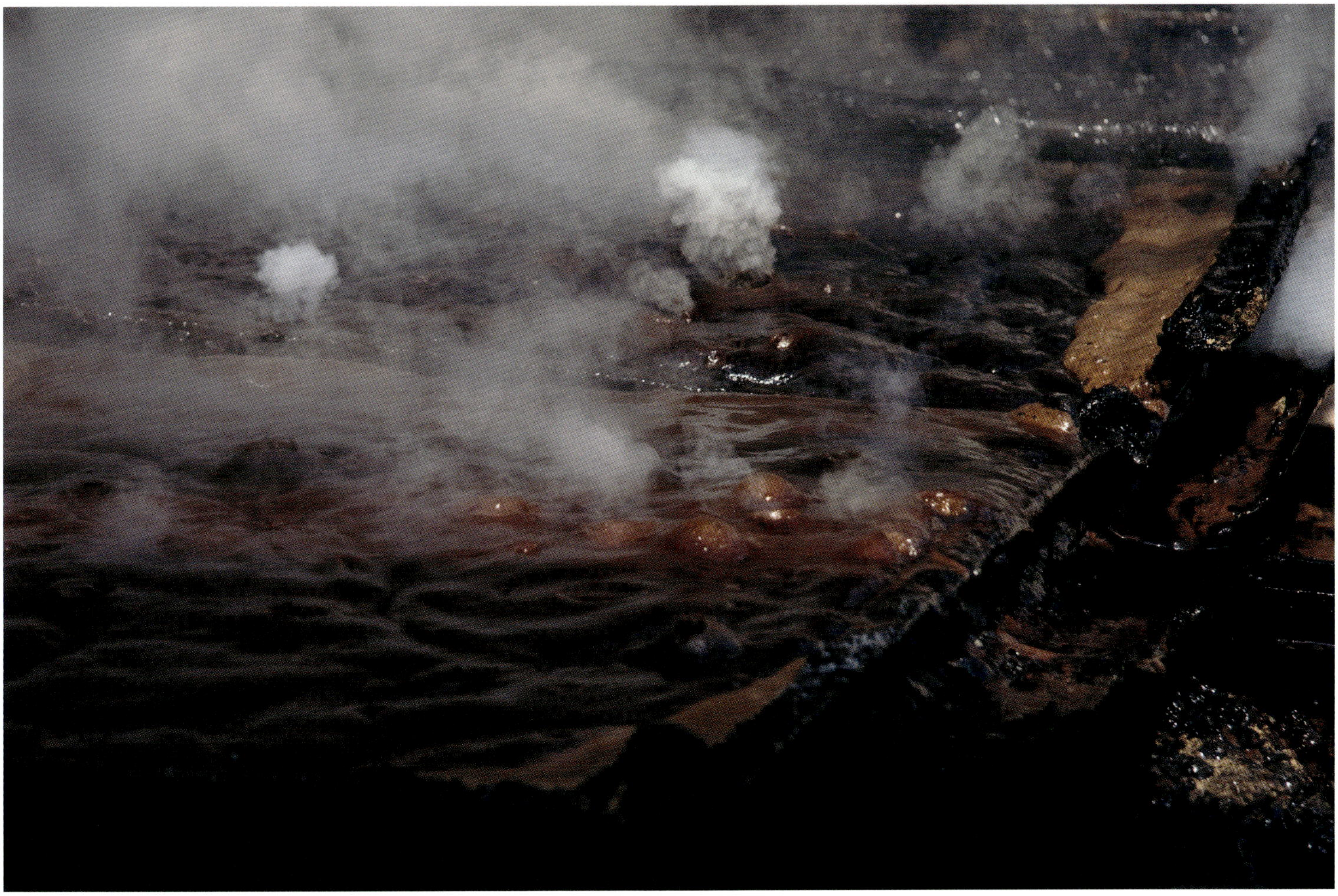

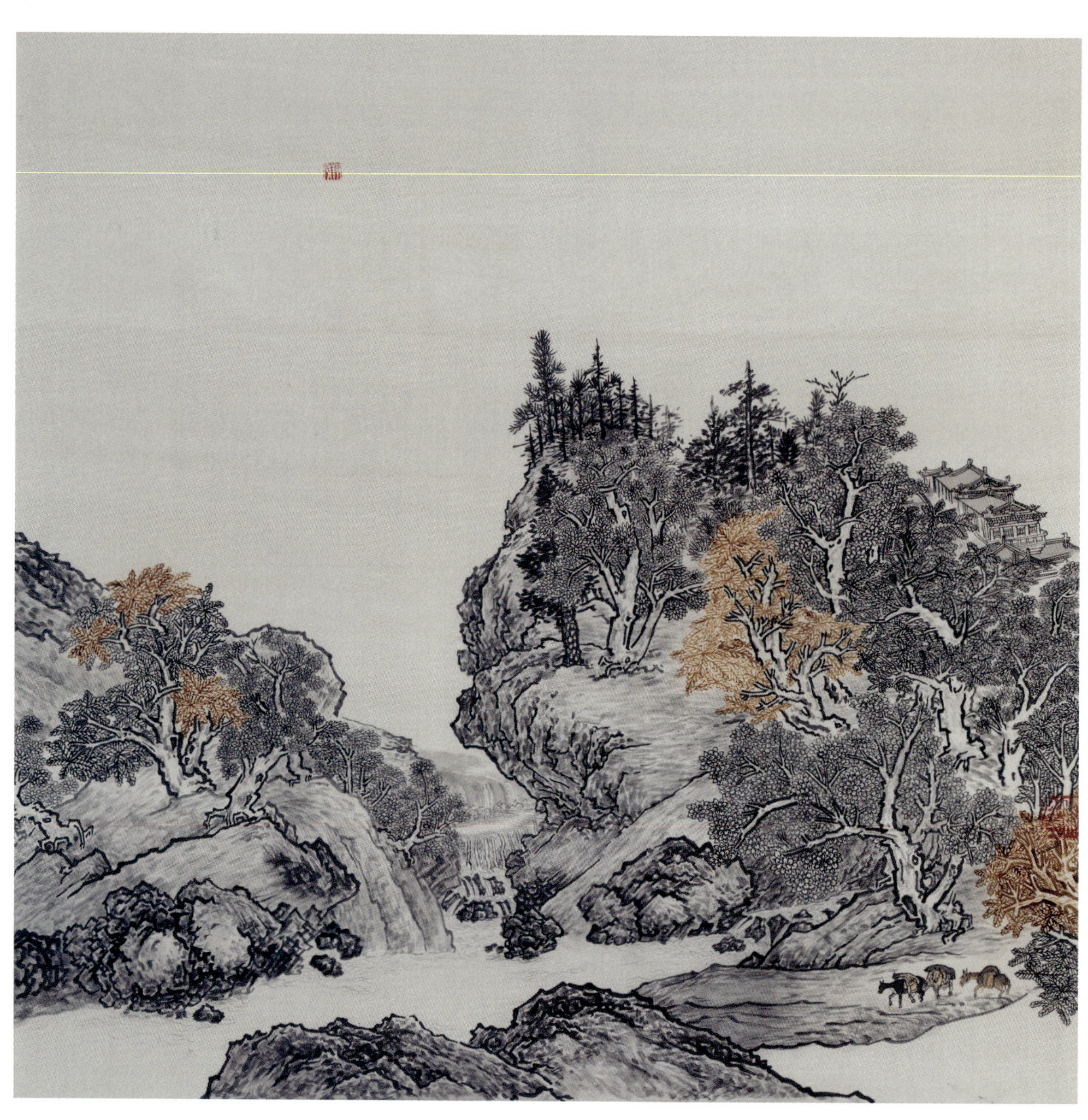

He Xiangyu, *Cola Project - Antique Series*, 2010, Chinese ink and Coca-Cola on silk, 32 3/4 x 41 1/2 in. (83 x 105.5 cm), acquired in 2011

何翔宇，《可乐计划-古董系列》，2010，中国水墨和可口可乐在绢本上，32 3/4 x 41 1/2 寸 (83 x 105.5 厘米)，收藏于 2011

He Xiangyu, *A Barrel of Dregs of Coca-Cola*, 2009, Coca-Cola resin, metal and glass, 82 1/2 x 39 3/8 x 39 3/8 in. (210 x 100 x 100 cm), acquired in 2011

何翔宇，《一桶可口可乐渣》，2009，可乐脂，金属和玻璃，82 1/2 x 39 3/8 x 39 3/8 寸 (210 x 100 x 100 厘米)，收藏于 2011

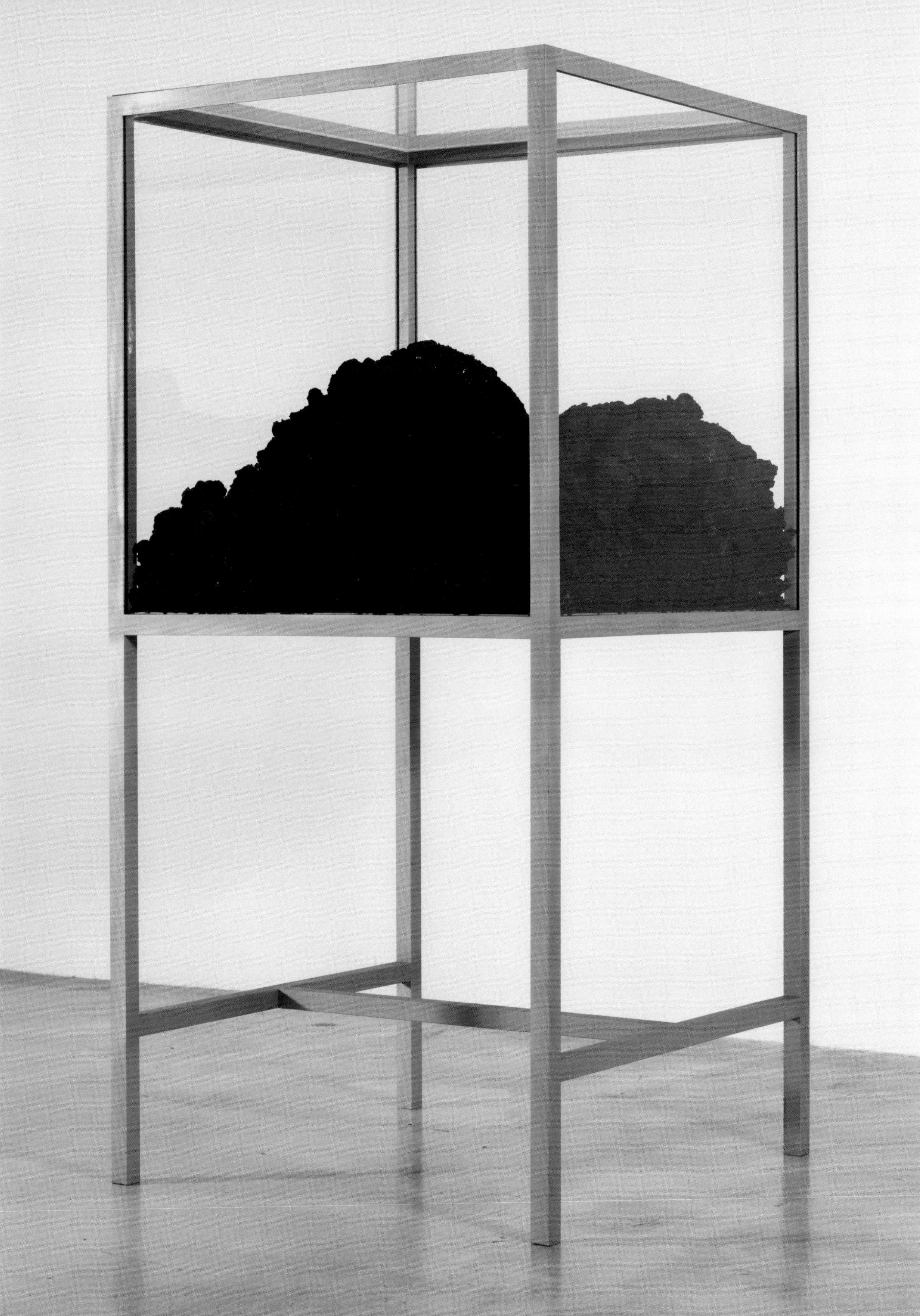

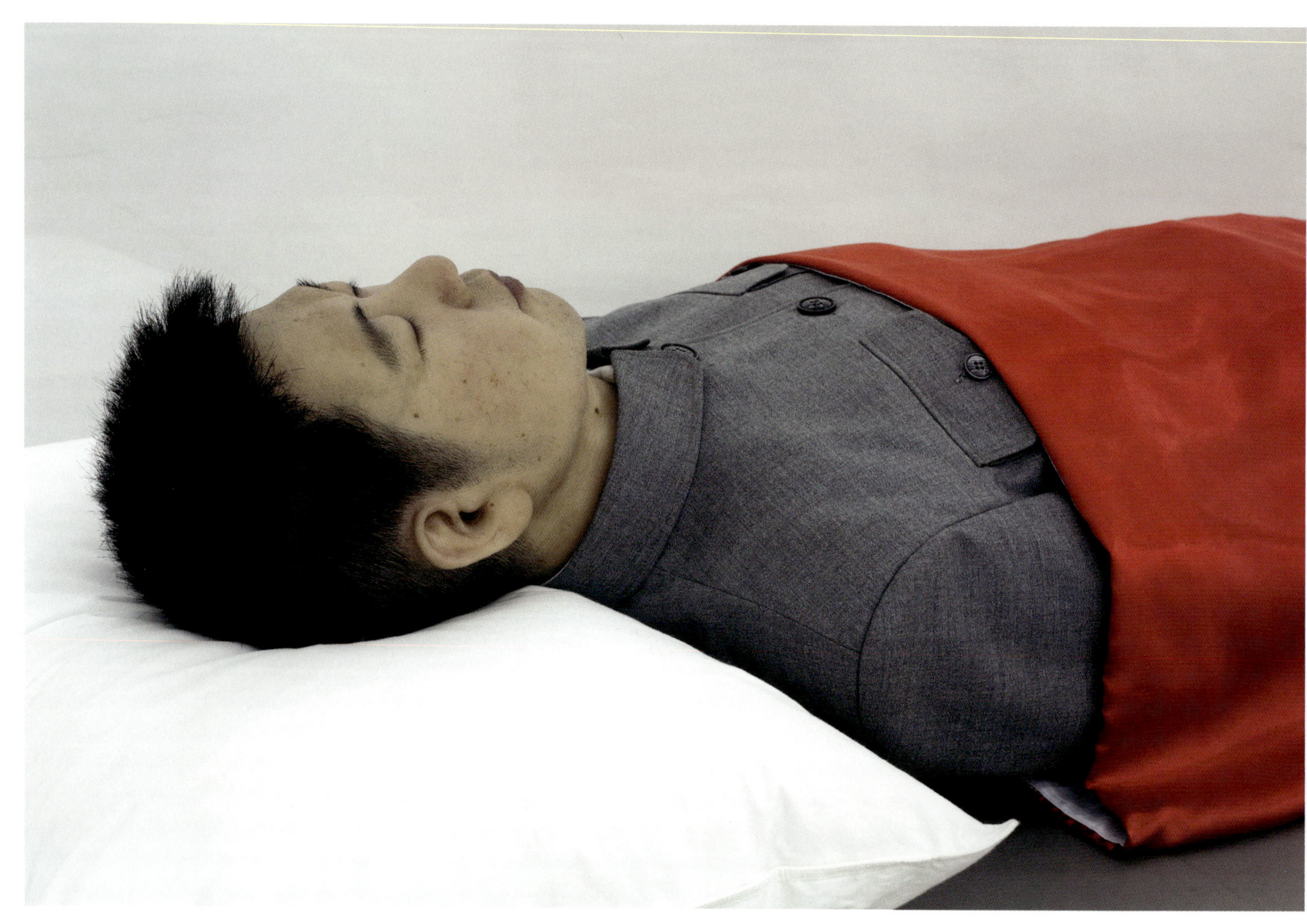

He Xiangyu, *My Fantasy*, 2012, fiberglass, silicone, fabric, human hair, glass and metal, Ed. 1/3, figure: 61 x 18 1/8 x 9 in. (155 x 46 x 23 cm), vitrine: 31 1/2 x 74 3/4 x 74 3/4 in. (80 x 190 x 190 cm), acquired in 2013
何翔宇，《我的梦想》，2012，仿真硅胶，玻璃钢，衣服，头发和金属，版本 1/3，人像：61 x 18 1/8 x 9 寸. (155 x 46 x 23 厘米)，玻璃柜: 31 1/2 x 74 3/4 x 74 3/4 寸. (80 x 190 x 190 厘米)，收藏于 2013

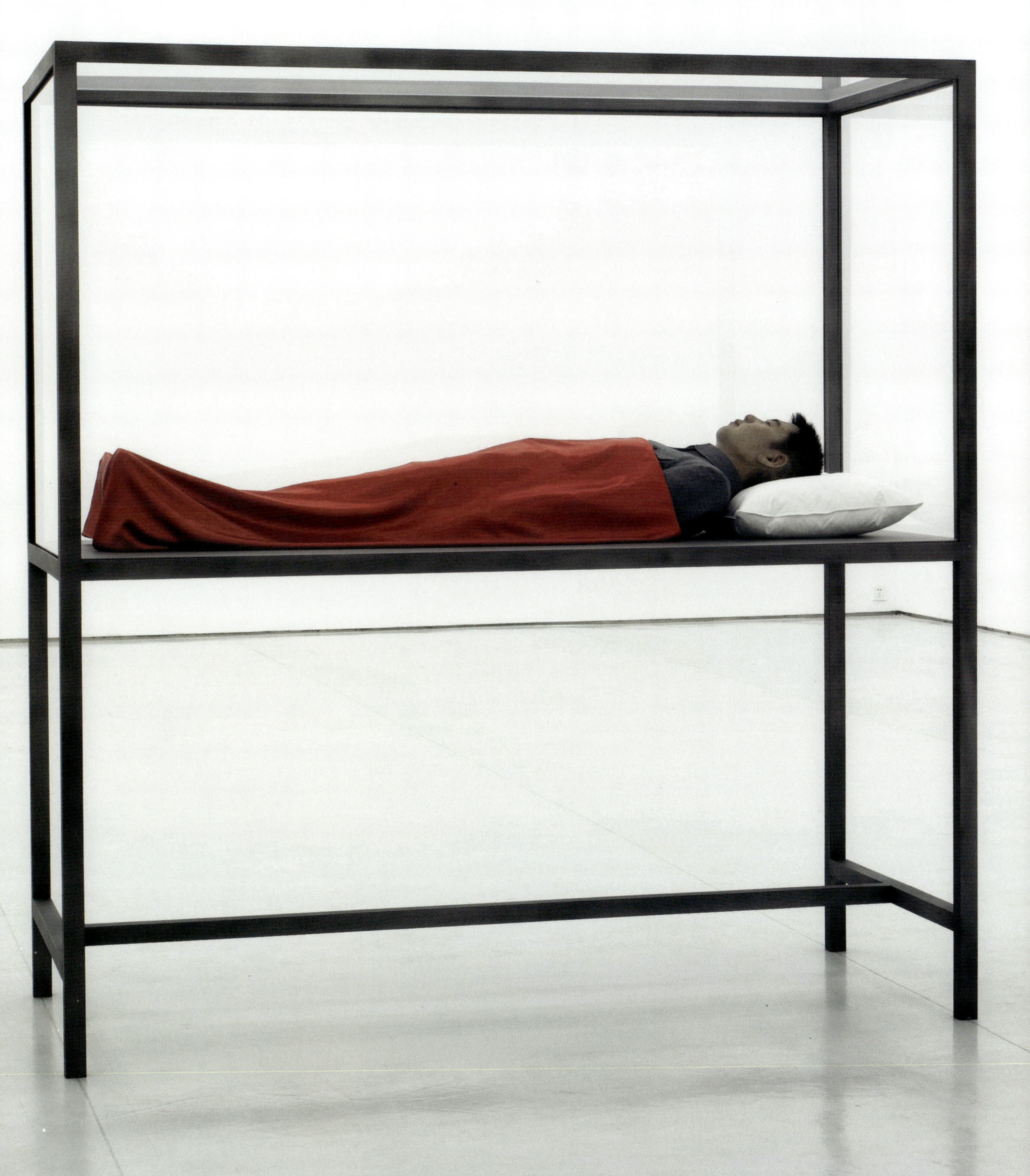

Hu Qingyan 胡庆雁

Born in 1982, Shandong, China
Lives and works in Beijing, China

一九八二年生於中国山东
居住和工作於中国北京

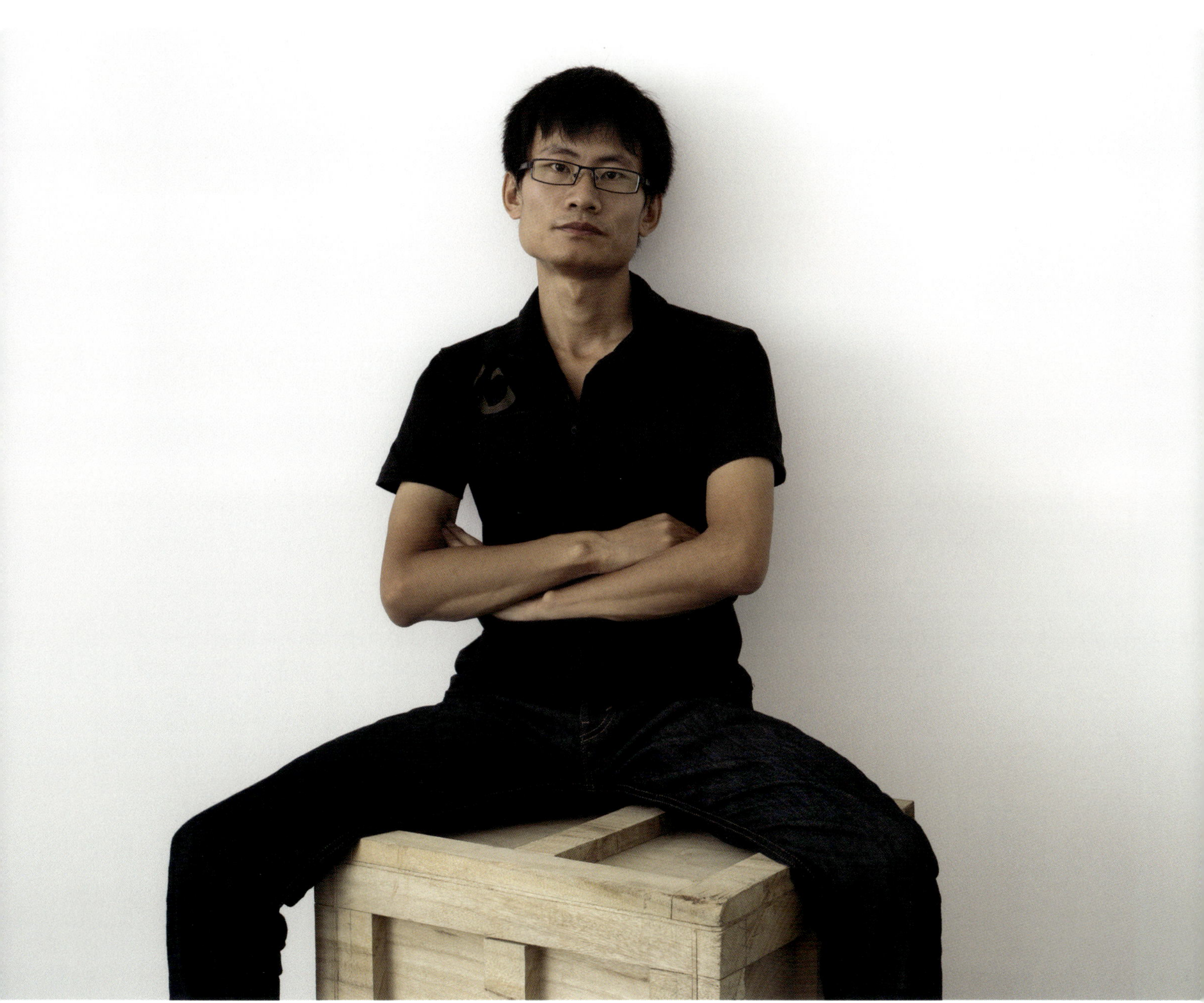

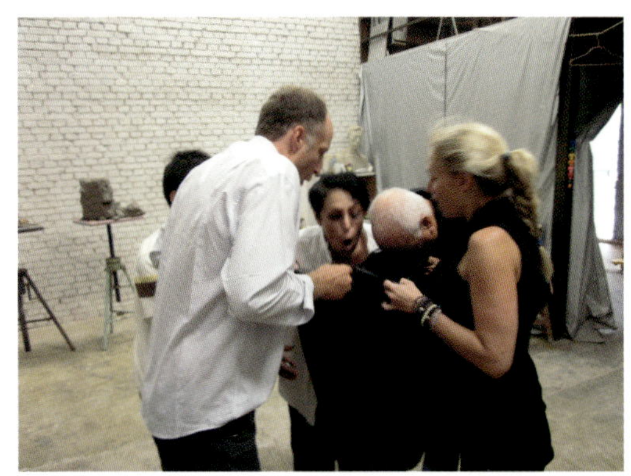
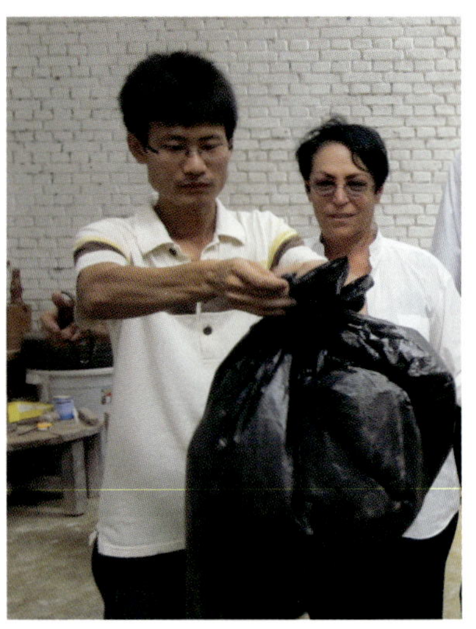

One Breath – Portrait of the Rubell Family is a sculpture of the Rubell family.

For a very long time, sculptures have tried to show the model's outside appearance. Here, I have shifted the viewpoint from depicting the outside appearance of the models to their inner appearances. I transferred the spaces in their bodies into a plastic bag by having them blow into it (just one breath from each person), and I used the bag as a model to make the marble sculpture. Thus, the volume of this marble is an objective recreation and representation of the spaces in their bodies. And this full-figured, solid marble "plastic bag" filled with one full breath from each of the members of the Rubell family is my depiction and representation of the portrait of the Rubell family.

There's an old saying in Chinese that goes, "Man lives just for one breath," and I use one breath to portray a family.

- Hu Qingyan

《一口气——鲁贝尔家族肖像》是鲁贝尔家族的雕像。

一直以来，雕像通常是对人物外部形象的呈现。在这里，我则把视点从被塑造对象的外部转移到身体内部，将身体内部的空间通过吹气（一口气）的方式转移到塑料袋当中，并以此为模型将其打制成大理石材质。那么这块大理石的体积就是对身体内部空间的客观塑造与呈现。而这个装着家族成员各自一口气的形象饱满、材质坚硬的大理石 "塑料袋" 是我对鲁贝尔家族肖像的描绘与呈现。

中国有句古语 "人活一口气"，我则通过一口气来呈现一个家族。

- 胡庆雁

Hu Qingyan, *One Breath-Portrait of the Rubell family*, 2011, marble, 13 x 19 3/4 x 14 in. (33 x 50 x 36 cm), acquired in 2011
胡庆雁，《一口气 —— 卢贝尔家族的肖像》，2011，大理石，13 x 19 3/4 x 14 寸 (33 × 50 × 36 厘米)，收藏于 2011

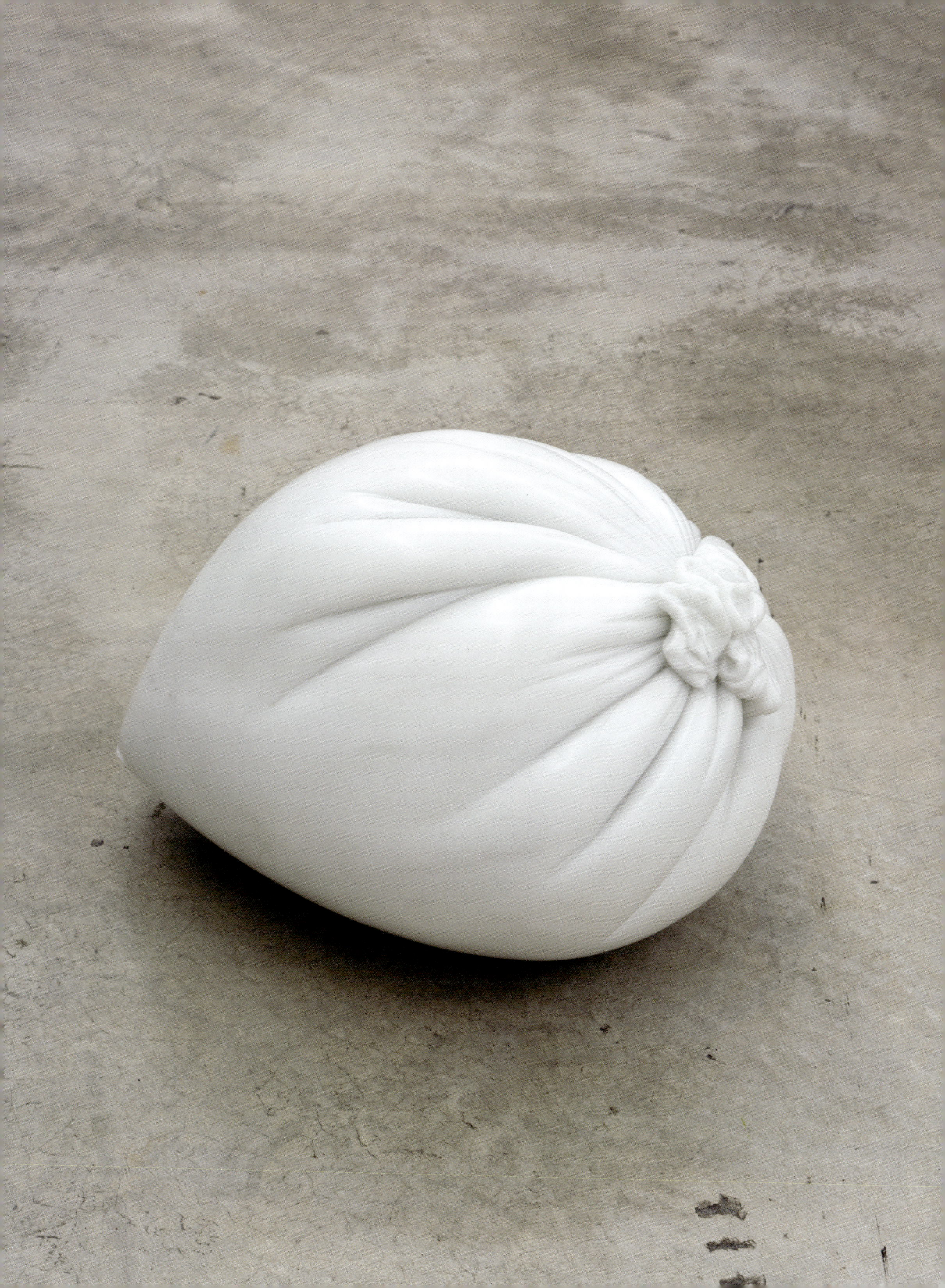

Hu Xiangqian 胡向前

Born in 1983, Guangdong, China
Lives and works in Beijing, China

一九八三年生於中国广东
居住和工作於中国北京

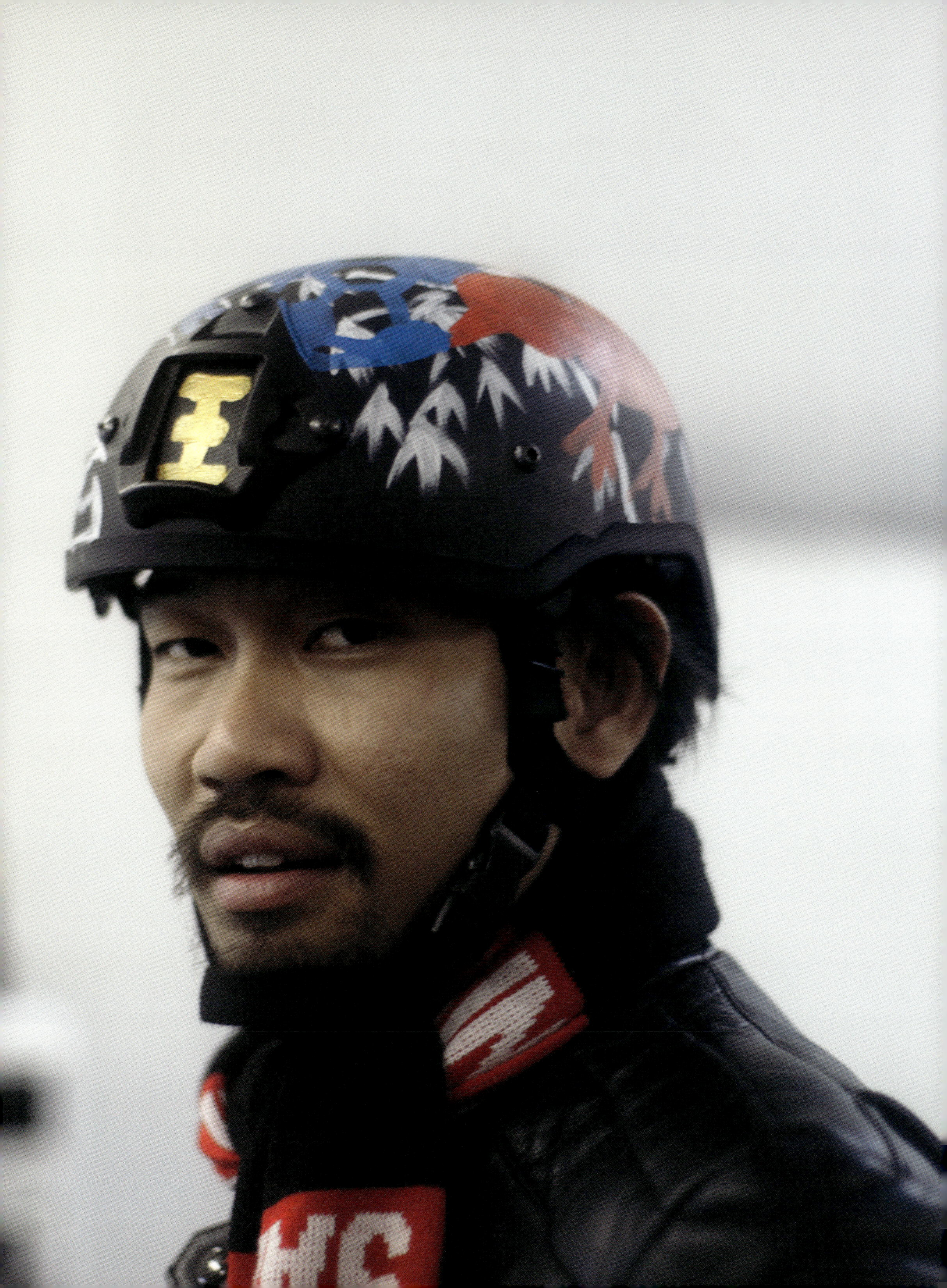

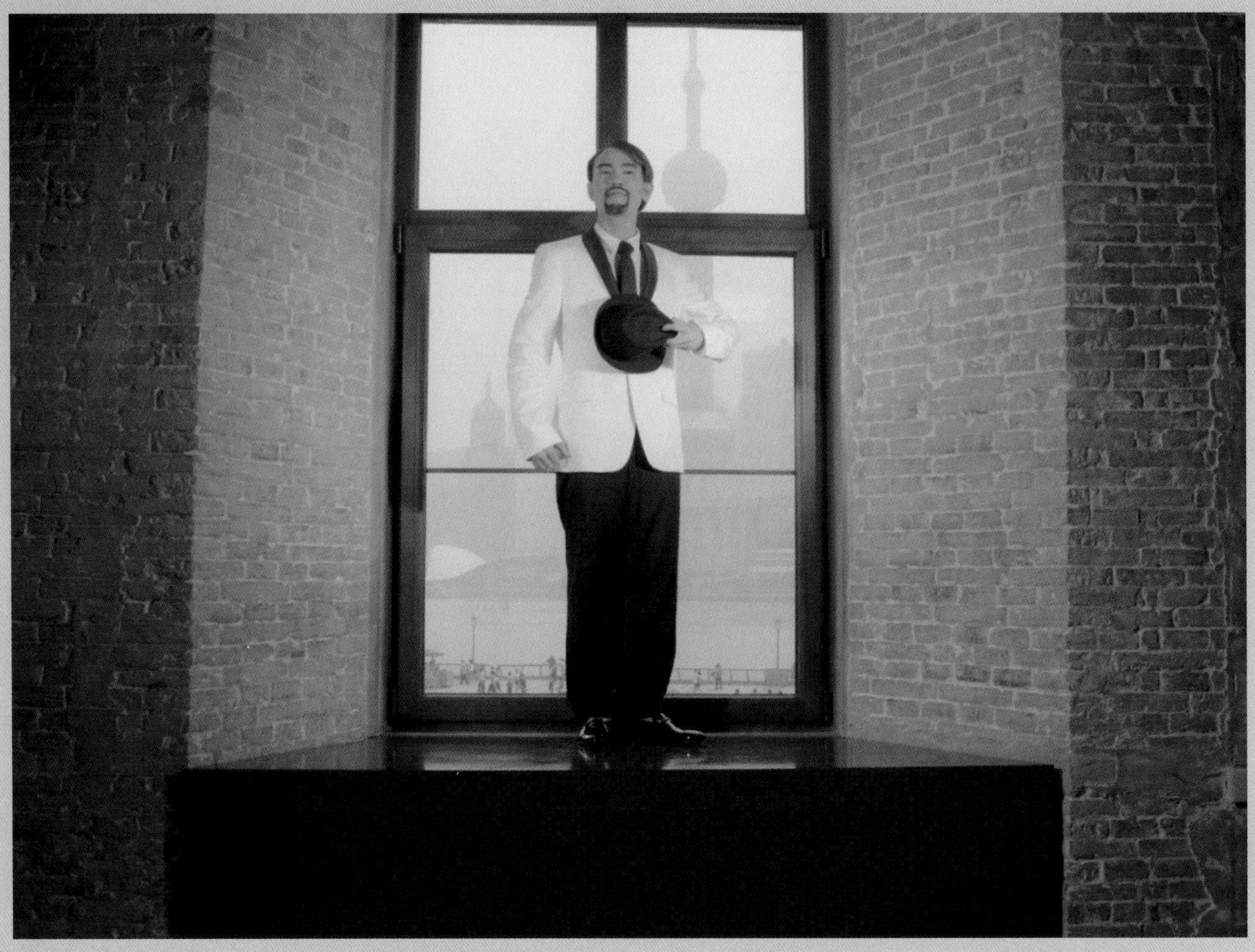

For this work I chose the artistic form of silent movies. I used some cinematic shots and scenes that everybody is familiar with, with slow and unnatural movements, with no plot, and where in fact nothing is happening. The art and artists that I see are often like this: boring, pretentious, affected, but looking very artsy – even though I don't know what's artistic about it. When this work is exhibited the artist himself becomes a member of the audience, enduring the boring and slow actions. Nobody likes this, but it still exists.

- Hu Xiangqian

这个作品我选择了默片的形式。应用一些大家都熟知的电影桥段和镜头，缓慢而做作的动作，没有情节，其实是什么事也没有发生。我看到的艺术和艺术家常常就是这样，无聊，做作，但是看起来很艺术，虽然我也不知道艺术在那里。当这个作品在展厅展出时，艺术家本人也变成了观众。一样在忍受那些无聊和缓慢的动作。没有人喜欢这样，但它还是存在的。

- 胡向前

Hu Xiangqian, *Acting Out Artist*, 2012, single-channel video (color, sound), duration: 14 min. 15 sec., acquired in 2012
胡向前，《表演艺术家》，2012，单视频 (彩色, 有声)，14 分15 秒, 收藏于 2012

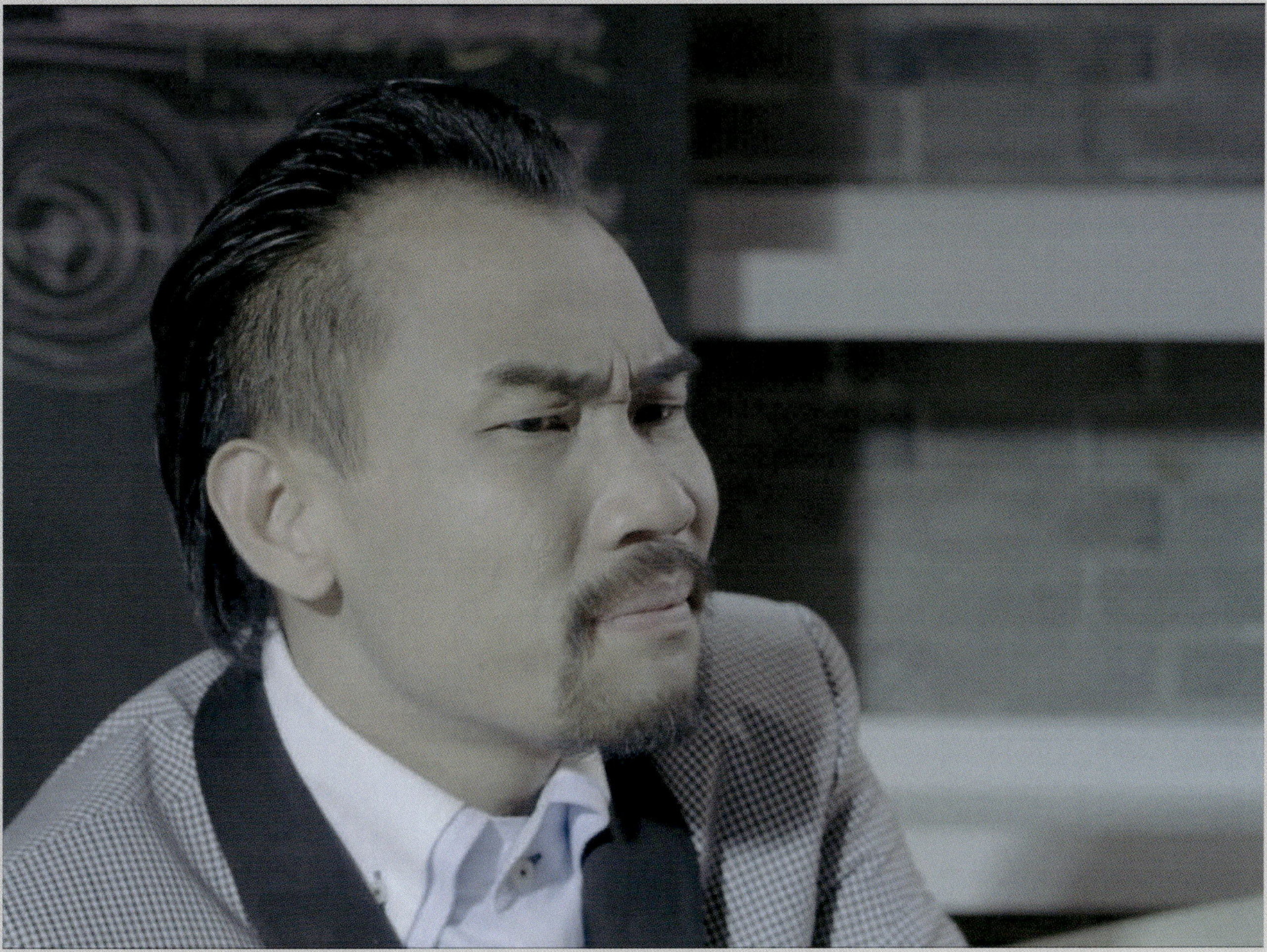

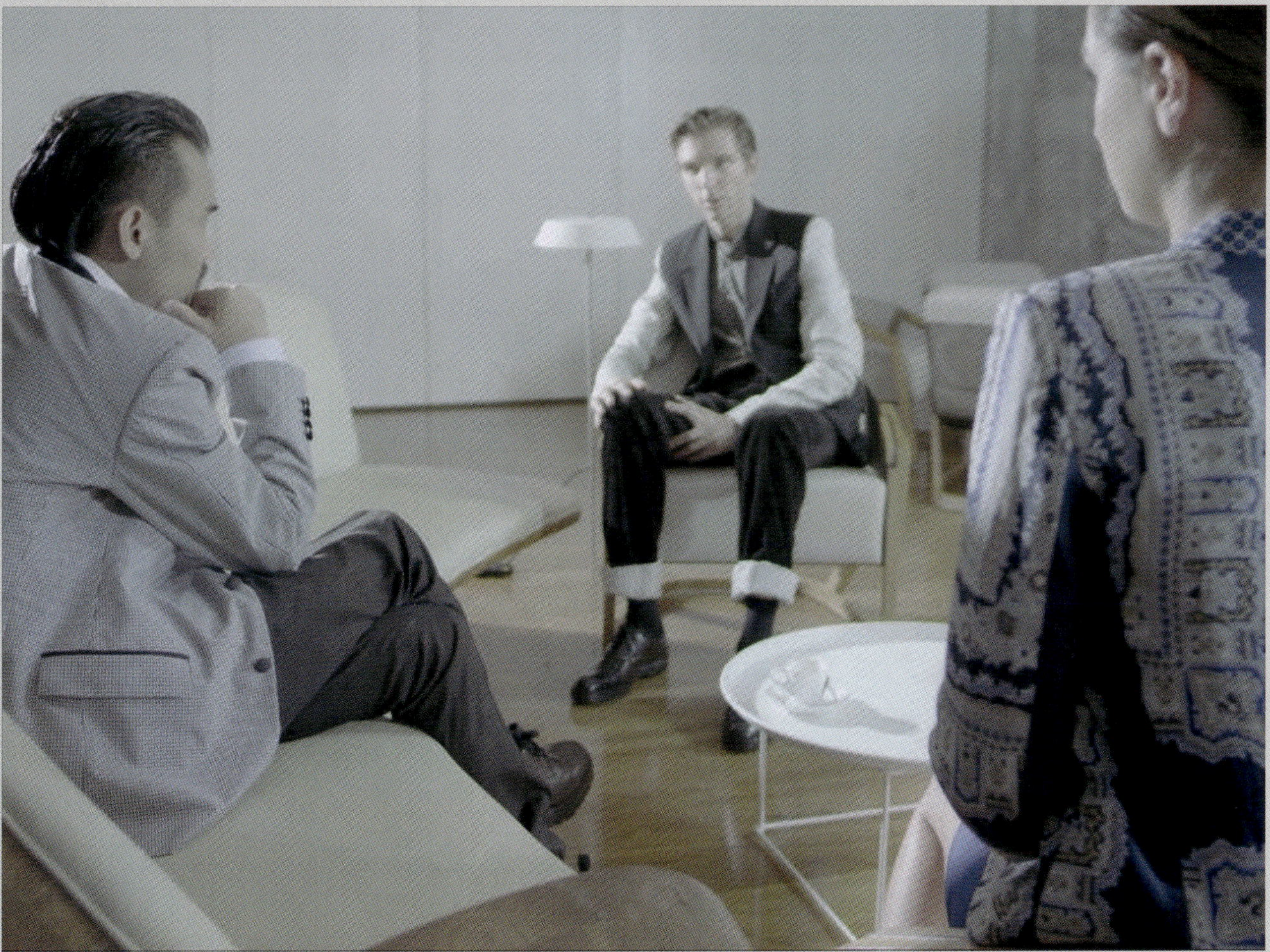

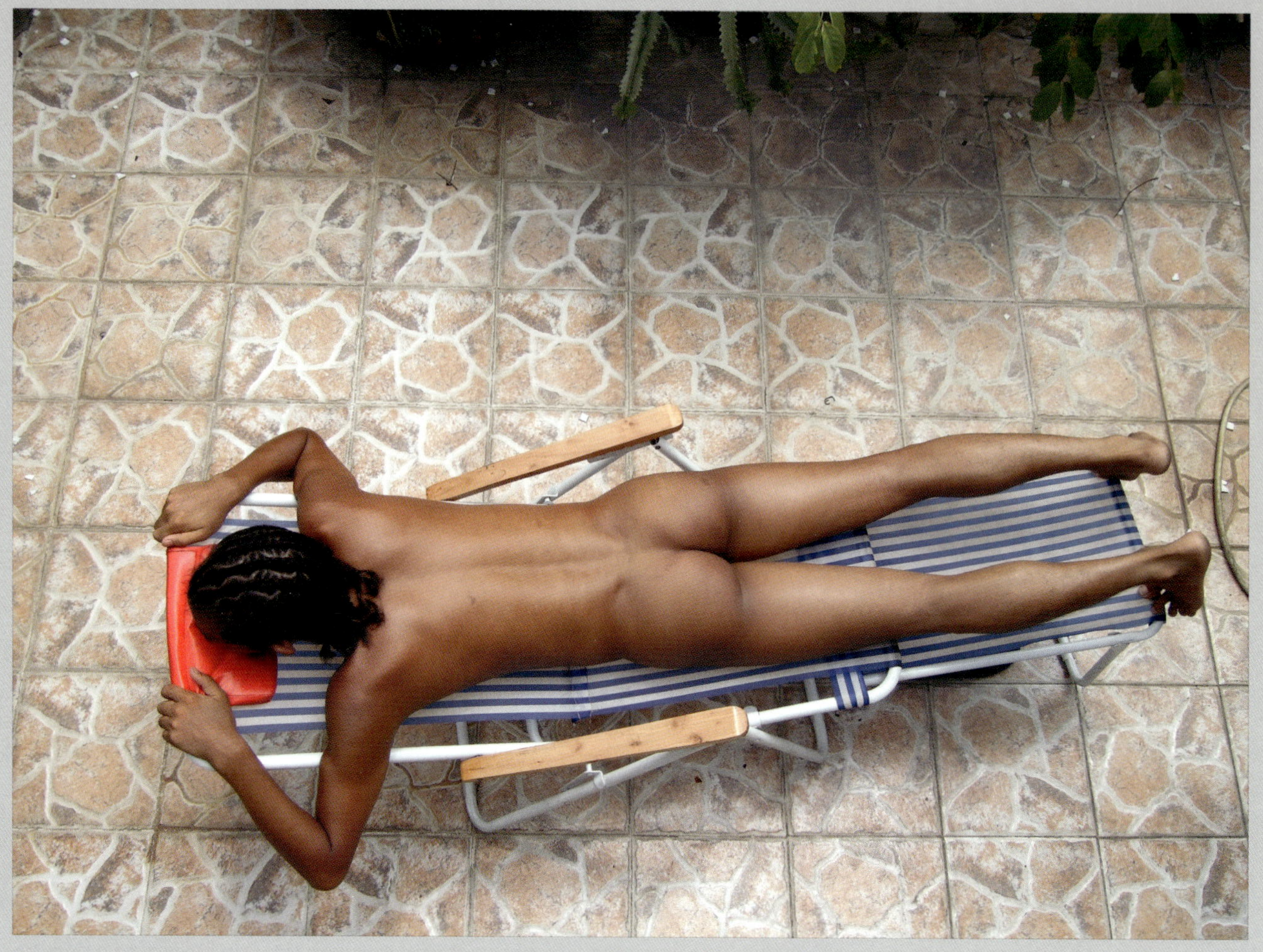

In this phase of my life I suddenly made a lot of black friends from Africa and I was fascinated by their skin color and appearance. To effuse such a lively power and beauty is what I want the most. It is the most essential thing in life that we often overlook. During the six months I spent with the sun I became acutely aware of this notion. Perhaps it is the most important thing in my artworks.

- Hu Xiangqian

生活在这段时间里突然交了很多来自非洲黑人的朋友，我对他们的肤色和形象感到着迷，散发着一股生命般的力量和美，这个是我最想要的，我们常常会忽略生命里最根本的东西。在和太阳相伴六个月的时间里，我结实体会到这种感觉，也许这就是我的艺术作品里最重要的。

- 胡向前

Hu Xiangqian, *Sun*, 2008, single-channel video (color, sound), Ed. 5/5, duration: 7 min. 59 sec., acquired in 2012
胡向前，《太阳》，2008，单视频 (彩色，有声)，版本 5/5，7 分 59 秒，收藏于 2012

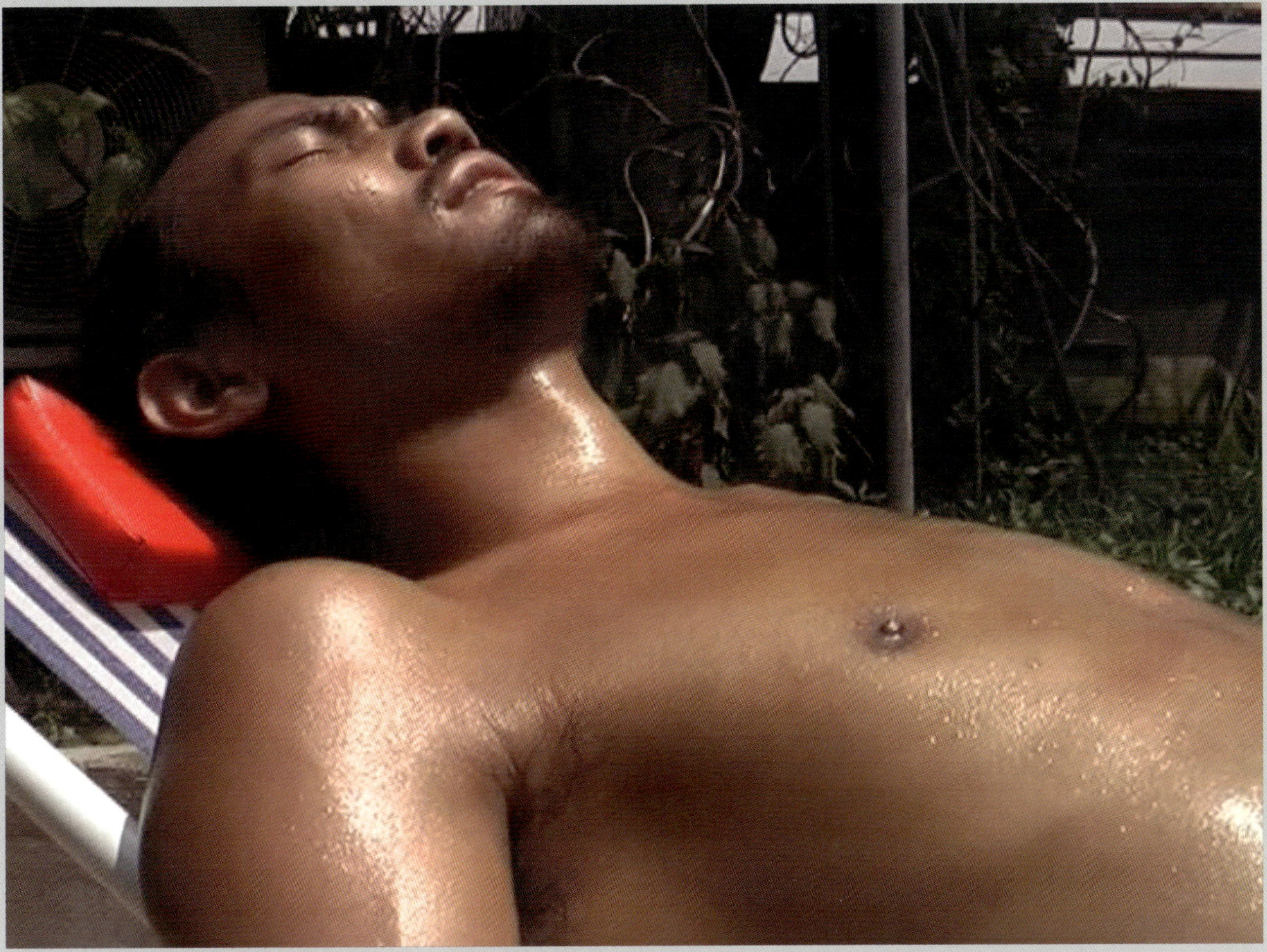

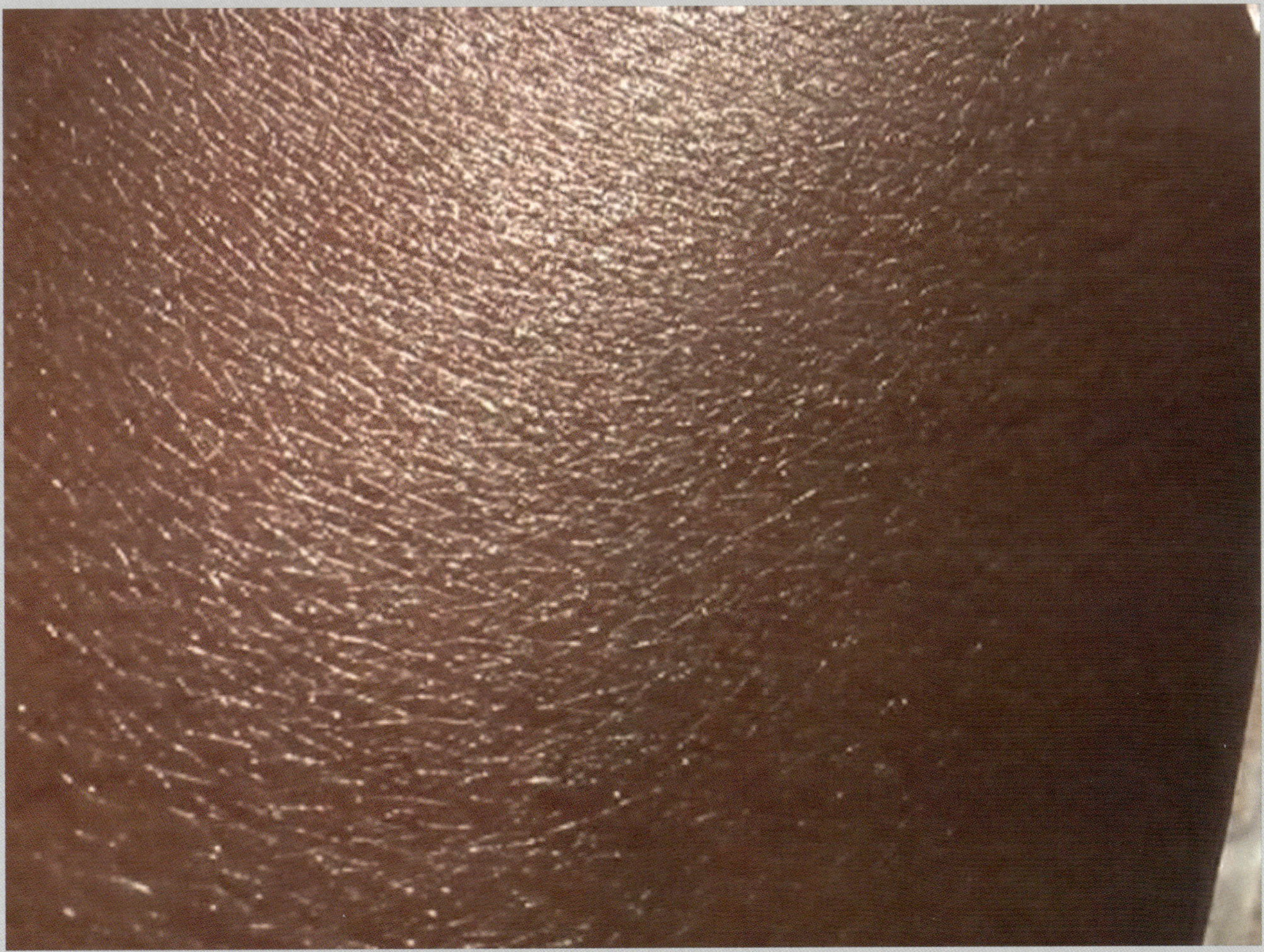

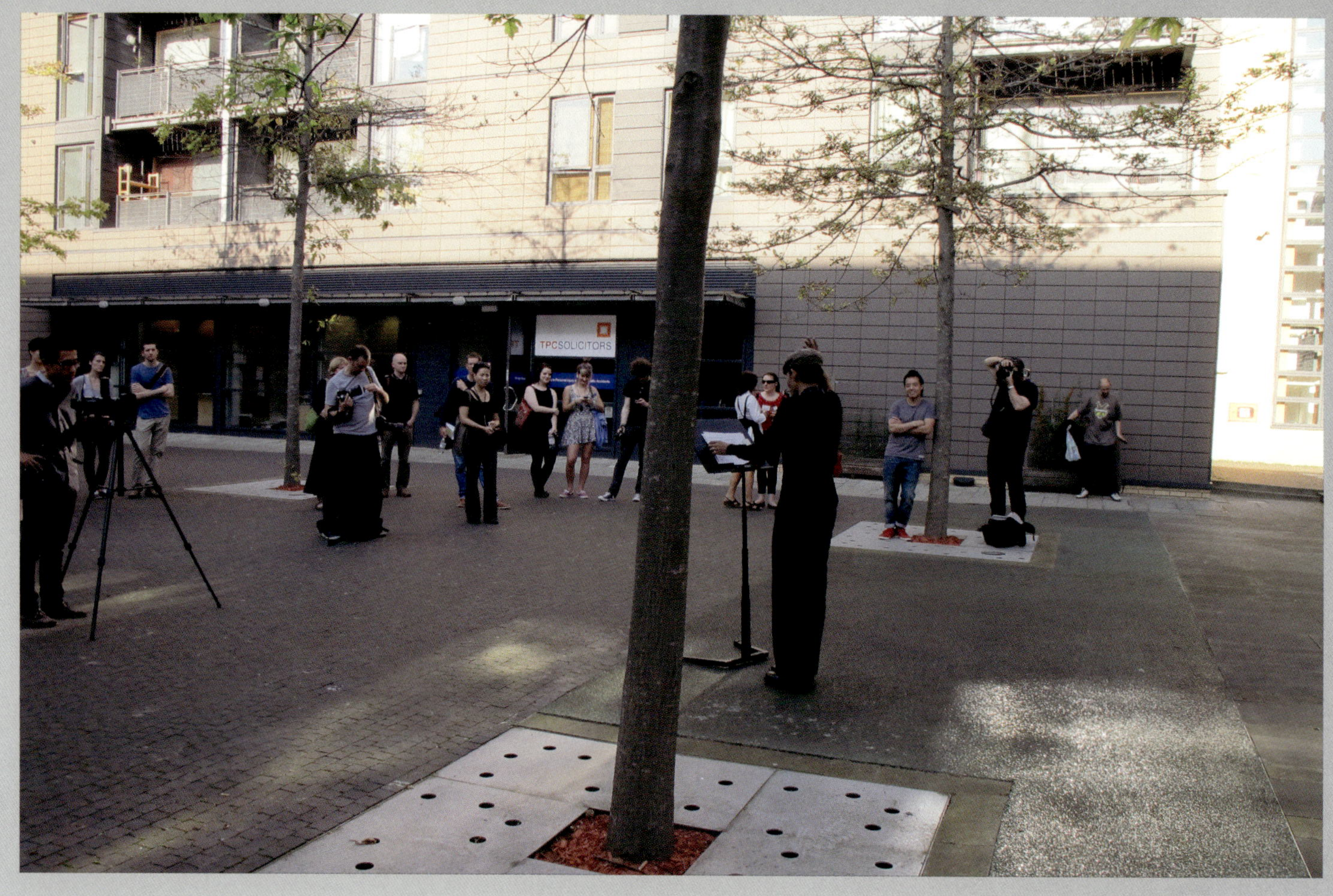

Everyone's body is initially empty and needs some material as well as immaterial things to fill it up. A museum is normally filled with material objects. However, through my eyes and brain, the tangible objects in a regular museum are turned into something immaterial. Through my performances, both the material and immaterial are then recycled and re-enacted in the bodies of the audience, the museum and myself. More importantly, this is something we can take with us.

- Hu Xiangqian

每个人的身体本来都是空的，都需要一些物质和非物质来填满他。一个美术馆通常情况是用实在的物质来填满。但经过我的眼睛和大脑，通常美术馆的实在物质就转化成非物质，再通过我的表演，这些物质和非物质循环再生在观众，美术馆和我的身体里。重要的是我们还可以随身携带。

- 胡向前

Hu Xiangqian, *Xiangqian Art Museum I, II, III*, 2010, three-channel video (color, sound), Ed. 4/5, duration: 14 min. 31 sec., acquired in 2012
胡向前，《向前美术馆 I, II, III》，2010，三视频 (彩色，有声)，版本 4/5，14 分 31 秒，收藏于 2012

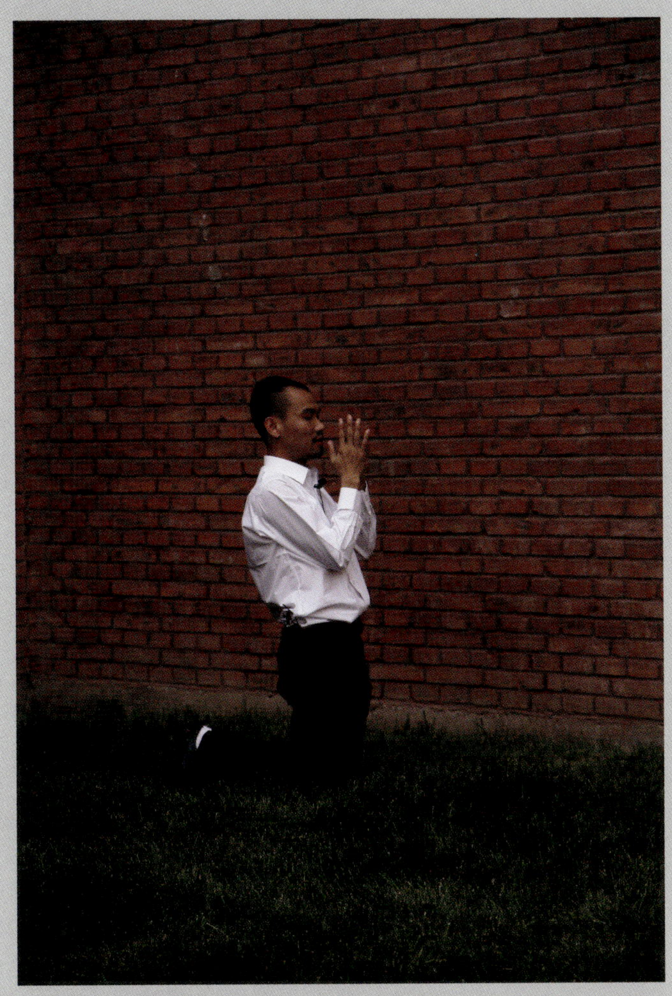
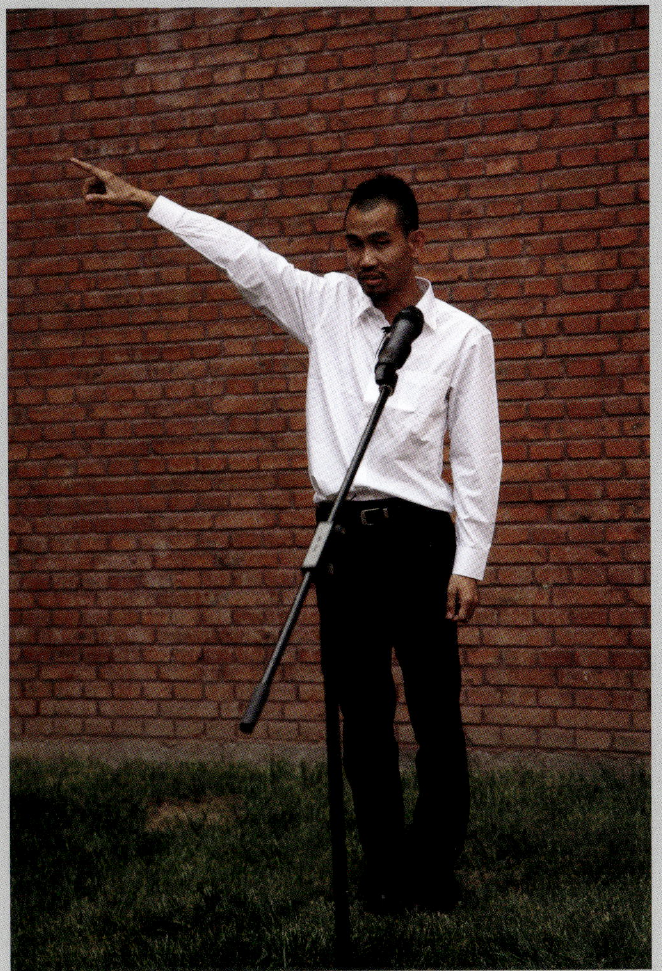
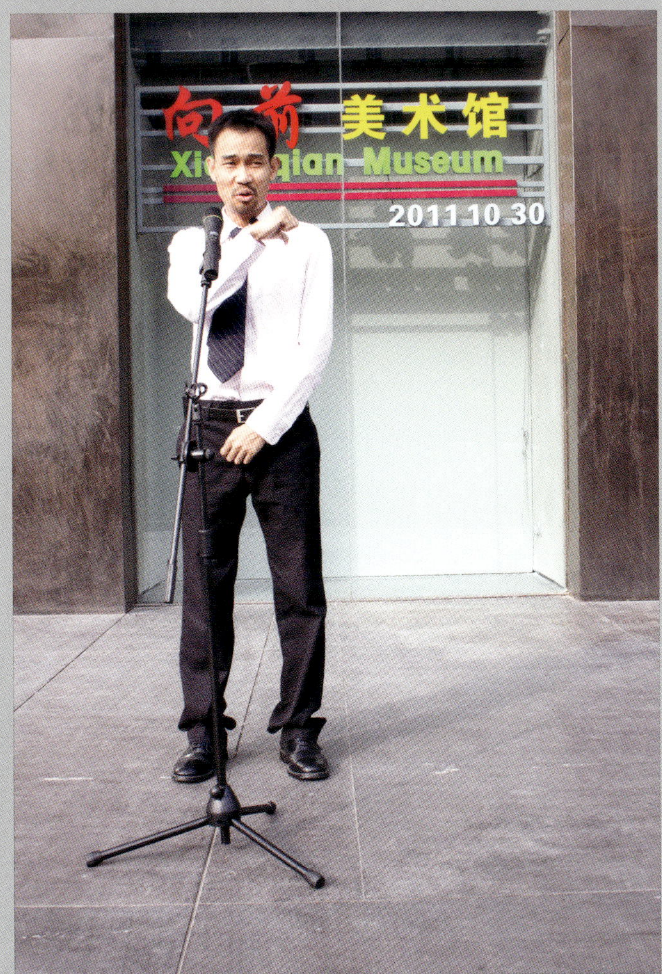

向前　美术馆
Xiangqian Museum
2011 10 30

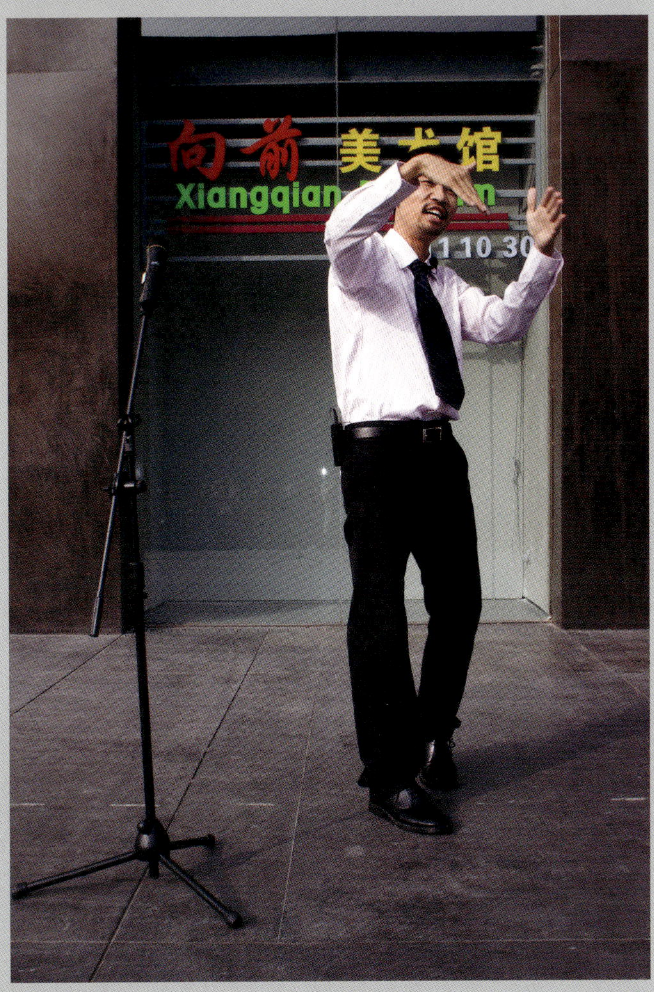

向前　美术馆
Xiangqian Museum
2011 10 30

Huang Ran 黄然

Born in 1982, Sichuan, China
Lives and works in Beijing, China

一九八二年生於中国四川
居住和工作於中国北京

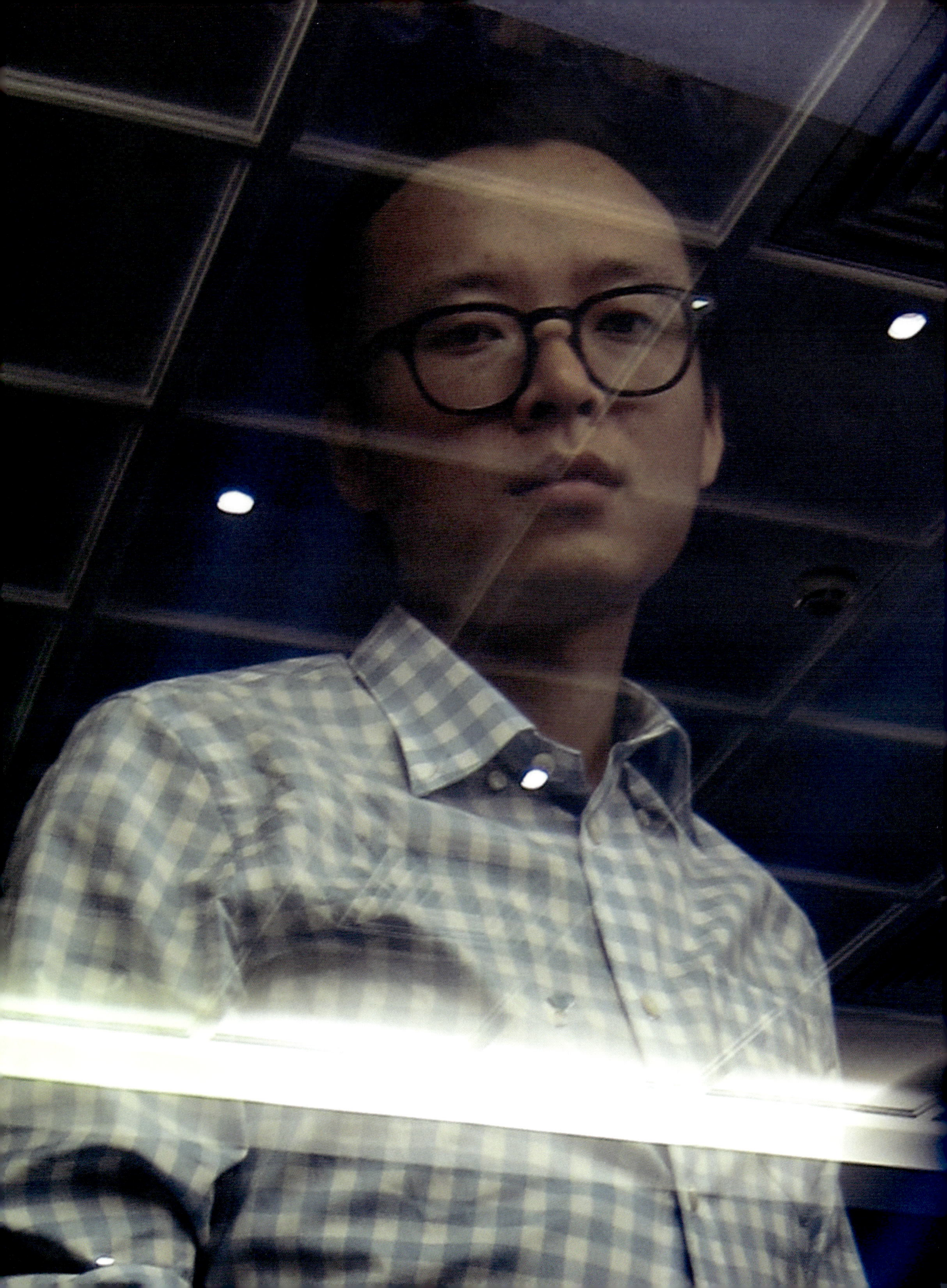

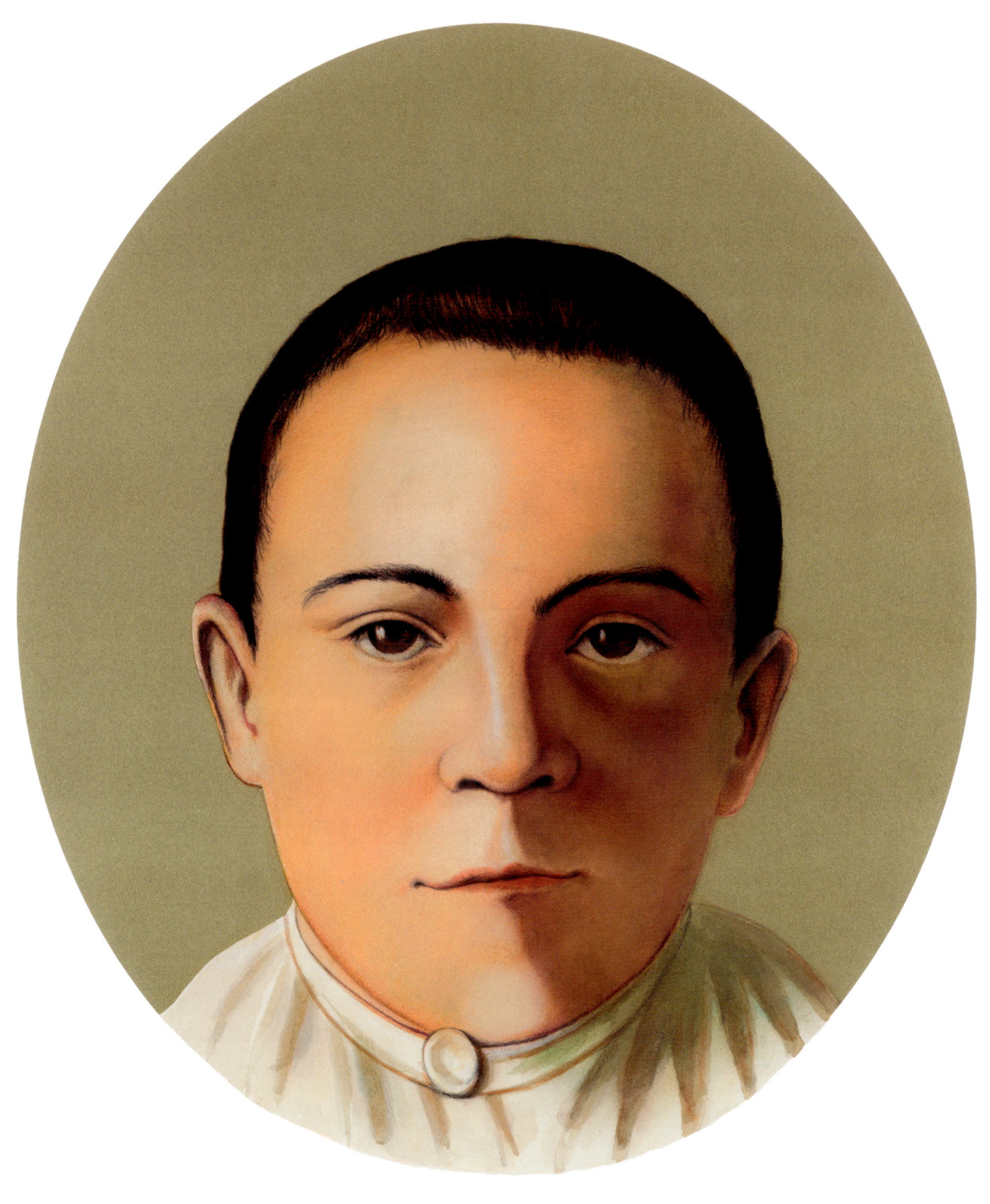

Huang Ran, *Something As Beautiful As Desirable, As Transcendent, As Evil*, 2011, screenprint on paper, Ed. 1/9, 46 3/4 x 34 1/2 in. (119 x 90 cm), acquired in 2011

黄然，《美的，让人渴望的，卓越的，邪恶的》，2011，版画，九个版本之一，46 3/4 x 34 1/2 寸 (119 x 90 厘米)，收藏于2011

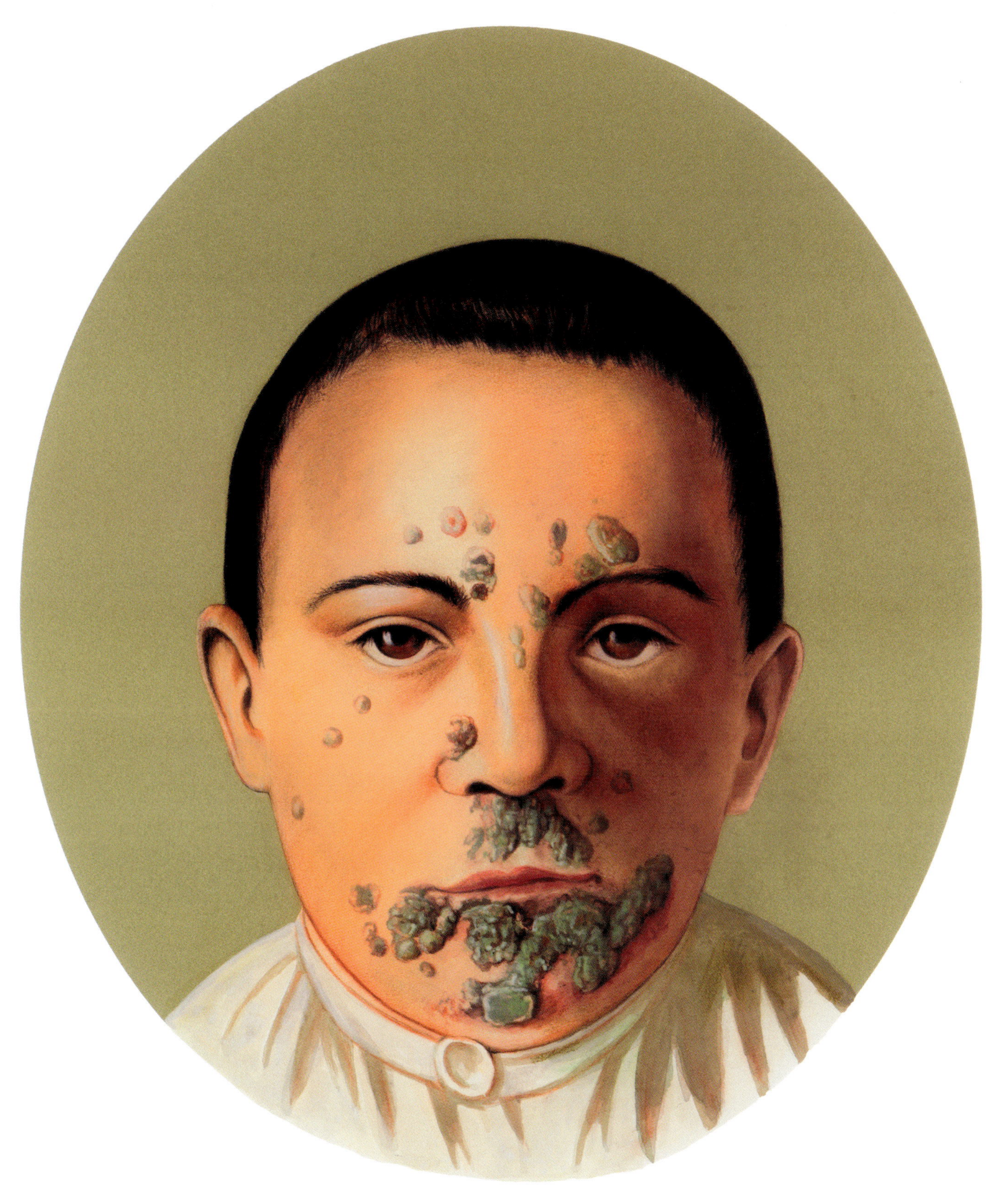

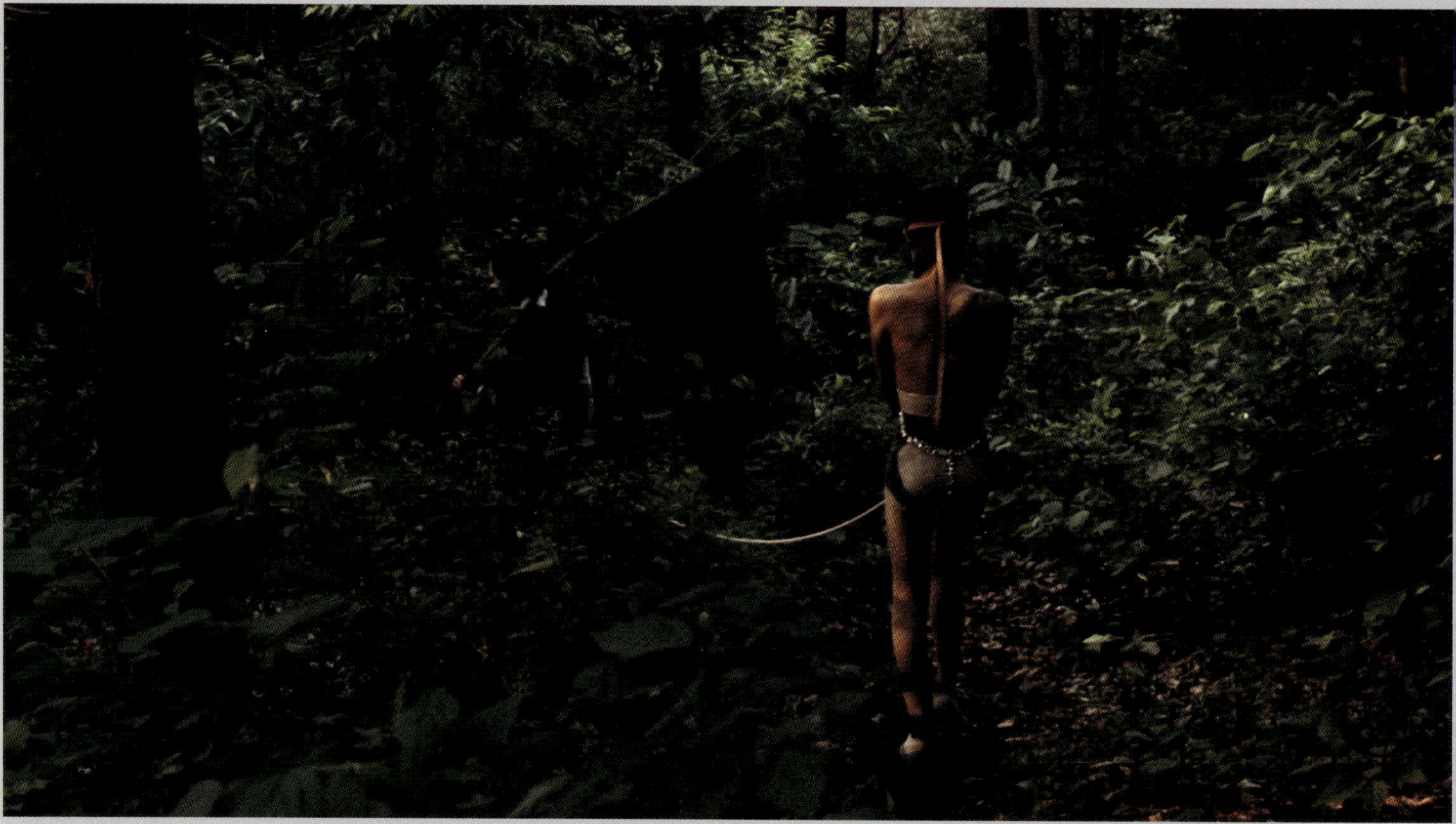

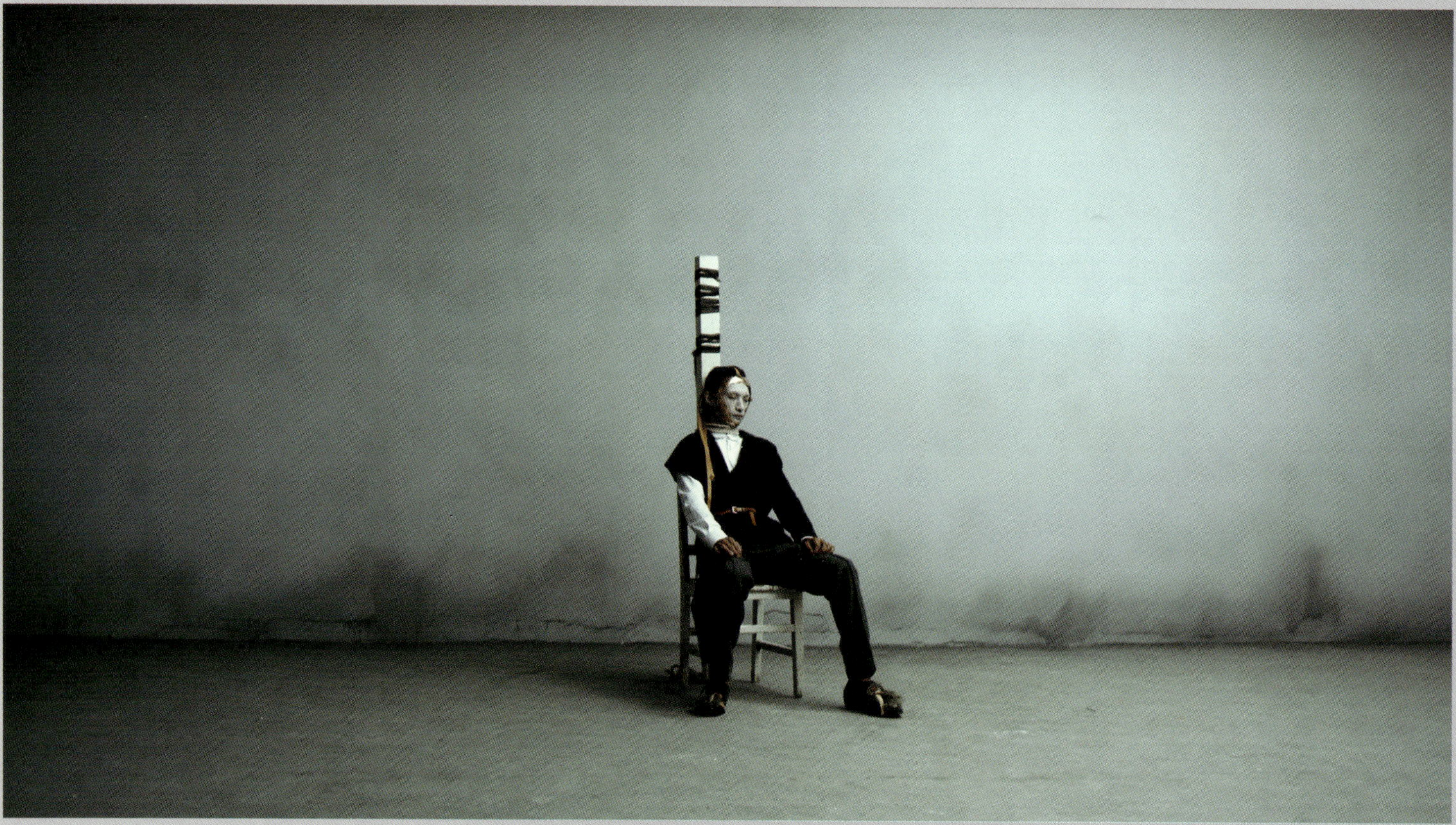

Huang Ran, *Blithe Tragedy*, 2011, single-channel video (color, sound), Ed. 1/5, duration: 14 min. 56 sec., acquired in 2011
黄然，《愉悦悲剧》，2011，单视频 (彩色, 有声)，五个版本之一，14 分 56 秒，收藏于2011

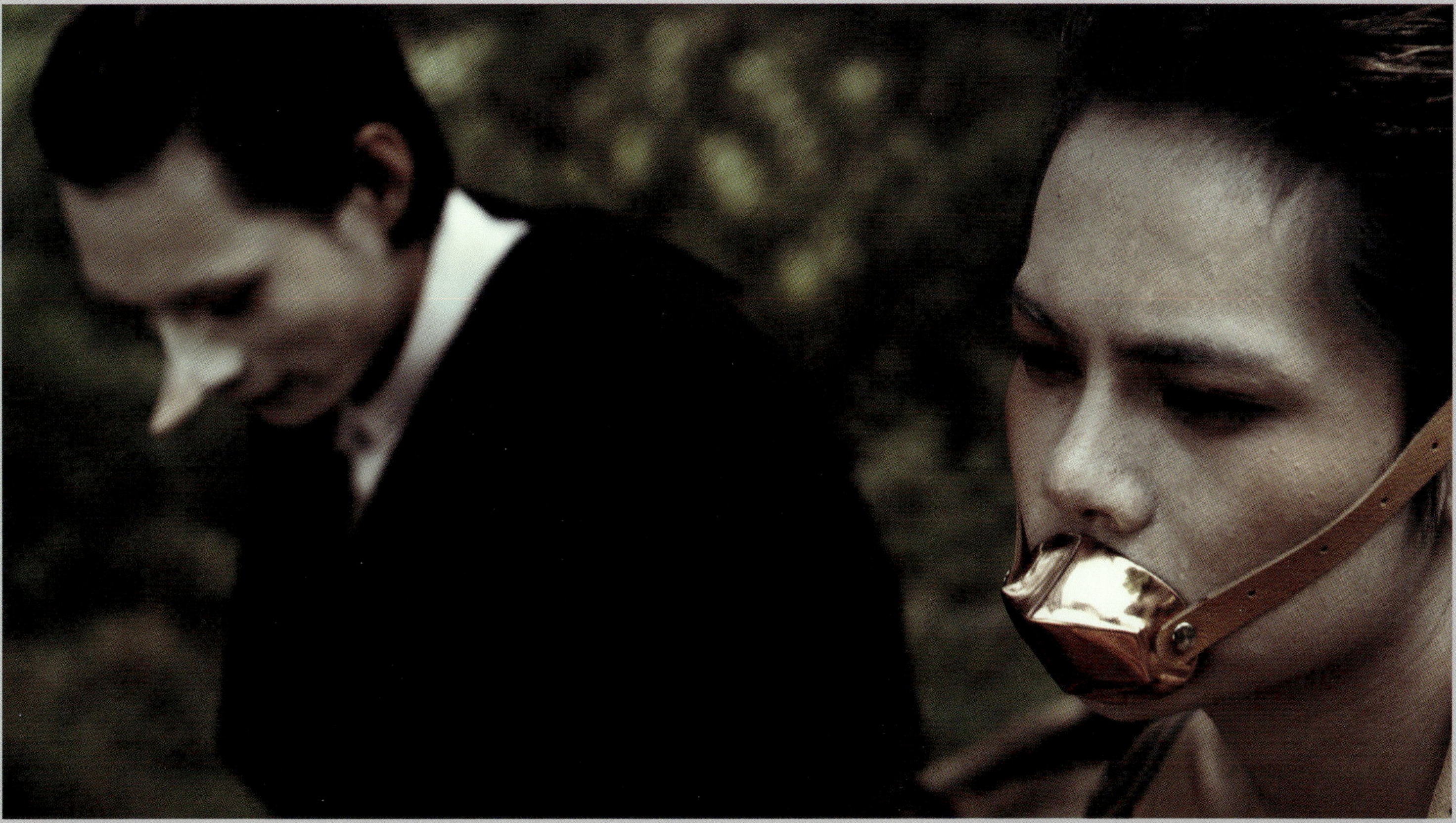

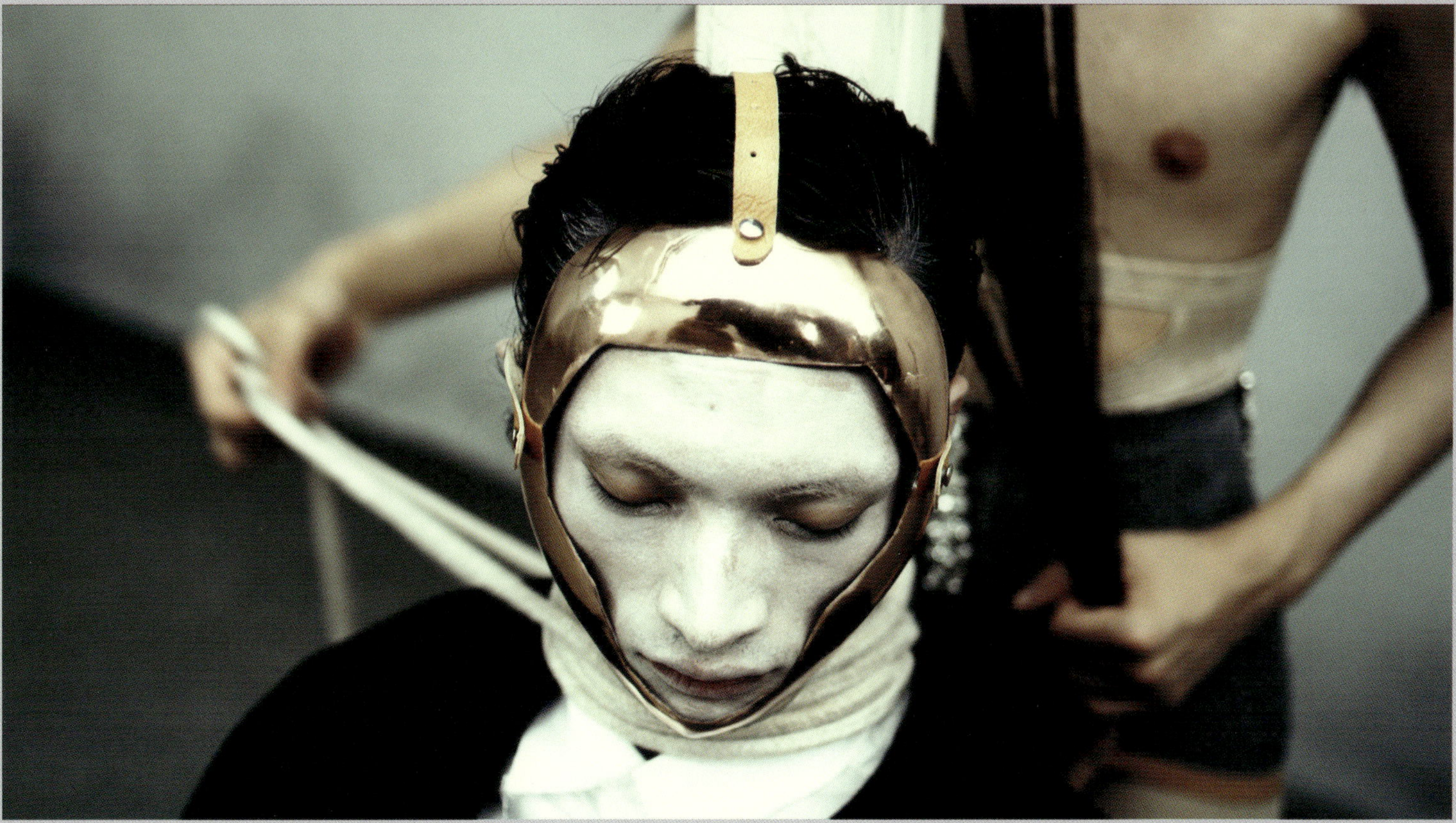

I think I am trying to examine a point where we are voluntarily gelded by a secured experience of aesthetic insecurity. Perhaps we just care about the feeling of caring.

- Huang Ran

我认为我在尝试着去检验我们如何甘愿被审美危机感所带来的安逸所阉割。也许我们仅仅是在乎一种被在意的感觉。

- 黄然

Huang Yong Ping 黄永砯

Born in 1954, Fujian, China
Lives and works in Paris, France

一九五四年生於中國福建
居住和工作於法国巴黎

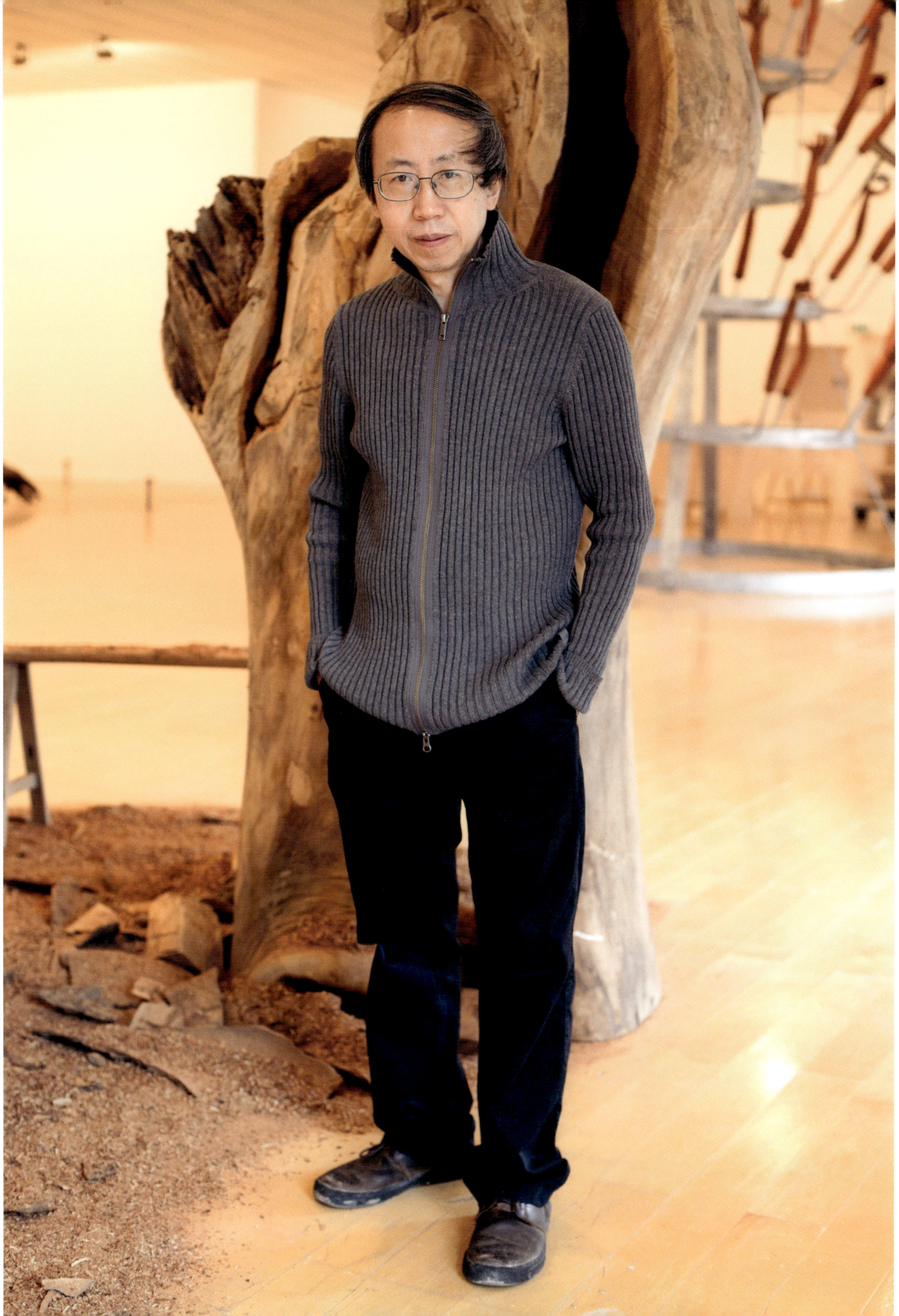

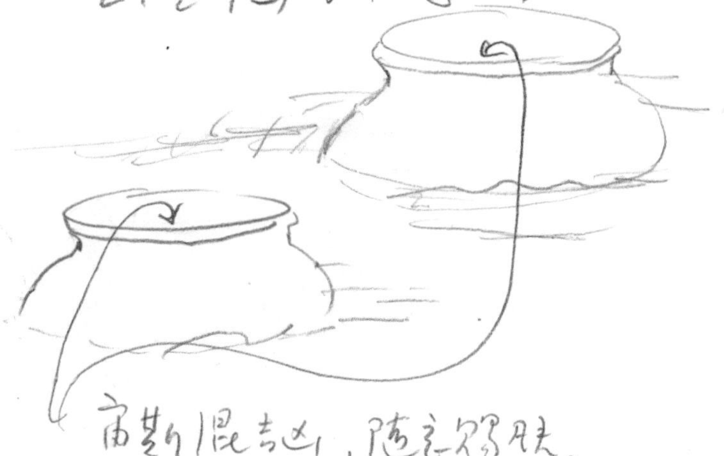

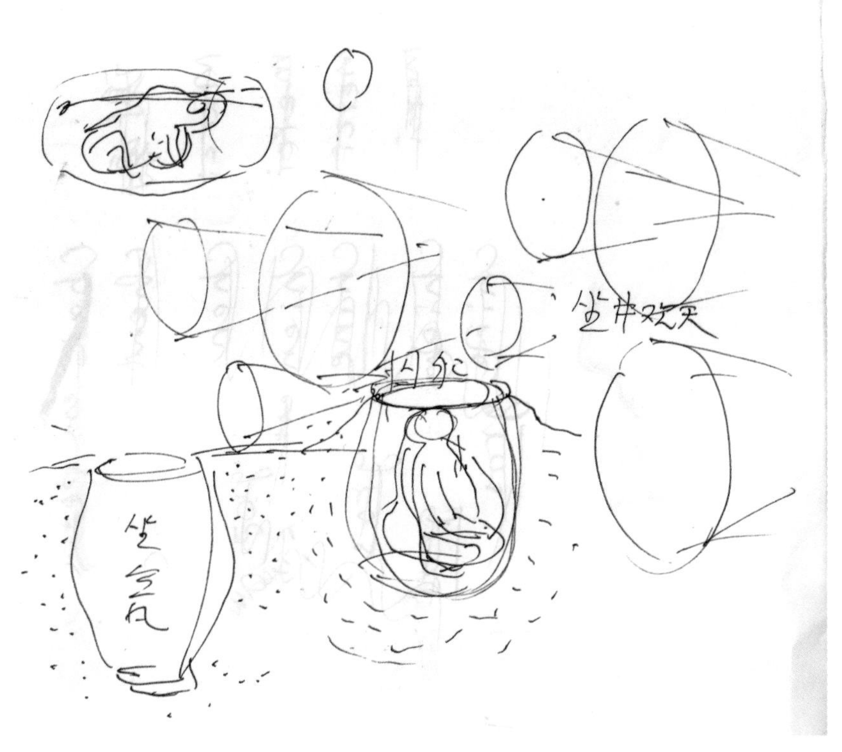

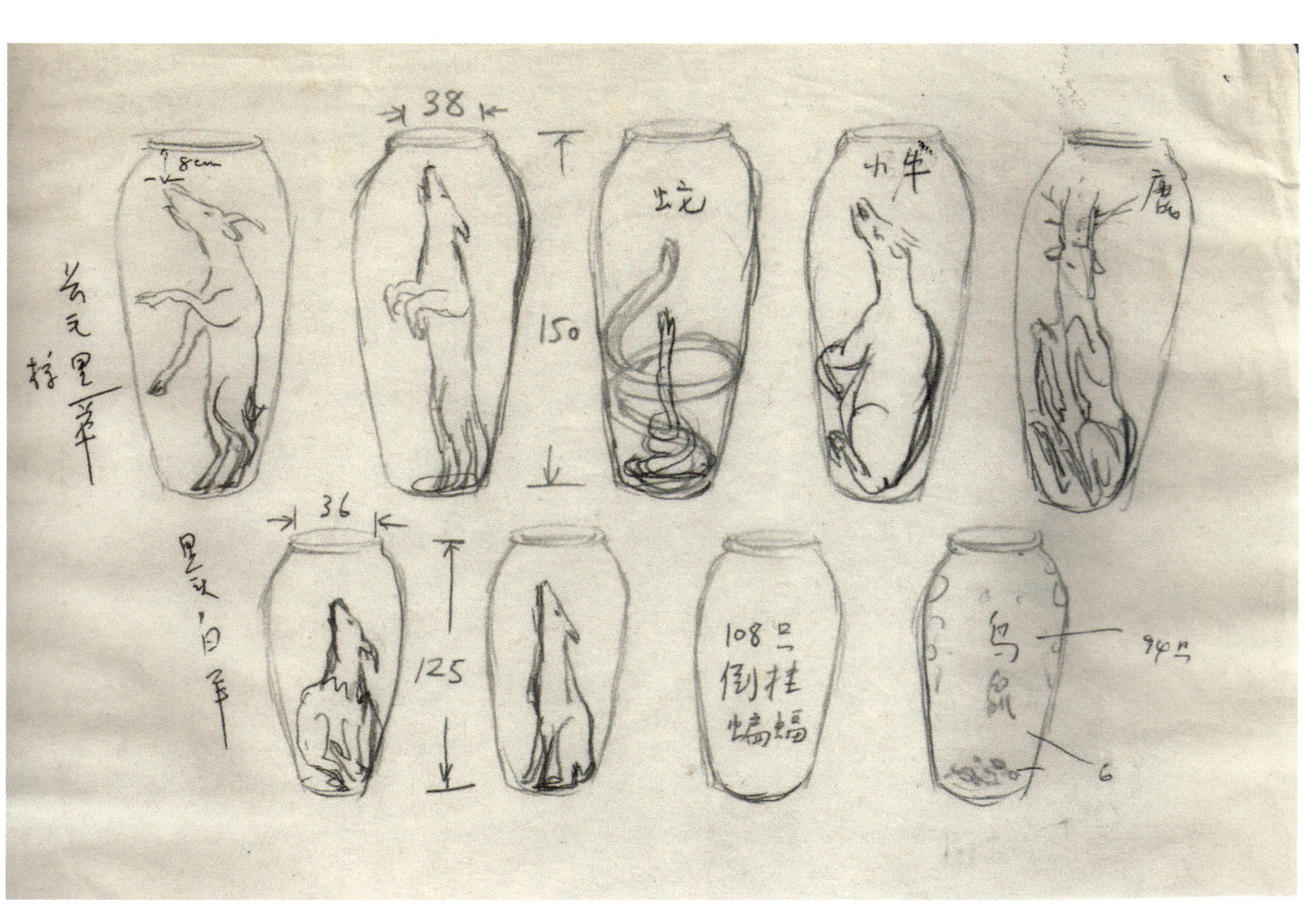

Huang Yong Ping, preparatory drawings for *Well*
黄永砅，《井》的构想筹备绘图

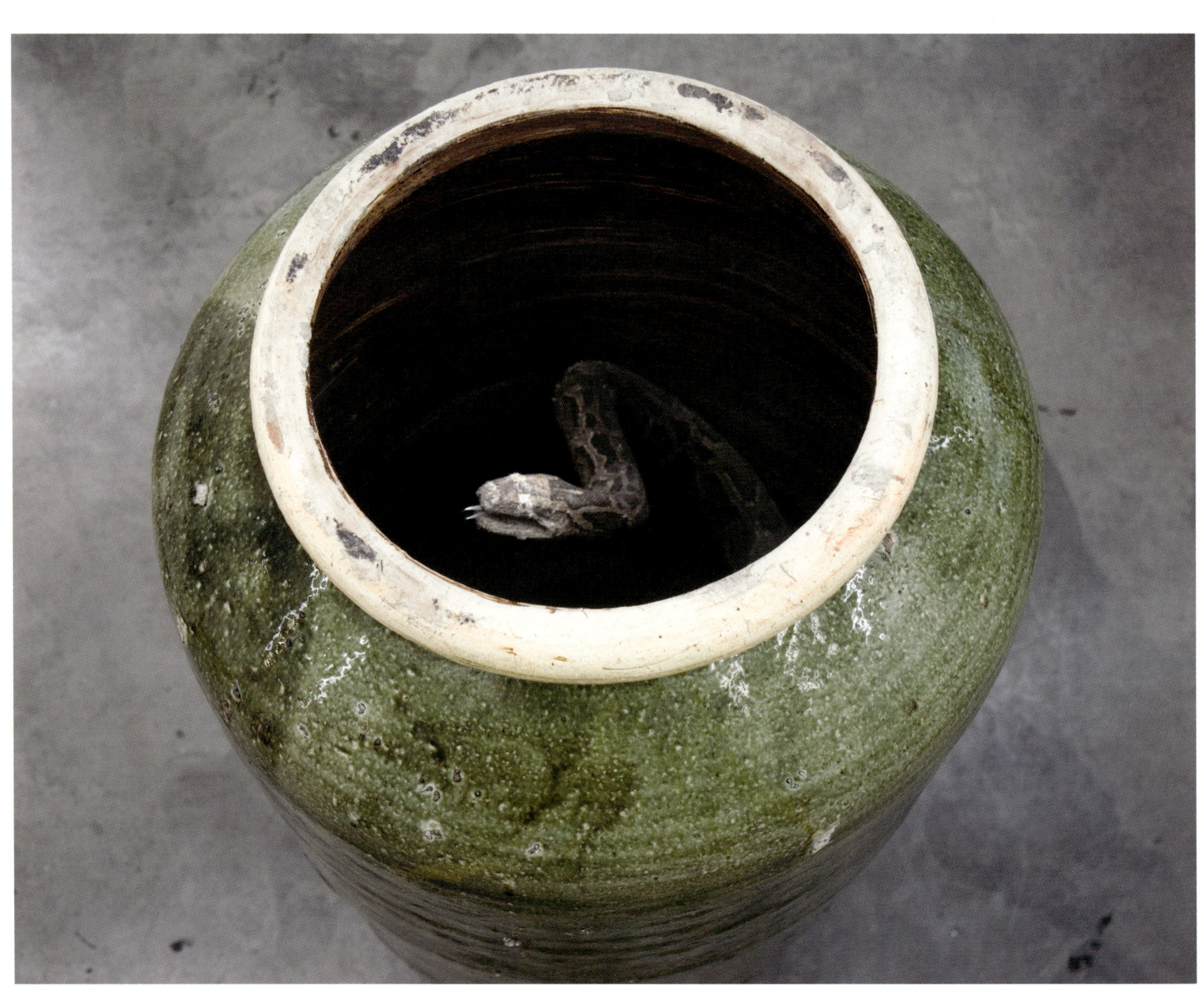

Huang Yong Ping, *Well*, 2007, ceramic and taxidermy, 60 x 26 1/2 x 26 1/2 in. (152.4 x 67.3 x 67.3 cm), acquired in 2007
黄永砯，《井》，2007，陶瓷和动物标本，60 x 26 1/2 x 26 1/2 寸 (152.4 x 67.3 x 67.3 厘米)，收藏于2007

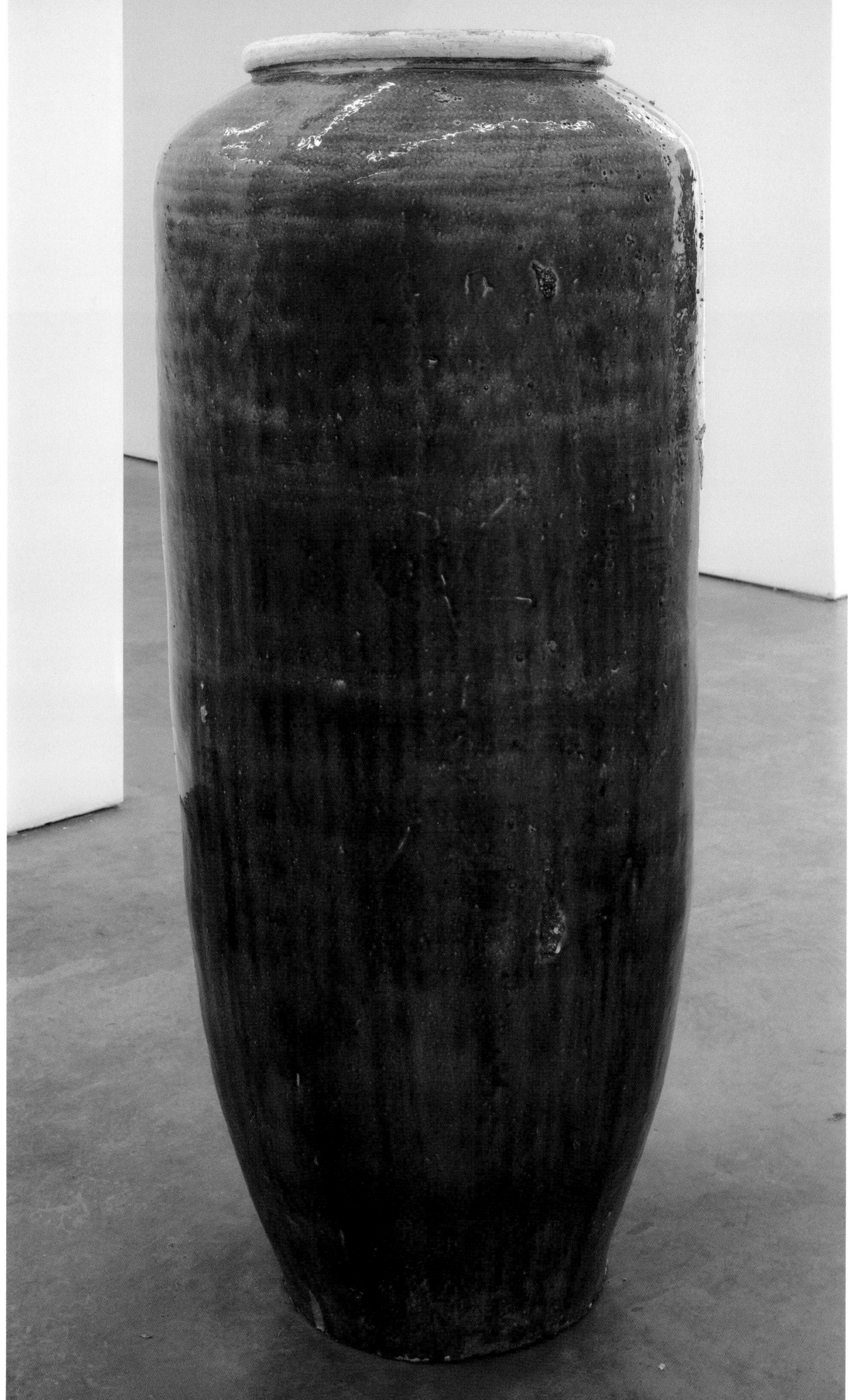

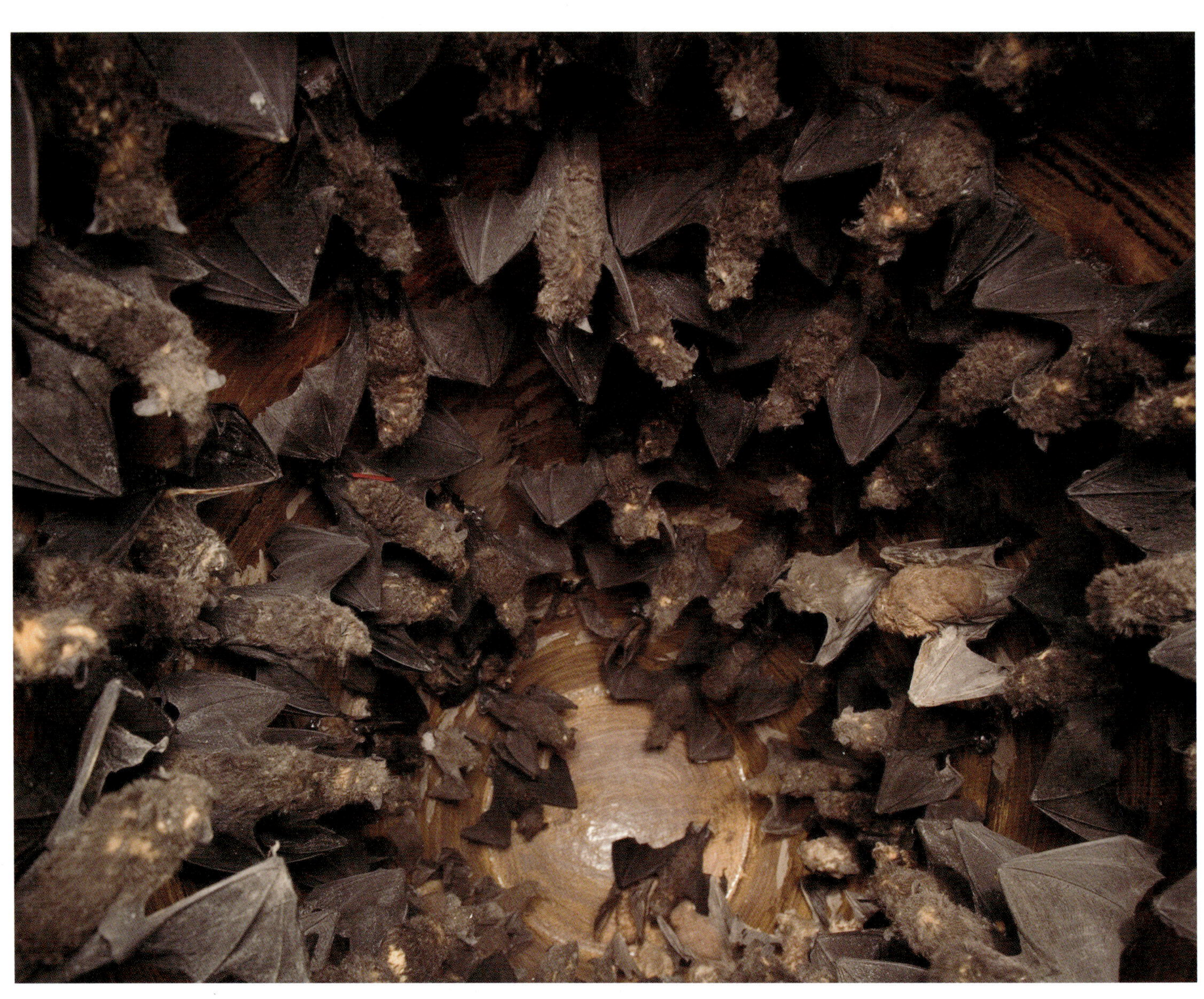

Huang Yong Ping, *Well*, 2007, ceramic and taxidermy, 60 x 26 1/2 x 26 1/2 in. (152.4 x 67.3 x 67.3 cm), acquired in 2007
黄永砅，《井》，2007，陶瓷和动物标本，60 x 26 1/2 x 26 1/2 寸 (152.4 x 67.3 x 67.3 厘米)，收藏于2007

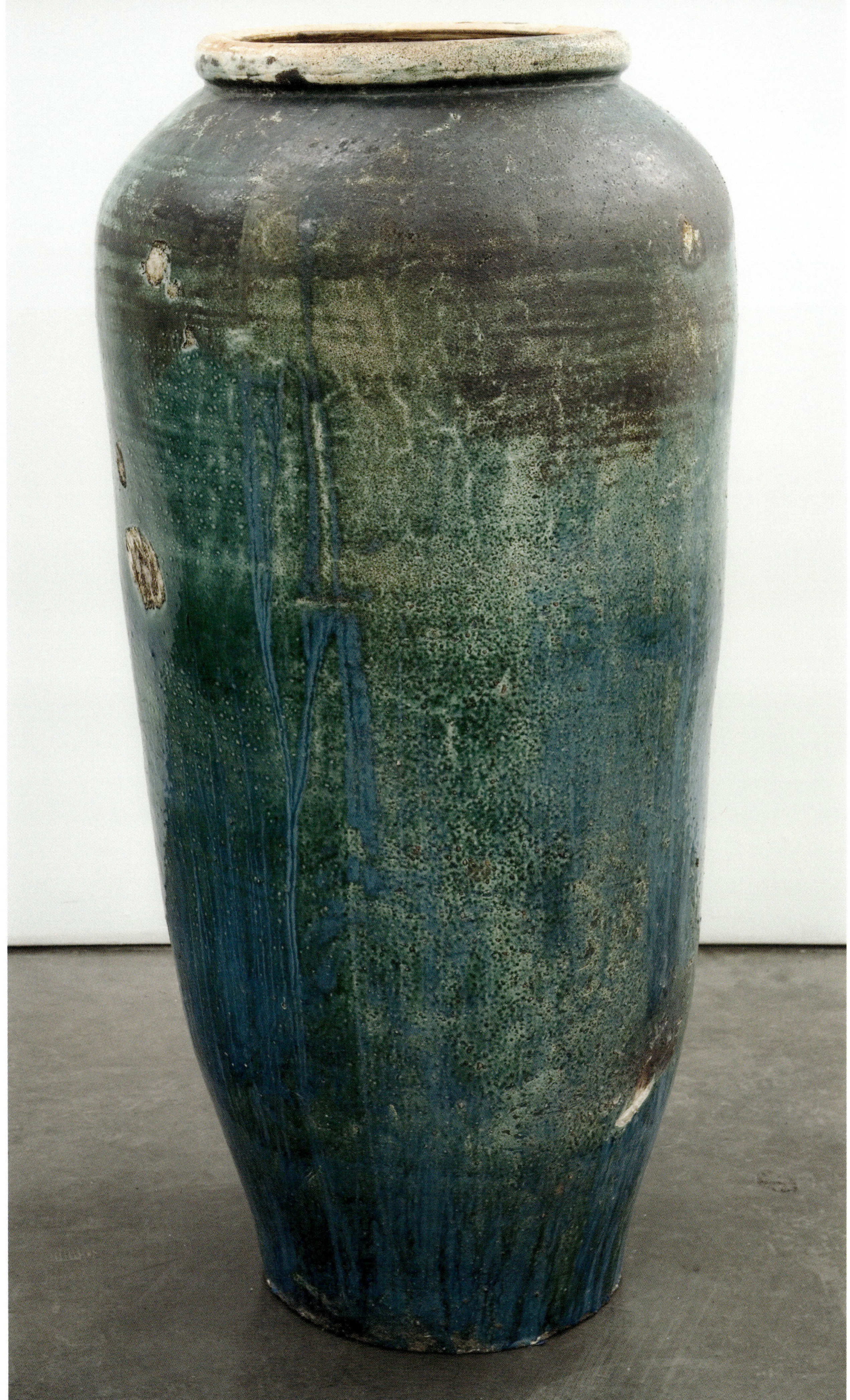

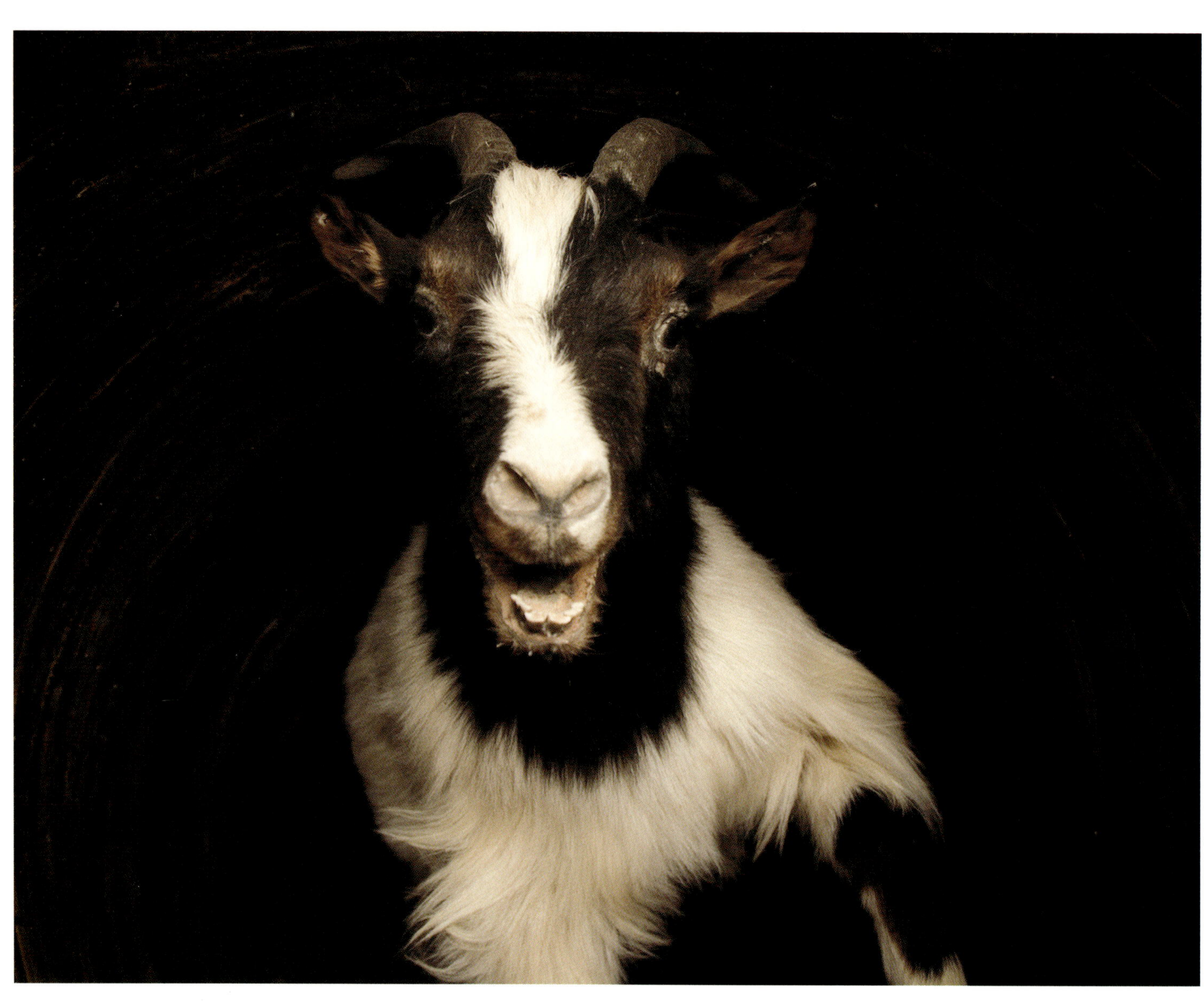

Huang Yong Ping, *Well*, 2007, ceramic and taxidermy, 60 x 26 1/2 x 26 1/2 in. (152.4 x 67.3 x 67.3 cm), acquired in 2007
黄永砅，《井》，2007，陶瓷和动物标本，60 x 26 1/2 x 26 1/2 寸 (152.4 x 67.3 x 67.3 厘米)，收藏于2007

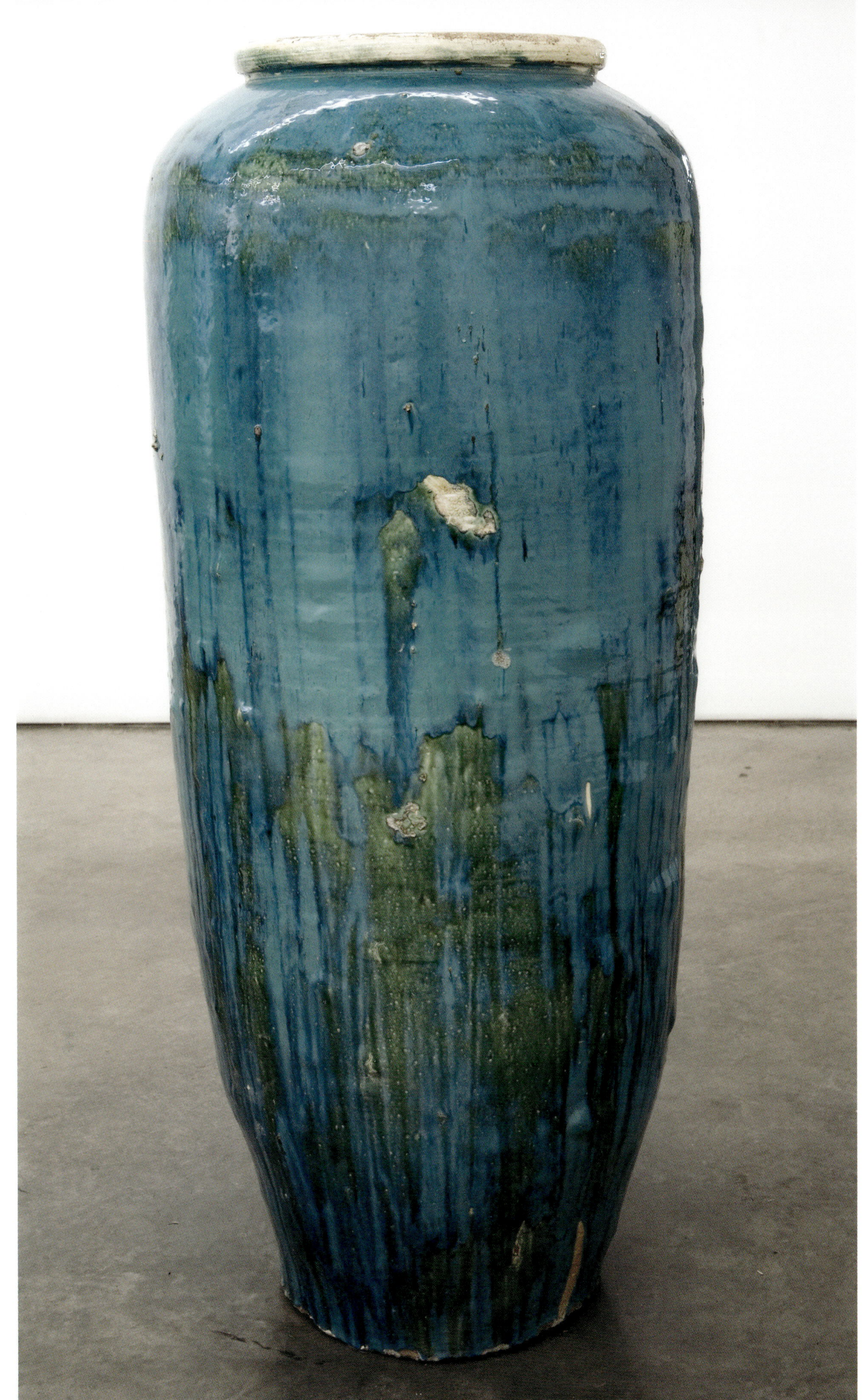

Lan Zhenghui　蓝正辉

Born in 1959, Sichuan, China
Lives and works in Beijing, China
and Toronto, Canada

一九五九年生於中国四川
居住和工作於中国北京
和加拿大多伦多

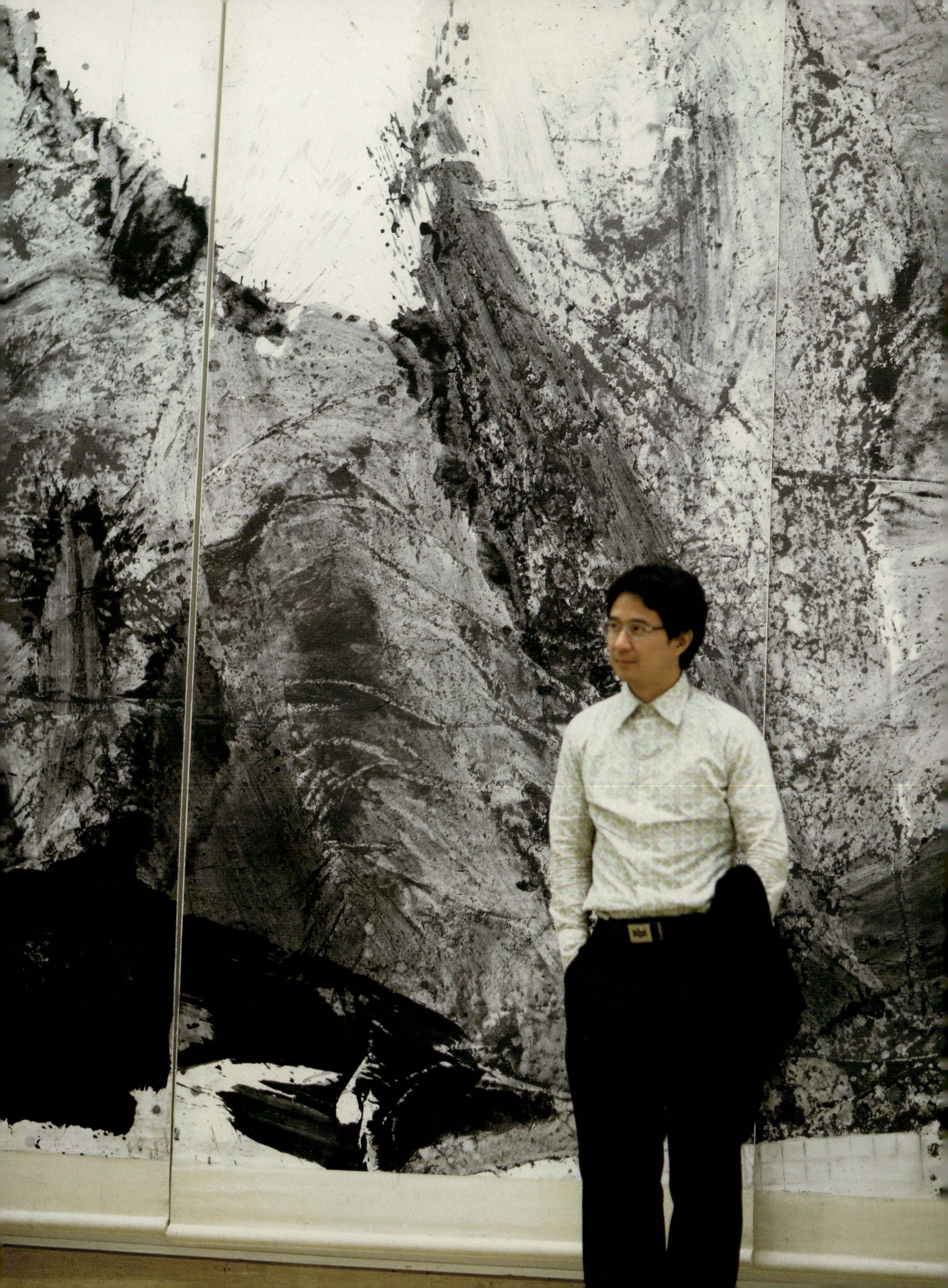

Untitled: Untitled obelisk. The hard edges of structuralism, the soft emptiness and the vast sides embrace each other in tiny variations.

Rain-washed Sky: Ji (rain-washed sky) is a kind of damp atmosphere, almost unbearably dense.

Cloud: The ample blending of the brushstroke looks like a billowing cloud; the logic of the three different shapes give a kind of answer.

Power: The early work from 2006 imploded, contorted, demolished, was quivering with unsteadiness. But it was also transparent with naïveté and candor.

- Lan Zhenghui

《无题》： 无题的方尖碑，结构主义的硬边，虚柔与巨大的旁置在微变中相拥。

《霁》： 霁是一种湿漉漉的氛围，凝重得无法承担。

《云》： 大量的晕染似云欲飘，造型不一的三段分布逻辑给出一种答案。

《权力》：早期2006年作品的坍塌纠结沦陷，摇摇欲坠极不稳定。也单纯与真切透明。

- 蓝正辉

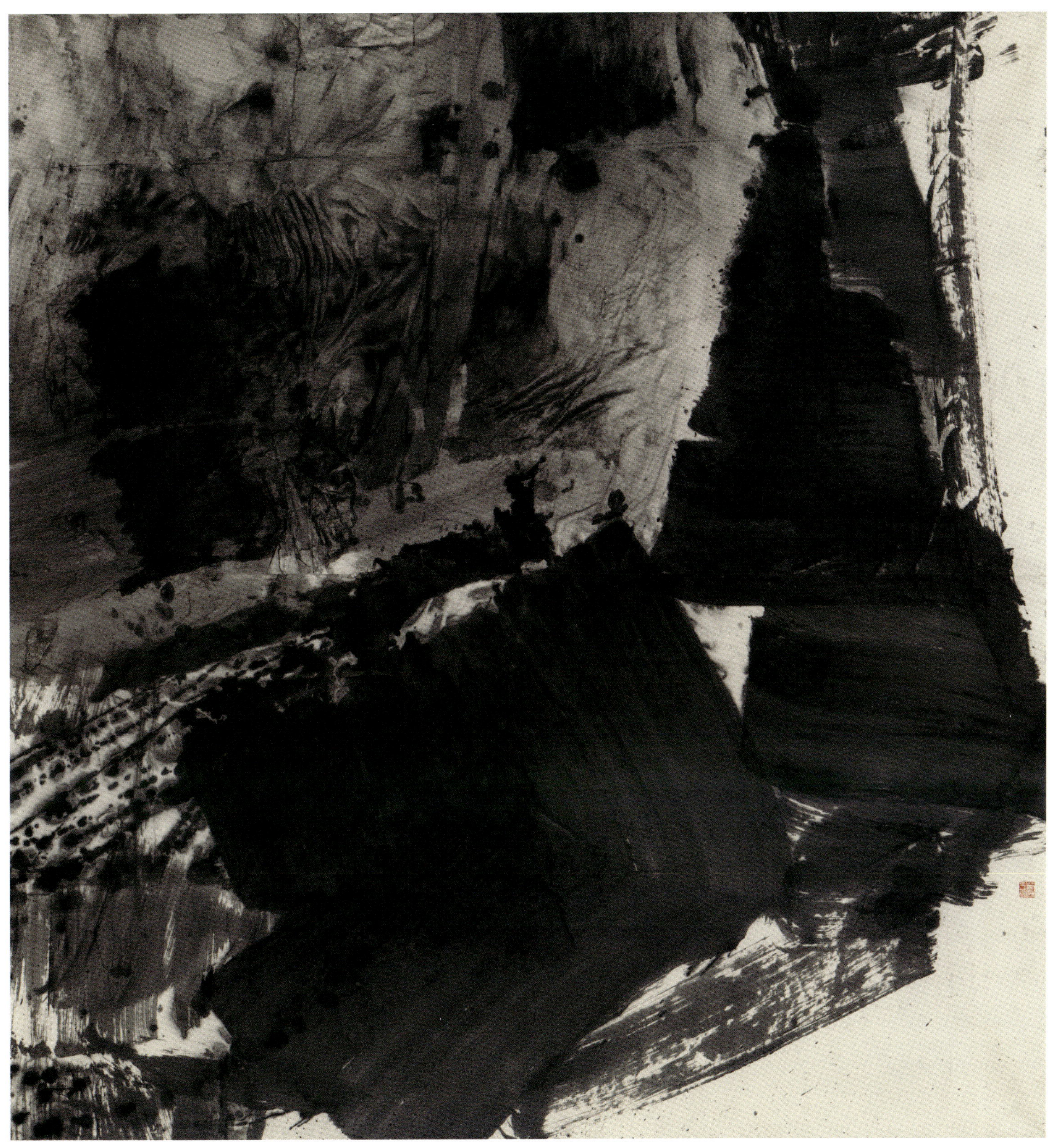

Lan Zhenghui, *Untitled*, 2008, ink on Xuan paper mounted on canvas, 70 7/8 x 75 7/8 in. (180 x 193 cm), acquired in 2011
蓝正辉，《无题》，2008，宣纸水墨裱布，70 7/8 x 75 7/8 寸 (180 x 193 厘米)，收藏于2011

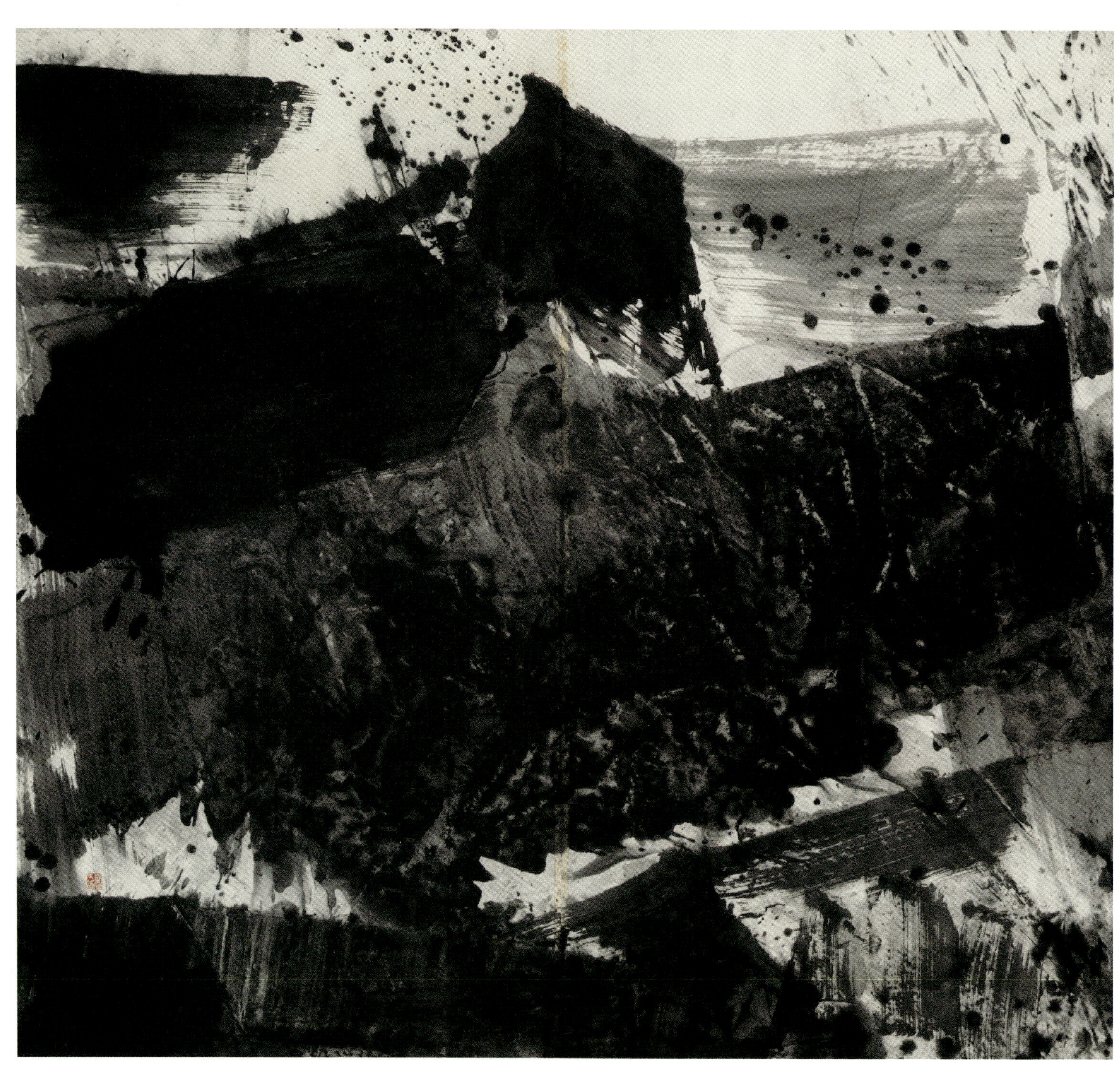

Lan Zhenghui, *Rain-washed Sky*, 2008, ink on Xuan paper mounted on canvas, 70 7/8 x 75 7/8 in. (180 x 193 cm), acquired in 2011

蓝正辉,《霁》, 2008, 宣纸水墨裱布, 70 7/8 x 75 7/8 寸 (180 x 193 厘米), 收藏于2011

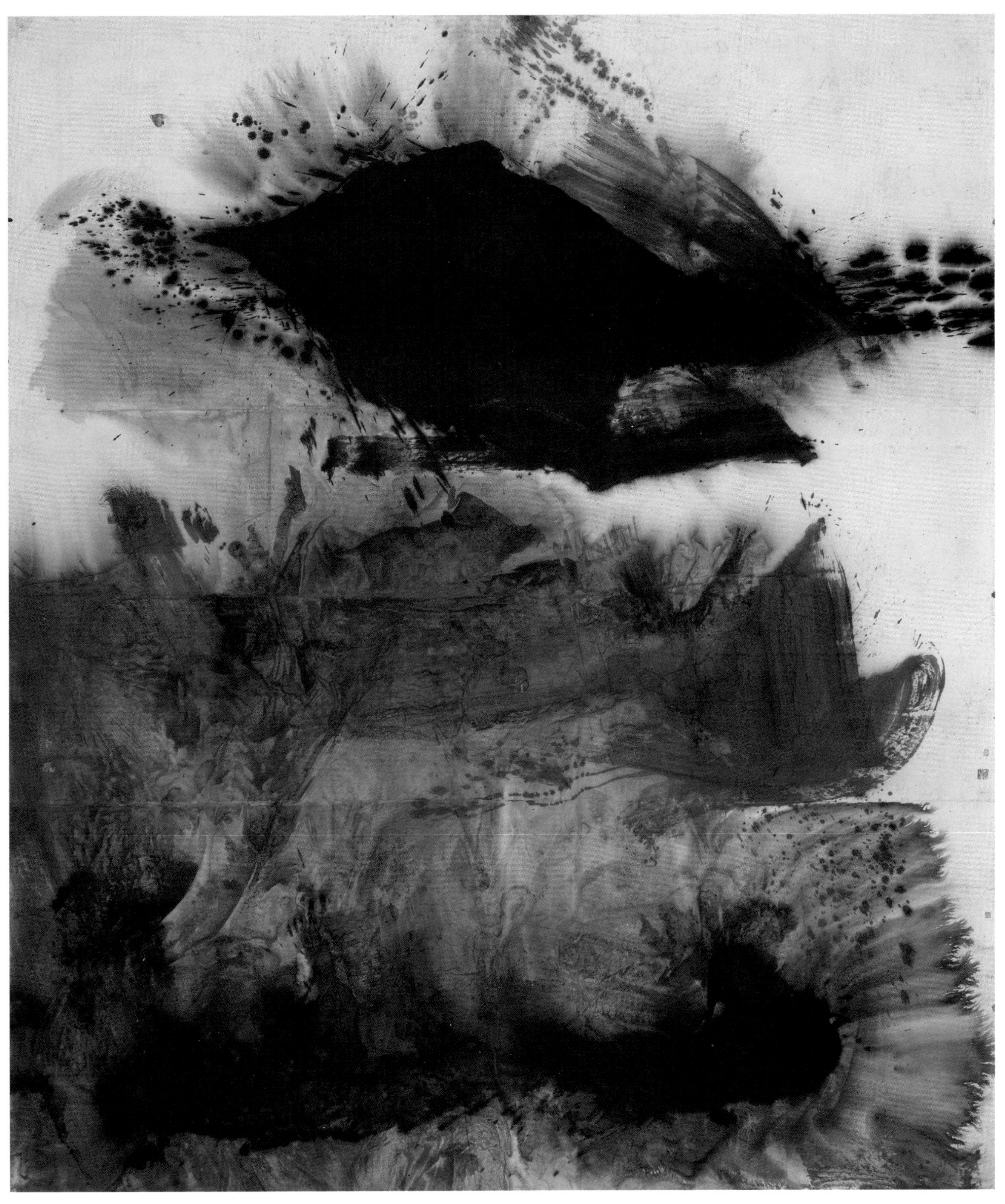

Lan Zhenghui, *Cloud*, 2009, ink on Xuan paper, 169 3/8 x 140 1/4 in. (430 x 365 cm), acquired in 2011
蓝正辉，《云》，2009，宣纸水墨，169 3/8 x 140 1/4 寸 (430 x 365 厘米)，收藏于2011

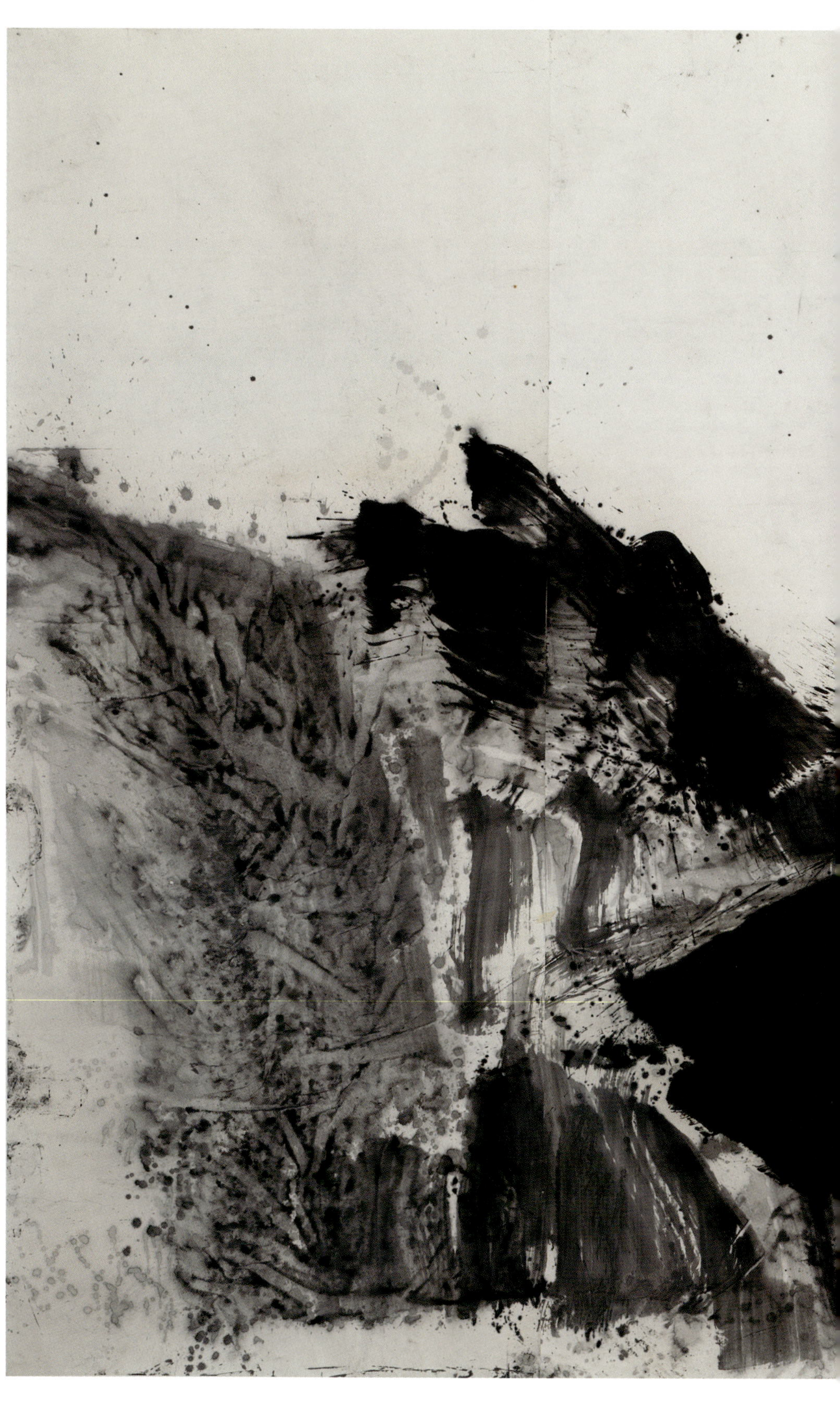

Lan Zhenghui, *Power*, 2006, ink on Xuan paper, 140 x 226 in. (356 x 575 cm), acquired in 2011
蓝正辉, 《权力》, 2006, 宣纸水墨, 140 x 226 寸 (356 x 575 厘米), 收藏于2011

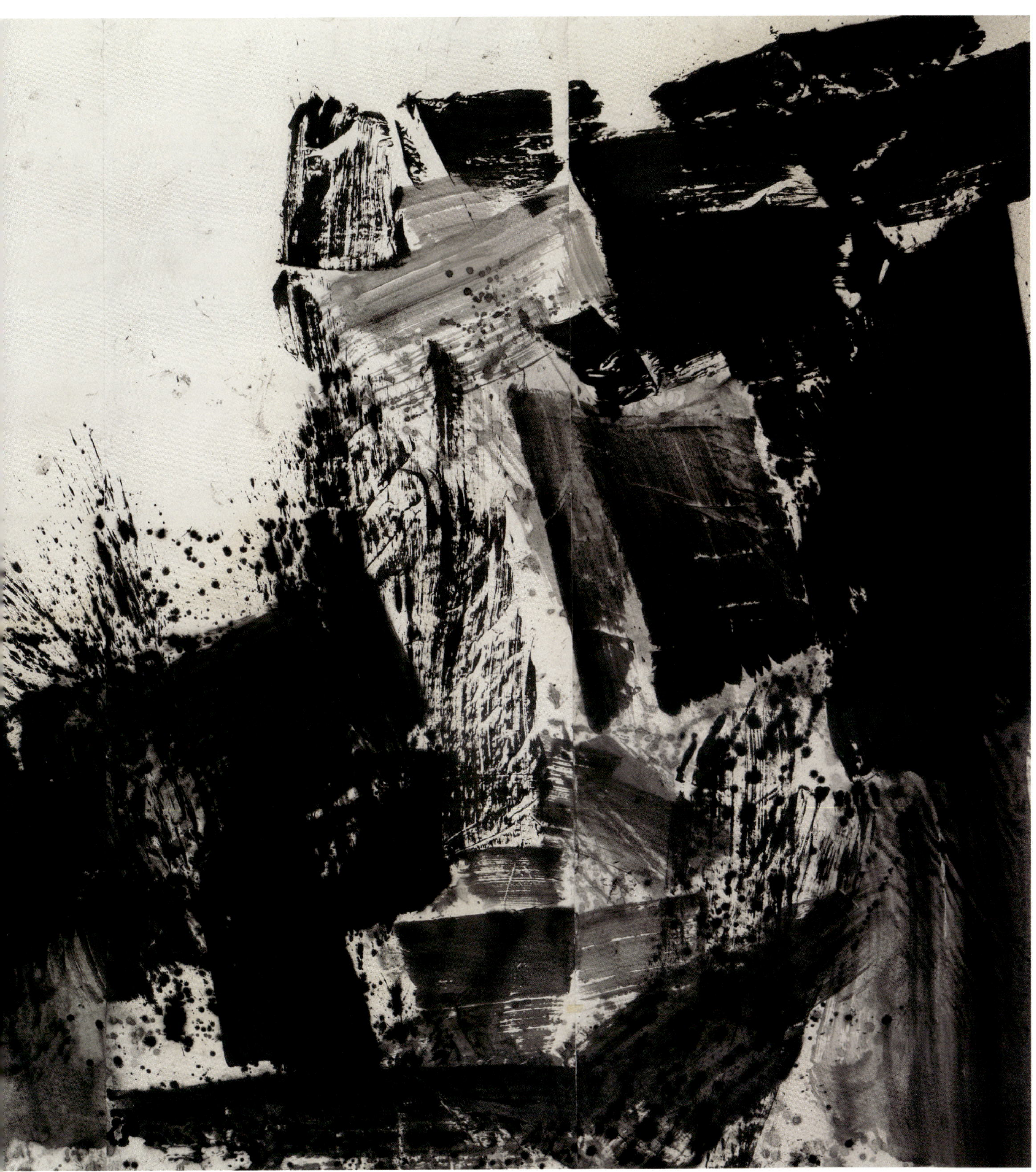

Li Ming

Born in 1986, Hunan, China
Lives and works in Hangzhou, China

李明

一九八六年生於中国湖南
居住和工作於中国杭州

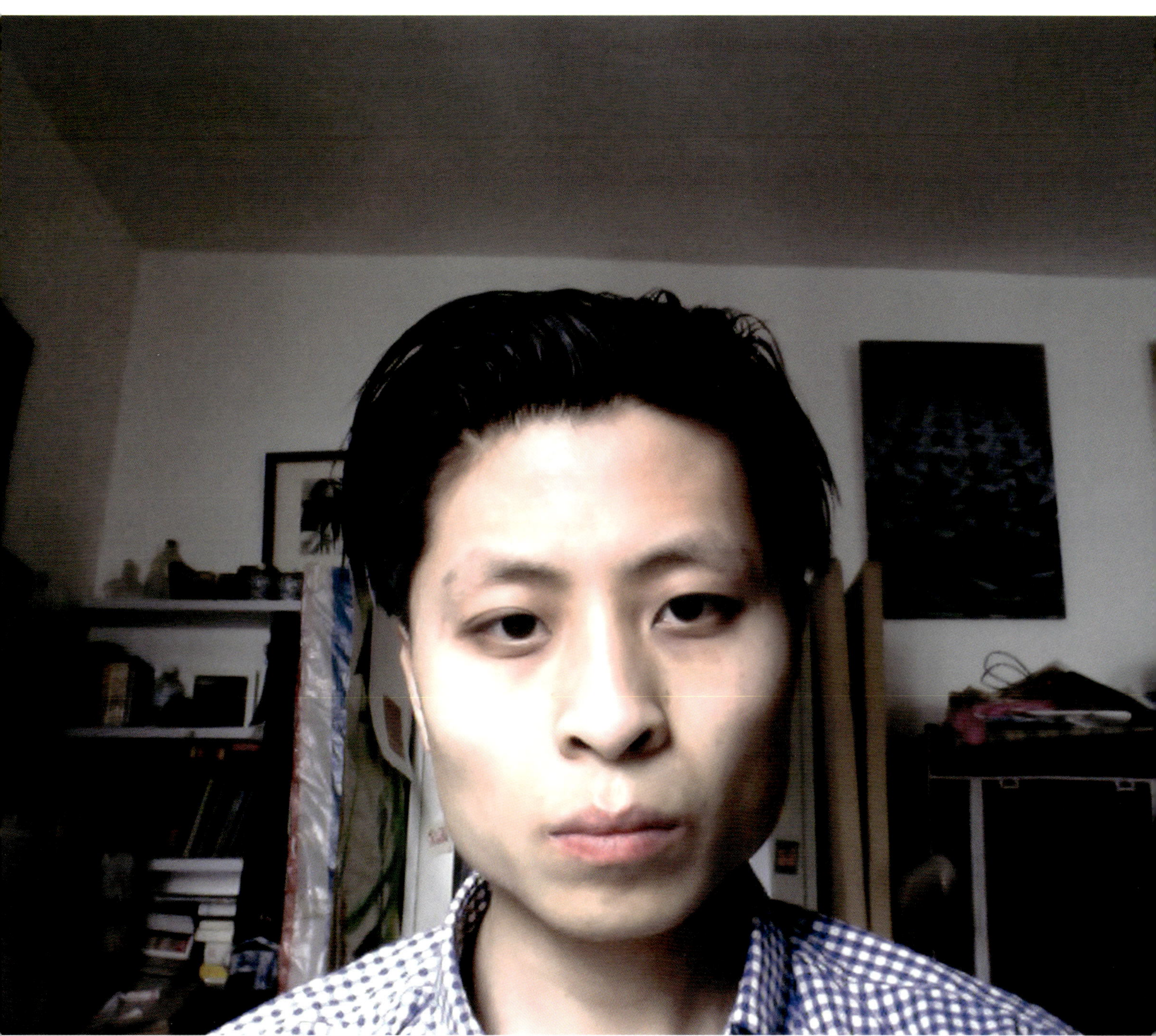

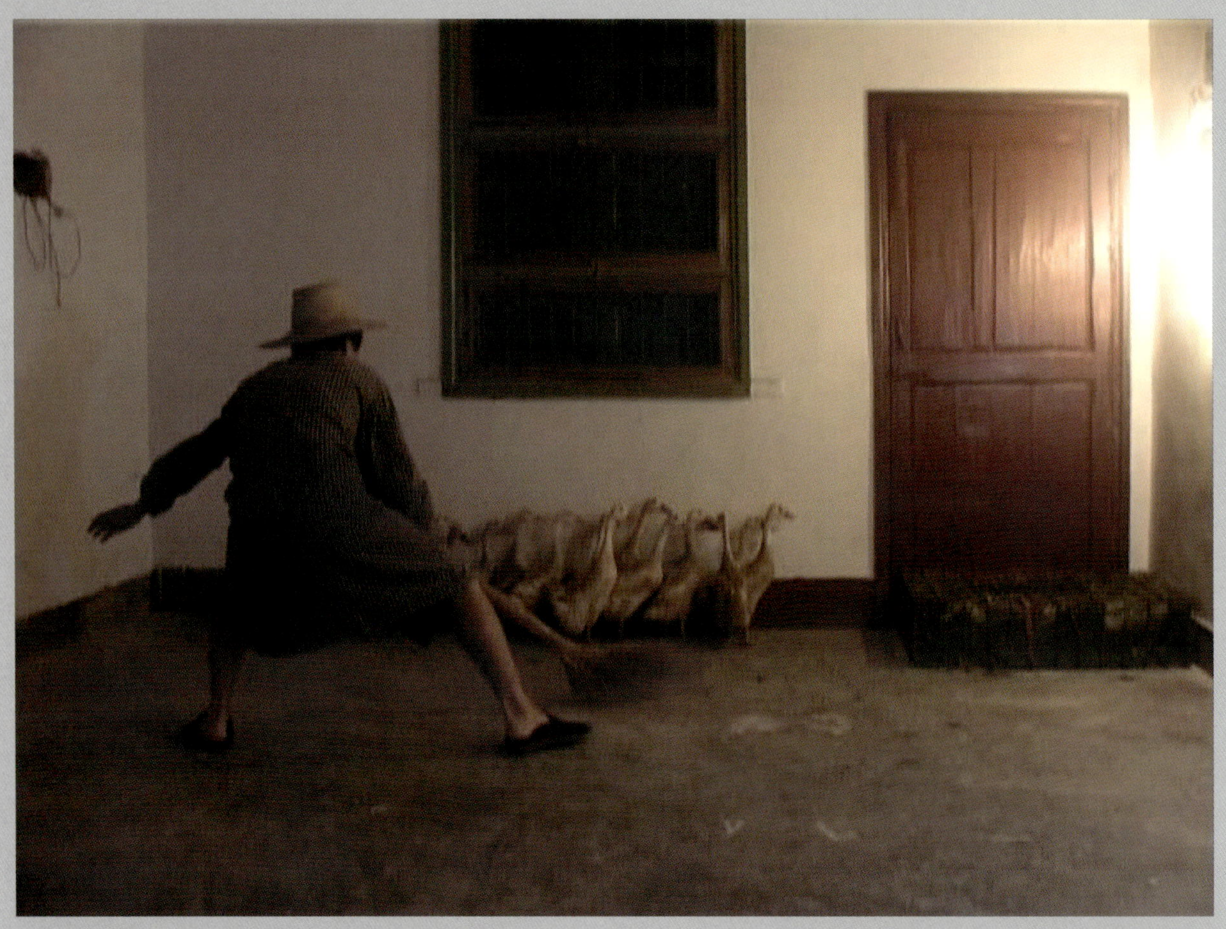

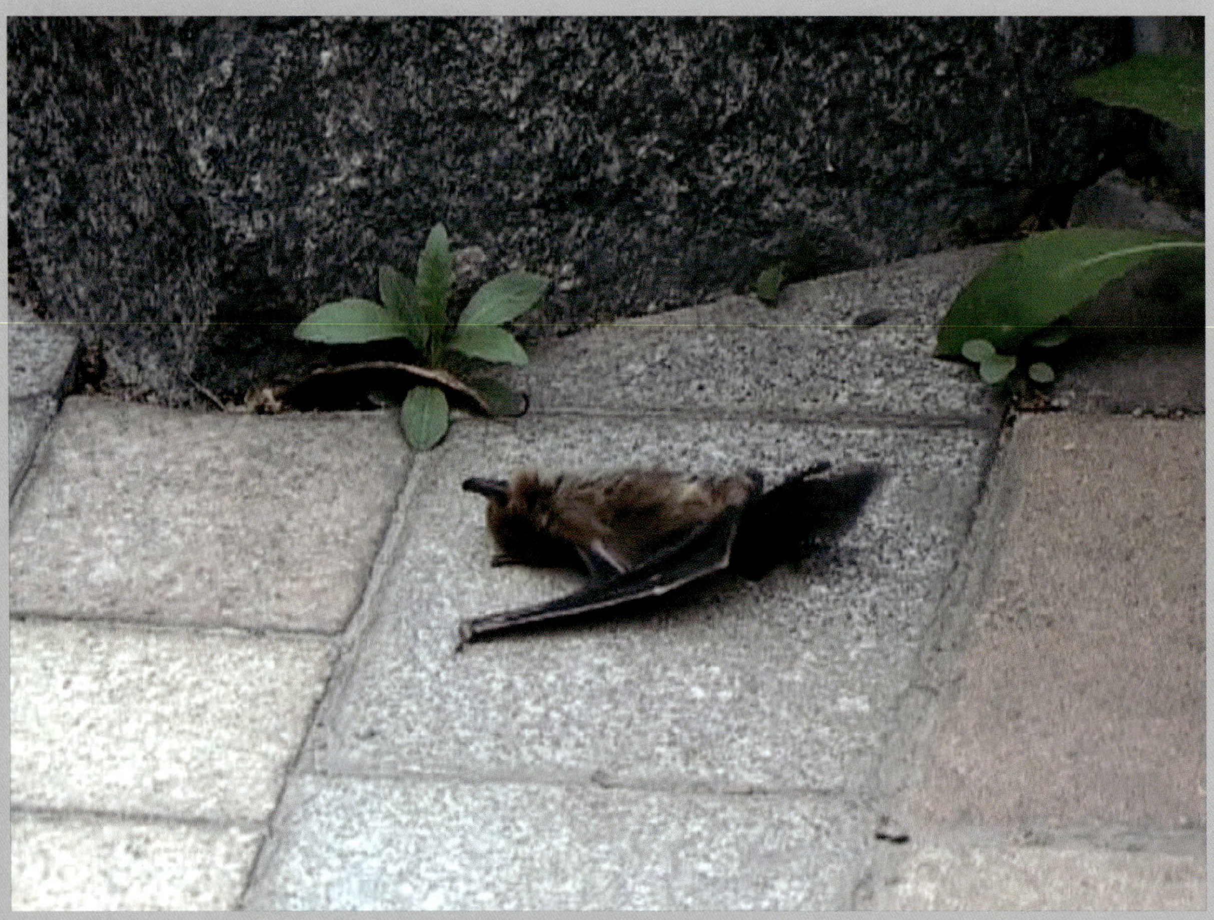

Li Ming, *Songs of Artist*, 2011, four-channel video (color, sound), Ed. 3/5 + 1 AP, No. 1, duration: 10 min. 38 sec., No. 2, duration: 9 min. 4 sec., No. 3, duration: 5 min. 25 sec., No. 4, duration: 2 min. 18 sec., acquired in 2013

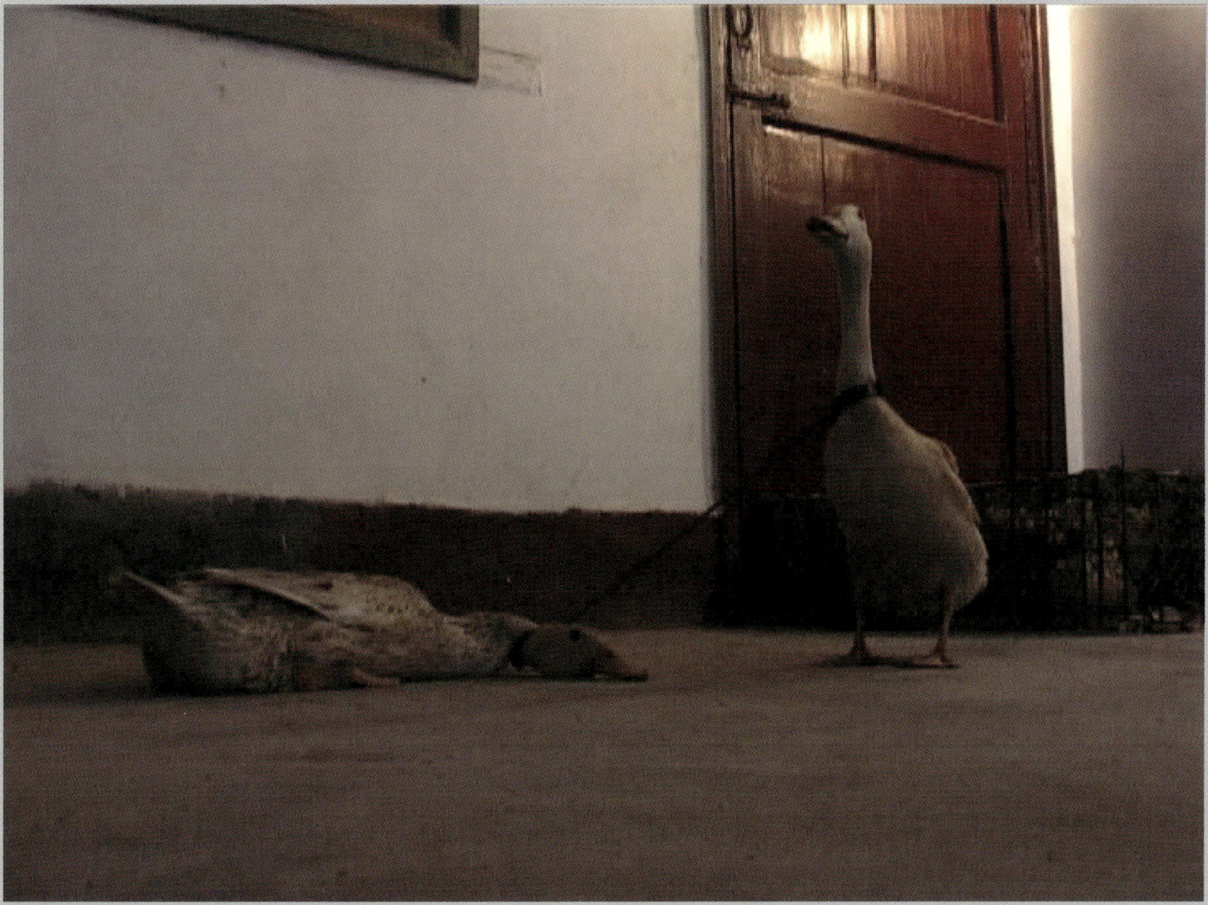

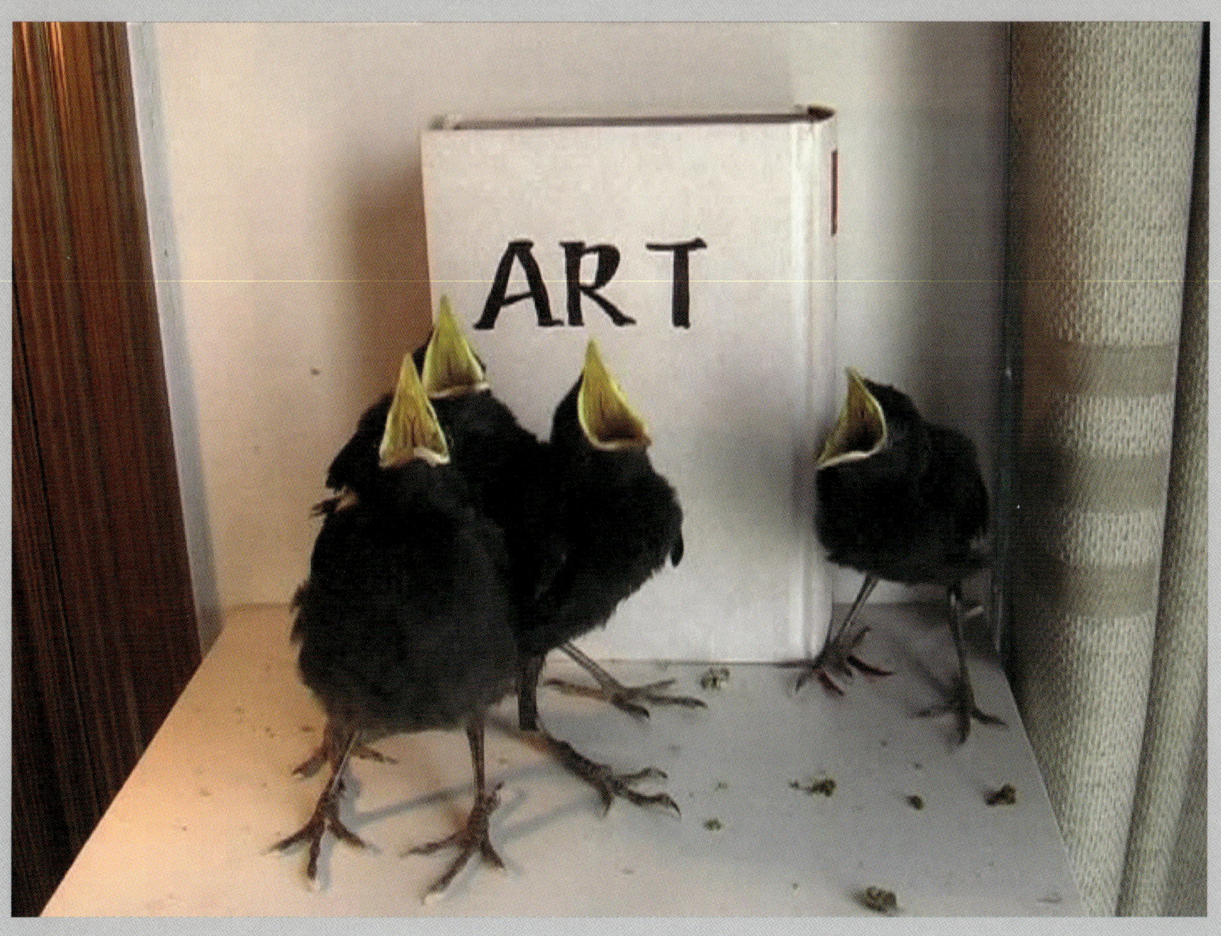

李明，《艺术家之歌》, 2011, 四视频 (彩色, 有声), 版本 3/5 + 1AP, 视频#1: 10分38秒; 视频#2: 9分4秒; 视频#3: 5分25秒; 视频#4: 2分18秒, 收藏于2013

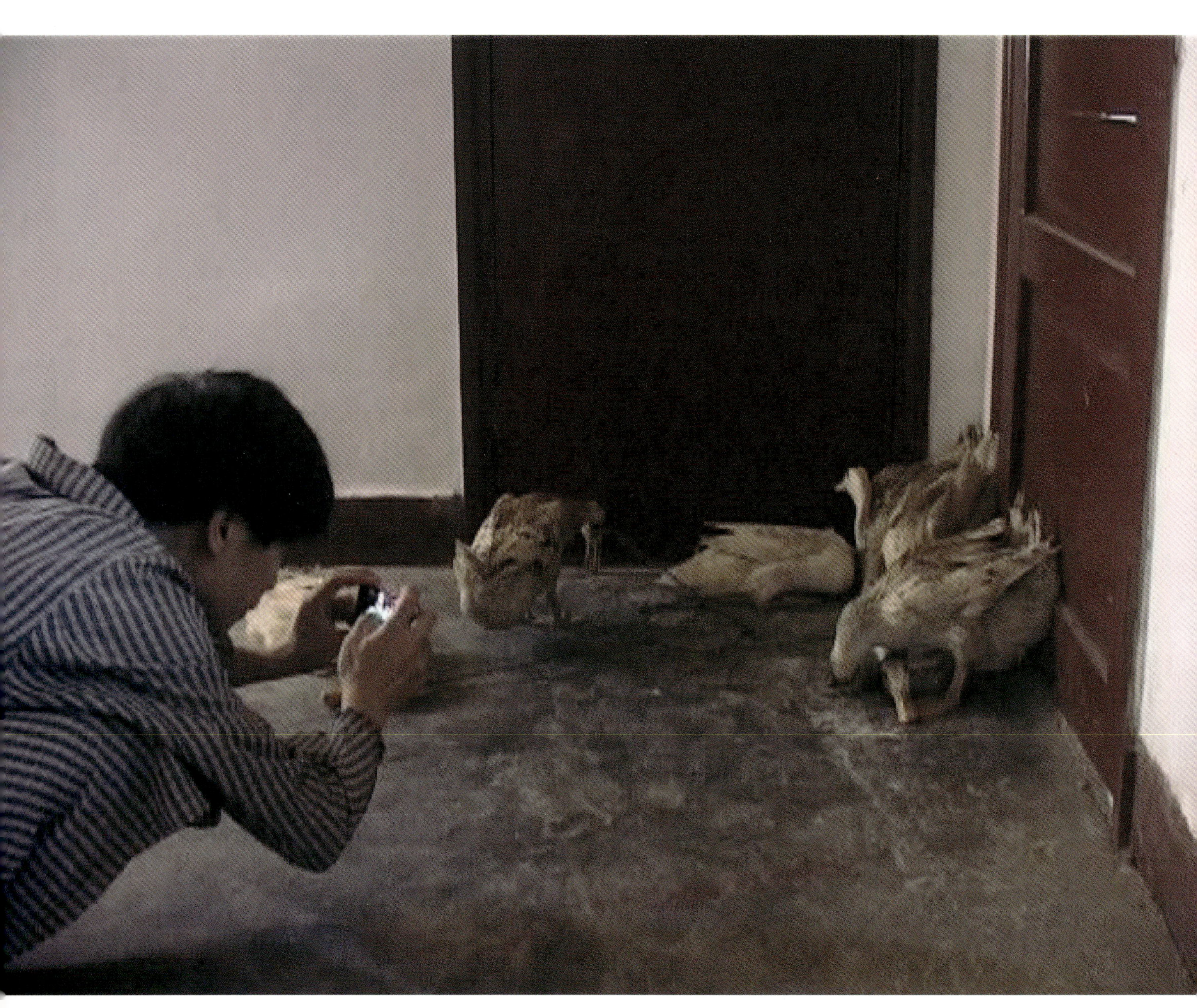

Li Ming, still from *Songs of Artist*, 2011
李明，视频定格，《艺术家之歌》，2011

In 2011, I started having doubts about the creative methods I had been using, and *Songs of Artist* was created during this period. Previously, my work was recognized because of some kind of emotional connection it was able to build with the audience, or because of its nuanced and delicate narrative tone. I value this quality in my work, however, at one point it will inevitably clash with reason and sense, on an individual and conscious level, or on an aesthetic and physical one posing an opposition against the social characteristics of an individual identity. I think it's a natural process, but of course "natural" doesn't mean it alleviates any of the creator's anxiety. The strange thing about this piece of work is that, on the one hand, my thoughts were very complicated, but on the other hand, the message the work expresses is so simple and direct that it's almost dreary. In *Songs of Artist*, I am chasing a group of ducks—this action in itself can easily be interpreted as an irony about the contemporary art world, and the title of the work further confirms the audience's guess. Of course I am indeed pointing out the awkwardness of an artist's personal identity in a collective situation and how their subjectivity struggles against the invasion from the outside world, which was exactly how I felt back then. I abandoned the obligation to make this piece more "artsy" or more like "a piece", which made it all the more strange. So, rather than mocking the art world, this work in fact serves as my own mumbles, without too much desire to communicate, because it doesn't need me to restate to the audience the absurdity and passivity in being an artist, but the clear implication of it is rather effective for me as an artist. Whether we juxtapose *Songs of Artist* with my earlier works, or we see it as a foreword for my works to come, it occupies a special location in my trajectory of creativity. I even think that the independence of this work is based on its dependence—it carries something beyond the action and the video themselves, which perhaps leaves larger room for discussion.

- Li Ming

2011年是我对自己以往创作方法感到怀疑的一个阶段，《艺术家之歌》就是这个时期的作品。此前作品被认同的部分往往在于同观者建立起了某种情感上的共通，或者以细微和轻盈的方式完成了一种叙事，我很珍视自己作品里的这种品质，但无论是个体的、知觉的，还是美学的、形式的，这些总会在一个时刻和理性发生冲撞，也和个体身份中的社会属性产生对峙。我认为这是一个很自然的过程，当然自然并不意味着可以减轻创作者丝毫的焦虑。这个作品比较怪异的地方在于，一方面我在那个时期想法非常复杂，但另一方面，作品的表达又简单直接到了一种几乎干燥的状态。在《艺术家之歌》里，我正在驱赶一群鸭子——这个行为本身很容易被理解成对当下艺术圈的讽刺，而作品的题目更印证了观众的这一想象。当然我的确是在指涉艺术家个人身份在集体情境中的尴尬，它的主体性和它被外部侵占的部分之间的力量拉扯，这也是我当时的切身之感。我抛弃了把这件作品做得更"艺术"或者更具"作品感"的负担，这反而让它显得有些异常。所以这件作品与其说是在讽刺艺术圈，不如说是我的自言自语，它实际并没有太大的交流欲望，因为不需要作为艺术家的我去向观众重申艺术家身份里存有的某种荒唐和被动，但这样明确的提示对作为艺术家的我却是有效的。无论是把《艺术家之歌》同我之前的作品并置来看，还是将它作为此后创作的一个序言，这件作品都处在一个很特别的位置上，我甚至认为，这件作品的独立性恰恰是建立在它的不独立之上——它携带了一些超出行为和影像本身之外的东西，这也许意味着一个更开放的讨论空间。

- 李明

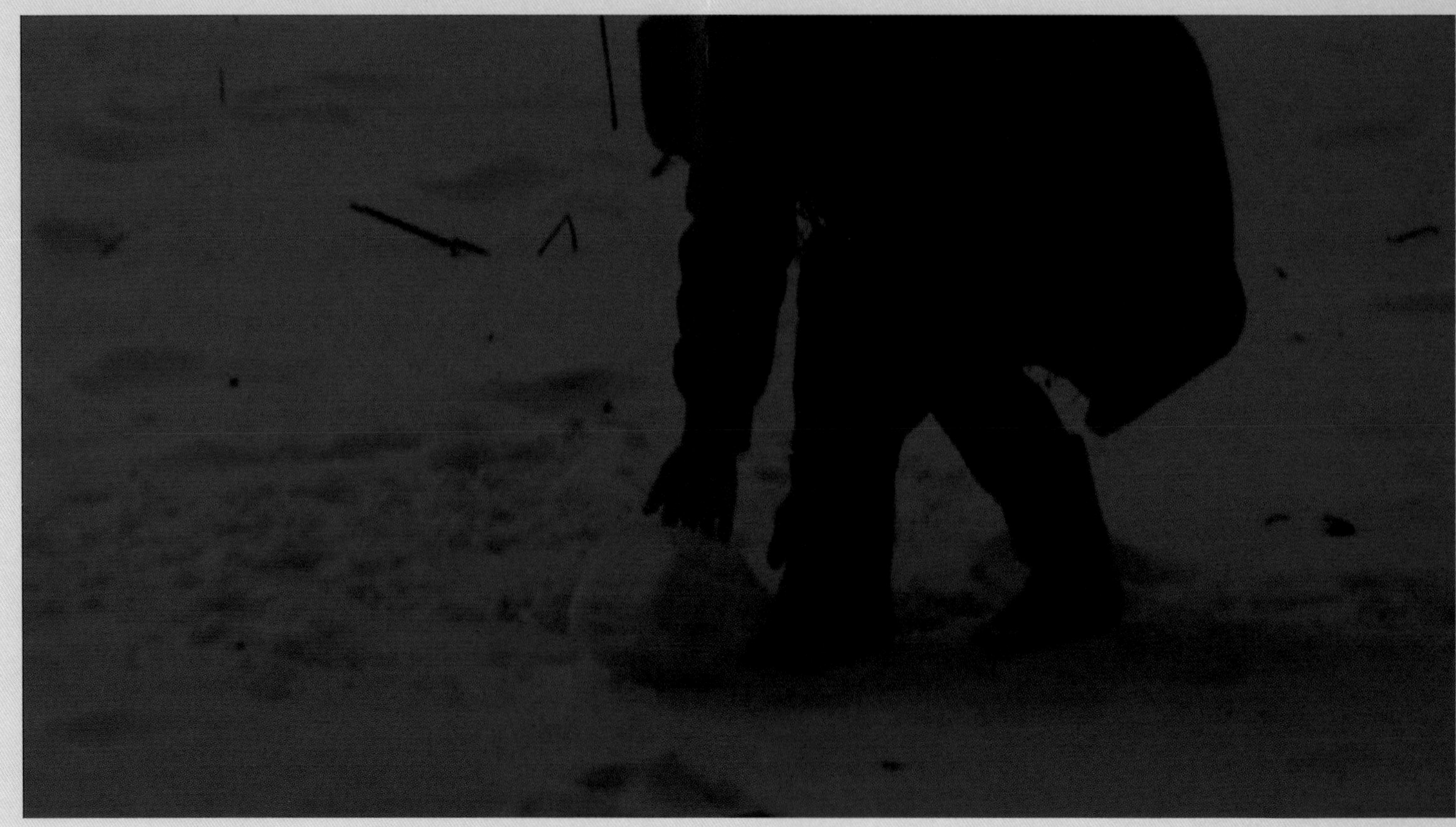

How does one distinguish between the recording of a piece of performance art and a piece of video art? Can the recording of an action be used to verify its subjectivity as video art, instead of as a supporting element? In *Snowball*, I try hard to distinguish the two, or discover the overlaps between them. Perhaps it's like the action of rolling a snowball itself, even if it is finally completed, it is based on a hypothetical precondition in which the existential meaning of rolling a snowball, or "[a] recording" could indeed exceed the boundary imposed by the time and space it has recorded. For me, *Snowball* does not exist as a carrier or platform through which we broadcast performance art, but rather, it exists as the film itself. During this process, the artist directly or indirectly participates in the shooting of the video by doing the action. The "action" that appears in the video is not isolated, because it connects all the natural objects presented in the frame resulting in a physical synthesis. I chose a work method that's suitable for myself, or perhaps it's what I am best at—creating a magical encounter, providing a fuse, entering the zone of hypothesis. The person holding the camera wanders in the grey area between interfering with reality and the concealment of such interference. While shooting, the artist is at once active and passive—in between going in and coming out. The part of his identity as the action itself overlaps with the part of him that is the video, and the two parts question each other— when this world of forged relationships starts, it has the same properties as the objective world, and we will realize that even at the moment the video stops the artist is not released from the conflict he has created for himself.

- Li Ming

Li Ming, *Snowball*, 2008, single-channel video (color, sound), Ed. 3/5 + 1 AP, duration: 14 min. 27 sec., acquired in 2013

如何区分用影像纪录下的行为作品和一个影像作品之间的差异？对行为的纪录是否可以确认它自身作为影像的主体性而不是仅仅作为一种服务性的载体？在《雪球》里，我努力去区分这两者间的差异，或者发现它们间的重叠部分，不过也许正像是滚雪球这一行为本身，即便最终获得了"成功"，它仍然处在一个假设的前提之下，即，滚雪球本身存在意义，或者，"纪录"的确可以超出它所记录下的时间和空间限定的边界。《雪球》这件作品对我来说，它呈现的影像不是传播行为表演的载体，存在的意义同样也在于影像本身。在这个过程中，艺术家以行动的方式直接或者间接地参与到录像拍摄中，出现在影像中的"行为"并不孤立，它连接着画面里所有呈现的自然物体，使得它们成为综合的物理状态。我选择了适合自身现实的工作方式，也许也是我所擅长的方式——制造一次奇遇，提供一个导火索，进入假设的范畴内部，持摄像机的人徘徊在对眼前现实的干预和隐藏这种干预的灰色地带，艺术家在捕捉影像时既是主动的，也是被动的，在进和出之间，他属于行为的身份和属于影像的部分不断重叠但又互相质疑——这个被制造出关系的世界一旦被启动，就同客观的世界有了同样的属性，我们会发现，即便在影像终止的一刻，艺术家也并没有从这种自己制造的矛盾中解放出来。

- 李明

李明，《雪球》，2008, 单视频 (彩色, 有声), 版本 3/5 + 1AP, 14 分 27 秒, 收藏于2013

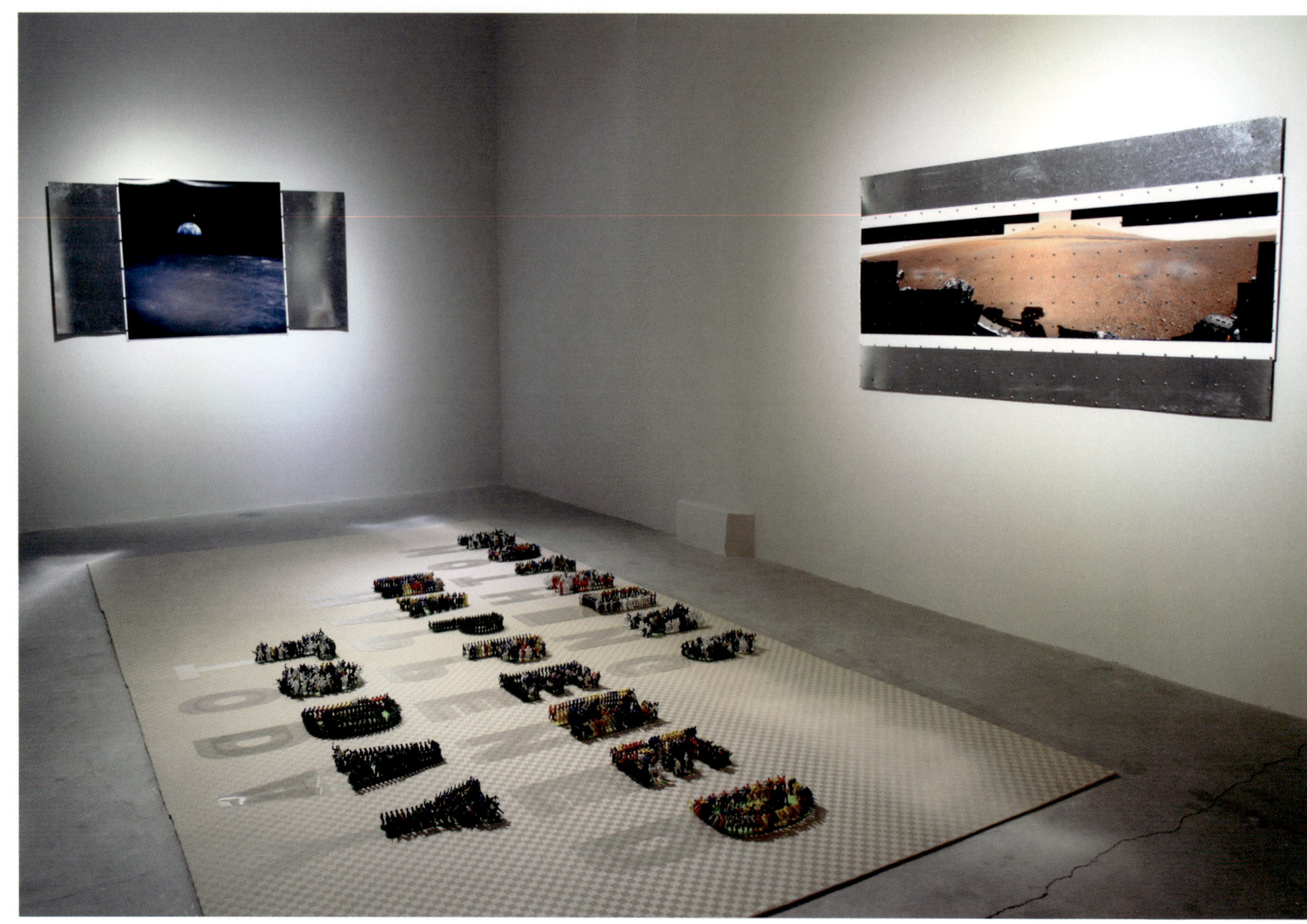

We are so accustomed to the pervasive presence of the Internet that we rarely consider its revolutionary significance, let alone exclaim in wonder about it, but as soon as we start thinking about this question we can still feel its magic. The Internet has flattened the sense of time on earth—not only horizontally, but also vertically—through the Internet we can not only reminisce about 10,000 years ago, but also share the first picture the Curiosity (robotic rover) snapped when it landed on Mars. The segmentation of time is not as abrupt. In *Nothing Happened Today #1*, I printed out a photo the Apollo (lunar roving vehicle) took of the earth after it landed on the moon in 1969. Although I didn't experience that moment myself, and didn't share the excitement of mankind at the time, I just started thinking about this piece when Curiosity landed on Mars. Interestingly, just a few days ago I saw on the news that Snowden, after receiving asylum "freedom" in Russia, revealed the confidential documents regarding how the U.S. faked the Apollo's moon landing. That time period in 1969 got transported to the present, and overlaps with the here and now. It won't take too long before we forget about all this, and again immerse ourselves in the imagination of the future.

- Li Ming

Li Ming, *Nothing Happened Today #1*, 2012, plastic toys, acrylic, PVC wallpaper, photographs and magnet, variable dimensions, acquired in 2012

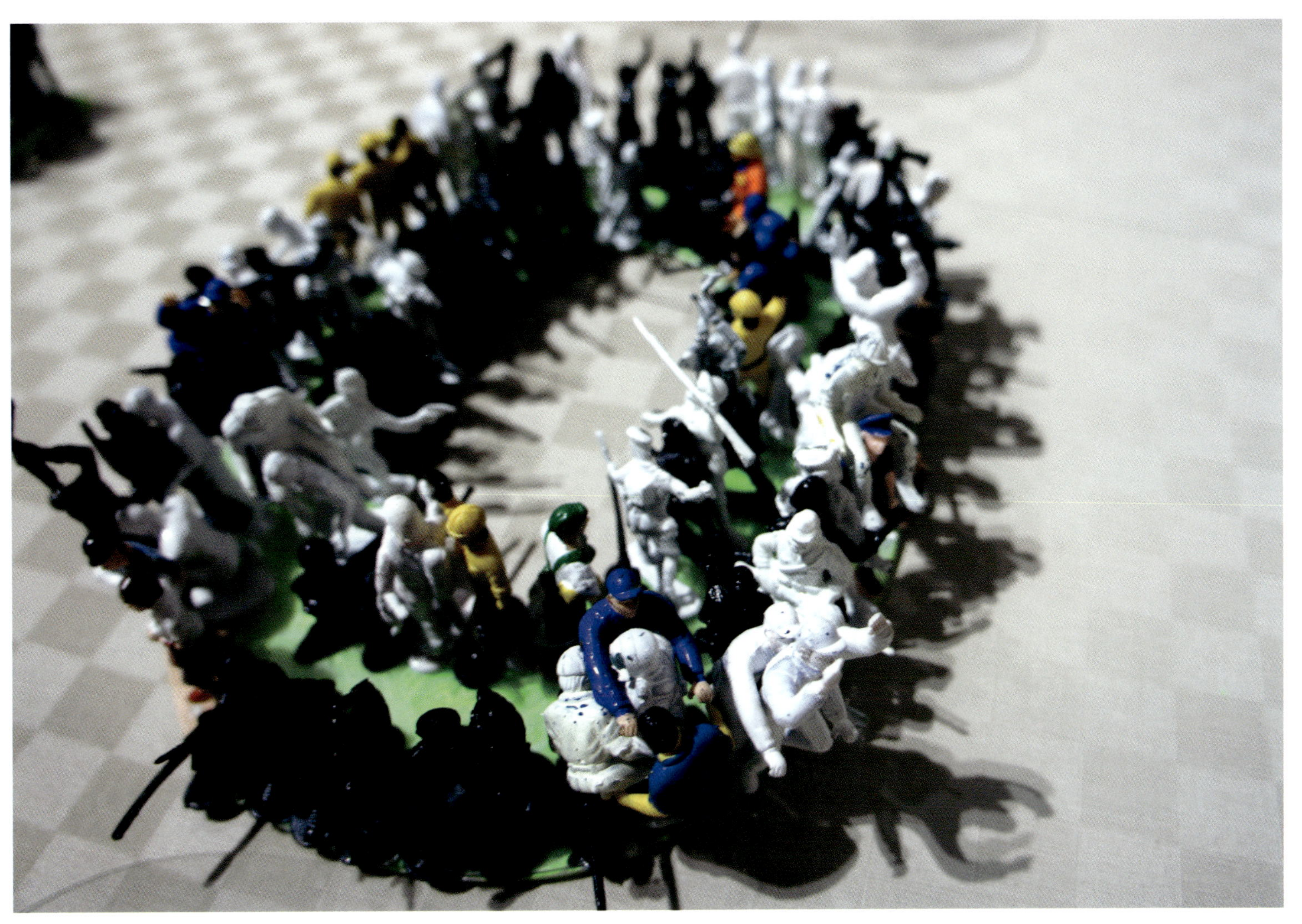

互联网在我们日常生活中的无处不在已经让我们
对它习以为常，很少再去认真考虑它的革命性意
义，更不用说感到惊叹，不过一旦开始思考这个
问题，我们仍然能够感受到它的神奇。互联网
把地球的时间拉平了，这不仅是横向的，也是纵
深的，通过网络，我们可以一起回忆一万年前的
时间，也可以共享好奇号登上火星时的第一张照
片，时间的断层感并不是那么突兀了。我在《今
天无事发生，1号》中，打印了一张1969年阿波
罗登陆月球时拍摄的地球的照片，我没经历过那
个时间，没有共享过当时人类的兴奋，正是在好
奇号登陆火星的时候我开始构想这件作品，有意
思的是，就在此前几天，我看到了新闻：斯洛登
在俄罗斯获得避难"自由"后揭露了美国1969年
登月造假的机密文件。那个1969年的时间又被抓

回到了现在，和此时此刻重叠了。也用不了太久
的时间，这一切又会烟消云散，我们还是会一起
沉浸在对未来的想象中去。

- 李明

李明，《今天无事发生 1号》，2012，塑料玩具，丙烯，PVC 墙纸，照片打印（照片来自网络），磁铁，尺寸可变，收藏于2012

Li Ran

李然

Born in 1986, Hubei, China
Lives and works in Beijing, China

一九八二年生於中国湖北
居住和工作於中国北京

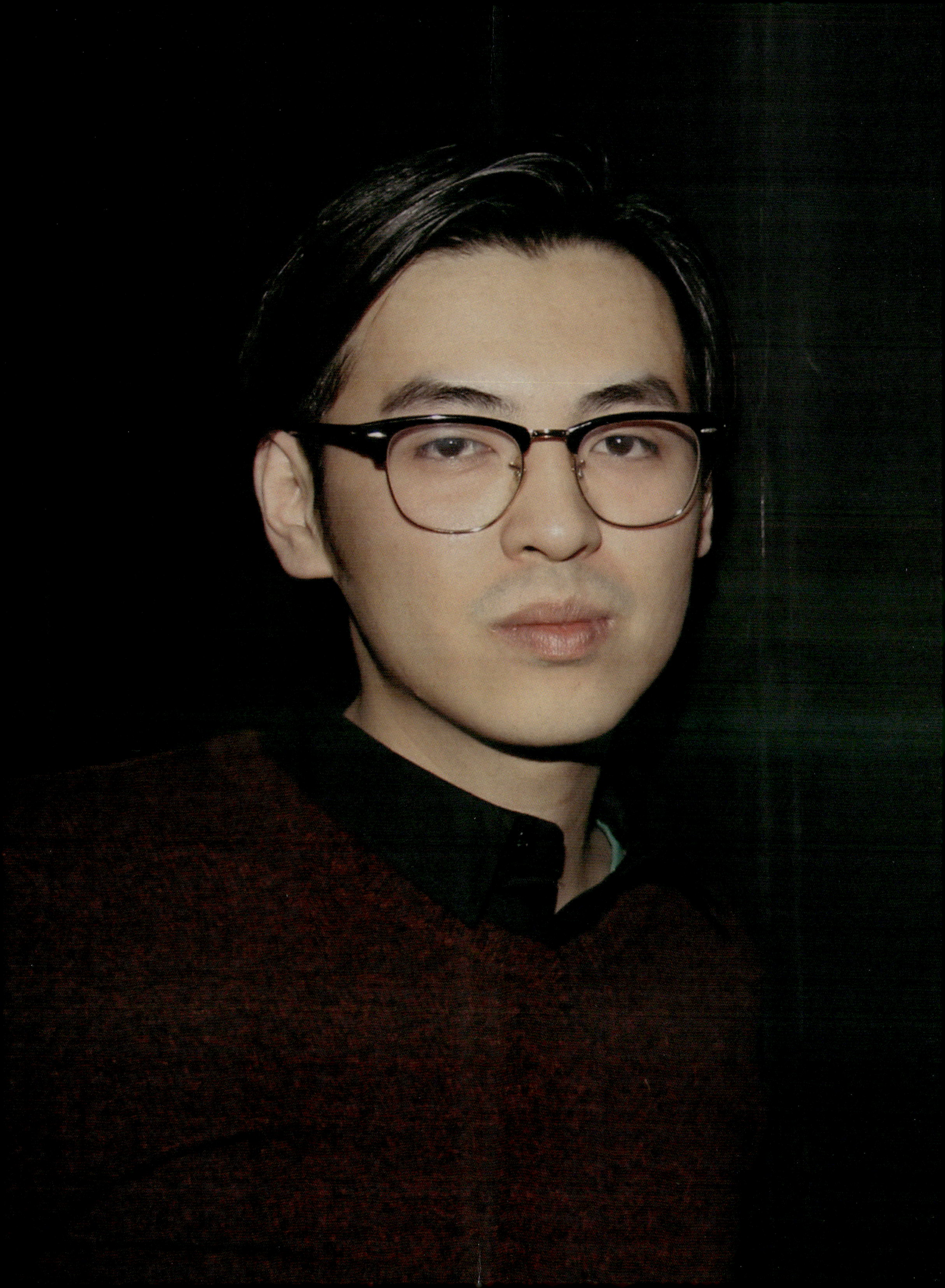

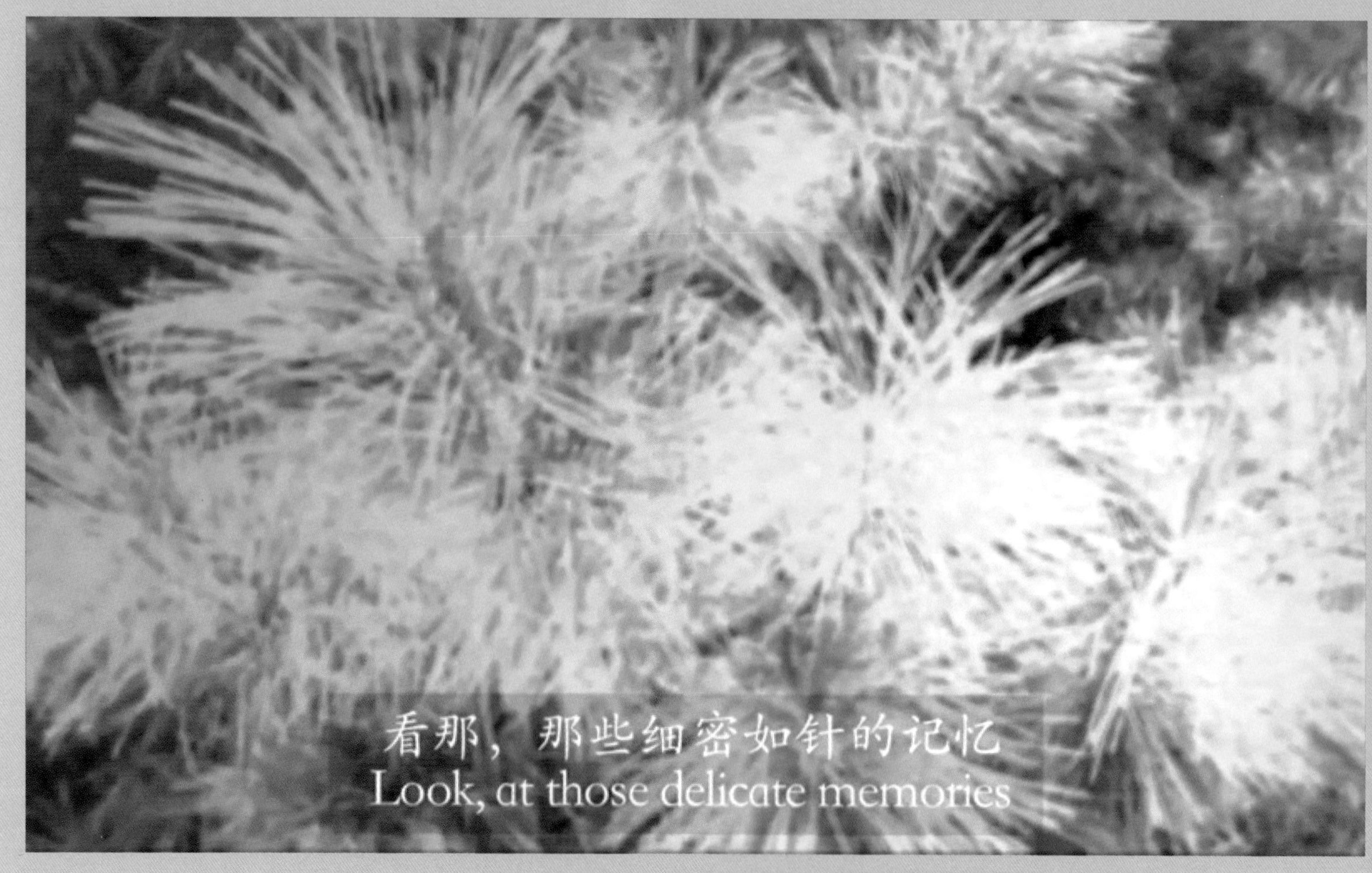

From Truck Driver to the Political Commissar of the Mounted Troops was adapted from the Soviet film *Destiny of a Man*. I once again play the role of a Soviet soldier, imitating an affected and artificial actor who is under the influence of the Communist ideology, and I use this hyperbolic style of acting to recount a person's political fate, emotions and homesickness. I also use this method to discuss the experience of an individual, and to restate in a humorous way questions about "standpoint" and "identity politics" in the industry.

- Li Ran

《从卡车司机到骑兵政委》取材与前苏联的电影《一个人的遭遇》，我再次扮演了一位前苏联的士兵形象，模仿共产主义意识形态下一个矫情做作的演员，并用这种夸张的表演方式讲述了一个人的政治遭遇，情感与乡愁。同时也是用这种方式谈及一种个体性的遭遇，再次将行业中"立场"与"身份政治"问题进行了一种调侃的表达。

- 李然

Li Ran, *From Truck Driver to the Political Commissar of the Mounted Troops*, 2012, single-channel video (black-and-white, sound), Ed. 2/ 5, duration: 8 min. 51 sec., acquired in 2012
李然，《从卡车司机到骑兵政委》，2012，黑白单视频，音频，版本 2/5，8 分钟 51 秒，收藏于2012

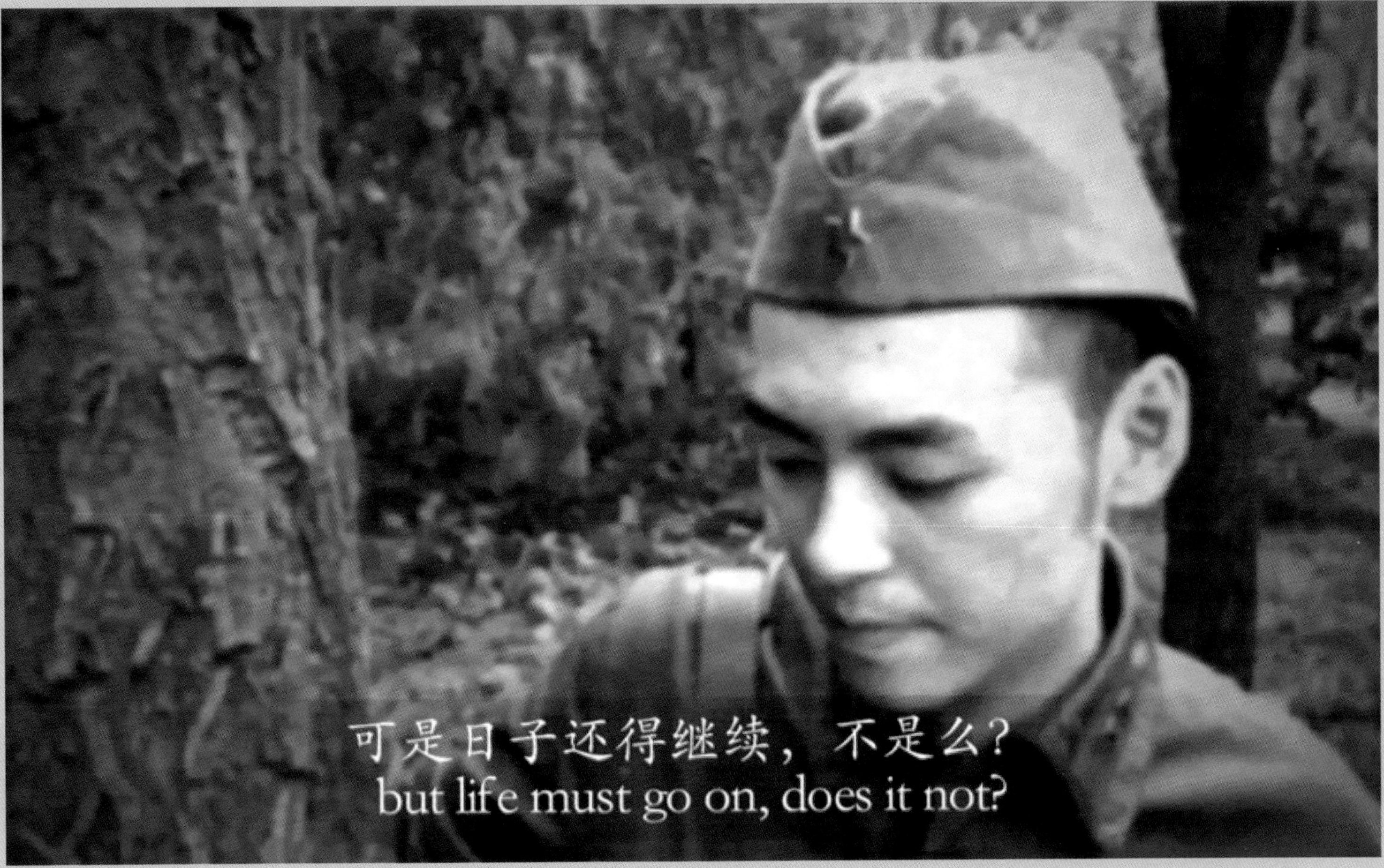

可是日子还得继续，不是么？
but life must go on, does it not?

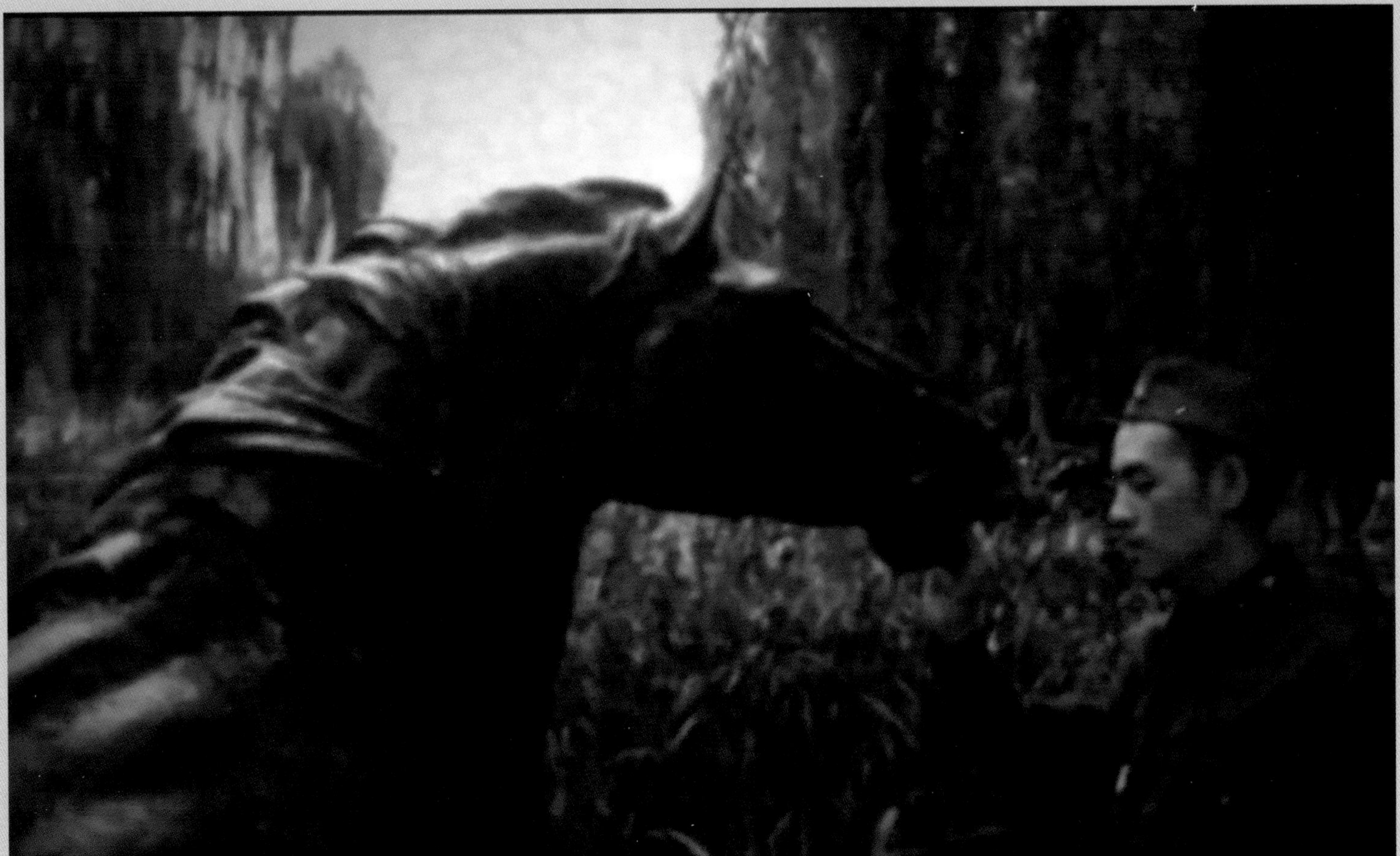

Li Shurui

Born in 1981, Chongqing, China
Lives and works in Beijing, China

李姝睿

一九八一年生於中國重庆
居住和工作於中國北京

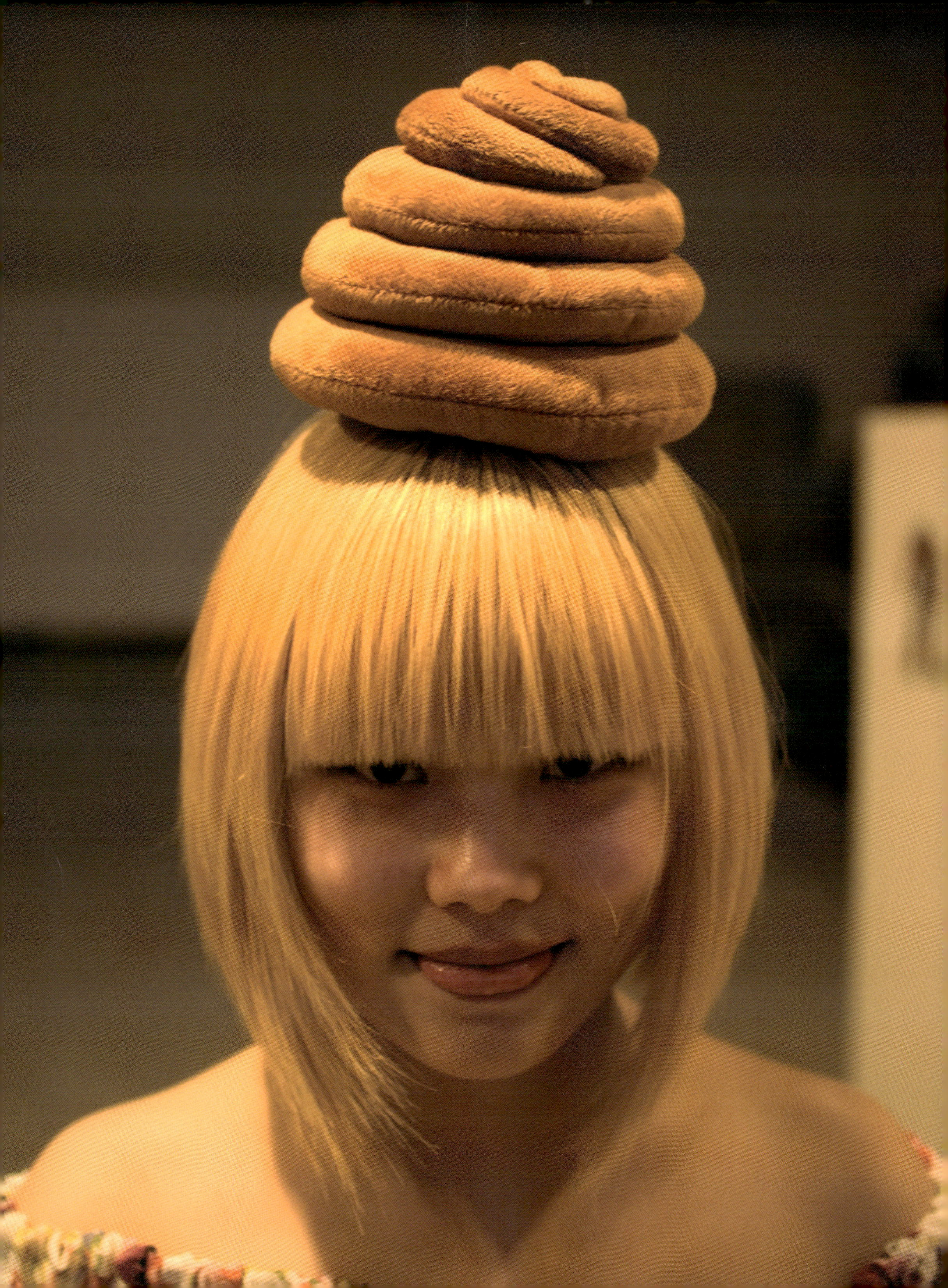

What caught your attention here?
This text is for you to feel closer to the paintings after you read it.
Besides the images of these works, have you seen the original paintings yet, hanging up on the clean walls of the museum?
They originate from my studio in Blackbridge (Heiqiao), Beijing, China.
There are concrete villages (not the kind in the midst of farmland and open spaces) on the outskirts of the city. Most of its inhabitants are manual laborers perpetually toiling at constructing, deconstructing, reconstructing, repairing and maintaining behemoth Beijing, along with a few young artists.
When I saw LA in the movie *Elysium*, I felt close to it.
I've never lived there [Blackbridge], I just drive past some of its few landfills to my studio every day. I've never drank the water either.
The water comes from wells dug out by the villagers themselves, thick with silt. After the silt precipitates I use the water to mix color and wash brushes.
The paintings you are looking at right now, are made from that water.
Anyhow, please enjoy!

- Li Shurui

是什么把你的目光带到这里？
这段文字，是为了让你看完之后，觉得跟旁边的图片距离更近一点。
除了这些作品的图片，你看到了原作吗，在美术馆的空间里，
干净的墙面上。
他们来自我的工作室，黑桥，北京，中国。
那里是都市边缘的村庄，没有农田。大多数居民是为这个巨型城市服务的体力工作者，另外还有一些年轻艺术家。
当我看到电影Elysium里的LA时，觉得很亲切。
我从没在那住过，只是每天开车经过几个垃圾站去工作室，我也从未喝过那的水。
那的水是从村民自己打的井里出来的，混着泥沙，沉淀一下，用来调颜料和洗笔。
你们看到的作品，就是这样的水画出来的。
好吧，请欣赏！

- 李姝睿

Li Shurui, *Untitled*, 2013, acrylic on canvas, 98 x 98 in. (250 x 250 cm), acquired in 2013
李姝睿，《无题》，2013, 布面丙烯, 98 x 98 寸 (250 x 250 厘米), 收藏于2013

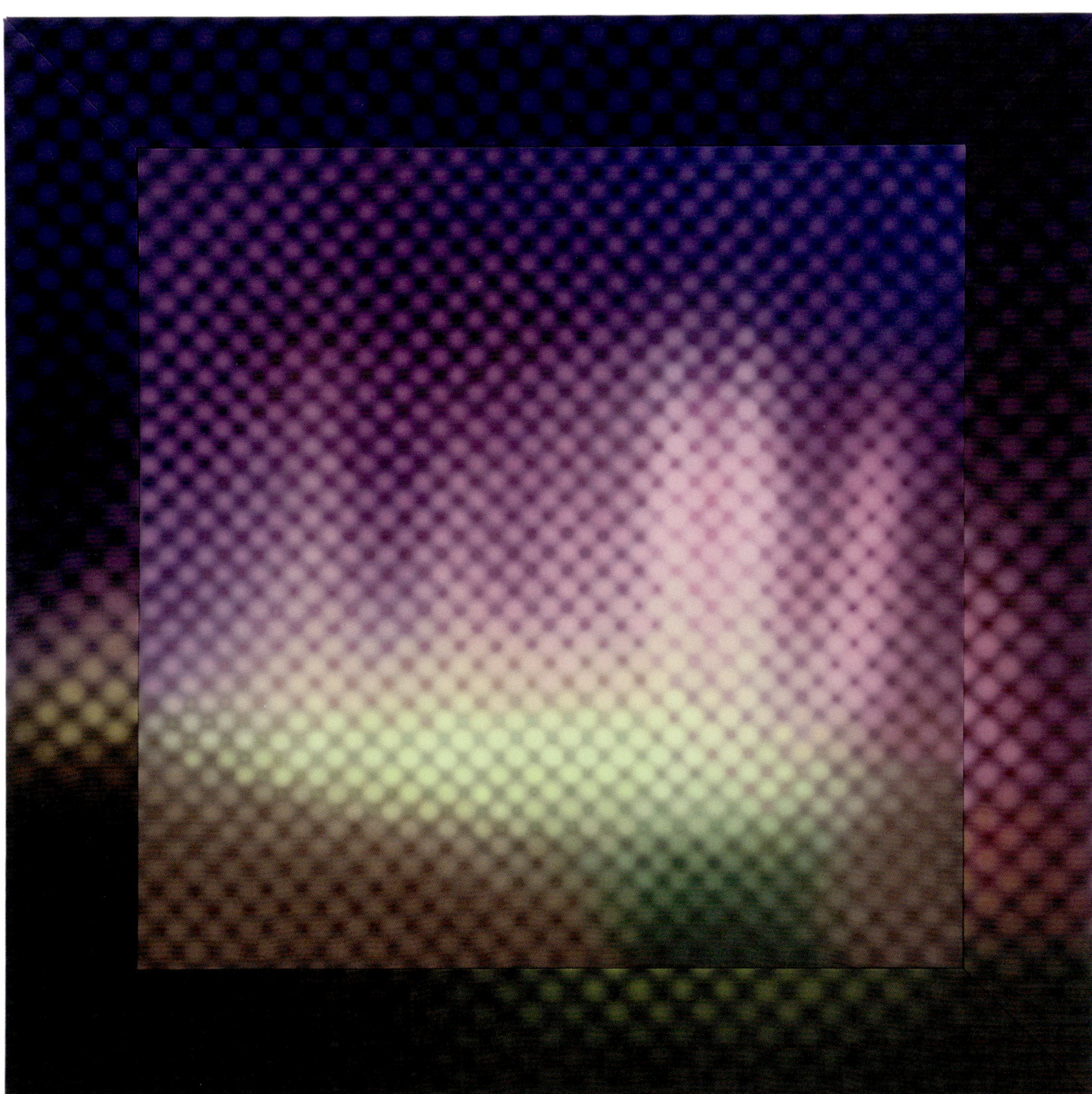

Li Shurui, *Untitled*, 2012, acrylic on canvas, 78 3/4 x 59 in. (200 x 150 cm), acquired in 2013
李姝睿，《无题》，2012, 布面丙烯, 78 3/4 x 59 寸 (200 x 150 厘米), 收藏于2013

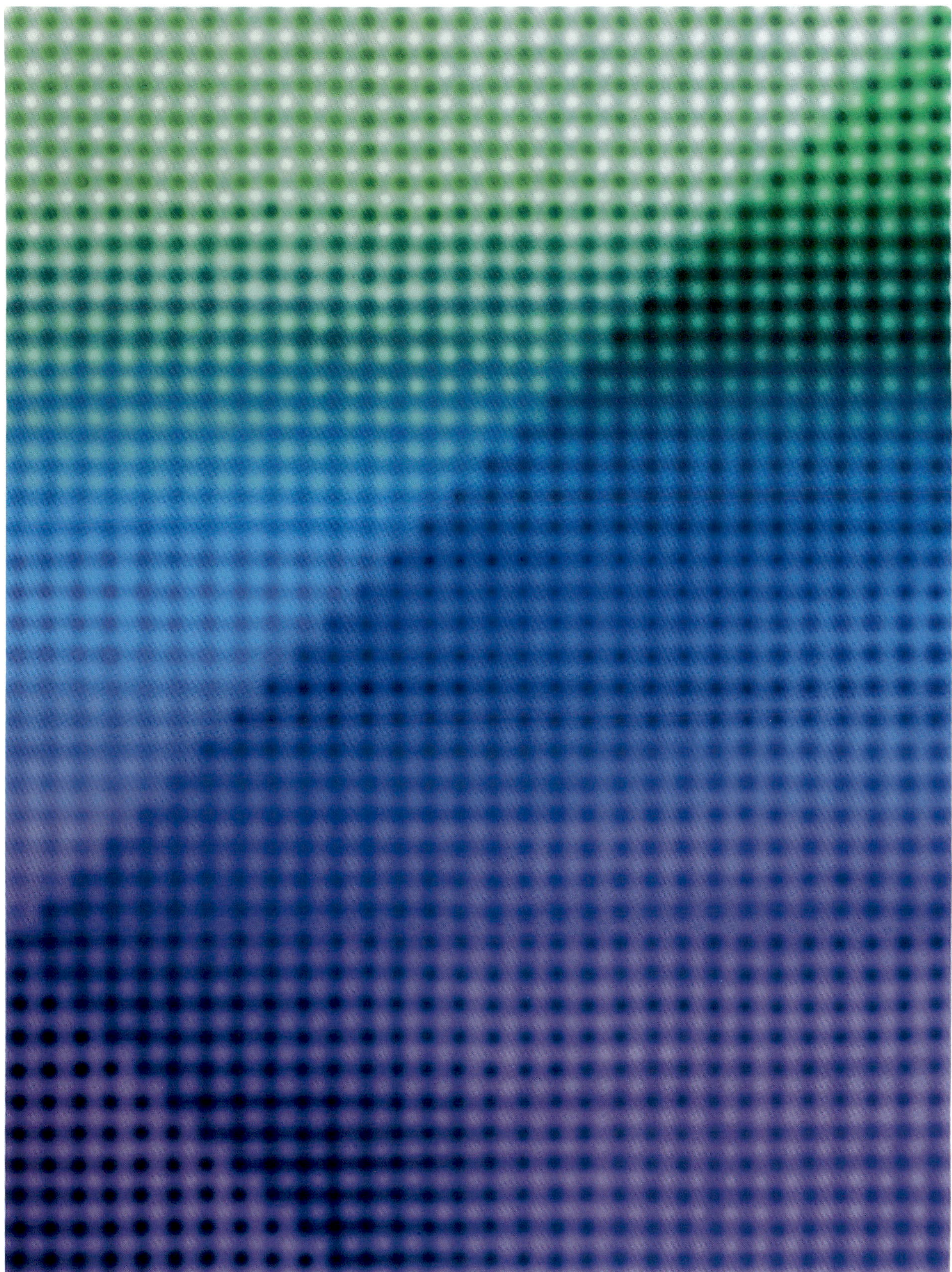

Li Shurui, *Inner Rainbow*, 2011, acrylic on canvas, 70 7/8 x 94 1/2 in. (180 x 240 cm), acquired in 2013
李姝睿，《室内彩虹》，2011，布面丙烯，70 7/8 x 94 1/2 寸 (180 x 240 厘米)，收藏于2013

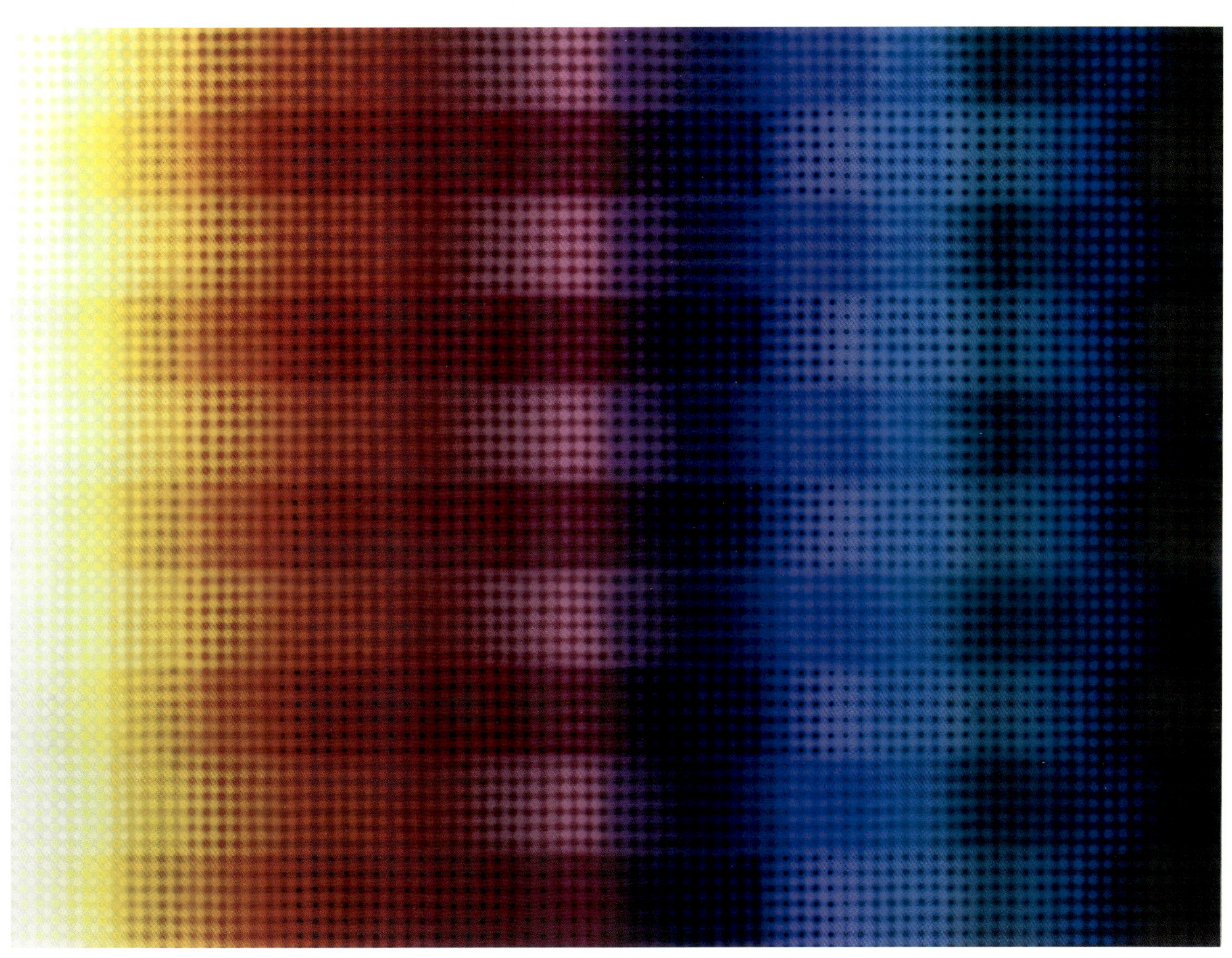

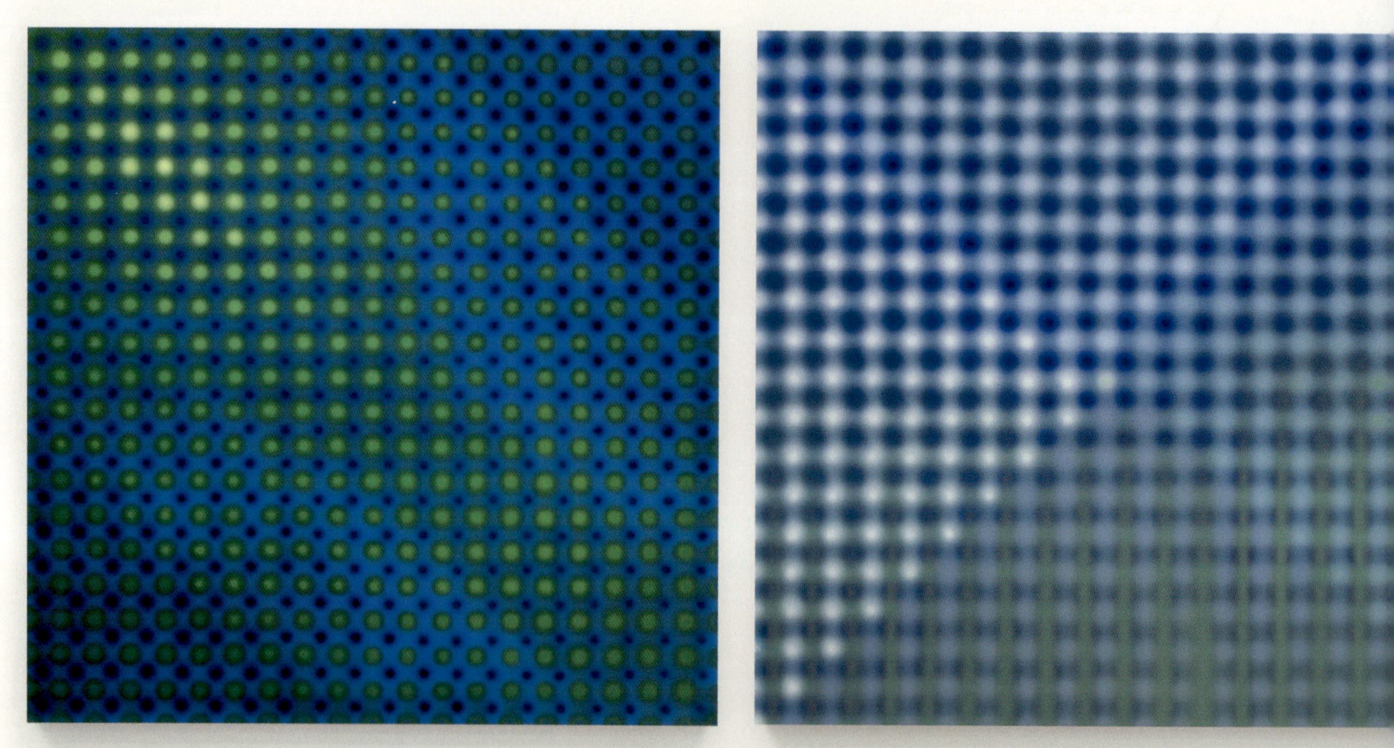

Li Shurui, *Sky Light 13,14,15,16*, 2012, acrylic on canvas, quadriptych, each: 35 1/2 x 35 1/2 in. (90 x 90cm), acquired in 2013
李姝睿，《天光 13, 14, 15, 16 》, 2012, 布面丙烯, 四连画, 每幅: 35 1/2 x 35 1/2 寸 (90 x 90 厘米), 收藏于2013

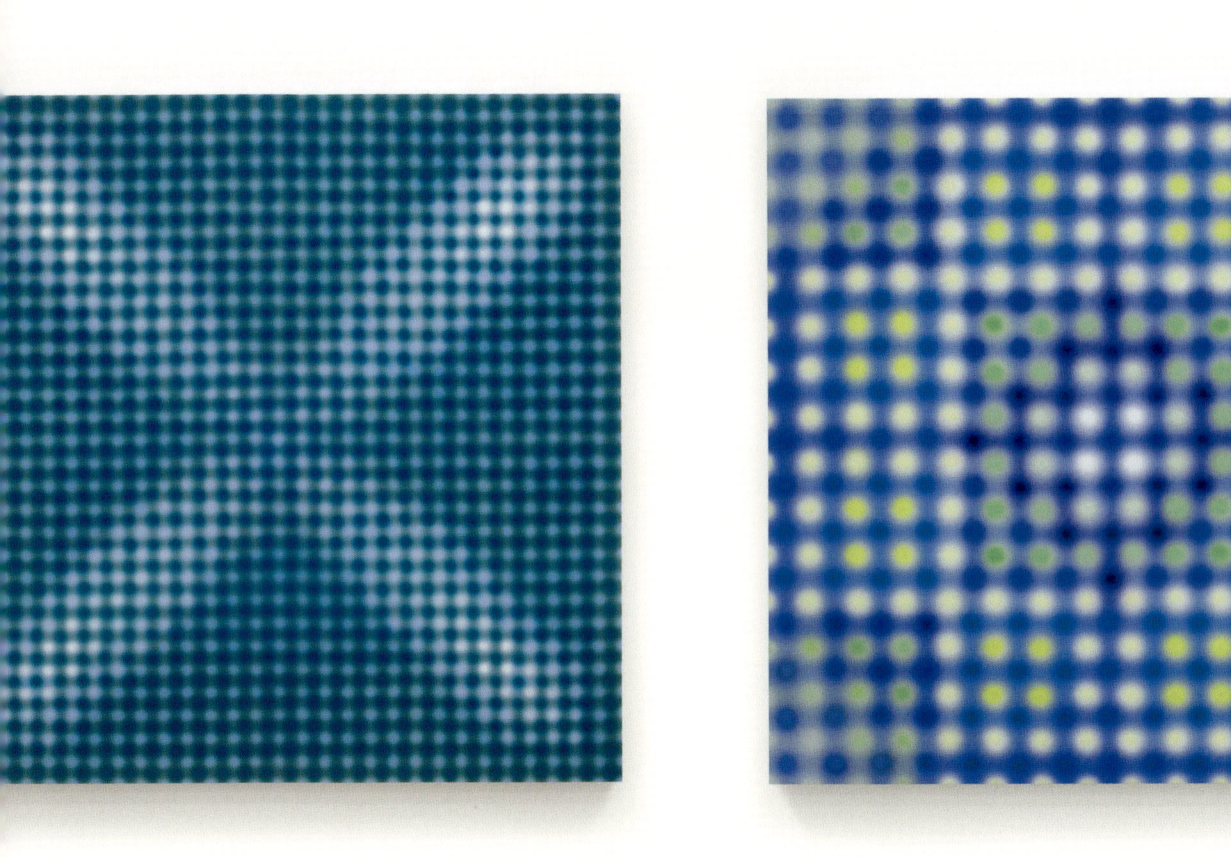

Li Songsong 李松松

Born in 1973, Beijing, China
Lives and works in Beijing, China

一九七三年生於中国北京
居住和工作於中国北京

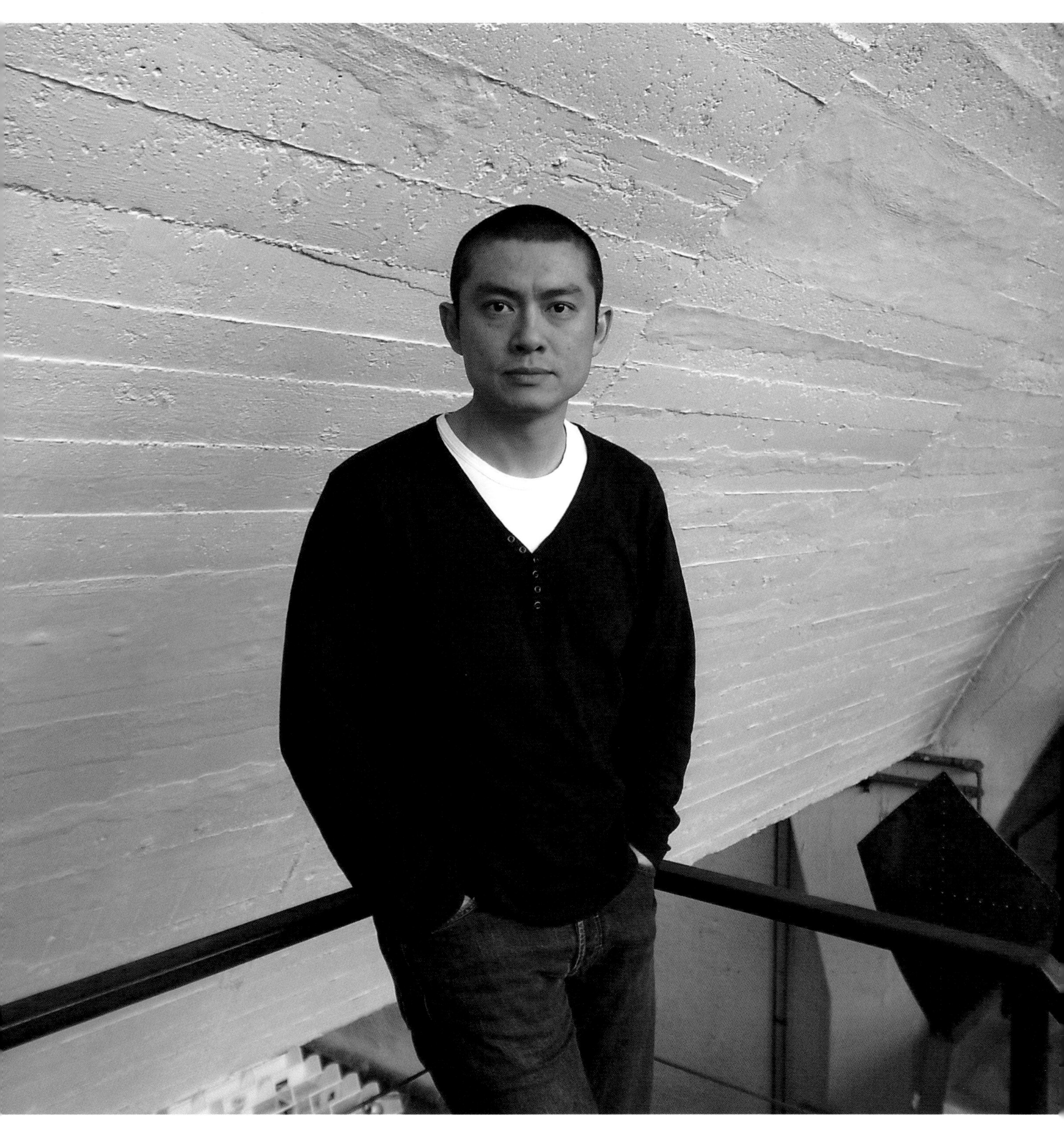

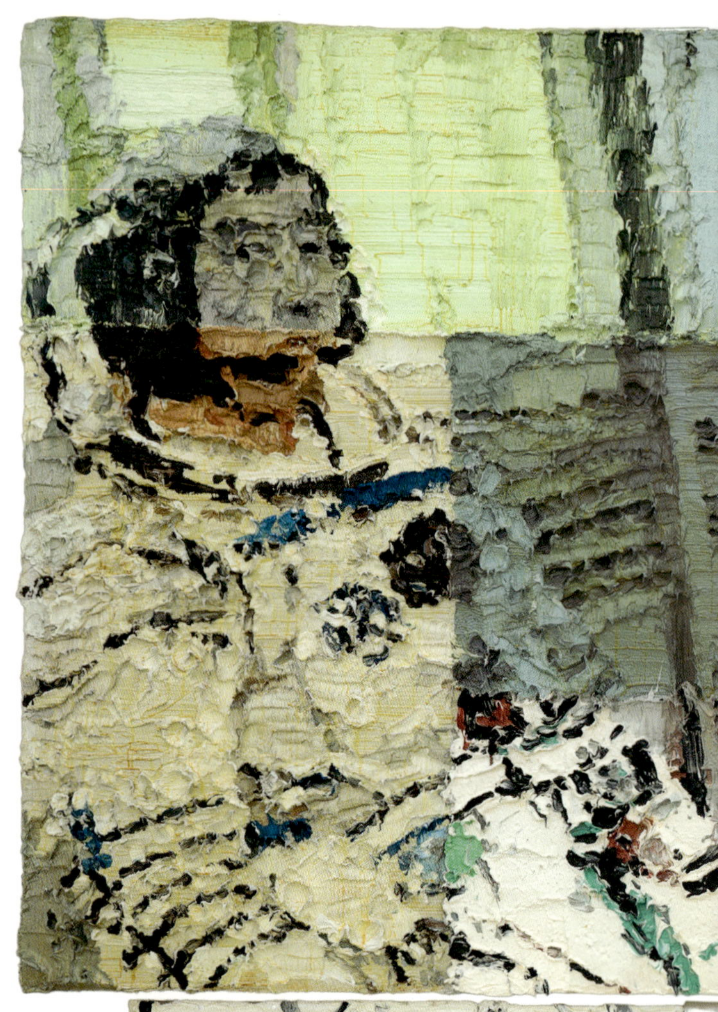

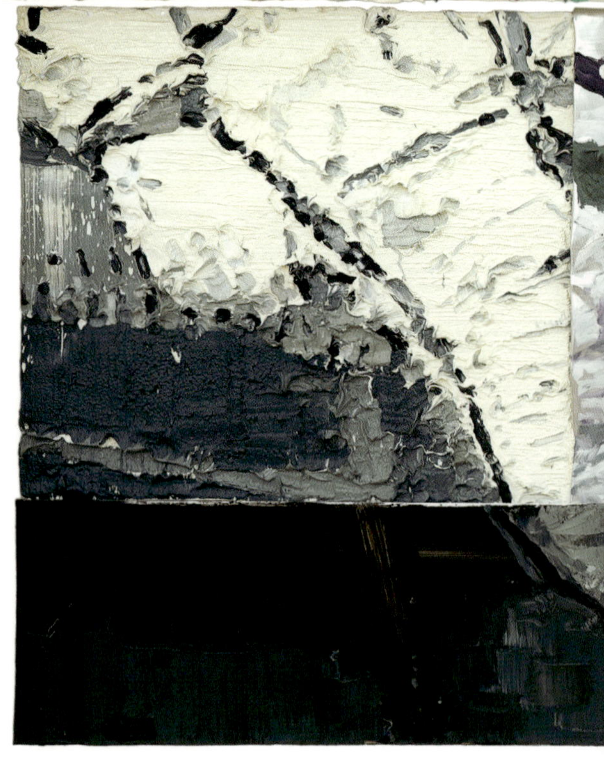

New Clothes originates from a news photo from that year about a Chinese astronaut. This is really just another average news photo—the astronaut and the cameraman—a dull moment really, but it gives off a feeling of frozen eternity. I think this is the feeling this painting is trying to provoke and occupy.

- Li Songsong

《新衣服》来源于当年的新闻图片，有关中国的太空人。这实在是一张乏善可陈的新闻图片，太空人和摄像师，一个无聊的瞬间，却散发一股近乎凝固的恒久感，我想这正是此画要占有的感受。

- 李松松

Li Songsong, *New Clothes*, 2008, oil on canvas and aluminum, two panels, overall: 126 x 149 1/2 in. (320 x 380 cm), acquired in 2008
李松松，《新衣服》，2008，布面油画和铝塑板，两联板，整体: 126 x 149 1/2 寸 (320 x 380 厘米)，收藏于 2008

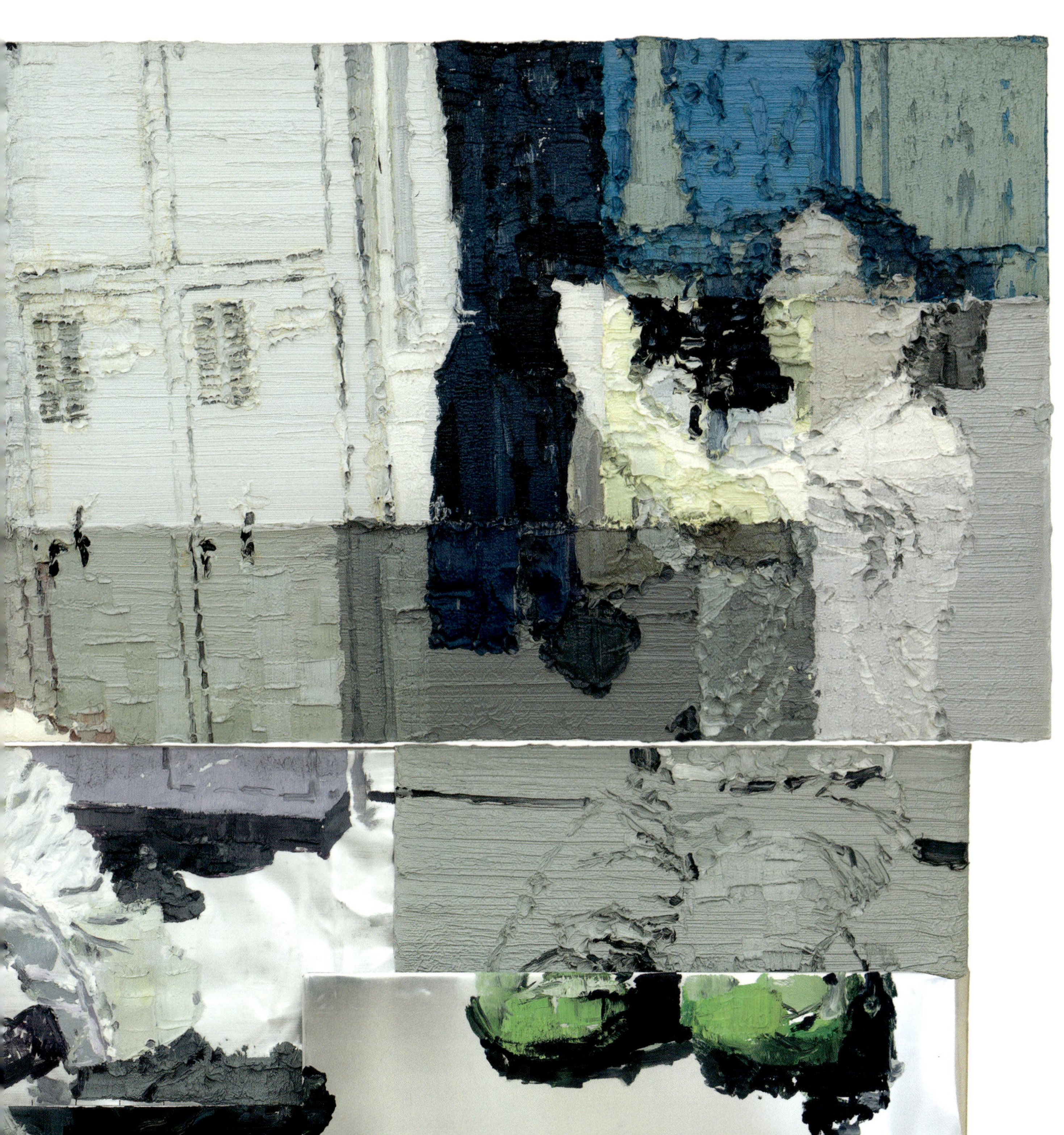

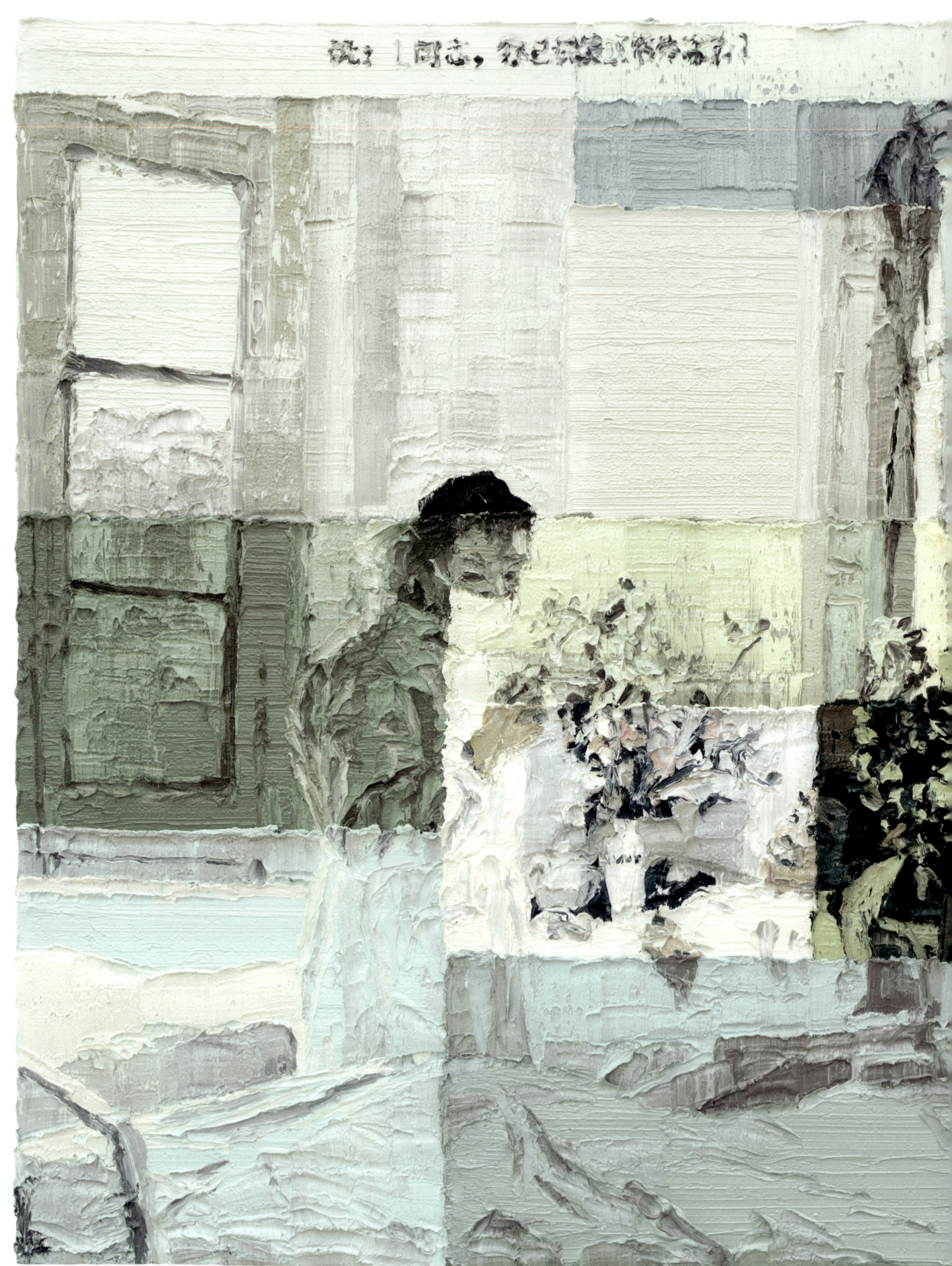
说：上同志，你已经成为工作的特务了！

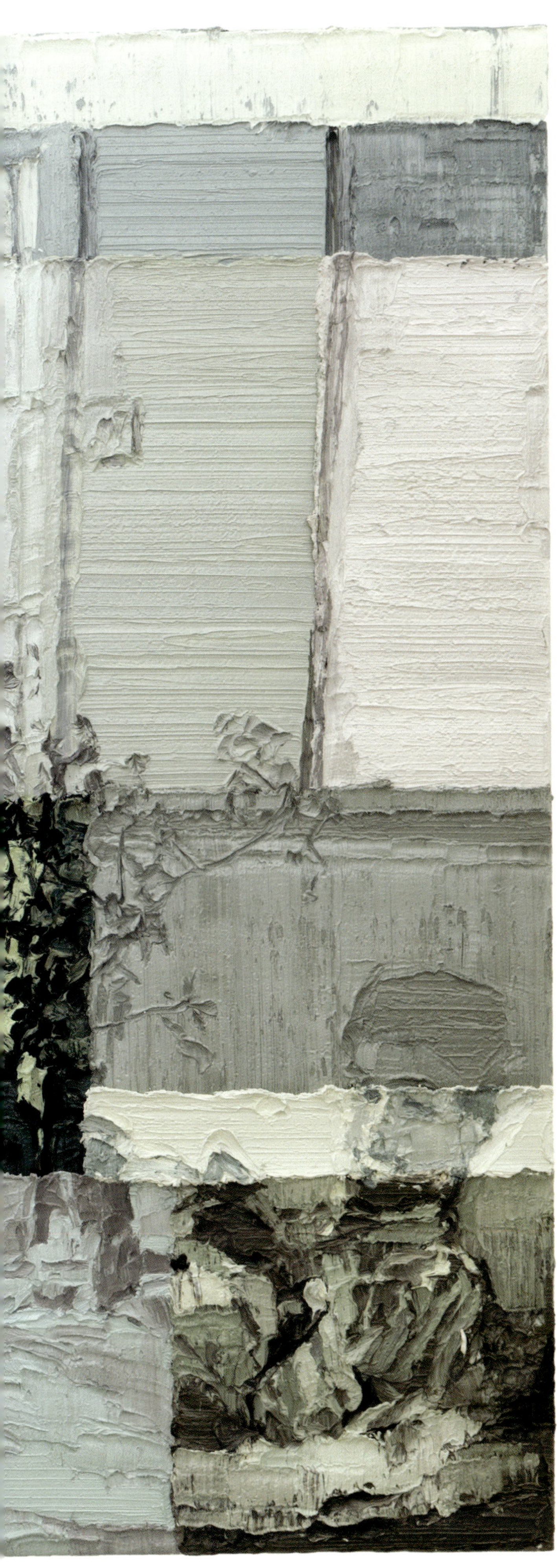

Comrade, Your Temperature is Back to Normal is drawn from a picture in a book from the 1960s, which was about how high the level of the medical care system for the Chinese working class was at that time. Like all advertising pictures, these goal-oriented publicity pictures were produced from perfect designs and sets, and it is just this unrealistically alluring scene that attracts me. If I remember correctly, there's a mercury themometer buried underneath the paint on the canvas where the nurse's hand is located.

- Li Songsong

《同志，你已经恢复正常体温了》取材于一幅的上世纪六十年代书中的图片，有关中国工人阶级的医疗保障达到了相当高的水平。和所有的广告图片相同，这些目的清晰的宣传图片来自完美的设计和摆拍，正是这种现实中并不存在的美好场面吸引了我。如果我没有记错，画中护士小姐手部分位置的颜色中埋着一只水银体温计。

- 李松松

Li Songsong, *Comrade your temperature is back to normal*, 2005, acrylic on canvas, 78 3/4 x 94 1/2 in. (200 x 240 cm), acquired in 2005
李松松，《同志，你已经恢复正常体温了》，2005，布面油画，78 3/4 x 94 1/2 寸（200 x 240 厘米），收藏于 2005

Li Zhanyang 李占洋

Born in 1969, Jilin, China
Lives and works in Beijing and Chongqing, China

一九六九年生於中国吉林
居住和工作於中国北京和重庆

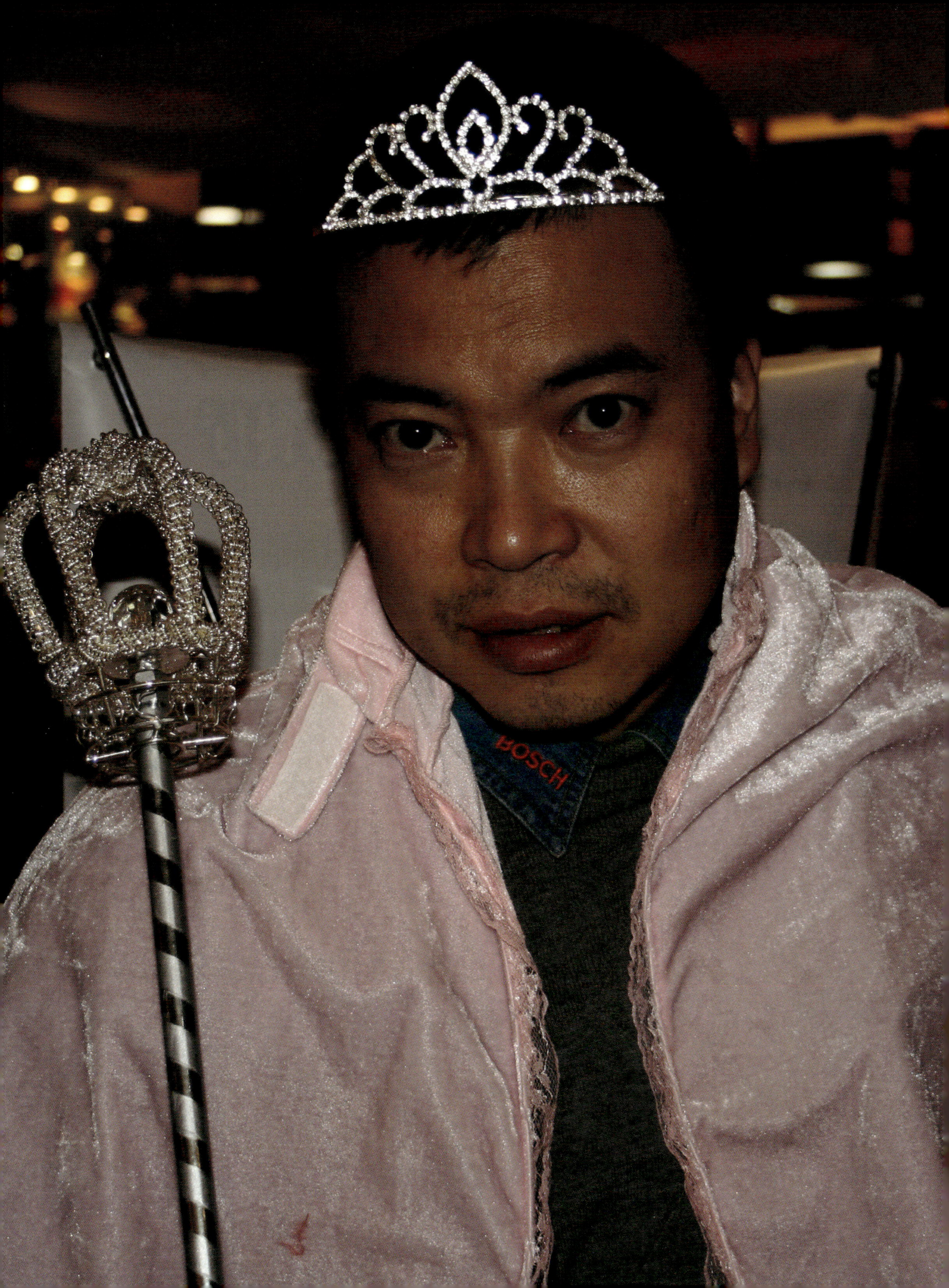

Mao and Joseph Beuys is a relatively independent part of my large sculptural installation *Rent-Rent Collection Yard* which I created from the end of 2006 to April of 2008. The basic concept of this piece is to apply the representation of class conflict in 1960's China as seen in the 1964 Socialist Realist sculpture *Dayi County Rent Collection Yard*—and use this typical installation as a shell, weaving influential artists, critics or curators of contemporary art into this shell, which means using the mode of transference to express what happens today via the form of an old work.

These, one old and one new, look as if there are some relevant imitations of actions, construction of the composition and the scene, but in fact they are completely disparate. What did I rent from *Rent Collection Yard*? What did I make from it? This is an interesting topic; you will know when you see it.

This is a group of very complex sculptures and when the piece became large enough I suddenly realized it was still circling in this system of class conflicts. If I treat this installation as one part, add another part, and make their meaning both separate and integral, that will lead the piece toward another direction, rendering it not simply as an adaption of the old version, but rather it becomes an installation that is more complex, or more specifically complex and complete. So, what is that part?

I decided to add Mao Zedong and Joseph Beuys into the piece. Making it another part of this monumental group of works, but isolating it as one part. Mao Zedong, this legendary figure in the East, has produced countless myths. He himself is a postmodern, mighty rendition, which has become an inexhaustible source of creative inspirations for Andy Warhol and artists today. He has a kind of secret explosive and destructive power—in the East, he is regarded as great as Che Guevara, with many wars, class conflicts and bloody violence behind him. This violence, using the blood of countless people, stained his ideals, transforming him into a sun that never sets in the Eastern sky. The Mao Zedong in my piece gazes forward unperturbed, like how he used to watch many of the class conflicts he planned with his own hands over numerous time periods. What is different is

毛和博伊斯是我的大型装置作品"租——收租院"的一个部分，一个比较独立的部分。2006年底到2008年4月，我创作了大型雕塑装置作品："租——收租院"。这件作品最基本的方法是运用中国20世纪60年代表现阶级斗争的——大邑县收租院——这一典型的装置作品为外壳，把今天在当代艺术中有影响力的艺术家批评家或策展人编入这个外壳之中，也就是运用挪用的手法，用旧作品的形式，表达今天所发生的事。

这一旧一新看似动作，构图，场景都模仿关联，实际上已经面目全非。我从"收租院"里租来什么？又做成什么？这是一个有意思的话题，大家一看便知。

这是一组相当繁杂的雕塑作品，当作品做到足够规模时，我突然发现它依然在阶级斗争这个系统里打转转，如果把这个装置作为一个部分，再加另外一个部分，使它们的意义既分开又统一，那会把作品引向另一个方向，使作品不仅仅是一个老版本的改编，而是使这个装置作品更加复杂化，或更加具体地复杂化，从而达到完整。那么，那个部分是什么呢？

我决定把毛泽东和博伊斯放进作品中。让它成为这组庞大作品中的另外一部分，但它是独立出来的一部分。毛泽东这个东方的传奇人物，制造了无数神话，他本身就是个后现代的巨大载体，他成为从安迪·沃霍到今天的艺术家取之不尽的创作源泉。他总有种神秘的爆发力和破坏力，在东方，他如格瓦拉一样伟大，他背后到处充满战争、阶级斗争，和血腥的暴力，这暴力使他的理想用无数人的血染成一轮东方不落的太阳。我作品里的毛泽东，如往昔观望他亲手策划的众多时间段中的任何一场阶级斗争一样，泰然自若，凝望着前方。不同的是，他的神情既淡定又充满疑惑。我觉得有这一角色的介入是很有必要的，充满戏剧感。我在设想，他对我设计的这幕现代版的收租院是否感到迷茫，他似乎在疑问，这是否还是收租院？这时博伊斯站出来在给毛解释这件作品，说这件作品充满了浪漫的情调，说其实在中国从来没有改变过剥削制度，从来没有改变过阶级斗争。在这两位东西方哲学艺术的大师碰撞中，你会觉得这件作品其实真的太离谱了。我们似乎还可以给予它别的解释，或任何解释。博伊斯是后现代大师，无论他的《对兔子说话》，还是他的《种植7000棵橡树》，还是他的《与狼共舞》，都使他的观念艺术深植我的内心。我认为他是西方世界中最有力量的观念艺术家，他的艺

that his expression is at once calm and filled with confusion and doubt. I think the introduction of this character is very necessary; it's really dramatic. I am postulating: Is he baffled about the modern *Rent Collection Yard* I designed? It's as if he's questioning, is this still a *Rent Collection Yard.* This is when Beuys comes out to explain to Mao about this piece, saying that this piece is full of romantic sentiments, saying that in fact China never brought about any changes in the system of exploitation and class conflicts.From the clash between these two philosophical and artistic masters you will feel that this piece is actually quite outrageous. Perhaps we can give it another explanation, or any explanation. Beuys is a master of postmodernism, whether it is his *How to Explain Pictures to a Dead Hare, 7000 Oaks Project,* or his coyote performance, they all planted his conceptual art deep in my heart. I think he is the most powerful conceptual artist in the Western world; his art is philosophical. Mao Zedong, in a sense is also a big philosophical artist, his Cultural Revolution should be regarded as the largest piece of performance art in the world. The class conflict-based Cultural Revolution he started left everlasting pain for the Chinese people. After the Cultural Revolution started, there appeared on the Chinese soil a great artwork that represents class conflicts—*Dayi County Rent Collection Yard. Dayi County Rent Collection Yard* is in a way the manifestation of the Maoist ideology in China.

I used the methods of "changing the broth but not the medicine" and "stealing the beams to replace the pillars" and changed the old characters with the characters of today. I am postulating that Mao feels lost, and Beuys is explaining this piece to him.

I used a lot of effort to make a boring thing while carefully fabricating a non-existent story. Mao and Beuys have been frozen in that moment, and the thing in my heart—the clash between contemporary cultures—started in the conversation between these two philosophers.

- Li Zhanyang

术具有哲学化。毛泽东，在某种意义上也是哲学化的大艺术家，他的"文化大革命"应该是世界上最大的行为艺术。他发动的阶级斗争"文化大革命"给中国人民留下了永远的伤痛，"文化大革命"开始，中国大地上就产生了表现阶级斗争的伟大艺术作品——大邑县收租院。大邑县收租院在某种意义上是毛思想在中国的具体体现。

我用了"换汤不换药"、"偷梁换柱"的方法，把过去的人物换成今天的人物，我在设想毛泽东在迷惑中，博伊斯在为毛讲解我的这个装置作品。这种混杂的时空，以时间重叠的方式呈现在这件装置作品中，呈现出明显的后现代的思维方法。

我很认真、很费力地做了一件无聊的事情，也很认真地编导了一个并不存在的故事。毛和博伊斯被凝固在那一刻，我心中的东西当代文化的碰撞就从这两位哲人的对话开始了。

- 李占洋

Li Zhanyang, *Rent-Rent Collection Yard-History Observed- Joseph Beuys & Mao Zedong*, 2007, fiberglass, resin and paint, 75 x 64 x 81 in. (190.5 x 162.5 x 206 cm), acquired in 2008

李占洋，《租——收租院 毛和博伊斯》，2007，玻璃纤维，树脂，涂料，75 x 64 x 81 寸 (190.5 x 162.5 x 206 厘米)，收藏于 2008

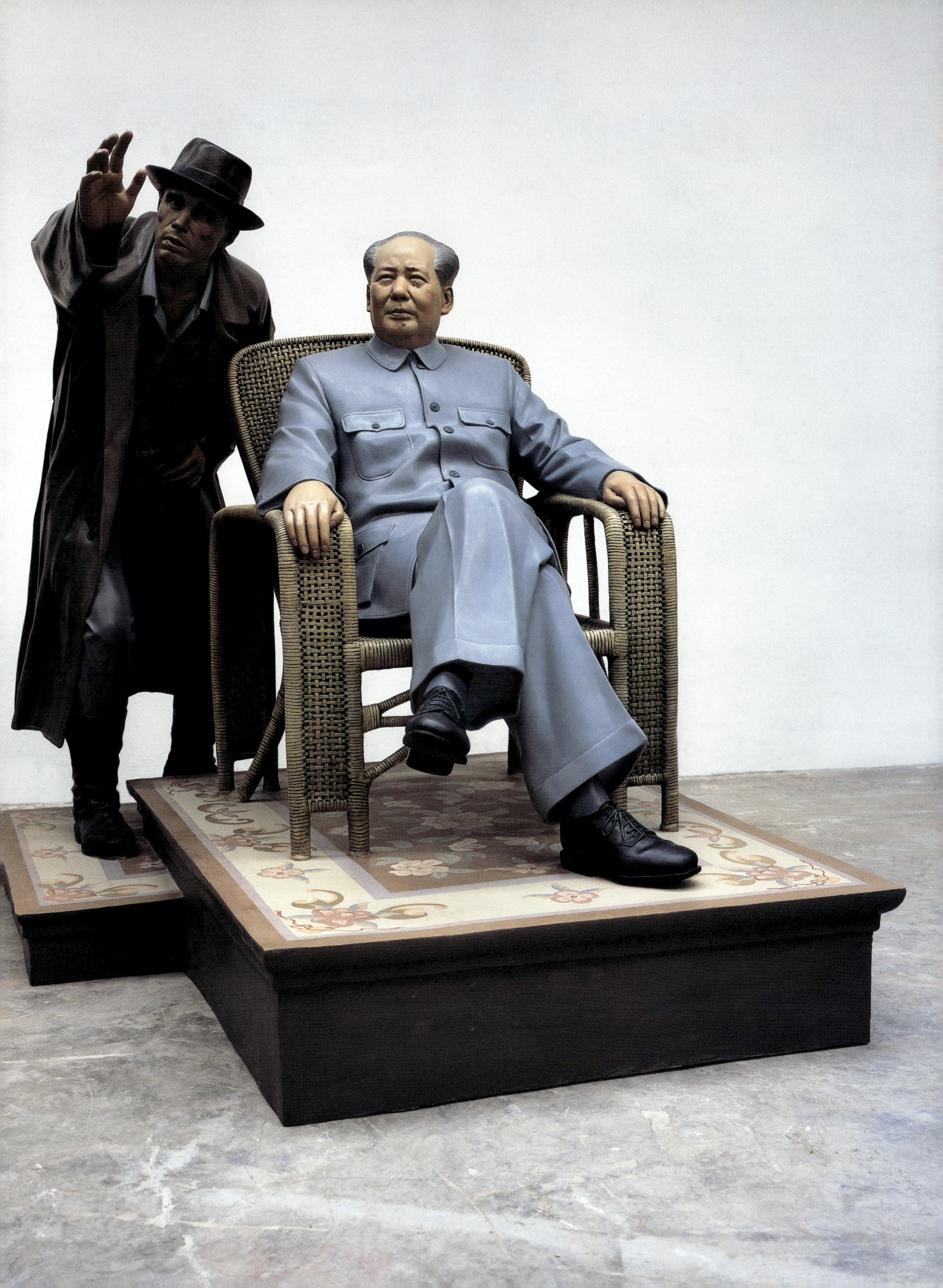

Liu Chuang 刘窗

Born in 1978, Hubei, China
Lives and works in Beijing, China

一九七八年生於中国湖北
居住和工作於中国北京

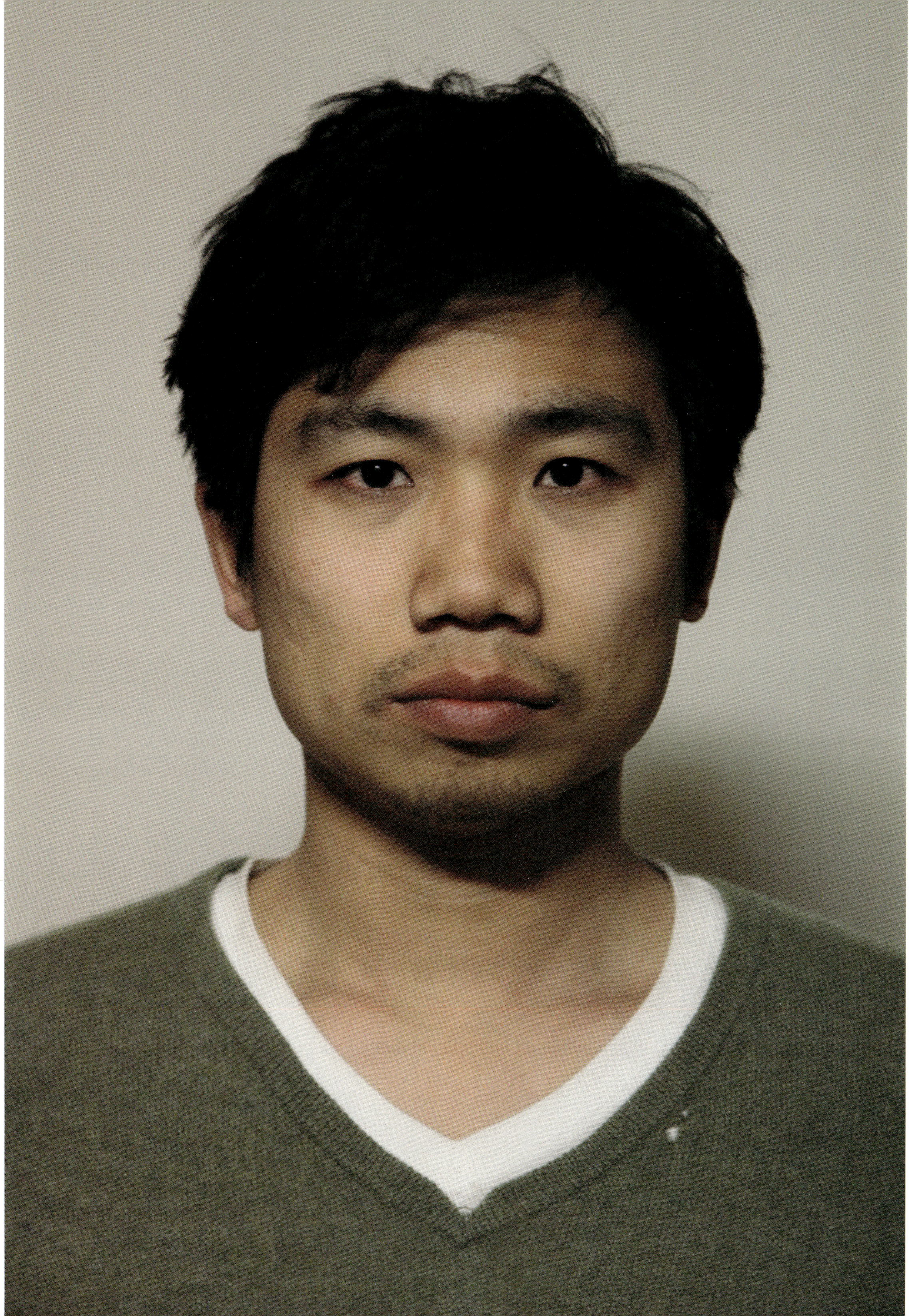

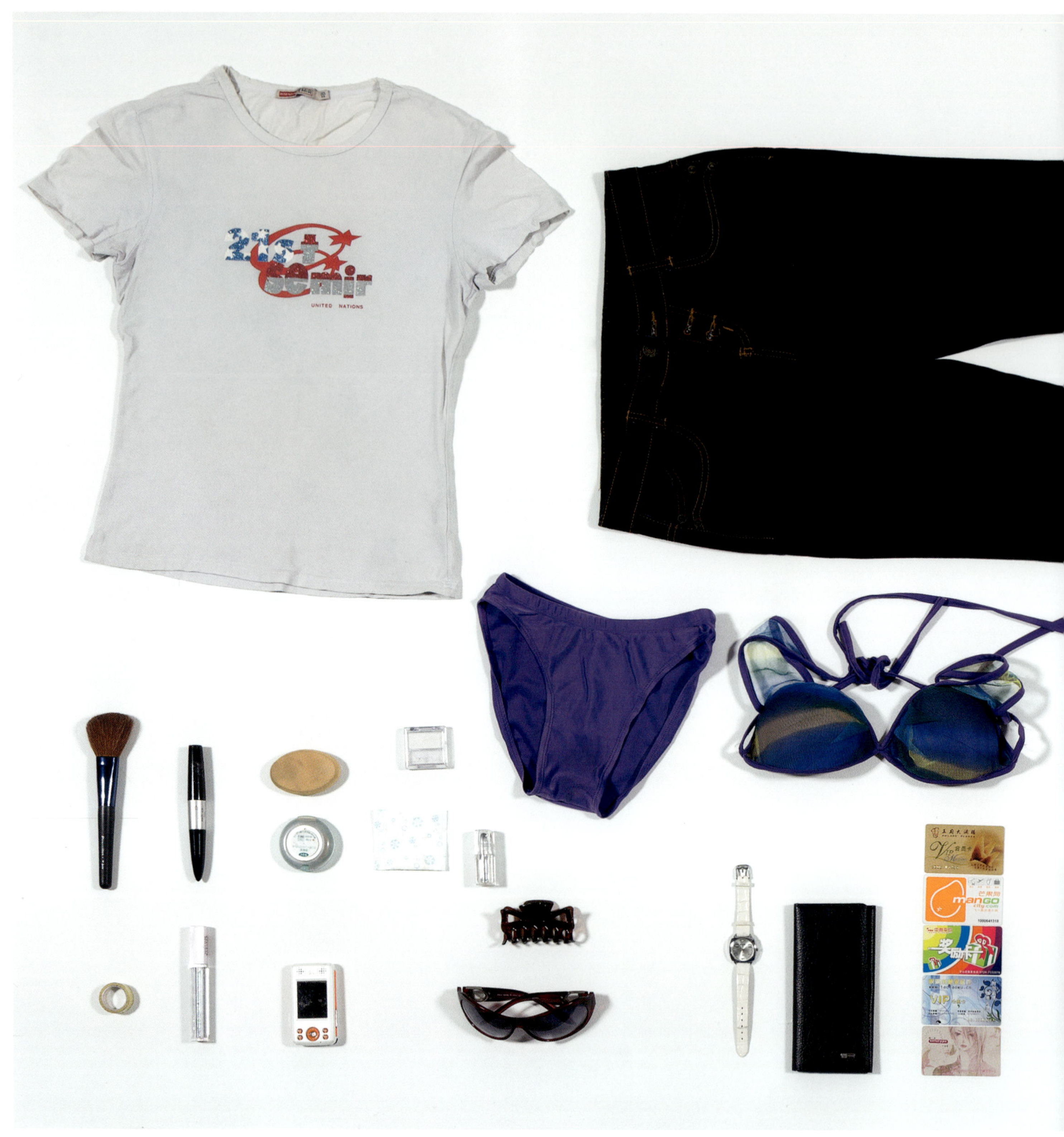

Liu Chuang, *Buying Everything on You – Dai Huan*, 2009, jeans, shirt, underwear, bra, shoes, socks, bag, sunglasses, currency, wallet, diploma, cellular phone, membership cards,prepaid cards, diploma, pamphlet, bank deposit slips and envelop, watch, tissue, personal photos, hair clip, tape, mascara, eyeshadow, eyeliner, make-up powder, powder brush, pantyliner, 94 1/2 x 47 1/4 x 8 in. (240 x 120 x 20 cm), acquired in 2011

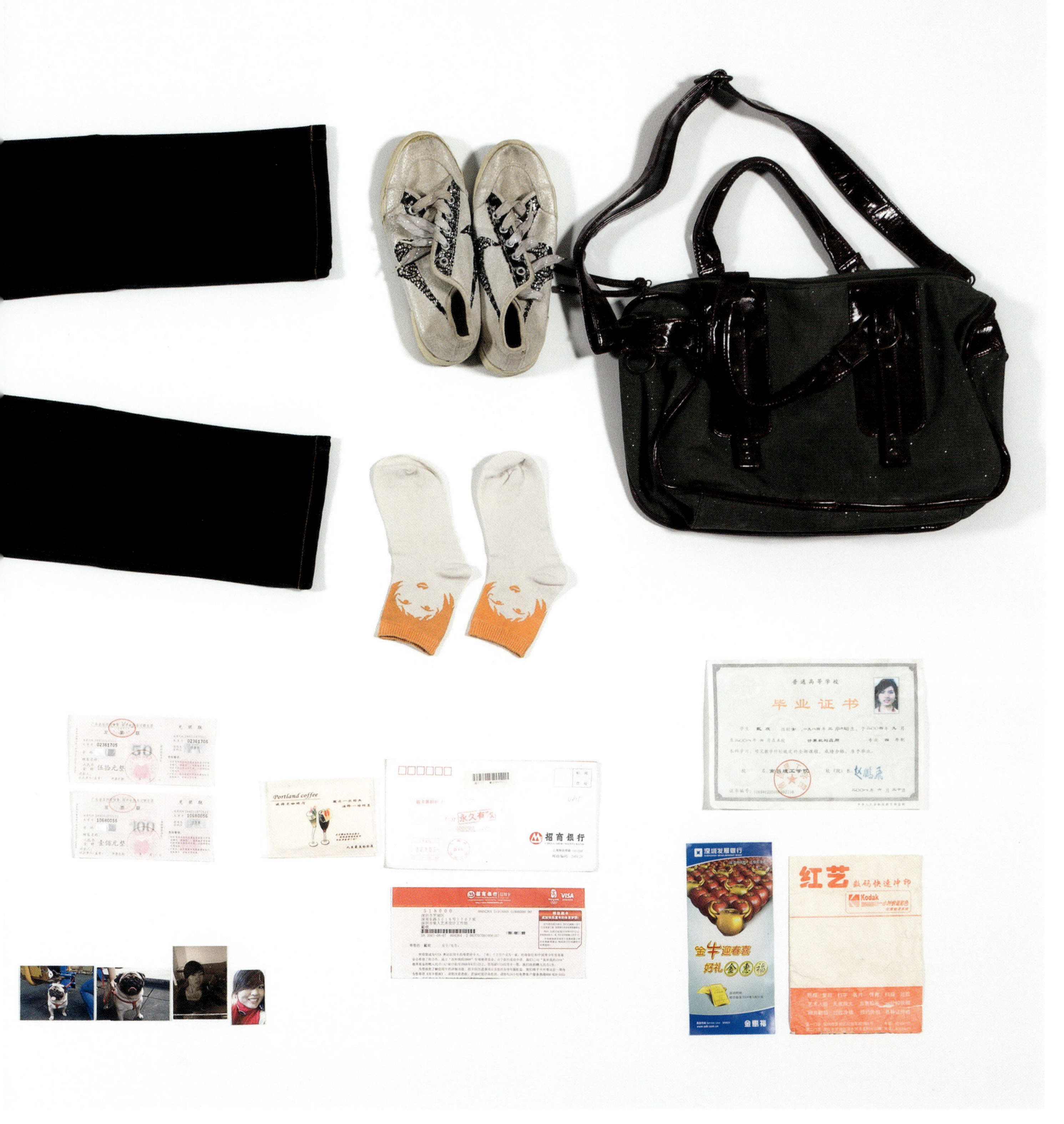

刘窗，《收购你身上所有的 东西 - 戴欢》，2009，牛仔裤，恤衫，内衣，胸罩，鞋，袜子，包包，太阳镜，货币，钱包，文凭，手机，会员卡，充值卡，毕业证书，小册子，银行存款单和信封，手表，纸巾，个人照片，发夹，胶带，睫毛膏，眼影，眼线，化妆粉，刷粉，卫生护垫，94 1/2 x 47 1/4 x 8 寸 (240 x 120 x 20 厘米)，收藏于 2011

This series started in 2005. I am interested in people who are looking for jobs in Shenzhen. There is an open square in front of the biggest labor market in Shenzhen where I approached these people and introduced my plan to them, telling them that their "things" would be shown in art museums. I communicated with them patiently, and a small number of people eventually agreed. We exchanged in the dress shop across the street. Some of these people just came to the city while others had been unemployed for a long time. What inspired me to do this work is my own personal experience. In addition, I try to see these objects as a kind of media, with which these individuals recount and record their stories, whether consciously or unconsciously.

- Liu Chuang

这一系列始于2005年，我对在深圳找工作的人感兴趣。在深圳最大的劳工市场前有一个广场，我就在广场上找这些人搭话，跟他们介绍我的计划，说他们的东西会被展览在美术馆里。我耐心地跟他们交流，最后有一小部分人答应了。我们在街对面的一个裙子店里进行了交换。他们有些是刚来到这个城市的，有些已经失业很久了。是我自己的经历启发我去制作这个作品的。而且，我尝试着把这些物品看作一种媒介，下意识或潜意识地诉说和记录着这些人物的故事。

- 刘窗

Liu Chuang, *Buying Everything on You – Guo Weixun*, 2006-2007, pants, shirt, shoes, belt, socks, underwear, bag, magazine, identification photos, identification cards, train ticket, diploma, bank cards, business cards, cellular phone, cellular phone charger, prepaid phone cards, membership cards, pens, batteries, razor, box of razor blades, headphones, keys, toothbrush, toothpaste, pocket knife, cigarette pack, 94 1/2 x 47 1/4 x 8 in. (240 x 120 x 20 cm), acquired in 2011
刘窗，《收购你身上所有的 东西 - 郭伟勋》，2009，裤子，恤衫，皮鞋，皮带，袜子，内衣，包包，杂志，护照照片，身份证，火车票，毕业证，银行卡，名片，手机，手机充电器，预付电话卡，会员卡，钢笔，电池，剃须刀，剃须刀片，耳机，钥匙，牙刷，牙膏，小刀，香烟包，94 1/2 x 47 1/4 x 8 寸 (240 x 120 x 20 厘米)，收藏于 2011

Liu Chuang, *Buying Everything on You – Huang Wei*, 2006-2007, pants, shirt, shoes, bag, socks, underwear, cellular phone, cellular phone charger, teabag, currency, business cards, passport photos, personal photos, notepad, diploma, pens, tissue, identification cards, prepaid phone cards, membership cards, bank cards, resume, course completion certificate, sticky notes, letter, 94 1/2 x 47 1/4 x 8 in. (240 x 120 x 20 cm), acquired in 2011
刘窗，《收购你身上所有的 东西 - 黄伟》，2009，裤子，恤衫，鞋，包，袜子，内衣，手机，手机充电器，袋泡茶，货币，名片，护照照片，个人照片，记事本，毕业证，笔，纸巾，身份证，预付电话卡，会员卡，银行卡，个人简历，课程结业证书，便笺，信件，94 1/2 x 47 1/4 x 8 寸 (240 x 120 x 20 厘米)，收藏于 2011

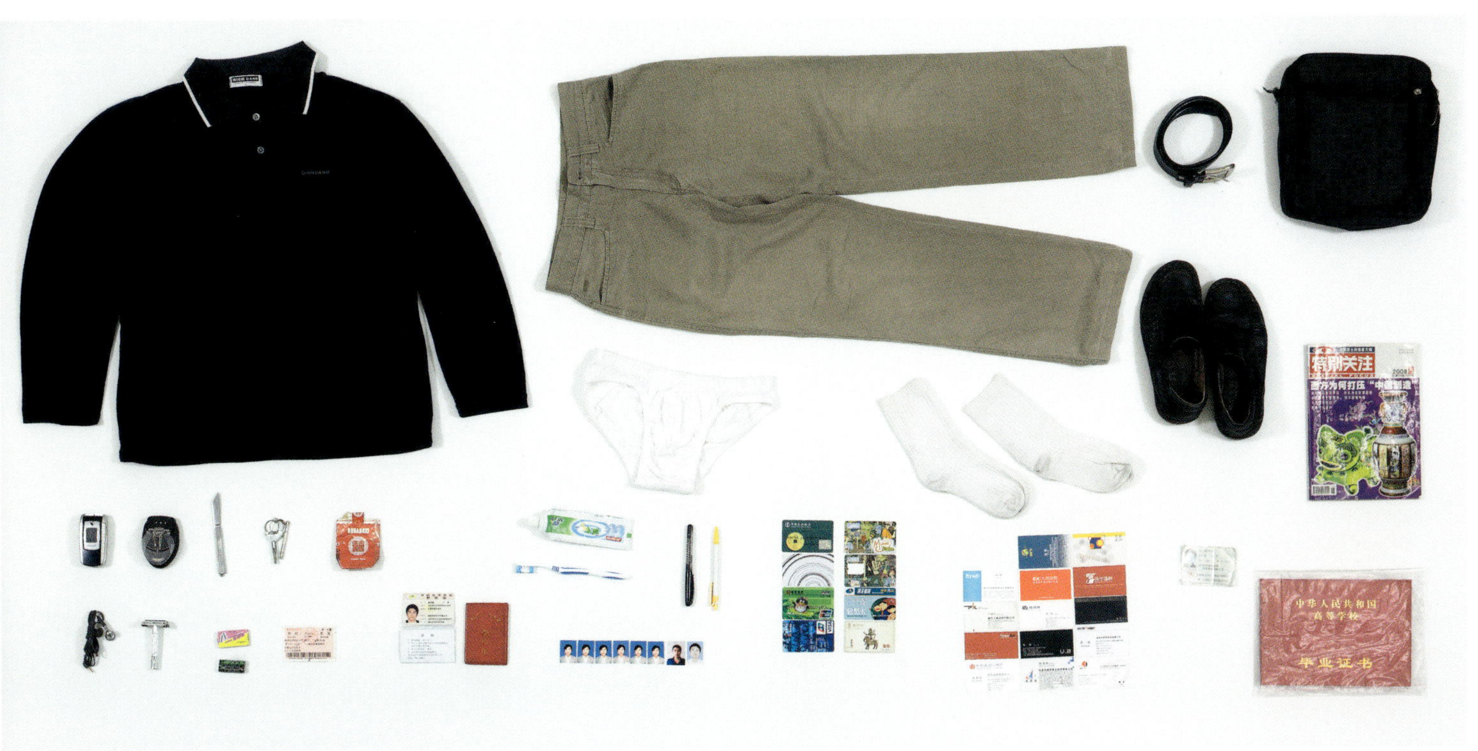

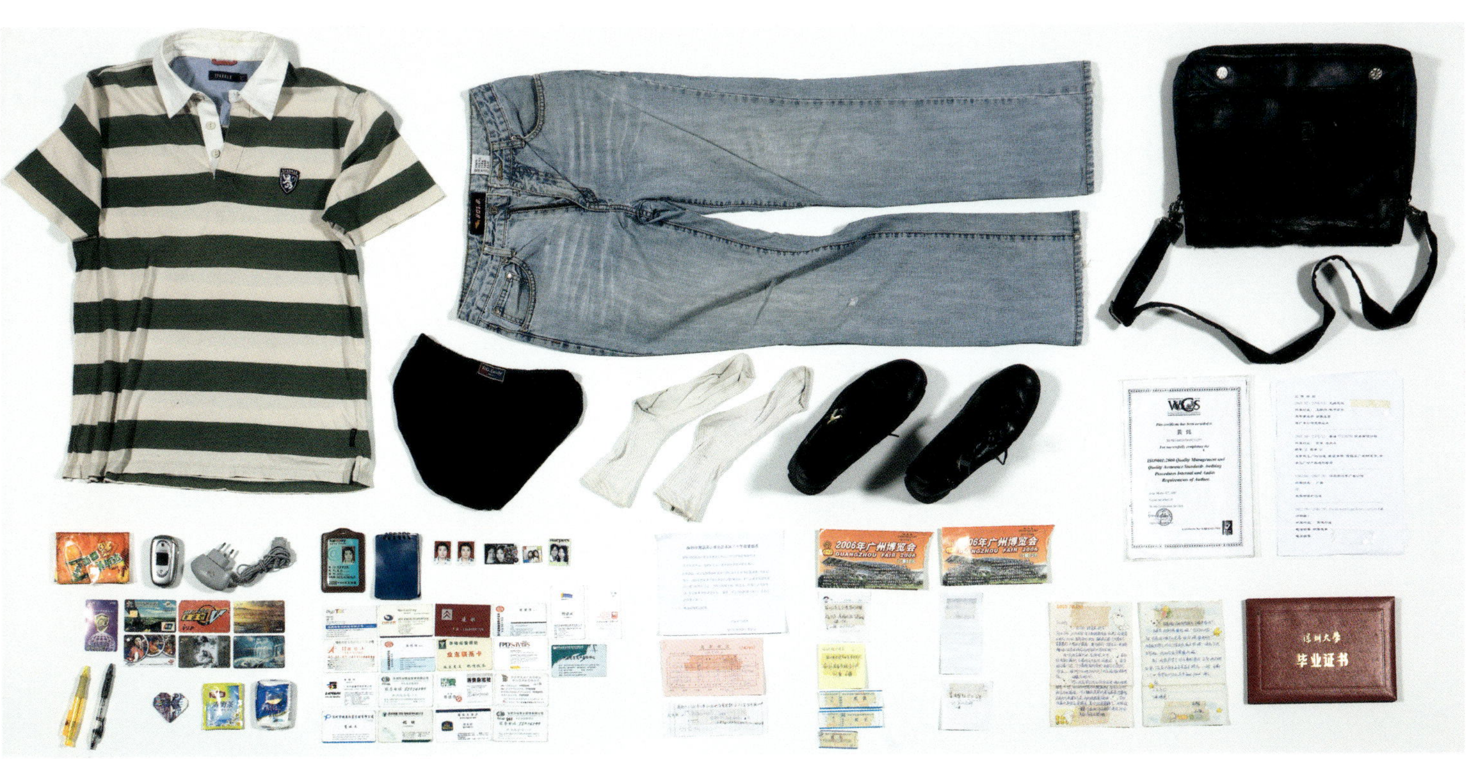

Liu Wei 刘韡

Born in 1972, Beijing, China
Lives and works in Beijing, China

一九七二年生於中國北京
居住和工作於中國北京

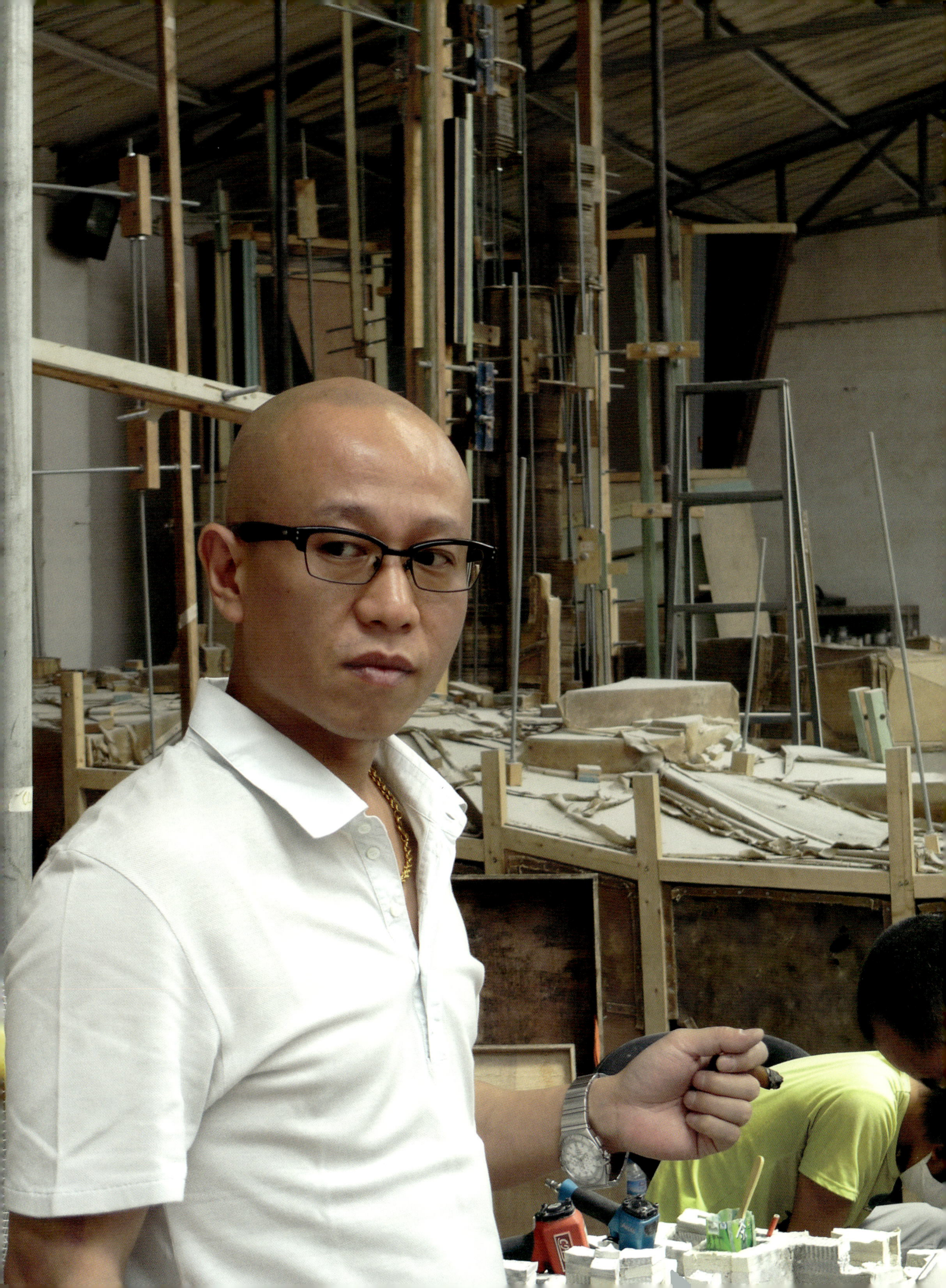

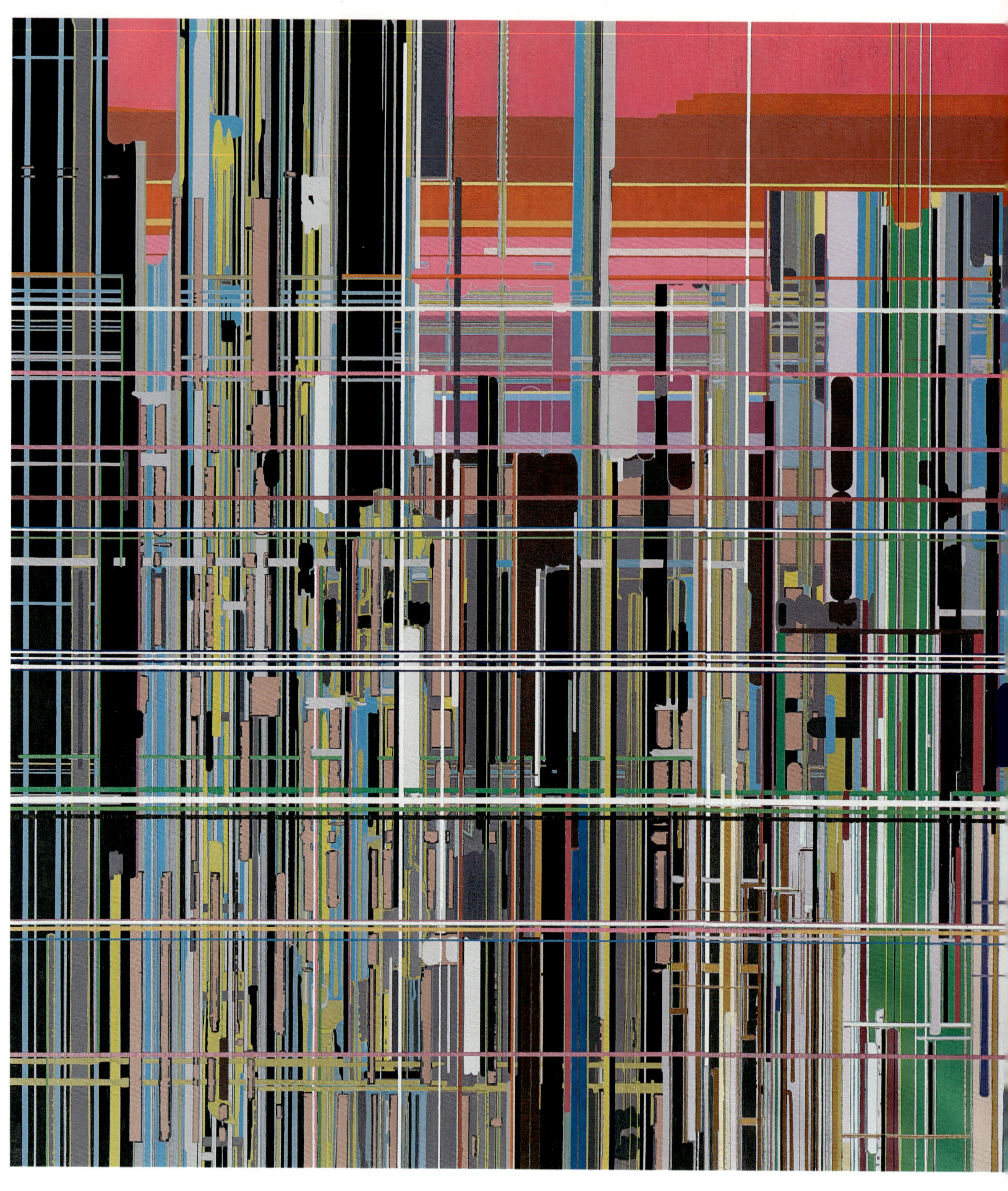

Liu Wei, *Liberation No.1*, 2013, oil on canvas, 118 x 212 1/2 in. (300 x 540 cm), acquired in 2013
刘韡, **解放** 1, 2013, 布面油画, 118 x 212 1/2 寸 (300 x 540 厘米), 收藏于 2013

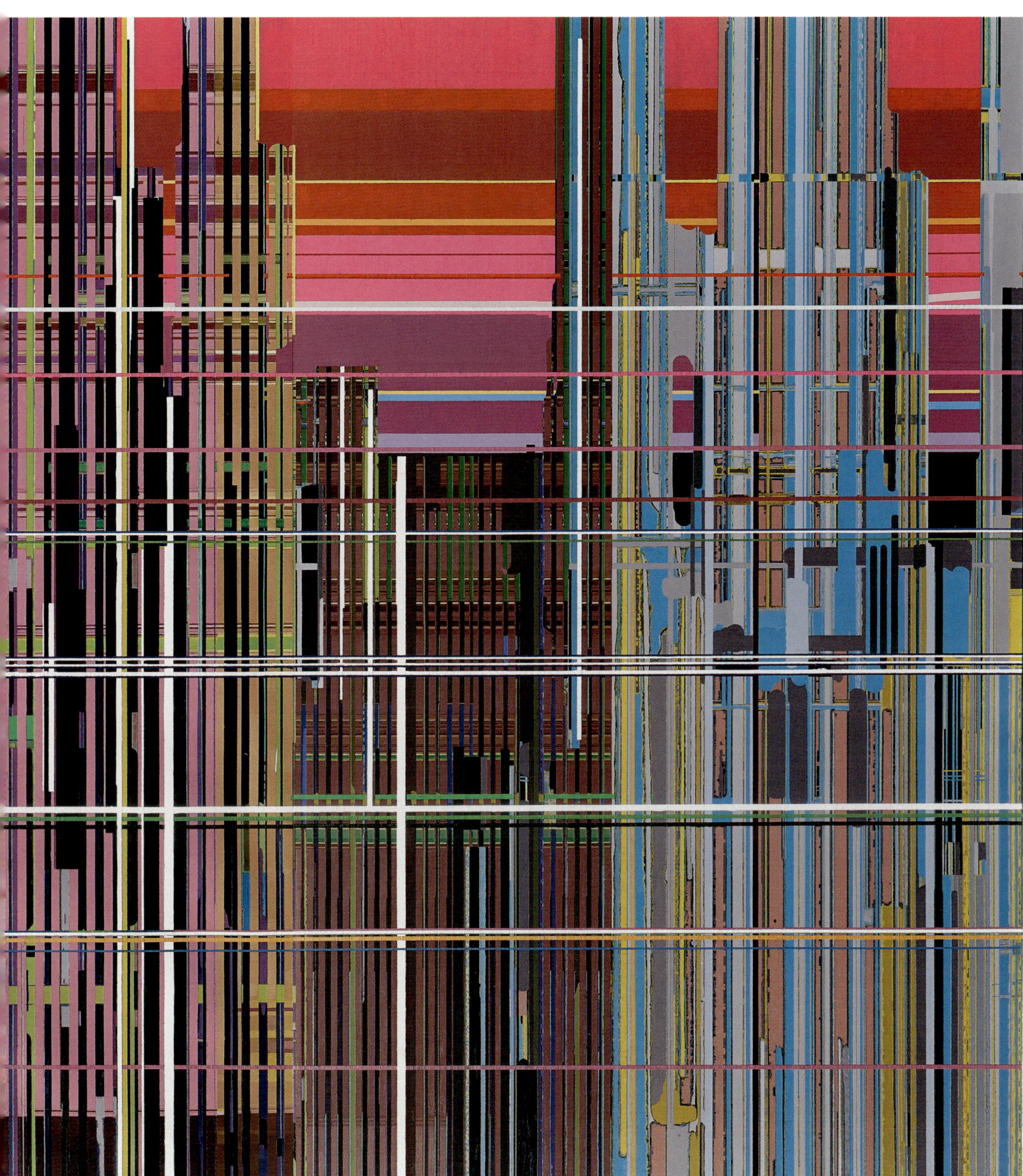

In painting, sculpture and installation, I give shape to the world around us, offering an acute visual commentary on underlying ideologies. My works have no specific meaning – this is left for the audience to decide. But they wipe a layer of dust from the surface of reality, forcing it to expose its true face. Reality exists independently of politics, ideology and philosophy.

-Liu Wei

在绘画，雕塑和装置［艺术］中，我给予我们周围的世界一种形态,为潜在的意识形态提供一种敏锐的视觉评论。我的作品没有明确的意思 – 这是留给观众自己决定的。但它们抹去盖在现实表面的一层尘埃，迫使它暴露出真实的面貌.现实独立存在于政治、意识形态和哲学之外.

- 刘韡

Liu Wei, *Truth Dimension No. 2*, 2012, oil on canvas, 87 1/8 x 70 2/8 in. (222 x 180 cm), acquired in 2012
刘韡，《**真实维度 No. 2**》，2012, 布面油画, 87 1/8 x 70 2/8 寸 (222 x 180 厘米), 收藏于 2012

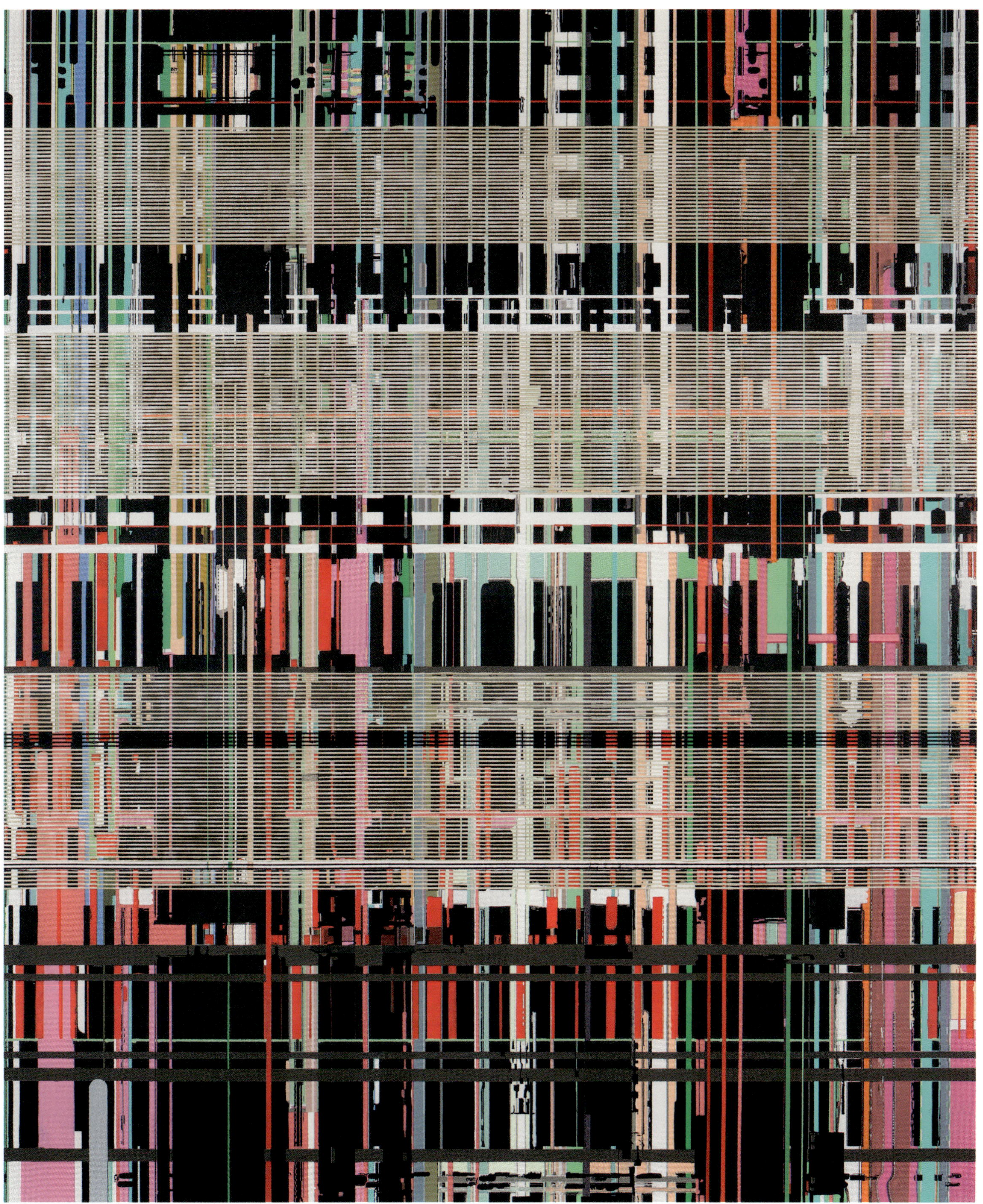

Liu Wei, *Truth Dimension No. 3*, 2012, oil on canvas, 87 1/8 x 70 2/8 in. (222 x 180 cm), acquired in 2012
刘韡，《真实维度 No. 3》，2012，布面油画，87 1/8 x 70 2/8 寸 (222 x 180 厘米)，收藏于 2012

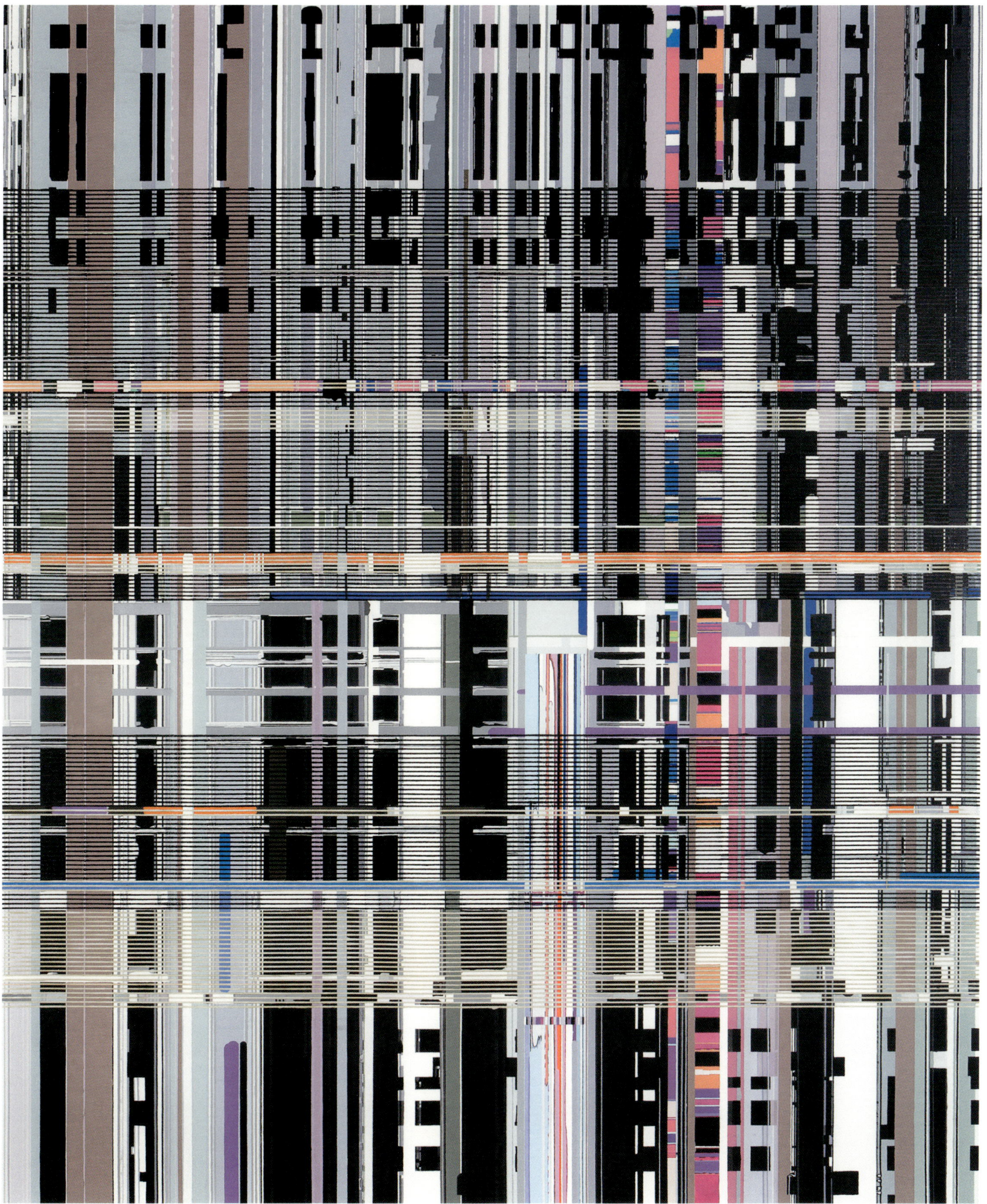

Liu Wei, *Merely a Mistake*, 2011, door frames, wooden beams and acrylic board, 66 1/2 x 57 x 212 1/8 in. (170 x 145 x 540 cm), acquired in 2012

刘韡，《仅仅是一个错误》，2011，门框，木梁和丙烯板，66 1/2 x 57 x 212 1/8 寸 (170 x 145 x 540 厘米)，收藏于 2012

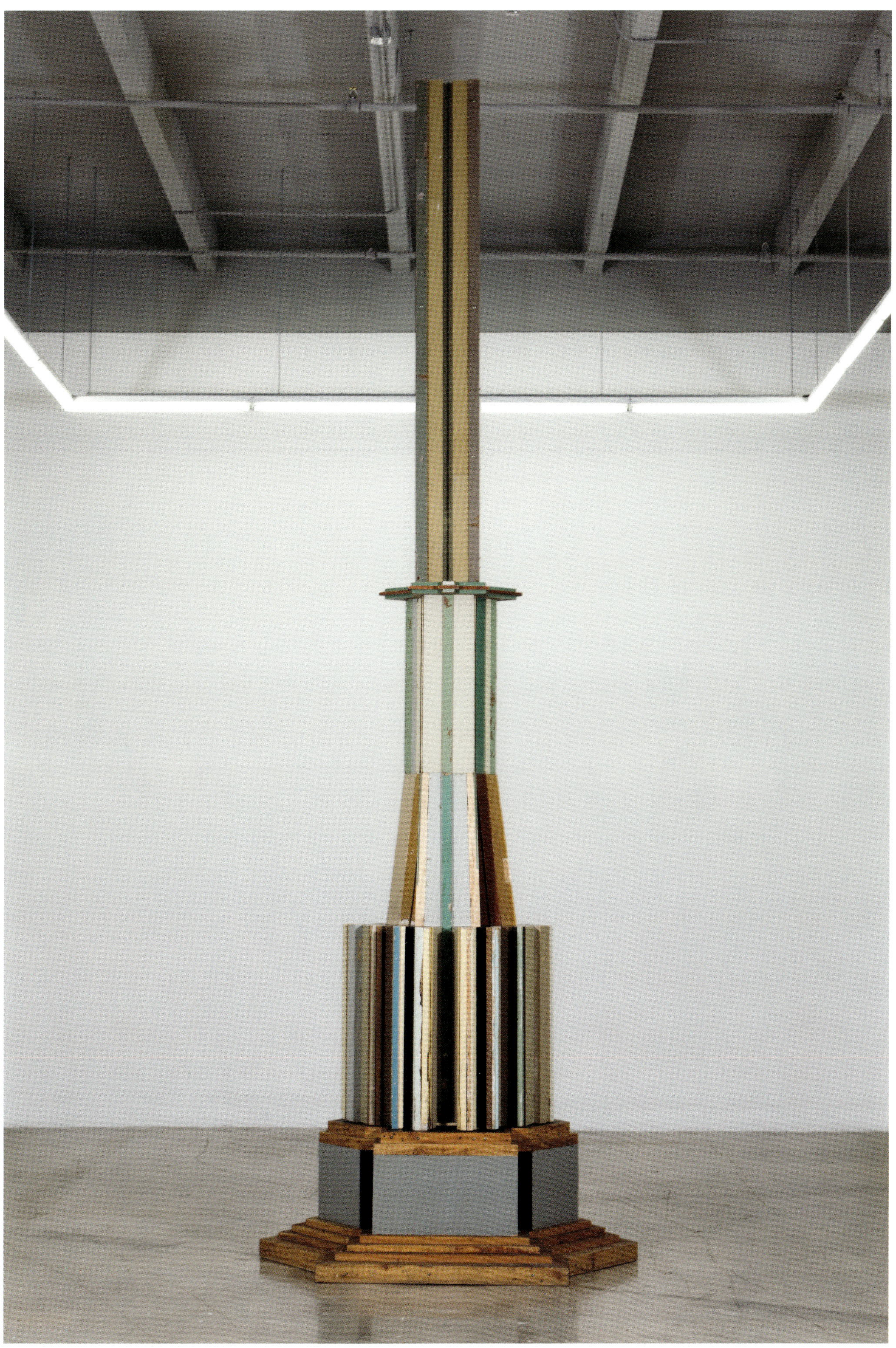

Qiu Zhijie

Born in 1969, Fujian, China
Lives and works in Beijing, China

邱志杰

一九六九年生於中国福建
居住和工作於中国北京

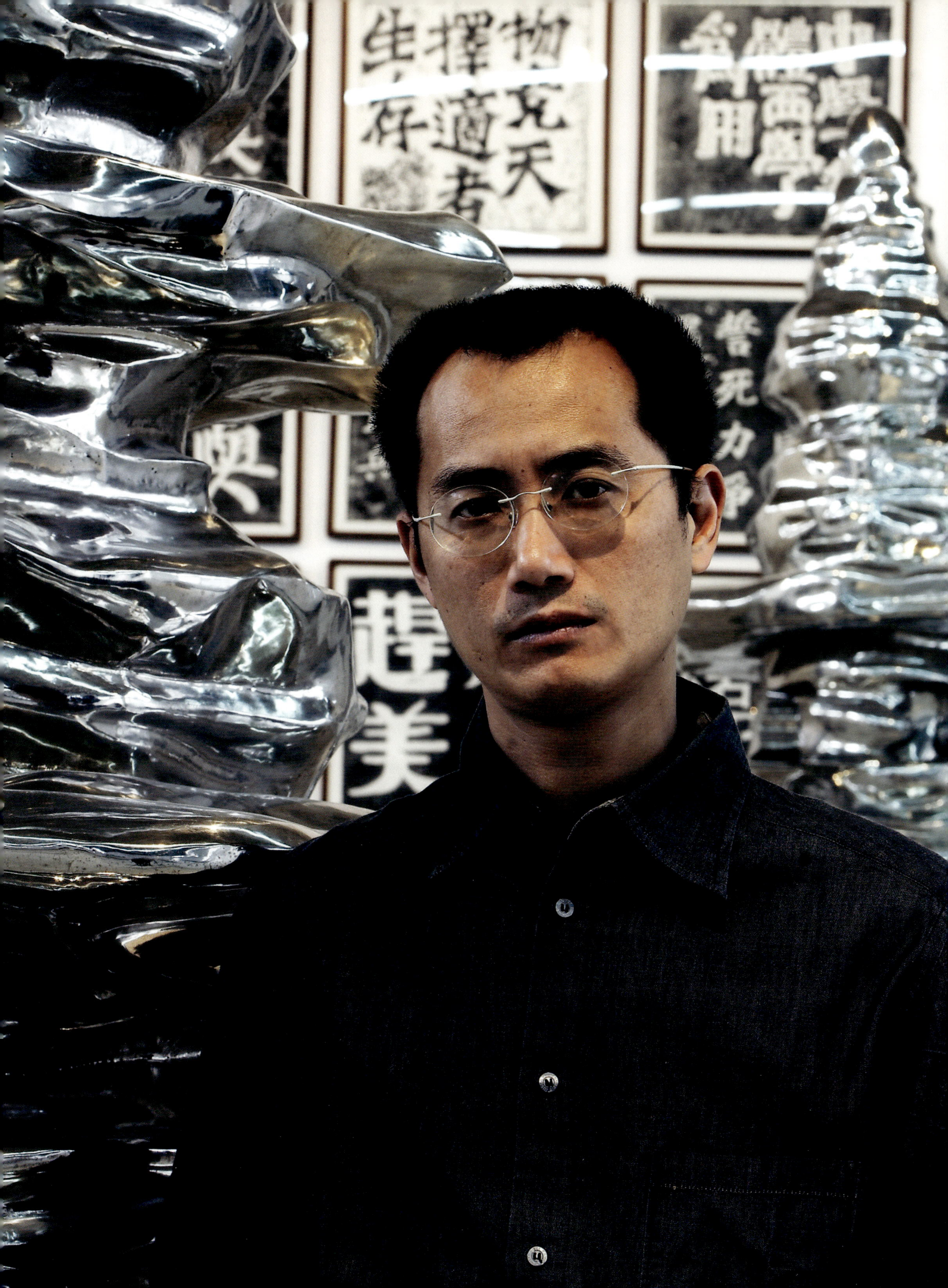

The TATOO series discusses the questionable relationship between a figure and its background. Keeping an appropriate relationship between the two is one of the preconditions of the traditional portrait game. Now, because of some shared characteristics of the two—being pierced through by the same object, or attempting to become the same Chinese character—the supposed distance between them disappears; the volume of the main body disappears, the weight of the person disappears, the smell of flesh disappears, all that is left is a two-dimensional plane that anybody can write or draw on endlessly. This person does not have the power to resist, because he has become an image only.

In *TATOO-2*, a red Chinese character was painted on the body and the wall, the meaning of the character is "No!" It covers and erases the boundary between body and wall.

In *TATOO-1*, some pushpins were put on both the body and the wall, which made the body lose its weight and its three dimensionality. The illusion here is used to discuss the relationship between an image and its background—how an image loses its independence and integrality by the extrinsic power.

- Qiu Zhijie

纹身系列讨论了一个形象和它的背景之间成问题的关系.这二者之间保持恰如其分的关系是传统肖像画游戏的前提之一.现在由于它们共享某种特征---被同一种物质所嵌入,或者妄图成为同一个汉字,它们之间应有的距离消失了,主体的体积感消失了,这个人的重量消失了,肉体的气味消失了,只剩下平面,谁都可以在上头无穷无尽地书写,图抹.这个人无力拒绝,因为它只不过是图像而已.

在"纹身2"中，一个中文汉字被涂在了肉体和墙上，字的意思是"不！"它覆盖且消除了肉体和墙之间的距离

在"纹身1"中，一些图钉被嵌入了肉体和墙上，使得肉体失去了自身的重量和三维立体感。这个错觉是用来讨论一个图像与它的背景之间的关系的——个图像如何在外界力量的影响下丧失了它自身的独立性和完整性。

- 邱志杰

Qiu Zhijie, *TATOO-2*, 1994, chromogenic print mounted on aluminium board, 73 1/4 x 62 3/4 in. (186 x 159.5 cm), acquired in 2011
邱志杰，《纹身2 -不》, 1994, 显色打印安装在铝板, 73 1/4 x 62 3/4 in. (186 x 159.5 cm), 收藏于 2011

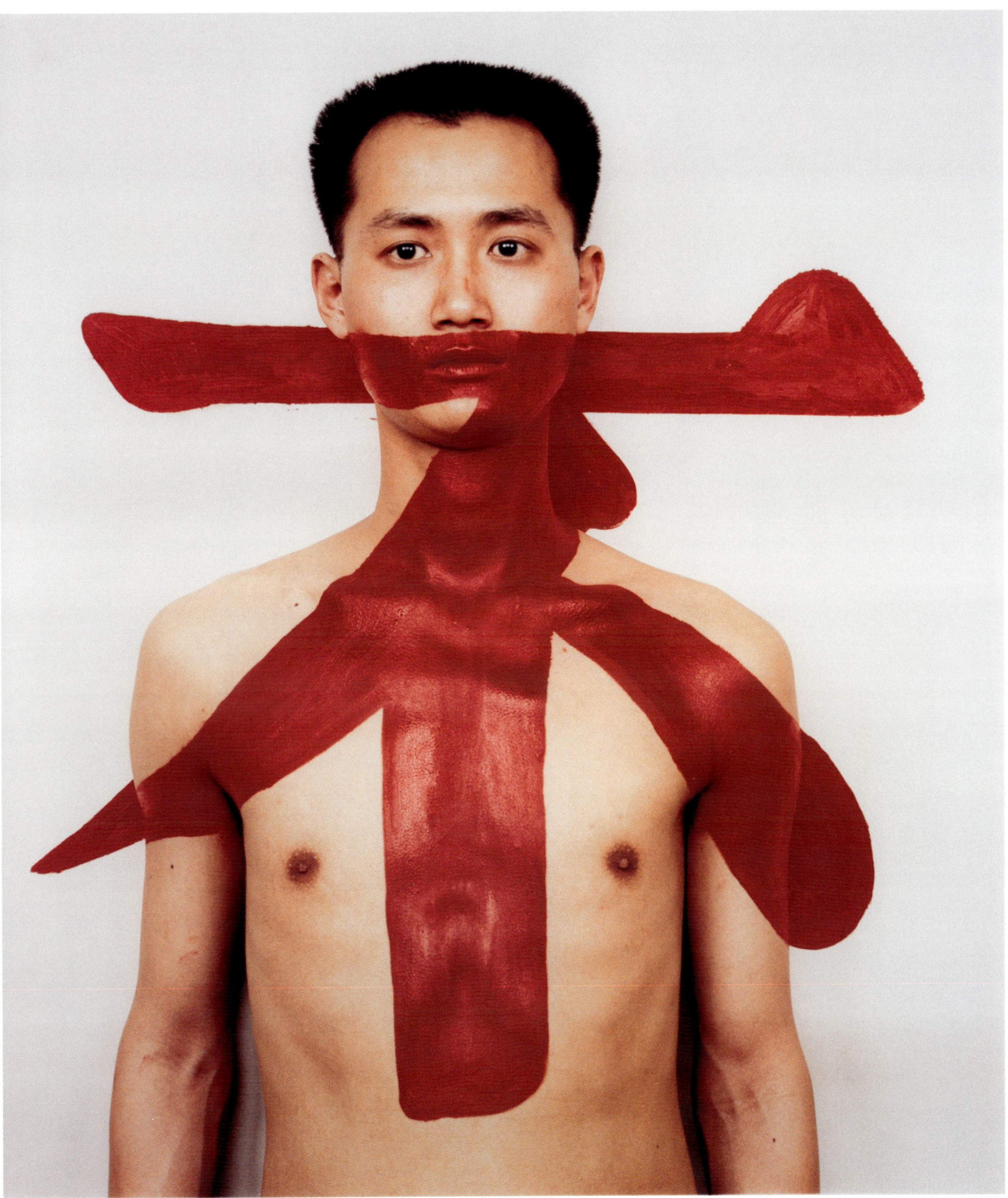

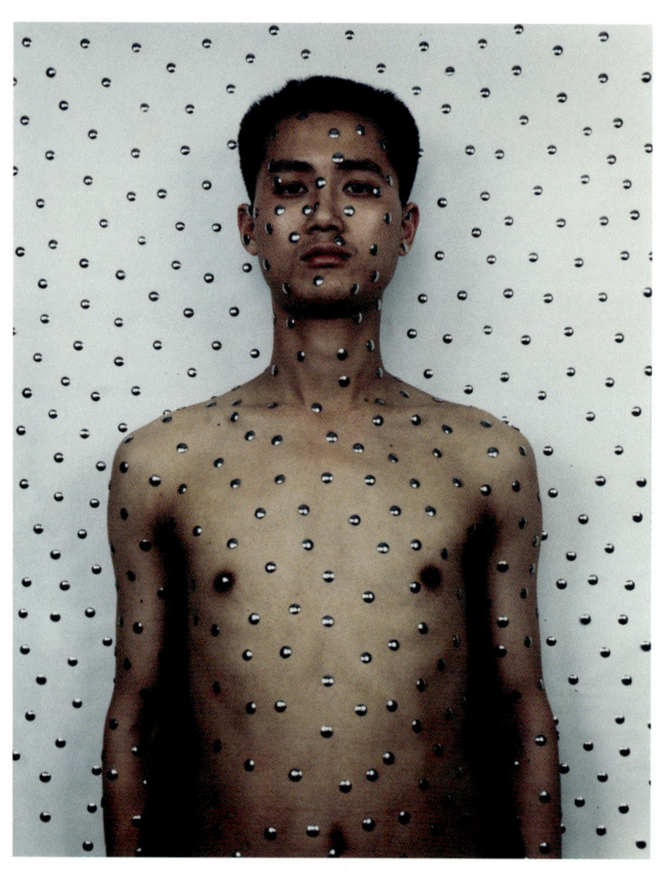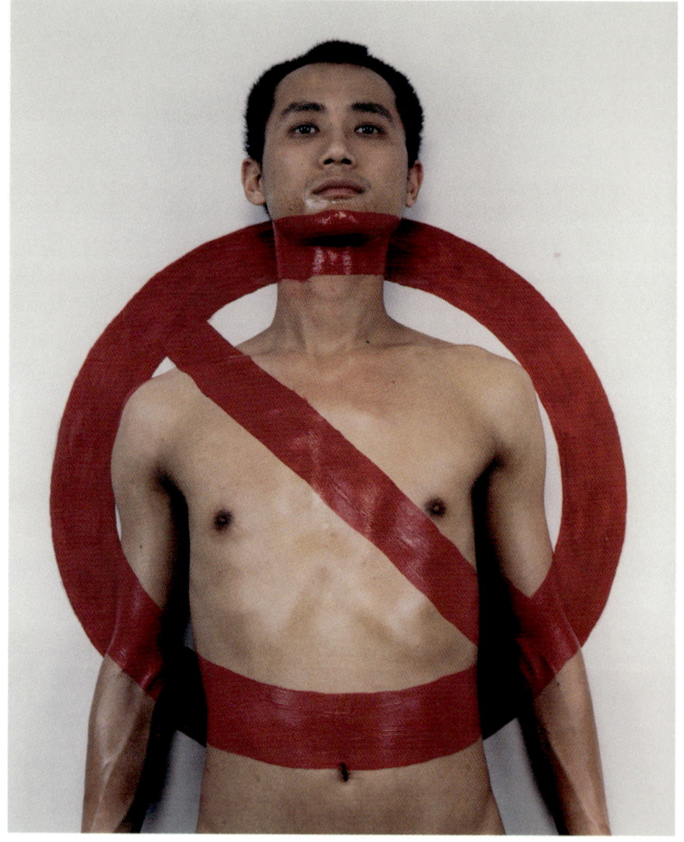

Qiu Zhijie, *TATTOO-1*, 2000, color coupler print, 55 × 45 3/4 in. (140 × 116 cm), acquired in 2011
邱志杰，《纹身1-图钉》，2000，彩色耦合器打印，55 x 45 3/4 寸 (140 x 116 厘米)，收藏于 2011

Qiu Zhijie, *TATTOO-3*, 2000, color coupler print, 43 5/8 x 35 3/4 in. (110.5 x 91 cm), acquired in 2013
邱志杰，《纹身3》，2000，彩色耦合器打印，43 5/8 x 35 3/4 寸 (110.5 x 91 厘米)，收藏于 2013

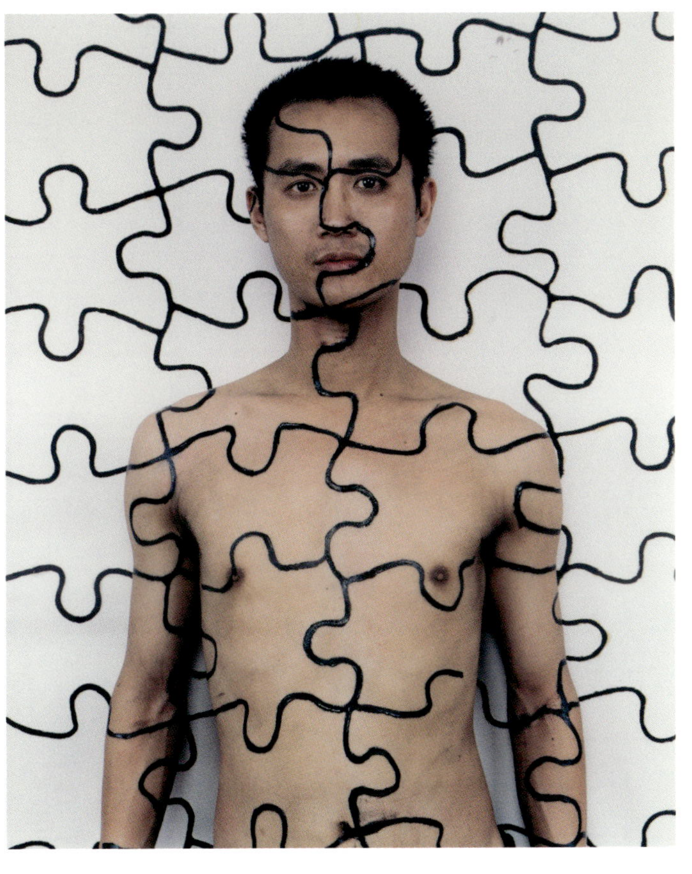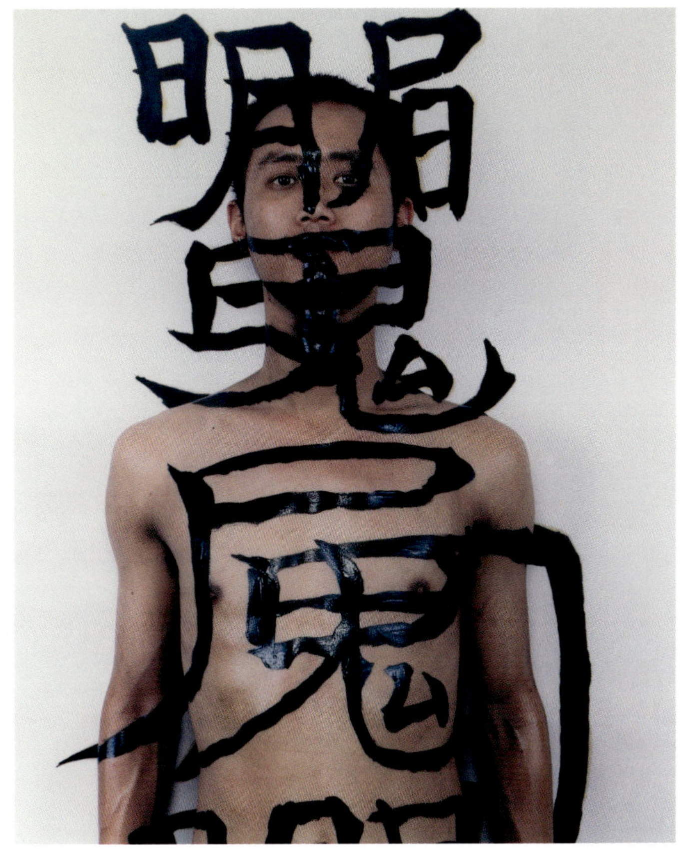

Qiu Zhijie, *TATTOO-5*, 2000, chromogenic print, 43 5/8 x 35 3/4 in. (110.5 x 91 cm), acquired in 2013
邱志杰，《纹身5》，2000，显色打印，43 5/8 x 35 3/4 寸 (110.5 x 91 厘米)，收藏于 2013

Qiu Zhijie, *TATTOO-6*, 2000, chromogenic print, 43 5/8 x 35 3/4 in. (110.5 x 91 cm), acquired in 2013
邱志杰，《纹身6》，2000，显色打印，43 5/8 x 35 3/4 寸 (110.5 x 91 厘米)，收藏于 2013

A Suicidology of the Nanjing Yangtze River Bridge(3): Darkness illuminates Me
A bulb is made of fiberglass, whose tungsten filament is replaced by neon lights and bent into the form of the English word "DARKNESS." The neon lights are blue.

- Qiu Zhijie

《南京长江大桥自杀者干预计划三：黑暗照亮了我》
制作一个有机玻璃的大灯泡。灯泡内部的钨丝由霓虹灯代替。用霓虹灯弯成英文词Darkness的形状。霓虹灯为蓝色。

- 邱志杰

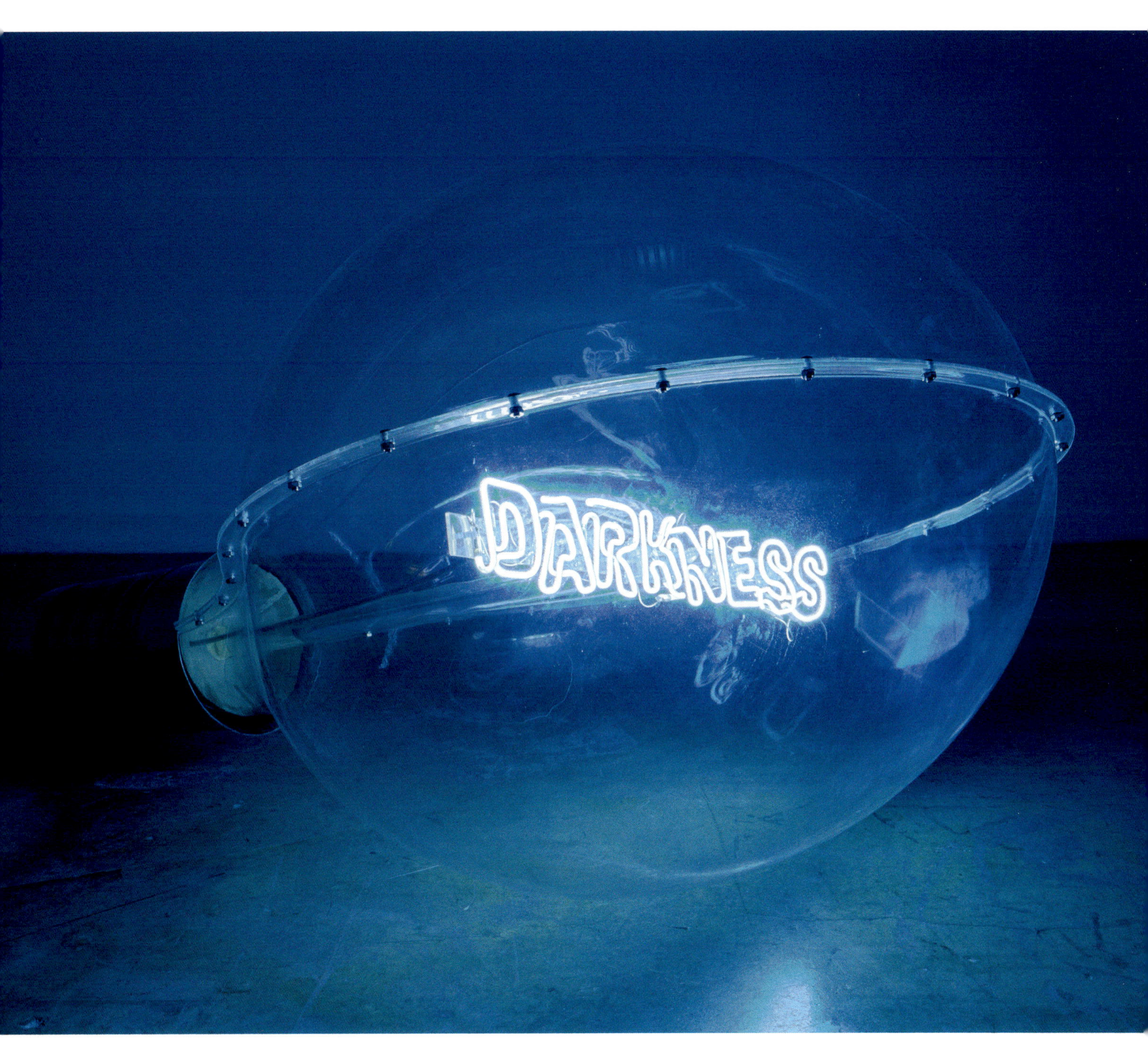

DARKNESS

From China's long history I picked all sorts of revolutionary speeches and slogans, from the Daze Village Uprising in the third century BCE until recently. Revolutions and uprisings have always happened periodically in China's history and this periodic shock became part of China's history. Every time a revolution happened new aphorisms came up, and these monumentalized the ideals and desires of that age.

I carved these characters onto the surface of a cement board and made an ink rubbing of the characters on the surface of this layer. Then I again put cement on top and waited until it was thoroughly dry before carving out a second layer of characters, which was a slogan of the next revolution, and again made a rubbing. This process was repeated until the "memorial stone" became a cement cube. On the surface it looks very much like a modern minimalistic sculpture but it has 20 layers. On the surface you cannot see the characters but on the side you can horizontally observe the traces of repeated pouring of cement and ink rubbings, as if it were the layers in an archeological pit.

Since with every carving I applied the style of calligraphy used at the time of the corresponding revolution, the entire set of rubbings produced through the whole process also form a history of calligraphy. Together with the history of revolutionary concepts they constitute a double history.

- Qiu Zhijie

我从中国漫长的历史中选择了各种各样的革命口号和革命话语，从公元前300年的陈胜吴光起义直到最近的。革命和起义在中国历史上总是周期性地爆发，形成了中国历史的周期性震荡。而每一次革命总是会提出一些著名的警句，这些词句铭记着那个时代的理想和欲望。

我把这些文字刻在一个水泥板的表面上，将这一层表面上的文字拓印下来，然后在上面再到上水泥，带干透后再刻上第二层的文字，也就是第二次革命的口号，再次进行拓印。这个过程一只反复直到这个"纪念碑"成为一个水泥立方体。表面上看他很像一个极简主义的现代雕塑，但是它有20层，从表面上看不出文字但是从侧面可以看到一次次的浇铸和拓印所留下的水平的痕迹，像是考古坑中的文化层。

因为我在往水泥面上刻文字的时候使用的是和每次革命时相应的时代的字体，所以在整个制作过程中所留下的一整套拓片也成为一个书法史，这和革命理念的历史一起构成一种双重的历史。

- 邱志杰

Qiu Zhijie, *Memorial for Revolutionary Speech*, 2007, 16 ink rubbings and cement cube, Ed. AP, ink rubbing: 31 1/2 x 31 1/2 in. (80 x 80 cm), cement cube: 31 1/2 x 31 1/2 x 31 1/2 in. (80 x 80 x 80 cm), acquired in 2011
邱志杰，《革命话语的纪念碑》，2007，16 拓本和水泥立方体，AP 版本，拓本: 31 1/2 x 31 1/2 寸 (80 x 80 厘米)，水泥立方体: 31 1/2 x 31 1/2 x 31 1/2 寸 (80 x 80 x 80 厘米)，收藏于 2011

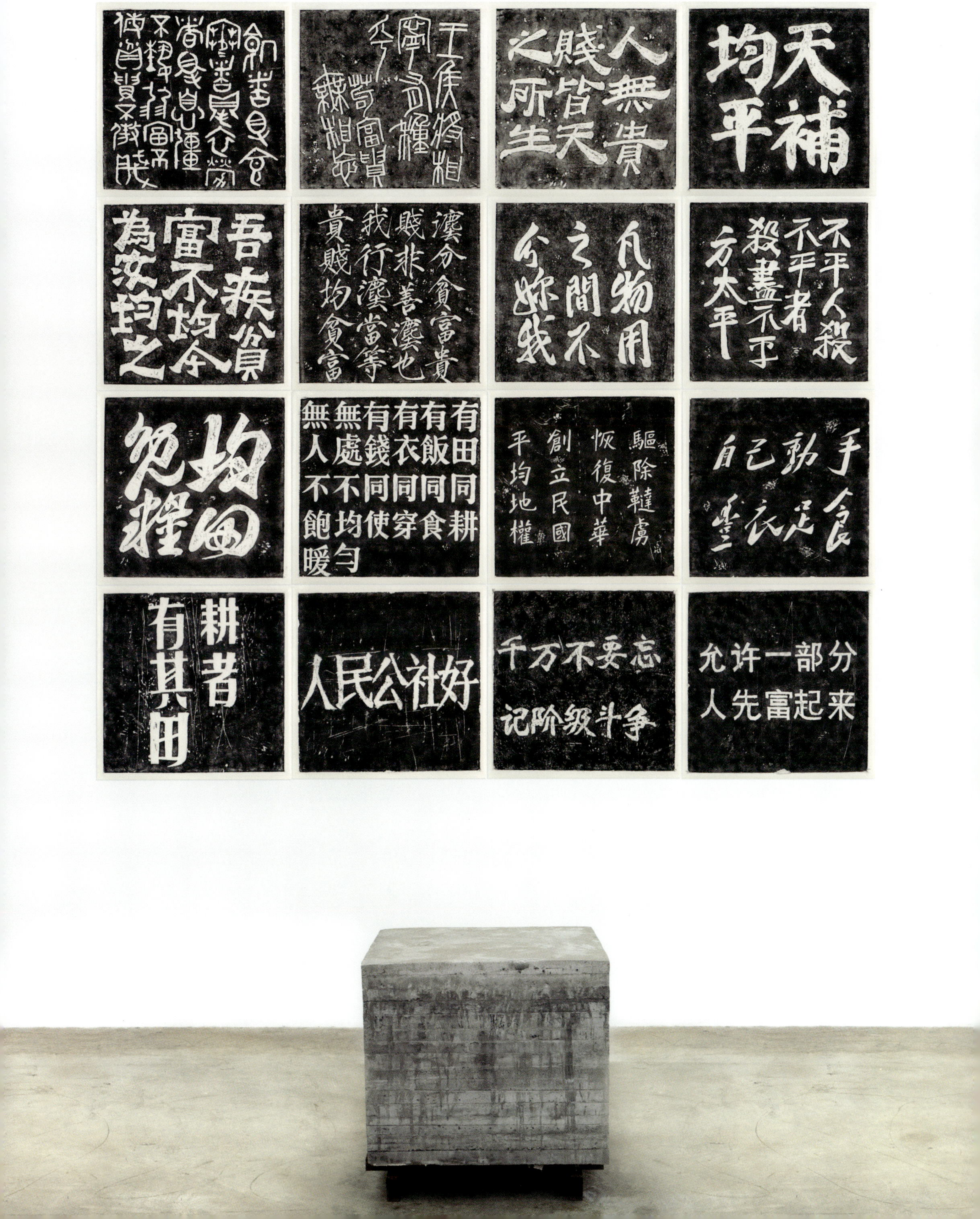

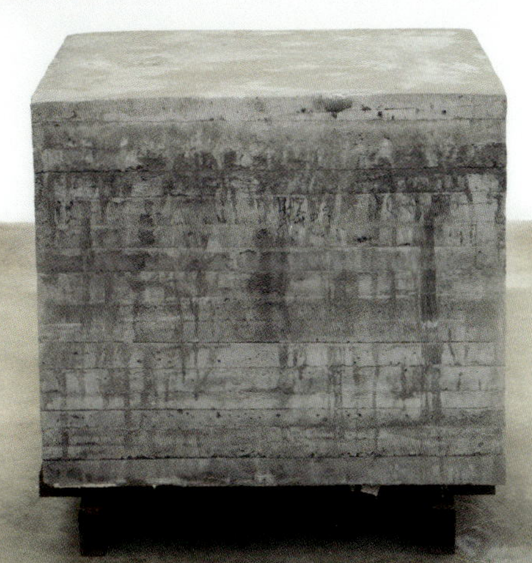
天補均平
人無貴賤皆天之所生
賤之所生
工農將相安寧富貴
吾疾貧富不均今為汝均之
漢分貧富貴賤我行漢當等貴賤均貧富
凡物用之間不公妳我
不平人殺不平者殺盡不平方太平
均田免糧
有田同耕有飯同食有衣同穿有錢同使有處同住無人不飽暖
驅除韃虜恢復中華創立民國平均地權
手足食自己勤衣
耕者有其田
人民公社好
千万不要忘记阶级斗争
允许一部分人先富起来

A large piece of bamboo mat whose color is rusty brown where it meets the floor. The bamboo transitions to a more iridescent color when it is near the wall. On the mat there are many kinds of bamboo utensils (the bamboo baskets are made from the same bamboo material as the utensils woven into the bamboo mat, making the mat and these utensils closely link to each other). The utensils include steamers, boxes, cradles, dustpans, baskets, tables, chairs, flutes, vertical flutes, Lushengs [Chinese musical instrument], bamboo rafts, bamboo ladders, fish baskets, chopsticks and other things that are frequently used in the daily lives of Chinese people. The lower half of one of the cradles has dissolved in the mat. When it reappears it has transformed into a bamboo ladder which dissolves into the mat and rises again as a bookshelf. This continuous process of dissolving and reincarnating shows Chinese peoples' worldview and the survival attitude of the ceaseless cycle of life.

- Qiu Zhijie

一大片竹席，竹席的颜色在靠近锈铁地面的时候是接近铁锈色的棕色，越往墙边越向竹子的青绿色过渡。竹席上面连接着多种竹器。（从构成竹器的竹材上劈出竹篾，编织进竹席中，使竹席和这些竹器紧紧相连。）竹器包括蒸笼、箱子、摇篮、簸箕、箩筐、桌椅、笛子、箫、芦笙、竹排、竹梯子、鱼篓、筷子等中国人日常生活中常用的种类。一个摇篮的下半部消融在竹席中，当它再次冒出来时，已经变身为一把竹梯子，等它再融化在竹席中，再次从竹席种升起，则变形为书架。这个不断融解、化生的过程，展示了中国人的世界观和生生不息的生存意志。

- 邱志杰

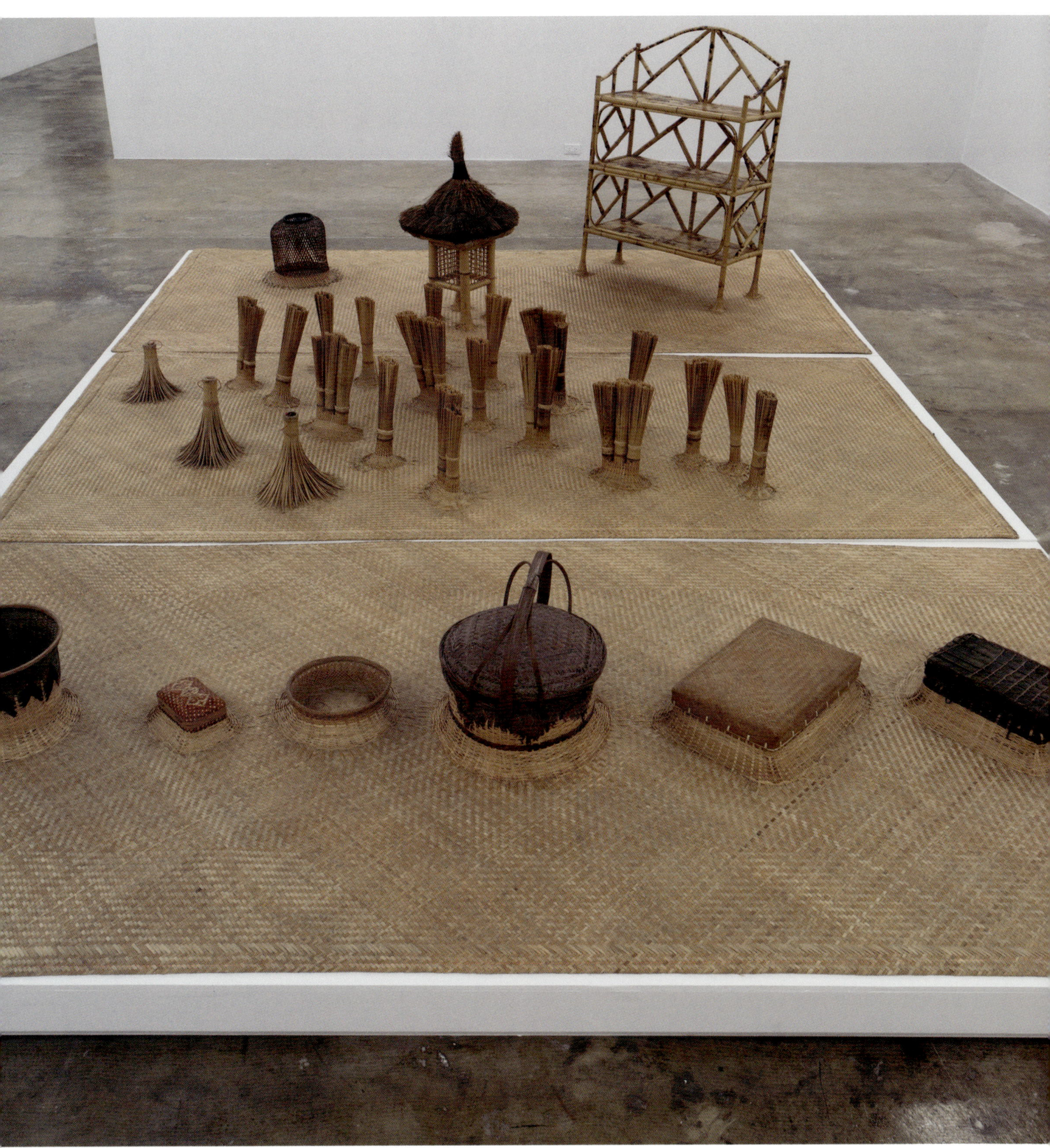

Shang Yixin 尚一心

Born in 1980, Zhejiang, China
Lives and works in Hangzhou, China

一九八零年生於中国浙江
居住和工作於中国杭州

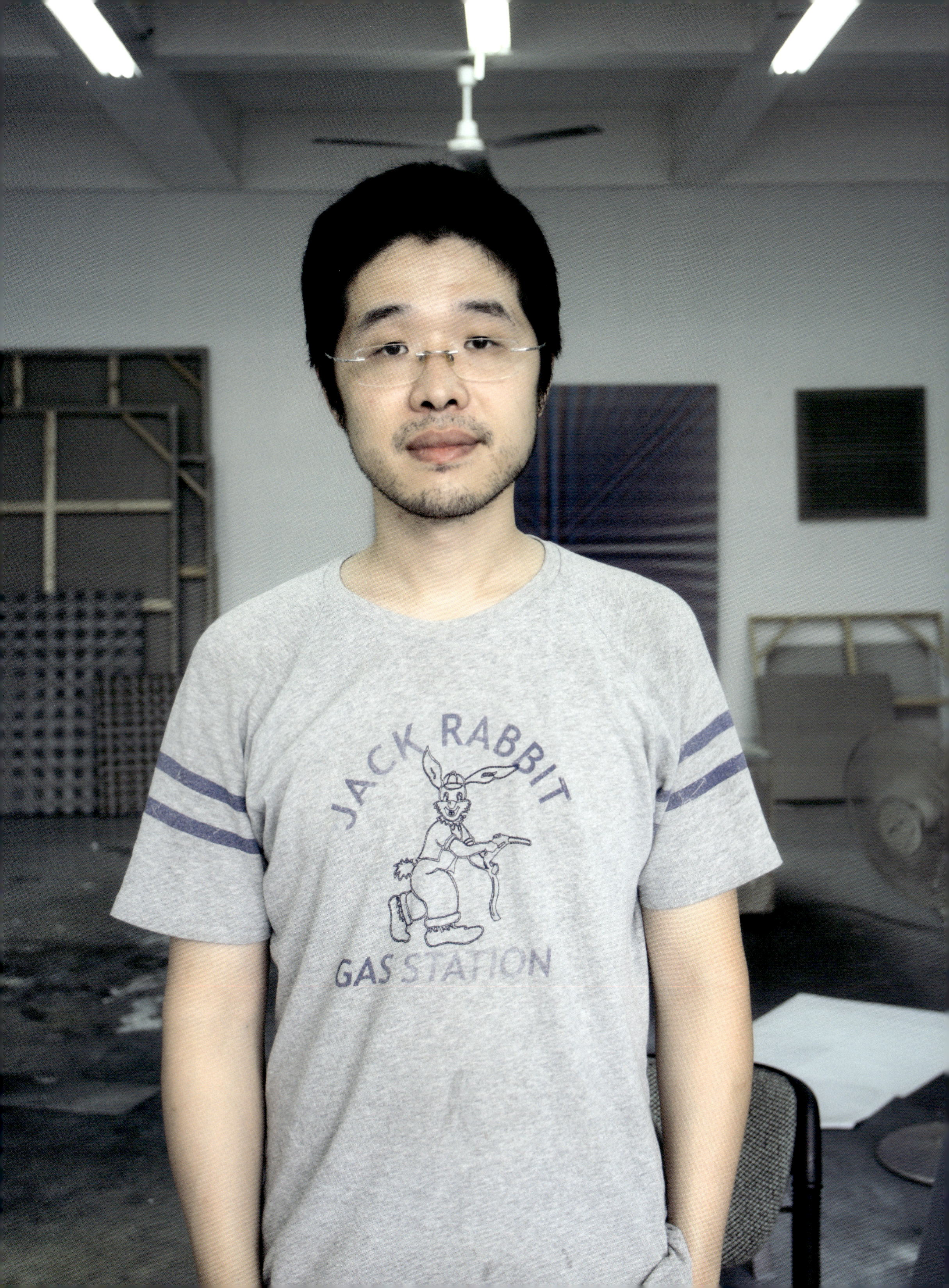

JACK RABBIT
GAS STATION

Ever since the end of 2011, I have chosen to use squares as the only element to create works. When copied, these squares form a matrix. They connect with each other to make up one single structure, an entire organization, in which a certain type of order and rules are embedded.

Every work is the product of a multiplication of the innumerable layers of a cubical matrix. The transparency and opacity of each layer of the matrix are under my control, in order to fit my needs. The cubical matrix in the painting changes according to specific rules—enlarge, shrink, shift, or appear as multiplications of half-transparent layers. The multiplication of every layer thus breaks through the order that was created and established by the previous one, establishing a new order. The shape of the cubical matrix gradually becomes blurrier in the painting; it melts and becomes less certain. What gradually appears and replaces it is a "path" of change, which little by little gains strength and becomes more prominent. Every action that I carry out on the cubical matrix influences the shape of this "path," and it dissolves into the "path" itself.

The relation between numbers—whether it is the ratio with which every layer in the cubical matrix is enlarged or reduced, the number of layers, the size of the squares, or the distance they shift—is hidden within. The relation between these numbers functions like "genes." They determine the relative relation between the different layers of the cubical matrix, as well as the development and final shape of its "path."

- Shang Yixin

从2011年底开始，我选择用方格作为唯一的元素来创作作品，方格被复制组成矩阵，它们互相交接形成一个结构，一个整体组织，其中暗藏了一种秩序和规则。

每件作品都是N层方格矩阵互相叠加的结果。我将每一层的方格矩阵都控制在我所需要的透明度和浓度上。方格矩阵在画面中按照一定的规则相对变化着——放大，缩小，移动，并呈半透明状互相叠加——每一层的叠加都在打破着上一层所制造和确立的秩序，同时建立起新的秩序。方块矩阵的形态渐渐得在画面中模糊、溶解，变得不确定；随之渐渐出现并取而代之的是一种变化的"轨迹"，渐渐的被强化和凸显出来。我对方格矩阵实施的每一个动作都影响着"轨迹"的形态，并消融于"轨迹"之中。

数字关系——每一层方格矩阵放大或缩小的比率，层数的多少，方格的大小，移动的距离等等——隐藏于其中，这些数字关系起着类似于"基因"的作用，决定着一层层方格矩阵之间的相对关系，决定着"轨迹"的生长和最终形态。

- 尚一心

Shang Yixin, *2096*, 2012, acrylic on canvas, 82 5/8 x 78 3/4 in. (210 x 200 cm), acquired in 2012
尚一心，《2096》，2012, 布面丙烯，82 5/8 x 78 3/4 寸 (210 x 200 厘米)，收藏于 2012

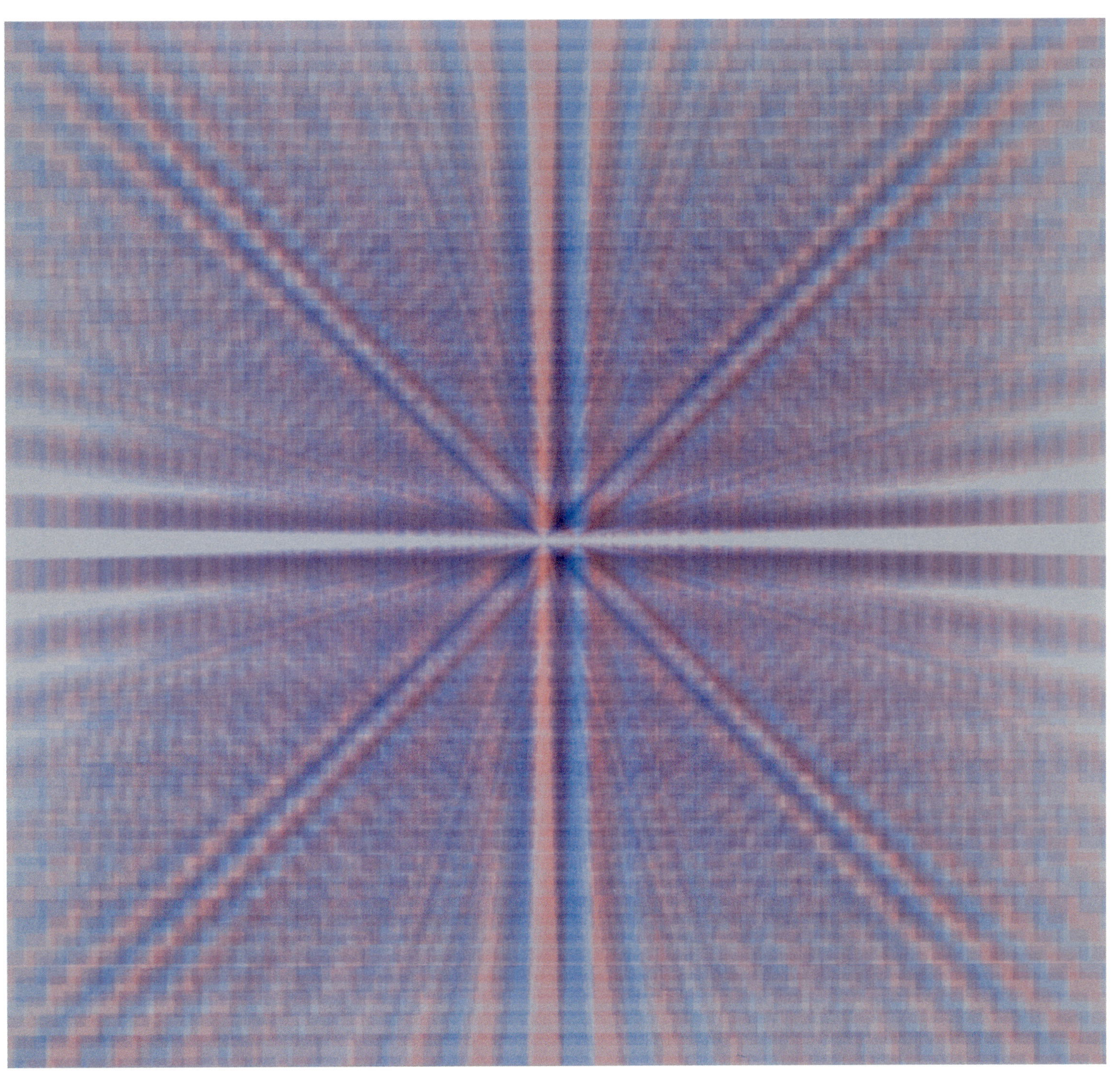

Shang Yixin, *+1*, 2012, acrylic on canvas, 25 1/2 x 25 1/2 in. (65 x 65 cm), acquired in 2012
尚一心，《+1》，2012，布面丙烯，25 1/2 x 25 1/2 寸 (65 x 65 厘米)，收藏于 2012

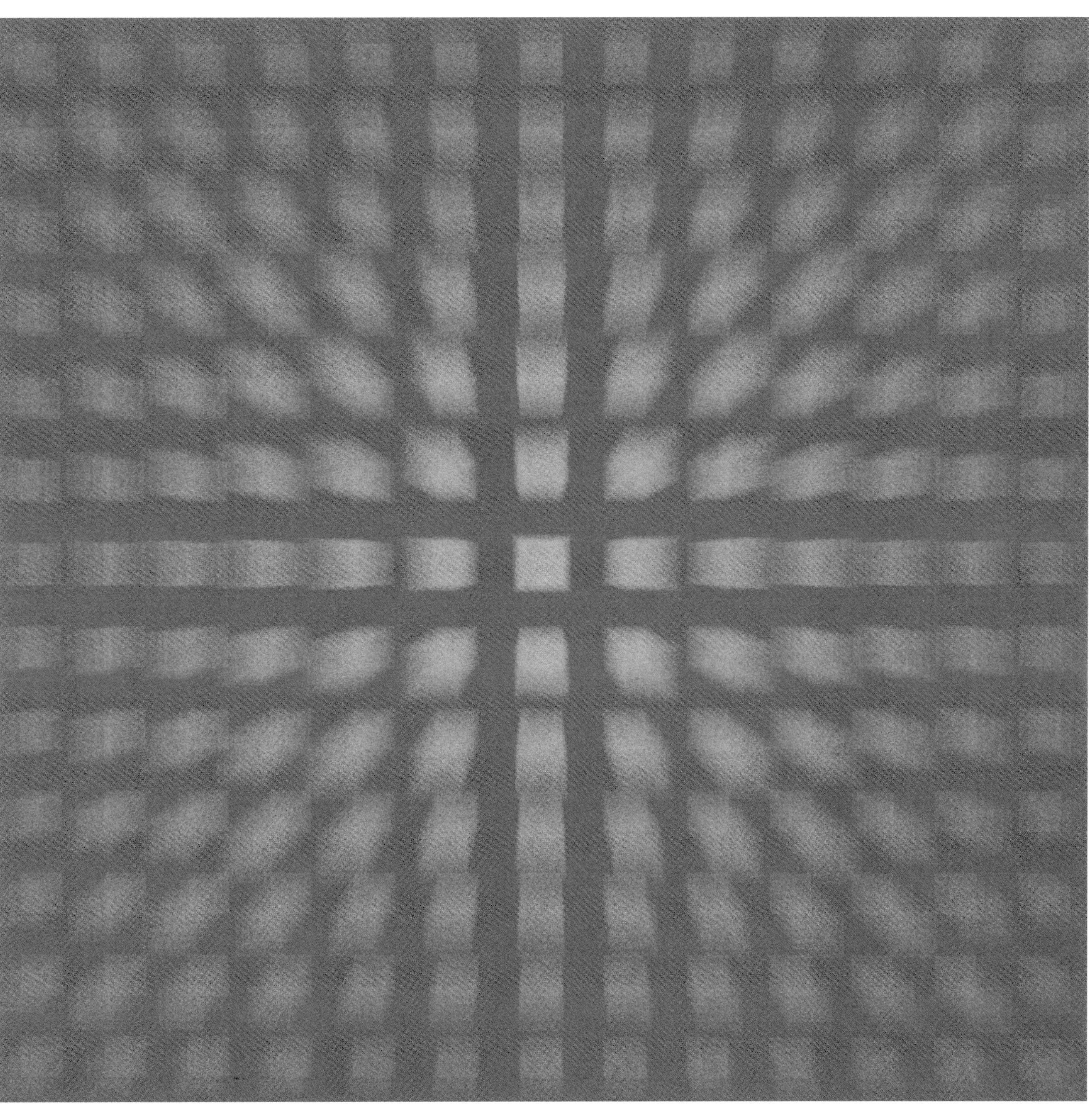

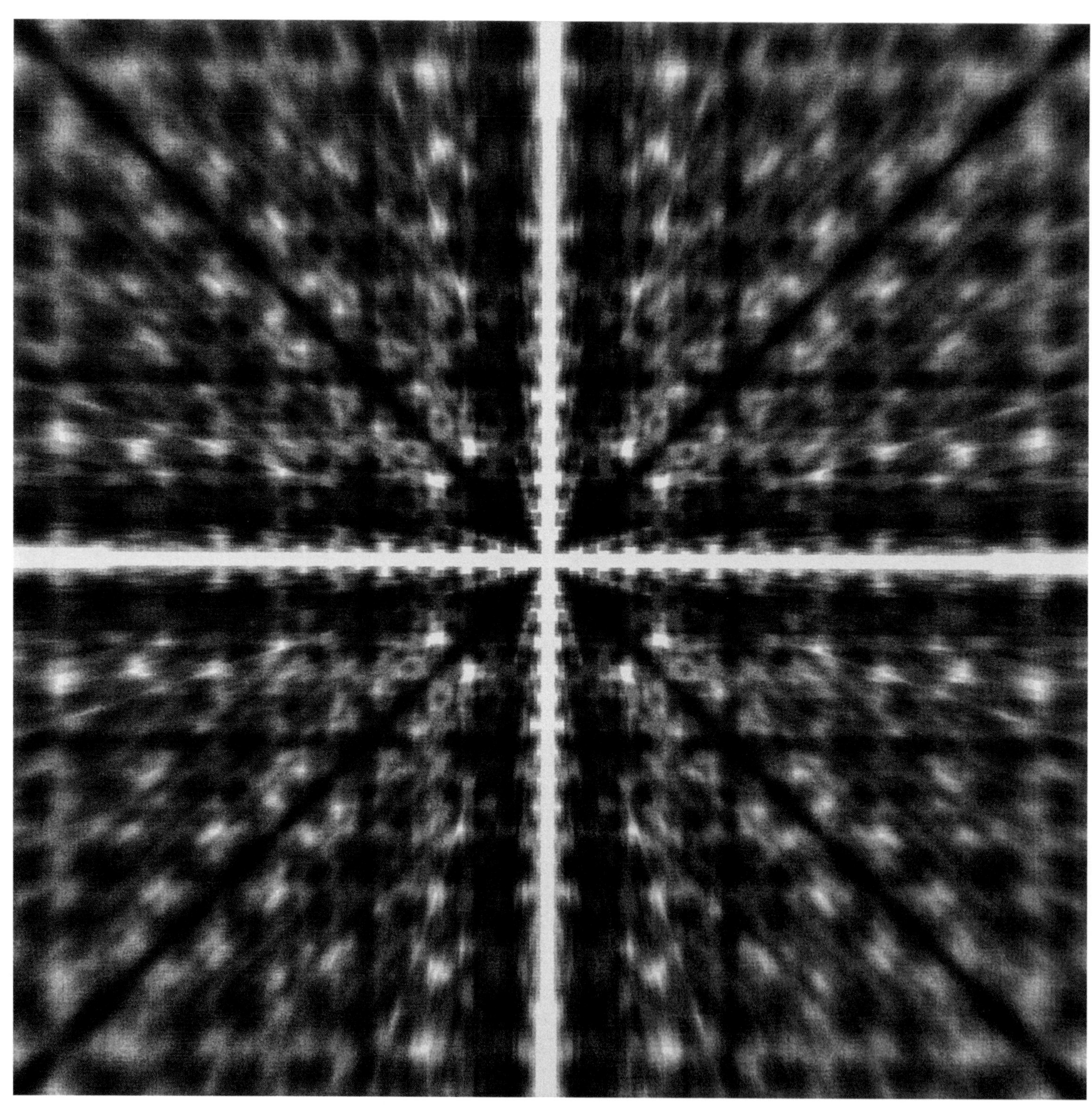

Shang Yixin, *1062*, 2012, acrylic on canvas, 39 3/8 x 39 3/8 in. (100 x 100 cm), acquired in 2012
尚一心, 《1062》, 2012, 布面丙烯, 39 3/8 x 39 3/8 寸 (100 x 100 厘米), 收藏于 2012

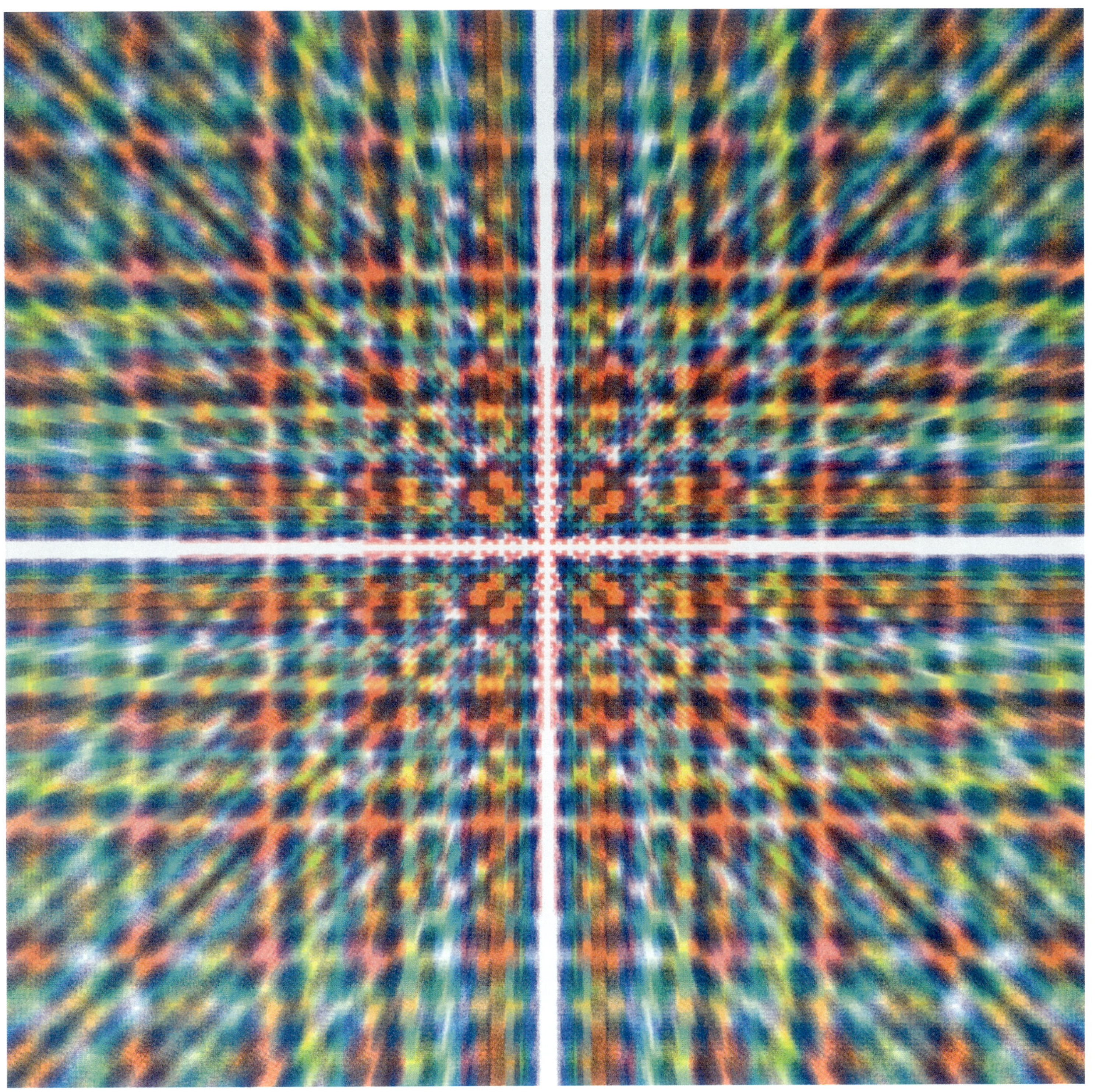

Shang Yixin, *1061*, 2012, acrylic on canvas, 47 1/4 x 47 1/4 in. (120 x 120 cm), acquired in 2012
尚一心，《1061》，2012，布面丙烯，47 1/4 x 47 1/4 寸 (120 x 120 厘米)，收藏于 2012

Wang Guangle 王光乐

Born in 1976, Fujian, China
Lives and works in Beijing, China

一九七六年生於中国福建
居住和工作於中国北京

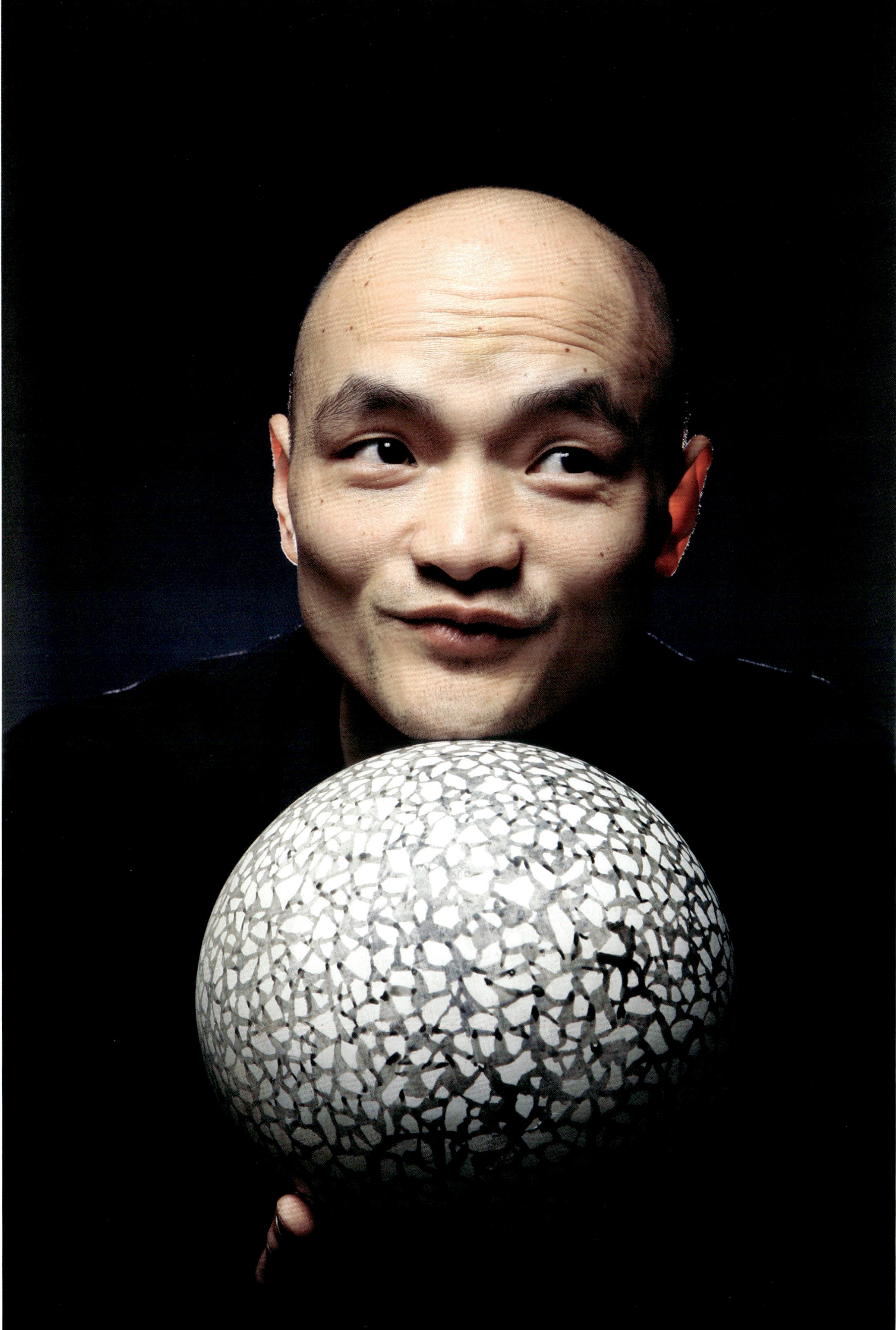

130905 originates from one of the paintings from my 2004 series "Shòuqī" (Longevity Paint), the title of the piece is the date I finished painting it.

I painted the canvas black, and then after it dried I painted it white, and then black, and so forth... But each time I covered the canvas with the new color, I would leave the top and bottom edges of the last layer unpainted, which formed the "lines" you see on the canvas. As the lines pushed toward the center of the canvas, the last layer stopped at the width of the paintbrush.

This series of paintings come from the burial traditions from my hometown in Southern China: when an old person is not feeling well, he prepares a coffin for himself. He paints the coffin himself, but if he doesn't die, the following year on the same day he paints the coffin all over again. Some old people even paint it over dozens of times. This is called applying "longevity paint."

I was touched by the notions contained within this tradition, so I borrowed that form of applying paint to create this series of paintings.

- Wang Guangle

《130905》这件作品是起始于2004年的我的《寿漆》系列绘画作品中的一件，作品名称是这件作品的结束的日期。

我把画布涂成黑色，等干了后再把它涂成白色，然后再涂黑色，如此反复。不过，每一次覆盖都留出上一层上下端的边缘，这样就形成了画面中的"线"，随着"线"向画面中间推进，最后一层停止在刷子的宽度上。

这个系列绘画来自我小时候南方家乡的土葬习俗：老人会在身体不好的时刻给自己准备一口棺材。他亲自为棺材刷一遍油漆，但，也许他没有死去，那么第二年的这一天他会再刷一遍，有的老人可以为自己刷上几十遍，这样的行为叫刷"寿漆"。

我被这个习俗包含的观念触动，也借用涂刷的形式形成这一系列绘画。

- 王光乐

Wang Guangle, *130905*, 2013, acrylic on canvas, 57 1/2 x 57 1/2 in. (146 x 146 cm), acquired in 2013
王光乐，《130905》，2013，布面丙烯，57 1/2 x 57 1/2 寸 (146 x 146 厘米), 收藏于 2013

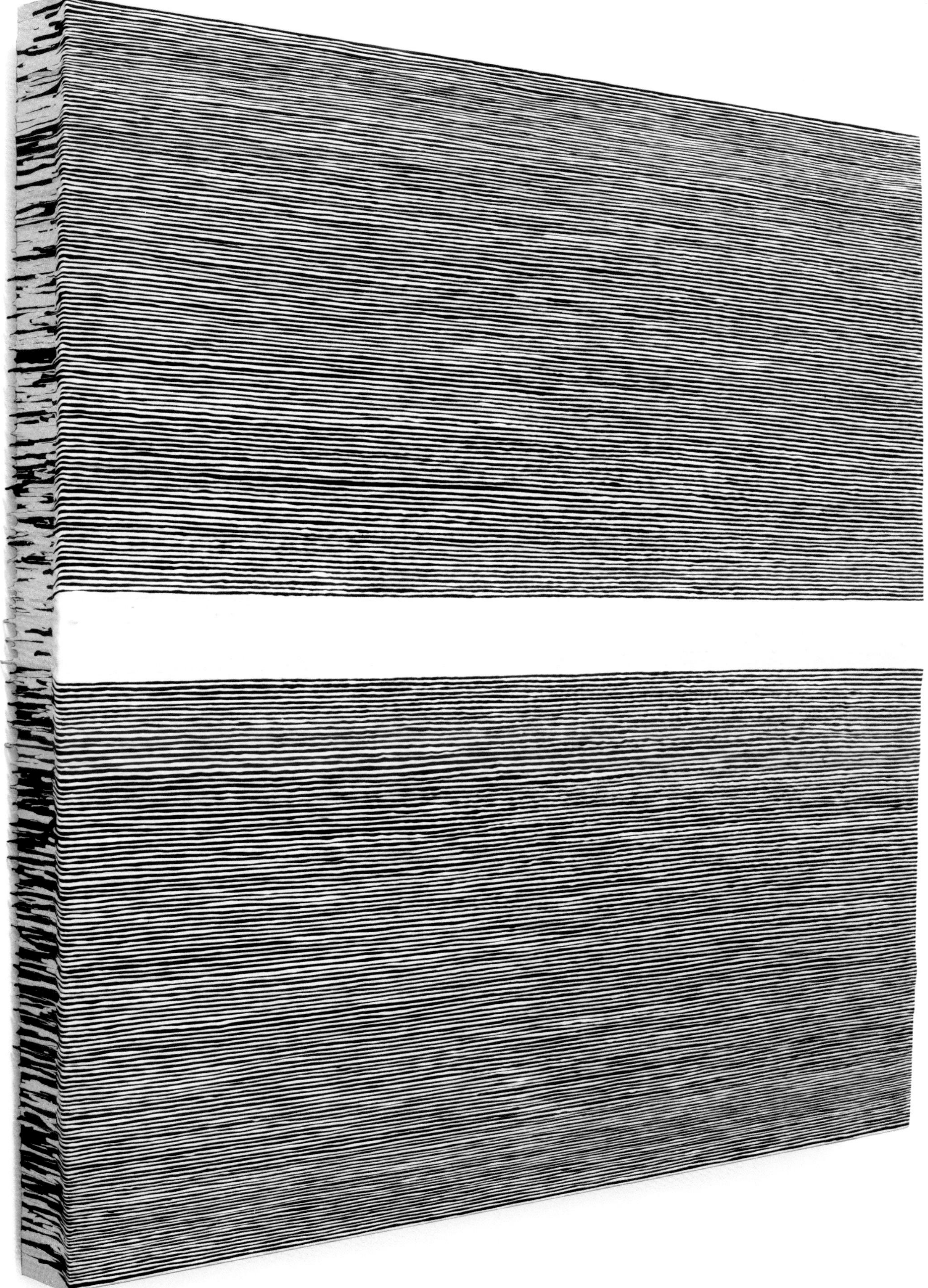

Wang Guangle, *120313*, 2012, acrylic on canvas, 78 3/4 x 79 in. (200 x 200.5 cm), acquired in 2012
王光乐，《120313》，2012，布面丙烯，78 3/4 x 79 寸 (200 x 200.5 厘米)，收藏于 2012

Wang Xingwei 王兴伟

Born in 1969, Liaoning, China
Lives and works in Beijing, China

一九六九年生於中国辽宁
居住和工作於中国北京

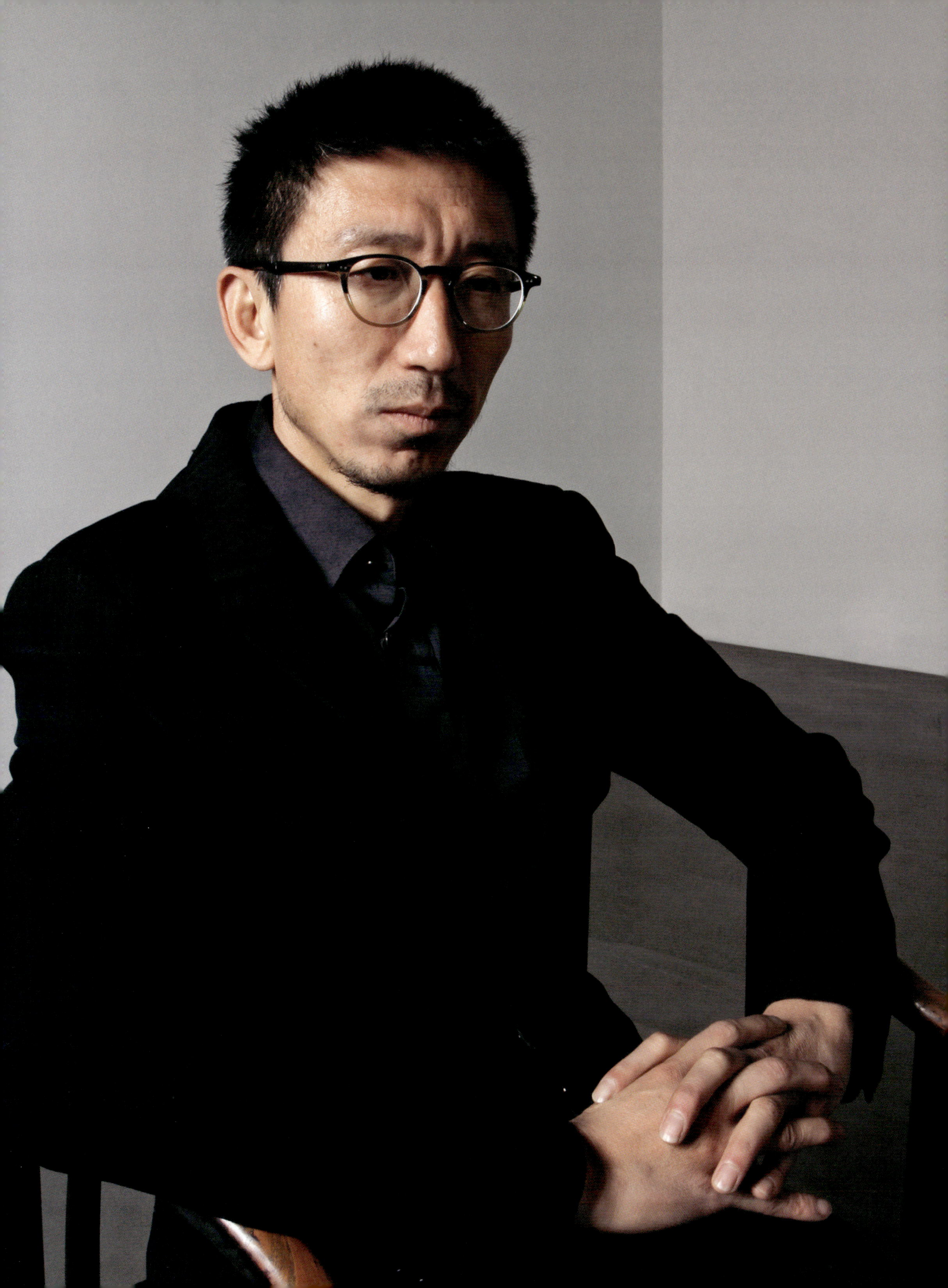

The character of Comrade Xiao He series is a female soldier of the Communist Party before the year of 1949, and she is actually a "nurse assistant." At that time, there was a certain number of female intellectuals in the pursuit of romantic revolution and love, so they left big cities and threw themselves into arduous and difficult revolutionary lives. The content of these paintings is that Xiao He is left behind the big troop, so she is on the way to catch up with the others.

The scenery of *Comrade Xiao He No.2* and *Comrade Xiao He No.3* is based on the vast and monotonous landscapes in Northern China, with the perspective of looking upward, which emphasizes the three-dimensional and perspectival effect of the figure in movement. The proportion and the shape of the body have been manipulated in an exaggerated manner.

The character seems to be frozen in time and space.

- Wang Xingwei

《小何同志》中人物是1949年之前的共产党部队中的女兵，是"卫生员"。当时有一些知识女性向往浪漫的革命和爱情，离开城市投奔到艰苦的革命生活。画面上表现的内容是她跟部队分散了，她正奔跑在追赶队伍的路上。

《小何同志》2和《小何同志》3中的景物都是北方辽阔、单调的景色，用的视角是仰视，强化了的运动中的立体和透视效果。人体比例，形体都遭到任意和夸张的变形处理。

人物被好像被凝结在时间和空间中。

- 王兴伟

Wang Xingwei, *Comrade Xiao He No. 3*, 2008, oil on canvas, 78 3/4 x 60 5/8 in. (200 x 154 cm), acquired in 2009
王兴伟，《小何同志》3，2008，布面油画，78 3/4 x 60 5/8 寸 (200 x 154 厘米)，收藏于 2009

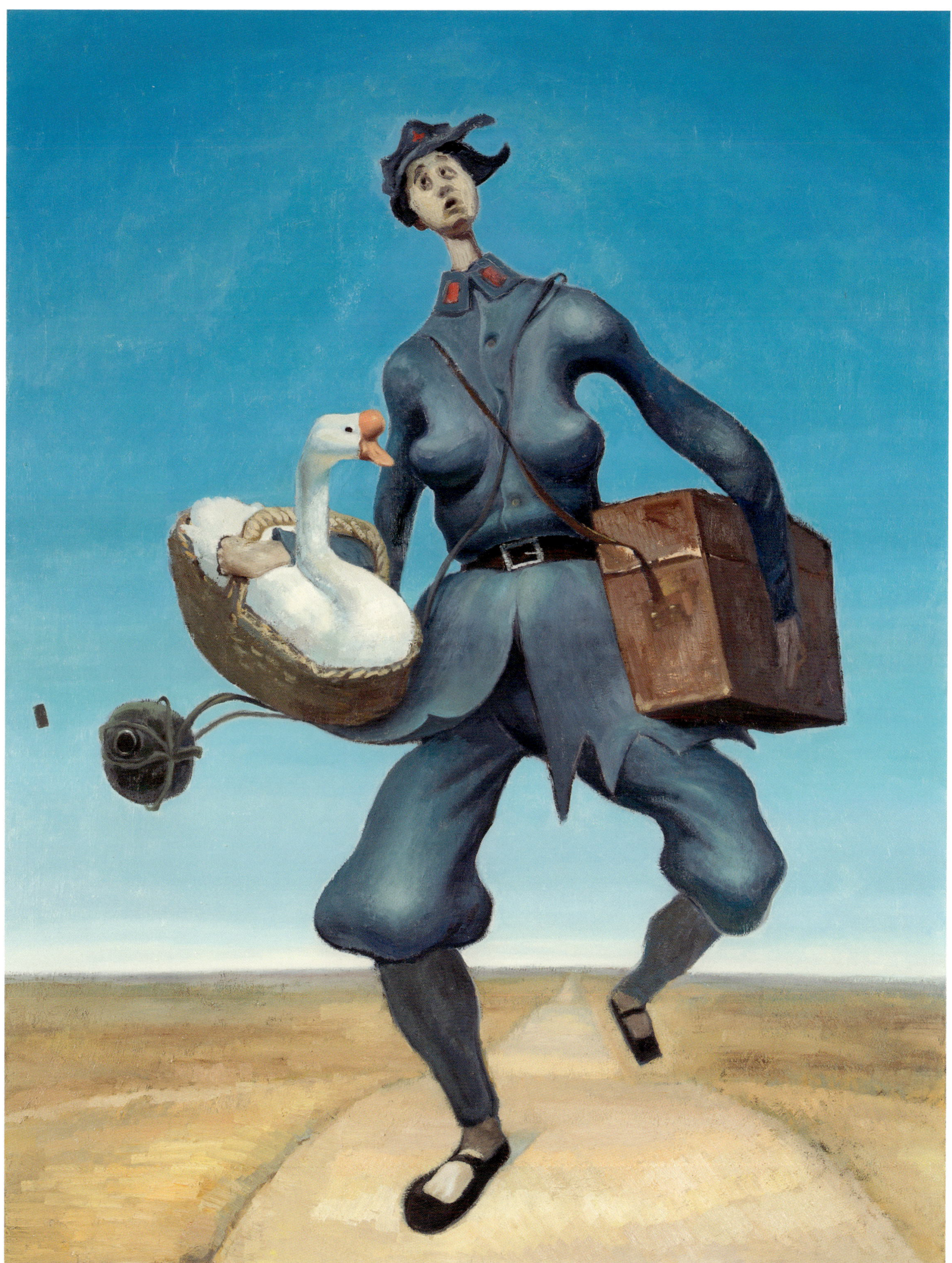

Wang Xingwei, *Comrade Xiao He No. 2*, 2008, oil on canvas, 78 3/4 x 60 5/8 in. (200 x 154 cm), acquired in 2009
王兴伟，《小何同志》2，2008，布面油画，78 3/4 x 60 5/8 寸 (200 x 154 厘米)，收藏于 2009

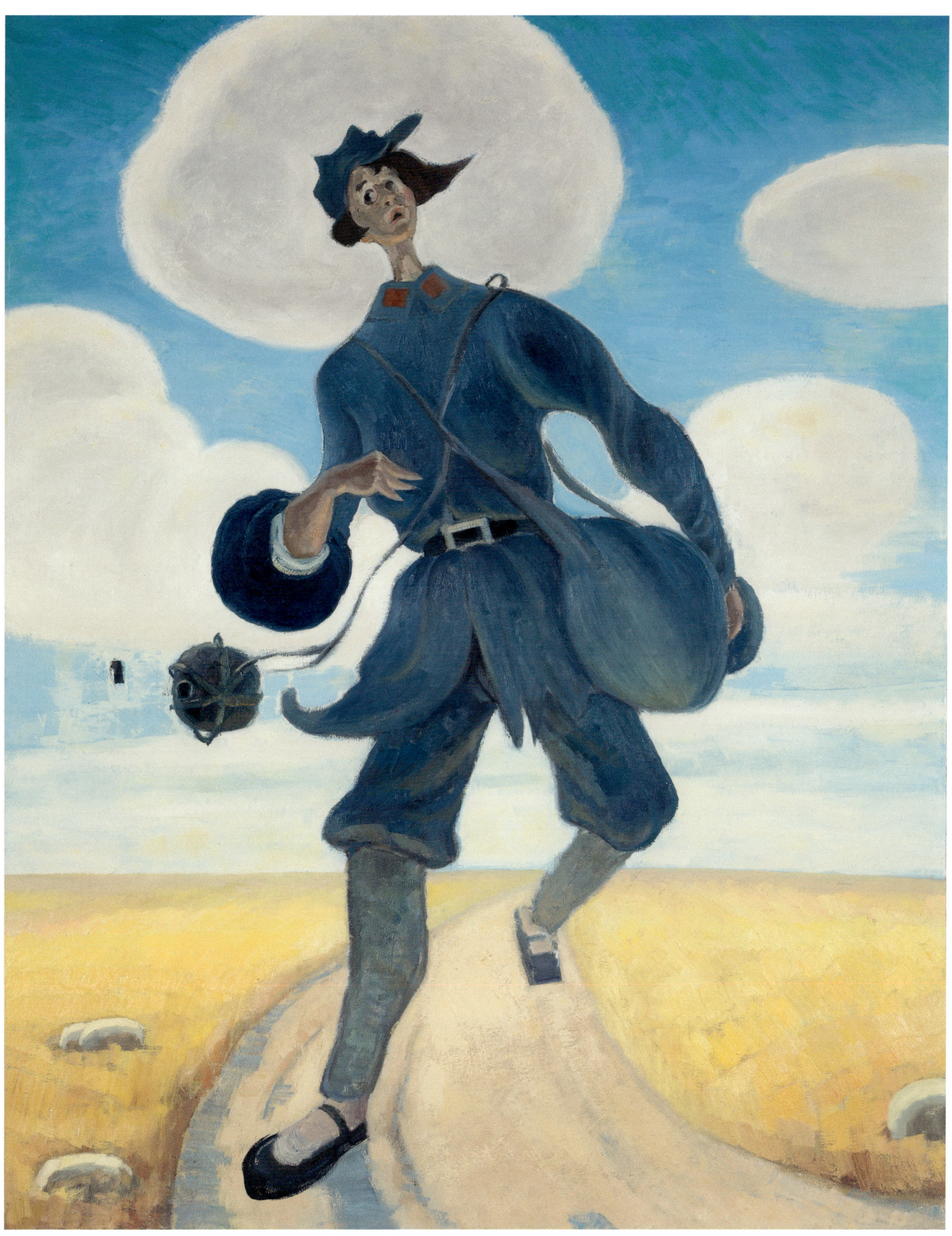

Near the Shanghai Art Museum there is an art shop and studio owned by an old painter. I commissioned him to do a group of abstract paintings and three nudes; he could decide what to paint. We signed a contract so that I can sign my name and sell or exhibit them as my own works.

This piece is one of them although I made some changes. Female nudes are a common theme in Western art. In China, besides the sketching practies in art schools, female nudes belong to the main category of "suiting the taste of the 'boss'" type of painting. There were originally two naked women in the painting. I eliminated one woman and added a goose with its head in the water and its butt above the water.

In Western traditional paintings, women and geese are common mythological topics but the combination of the Chinese style village scene, a Chinese woman and goose seem more like a country style painting. The naked woman is staring at the half of the goose's butt that is above the water. There is a sharp contrasting relationship between the naked woman and the goose. The most direct Western association of a naked woman and goose would be "Leda and the Swan." But the Chinese person, the Chinese style pond and the white farm goose's distasteful gesture seem extremely unfitting for Western mythology.

- Wang Xingwei

上海美术馆边上有一家画店兼画室，是一个老画家开的，我向他定制了一批抽象画和三张人体画，画什么他自己决定，我们签了一个合同，我可以签我的名字作为我的作品展出和出售。

这幅作品是其中之一，我做了一些改动。裸女题材在西方艺术中很常见，在中国除了学院的写生练习，主要的一个门类是迎合"老板"口味的"行画"。原来画面有两个裸女，我去掉一个女人，加上一只白鹅，头扎进水里，屁股露出水面。

西方传统绘画中女人和鹅是个常见的神话题材，而中国乡村风景、中国妇女和鹅组合在一起，更像农村风俗画，裸女注视着半截露出水面的鹅屁股，使得裸女和鹅之间建立了明显对应关系，而裸女和鹅最直接的西方式联想就是丽达和天鹅。而画面的中国人，中国式水塘、农家白鹅的不雅姿态和西方神话都是格格不入的。

- 王兴伟

Wang Xingwei, *Untitled (Nude Woman by the River)*, 2003, oil on canvas, 27 3/8 x 39 in. (69.5 x 99 cm), acquired in 2011
王兴伟，《无题（河边裸女）》，2003，布面油画，27 3/8 x 39 寸 (69.5 x 99 厘米)，收藏于 2011

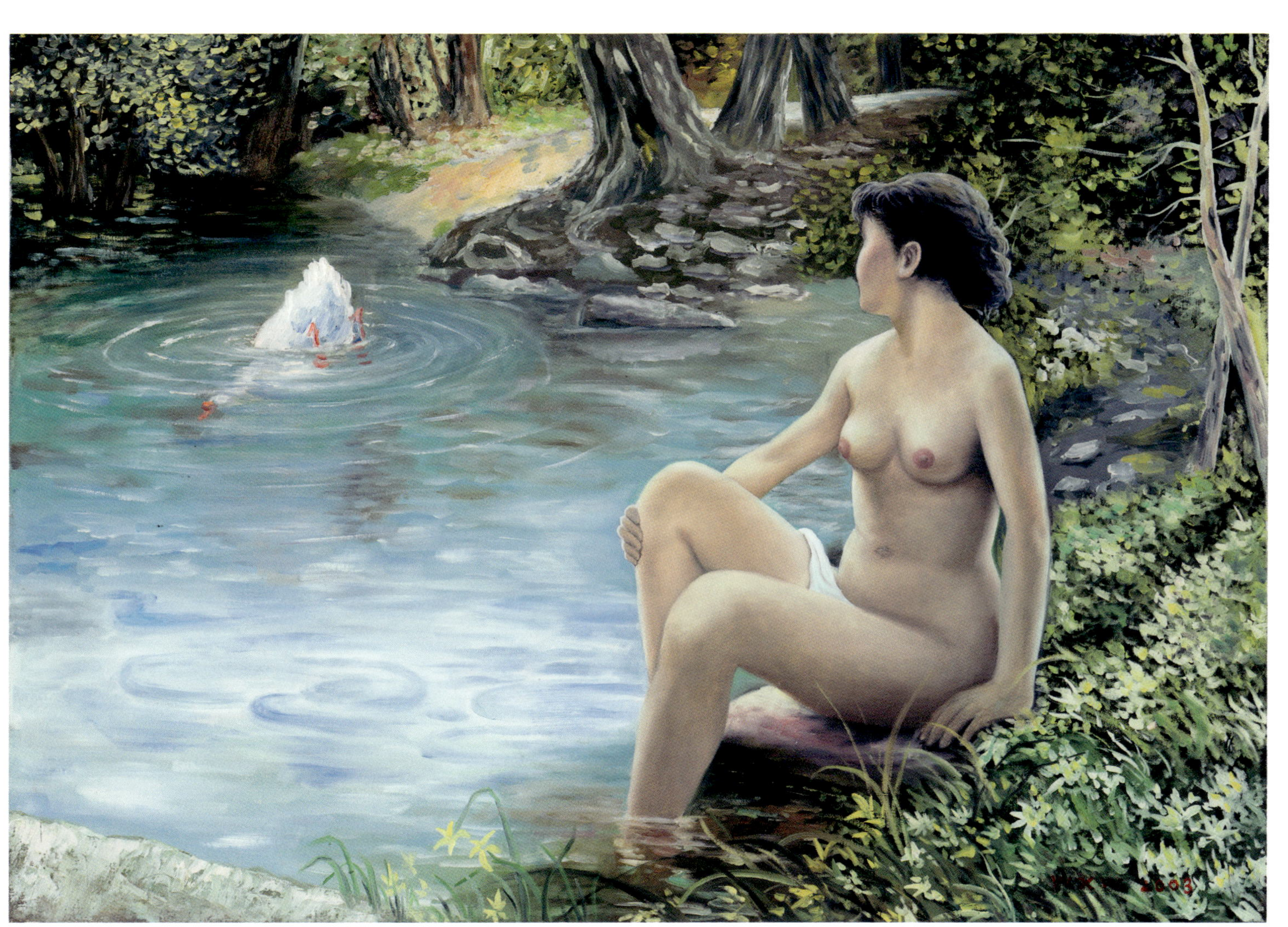

Xie Molin 谢墨凛

Born in 1979, Zhejiang , China
Lives and works in Beijing, China

一九七九年生於中国浙江
居住和工作於中国北京

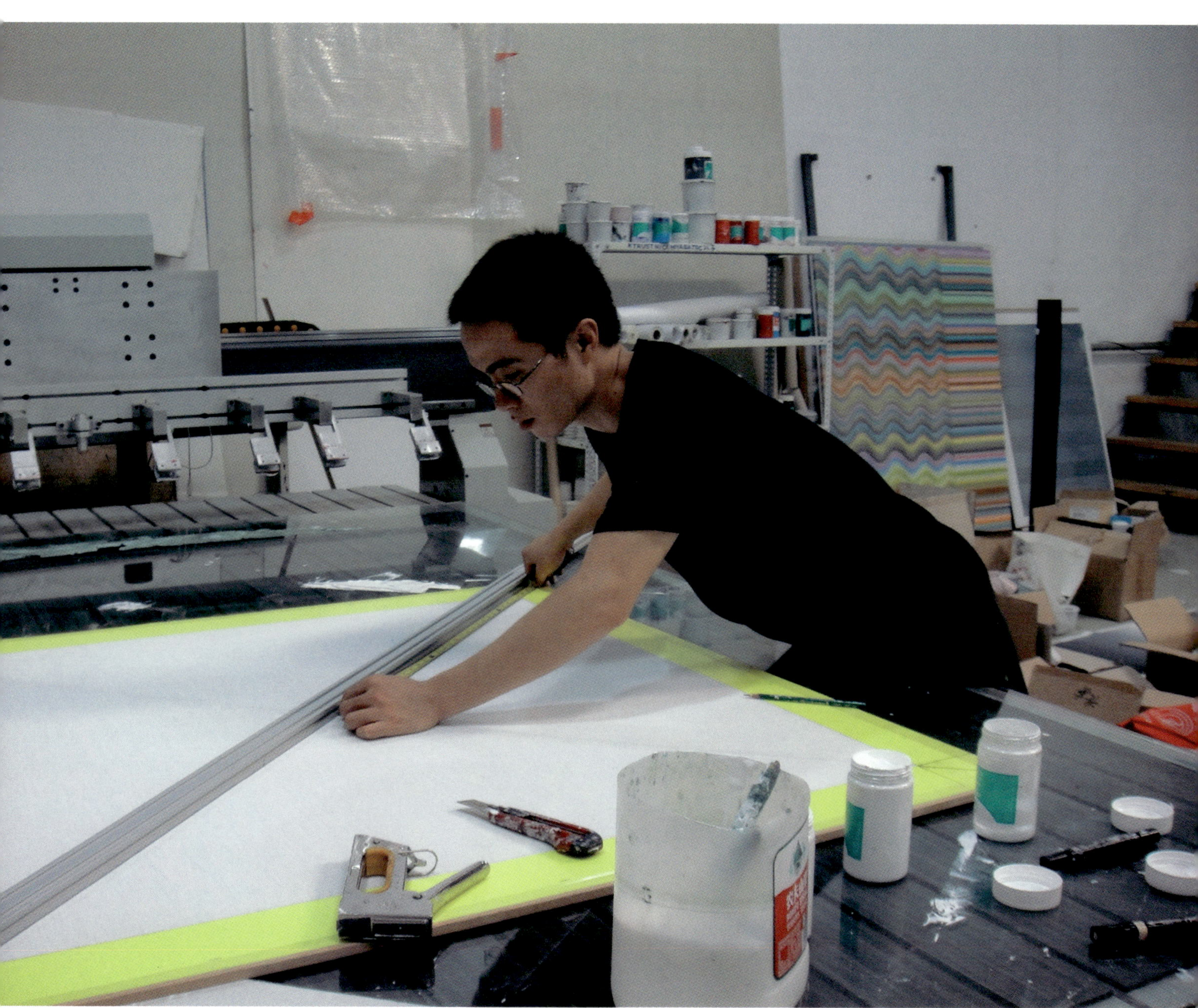

Xie Molin, *Gradation No. 3*, 2012, acrylic on canvas, 68 7/8 x 171 5/8 in. (175 x 436 cm), acquired in 2012
谢墨凛，《渐 3》，2012，布面丙烯，68 7/8 x 171 5/8 寸 (175 x 436 厘米)，收藏于 2012

Xie Molin, *Four Shades of Gray*, 2011, acrylic on canvas, 37 1/2 x 48 7/8 in. (94 x 124 cm), acquired in 2012
谢墨凛, 四种灰度, 2011, 布面丙烯, 37 1/2 x 48 7/8 寸 (94 x 124 厘米), 收藏于 2012

The works shown in this exhibition have been made with a digitally controlled triaxial drawing device that I built myself. There is a serrated blade attached to the machine that cuts out paint in lines according to patterns previously programmed on the computer. The accurate movements of the digital machine and the blade's teeth carve out the patterns and structures in the propylene paint on the canvas, thus directly determining the final viewing effect of the painting.

The idea of building this drawing device started in 2005 when I used a character-carving machine in my painting. These carving machines are commonly seen in the common shabby small street shops that print billboards and other advertisements—you can find these shops all over China. Through applying and understanding these carving machines I started to try to build my own drawing device as a creative tool in 2008. Since industrial technology has become more widespread and developed in China over the last 30 years, it was quite easy for me to get in contact with the technology I needed. In early 2011 I finished this machine that I am currently using. The present series of abstract works focuses on the unification of the concept of a painting and its visual experience. By applying the technology of digital machines to painting, I hope to enrich the possibilities for paintings in the digital age.

- Xie Molin

这次展览上的作品是通过我制作的数控三轴联动绘画机器来完成的。这台机器上装有一个很长的锯齿状刮板，机器在电脑的控制下在颜料上刮出事先在电脑中制作好的路径轨迹。精确的数控机械运动轨迹和刮板的锯齿形状塑造了画面上丙烯颜料的形状和结构，直接决定了最终的画面观看效果。

制作绘画机器的想法开始2005我将刻字机运用到绘画中，这些刻字机常见于中国街边简陋的广告牌制作小店中，通过对它的运用和理解，我开始在2008年尝试自己制作绘画机器，作为创作工具，由于中国在过去三十年中工业技术普及和发展，使我有机会比较容易的接触到我需要的技术。在2011初我完成这台目前创作使用的机器。目前创作的抽象系列作品关注的是绘画的观念和视觉体验的统一，希望通过将数控机械技术运用于绘画而丰富绘画在数字时代的可能性。

- 谢墨凛

Xie Molin, *S*, 2012, acrylic on canvas, 63 1/2 x 87 1/4 in. (161.5 x 221.5 cm), acquired in 2012
谢墨凛, S, 2012, 布面丙烯, 63 1/2 x 87 1/4 寸 (161.5 x 221.5 厘米), 收藏于 2012

Xu Zhen 徐震

Born in 1977, Shanghai, China
Lives and works in Shanghai, China

一九七七年生於中国上海
居住和工作於中国上海

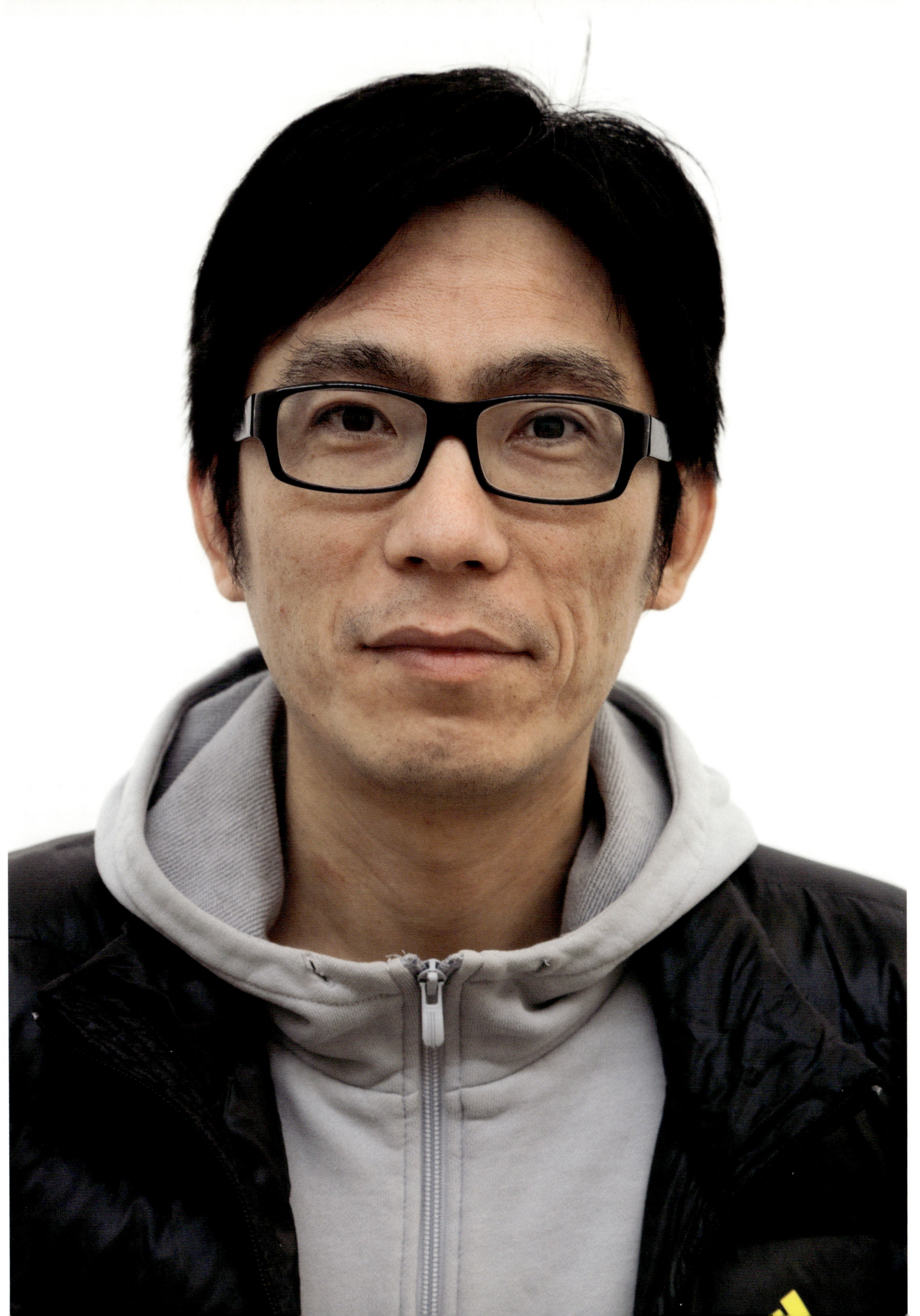

The series of works "Spread," started in 2009 with the exhibition *Seeing One's Own Eyes – Middle East Contemporary Art Exhibition*, and consists of pictorial scenes combining international political cartoons, caricatures, medieval images, exotic bestiaries and other imagery in the form of cloth collages, installations and paintings.

- Xu Zhen

"蔓延"从2009年的"看见自己的眼睛"中东当代艺术展中发展而来，蔓延系列以全球的政治漫画，插图，流行图像为线索，拼接出一系列新的景观式的图景。后来经过蔓延的不断发展，由雕塑，抽象喷绘，布类拼贴等不同类型组成整个框架。织物这种材料特有的可塑性能非常精准的还原漫画中的那种条线感。

- 徐震

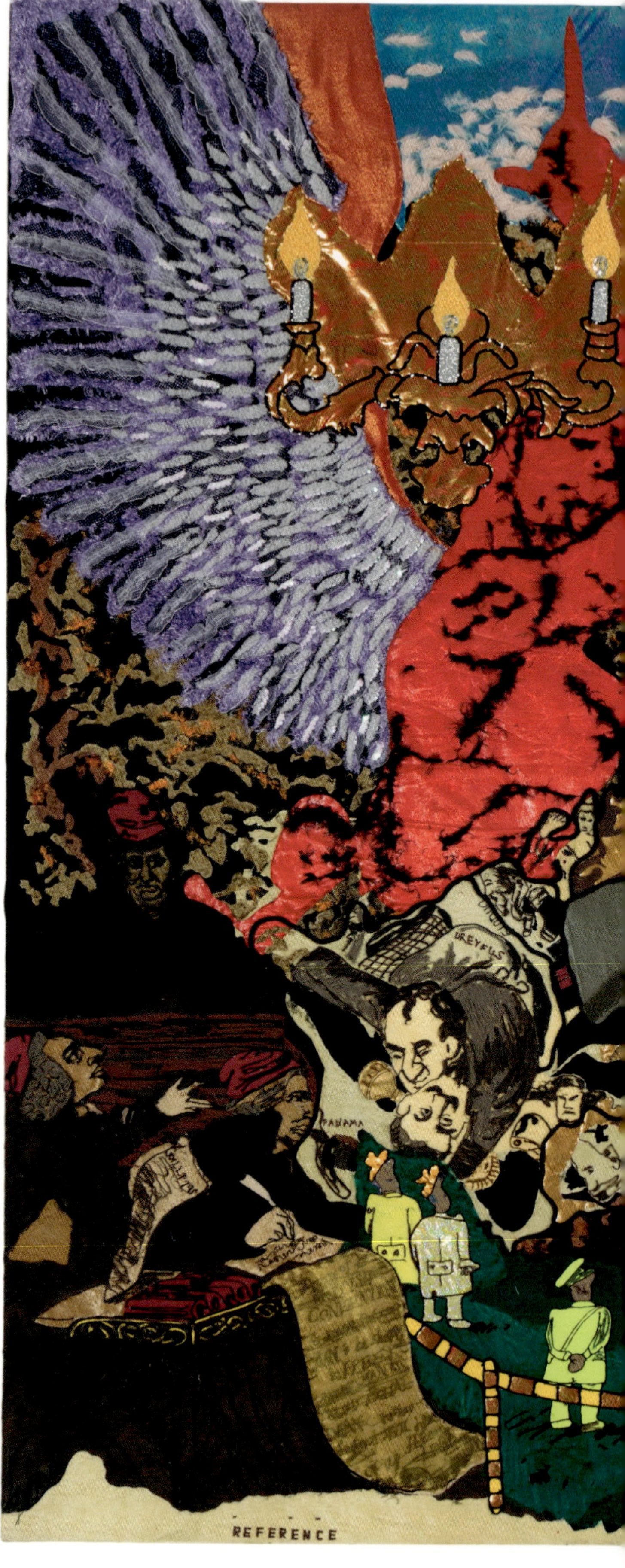

Xu Zhen, *Empire's Way of Thinking*, 2011, embroidery and plastic on canvas, 106 3/4 x 139 in. (271 x 353 cm), produced by MadeIn Company, acquired in 2011
徐震，《帝国的思考方式》，2011，刺绣和塑料在画布上，106 3/4 x 139 寸 (271 x 353 厘米)，没顶公司出品，收藏于2011

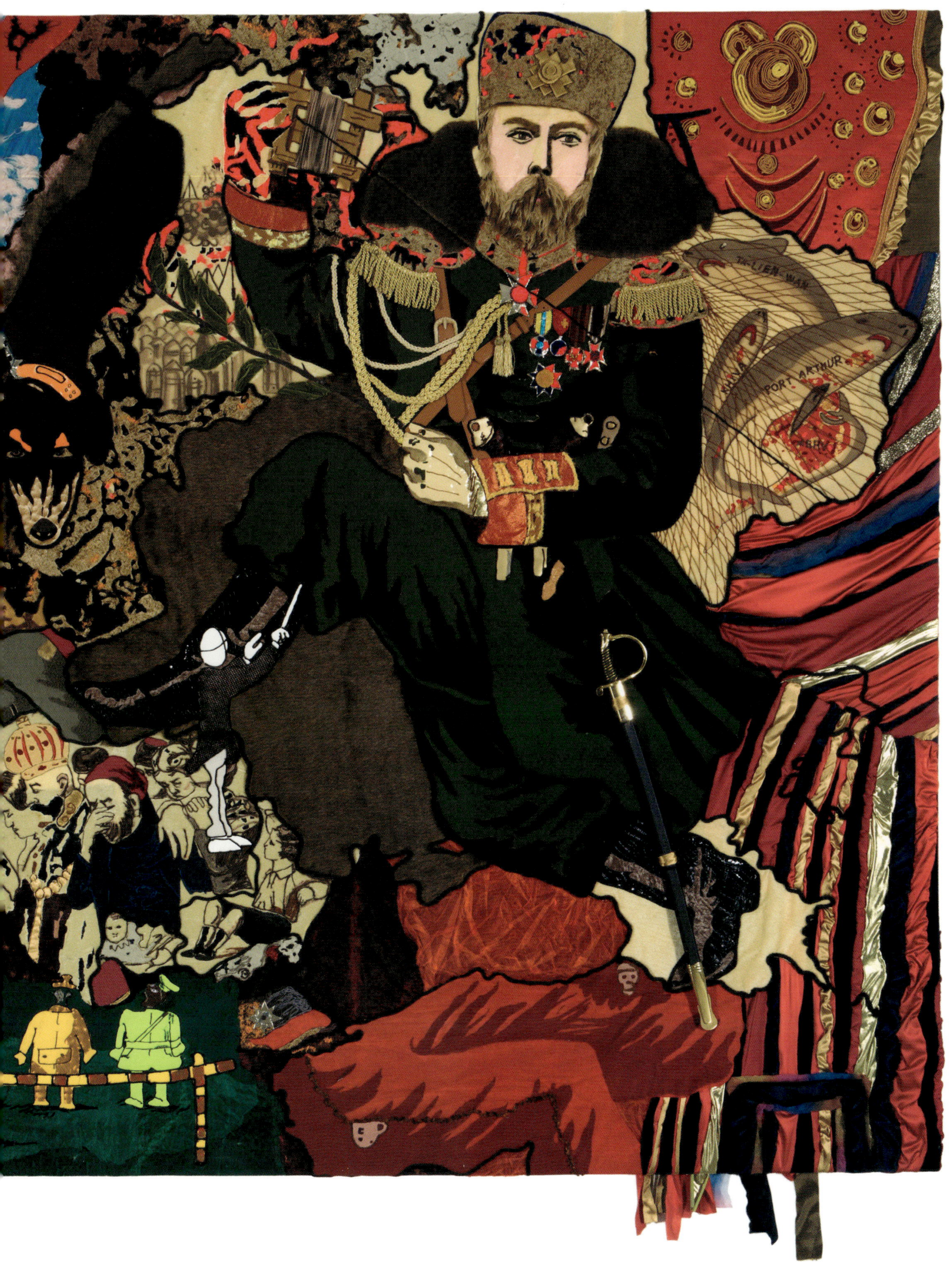
TA-LIEN-WAN
PORT ARTHUR

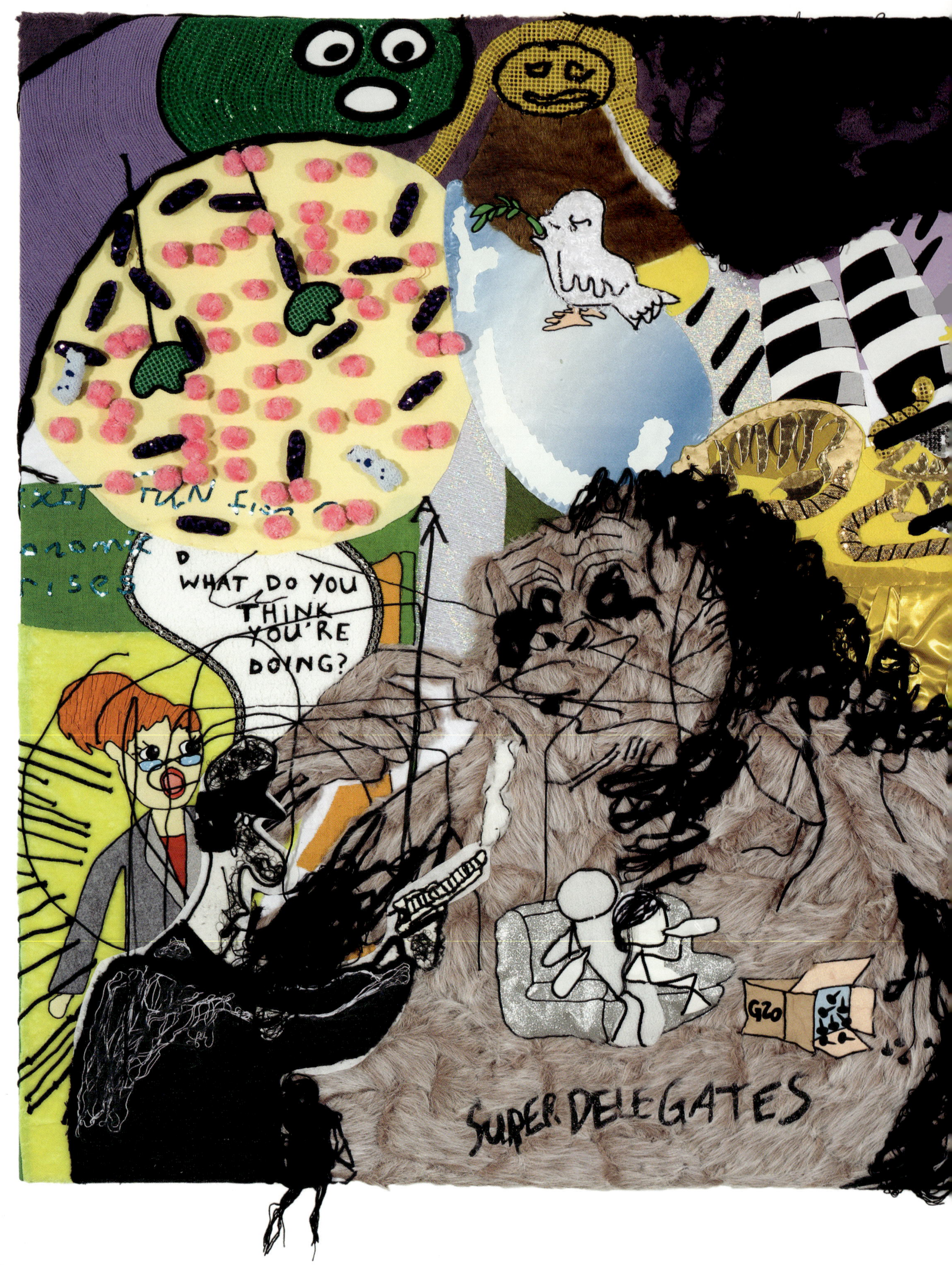
WHAT DO YOU THINK YOU'RE DOING?
SUPER DELEGATES
G20

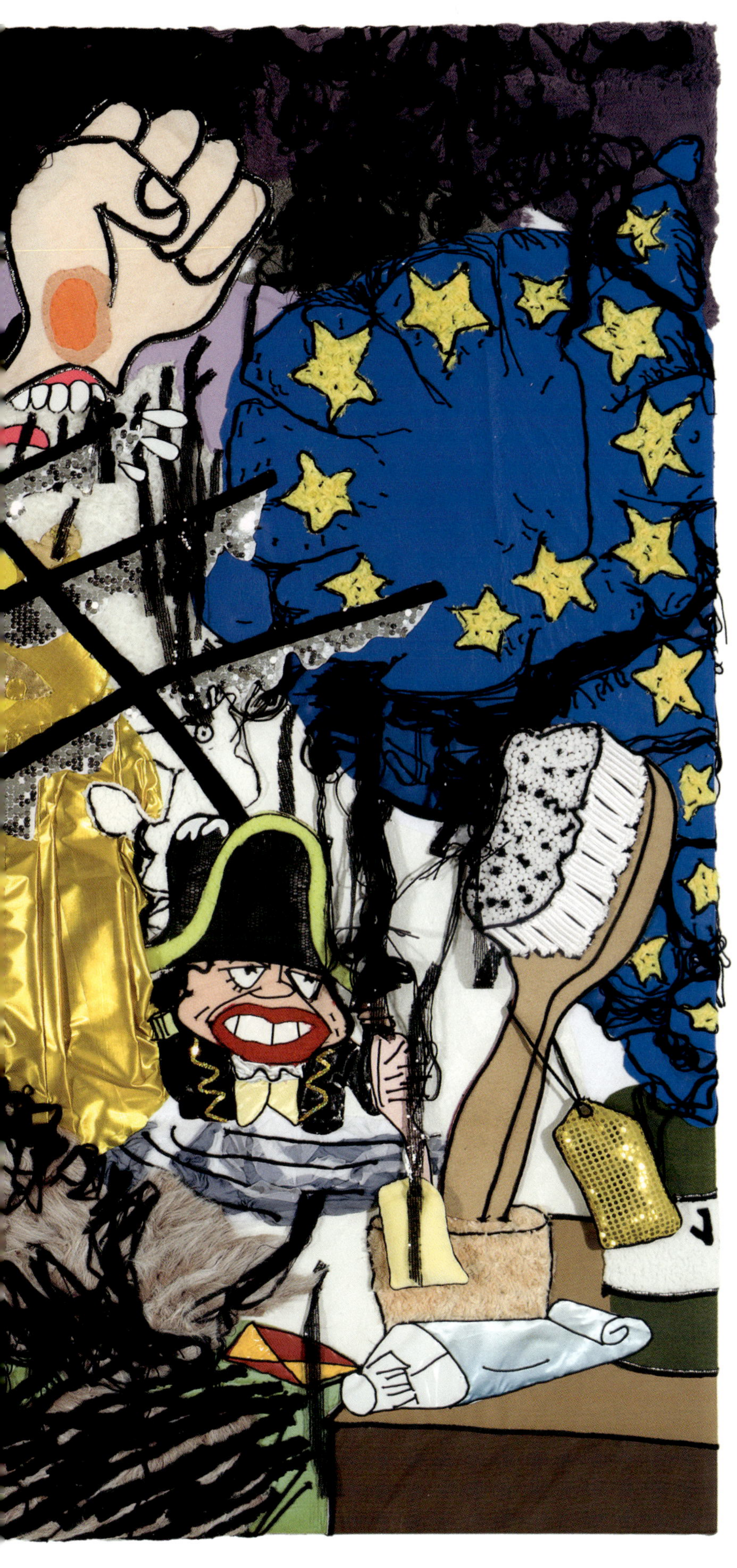

Xu Zhen, *Spread B-043*, 2010,
embroidery on canvas, 82 x 110 1/4 in.
(208 x 281 cm), produced by MadeIn
Company, acquired in 2011
徐震，《蔓延 B-043》，2010, 刺绣在画布
上，82 x 110 1/4 寸 (208 x 281 厘米)，没
顶公司出品，收藏于2011

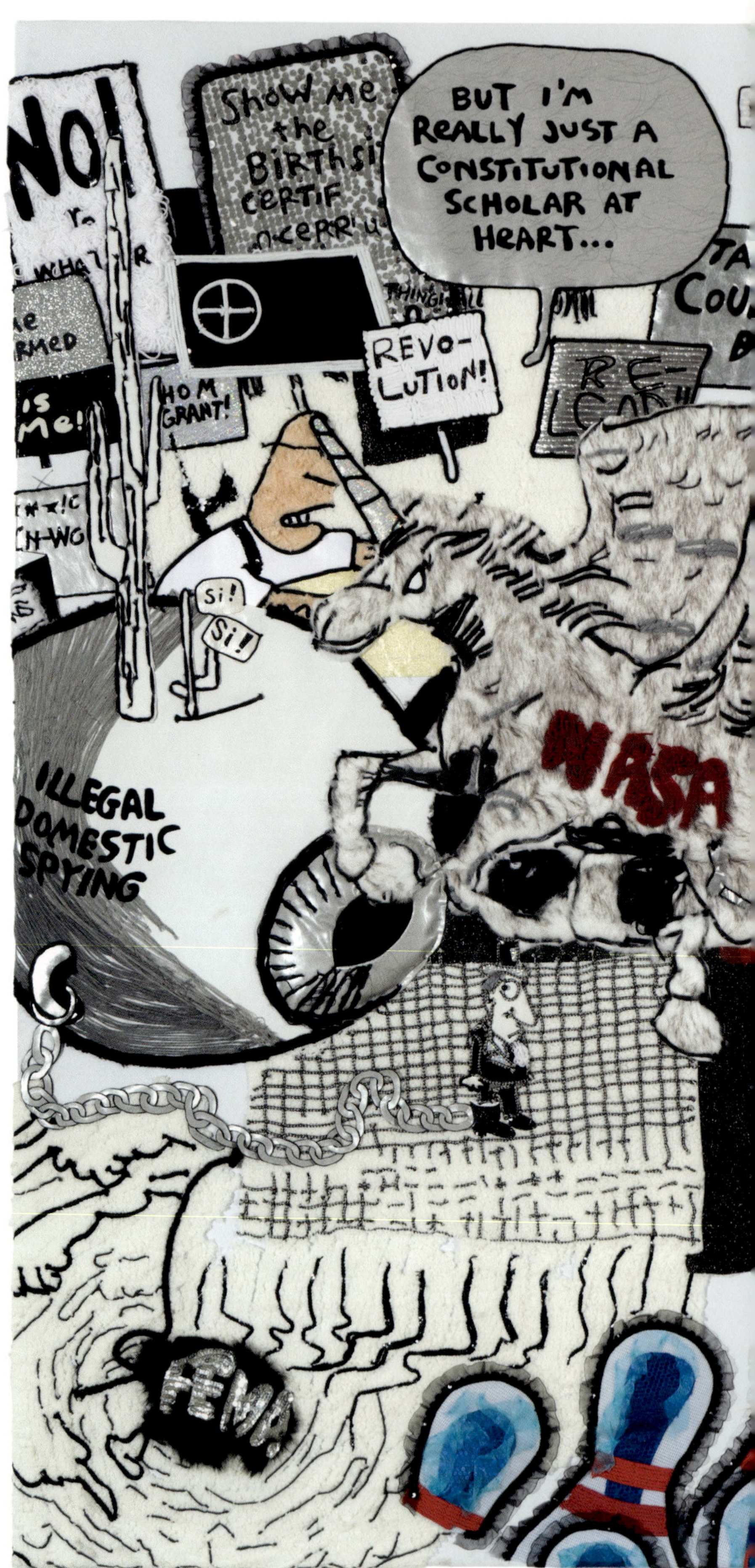

Xu Zhen, *Spread B-051*, 2010, embroidery on canvas, 80 3/4 x 108 1/2 in. (205 x 276 cm), produced by MadeIn Company, acquired in 2011
徐震，《蔓延 B-051》，2010，刺绣在画布上，80 3/4 x 108 1/2 寸 (205 x 276 厘米)，没顶公司出品，收藏于2011

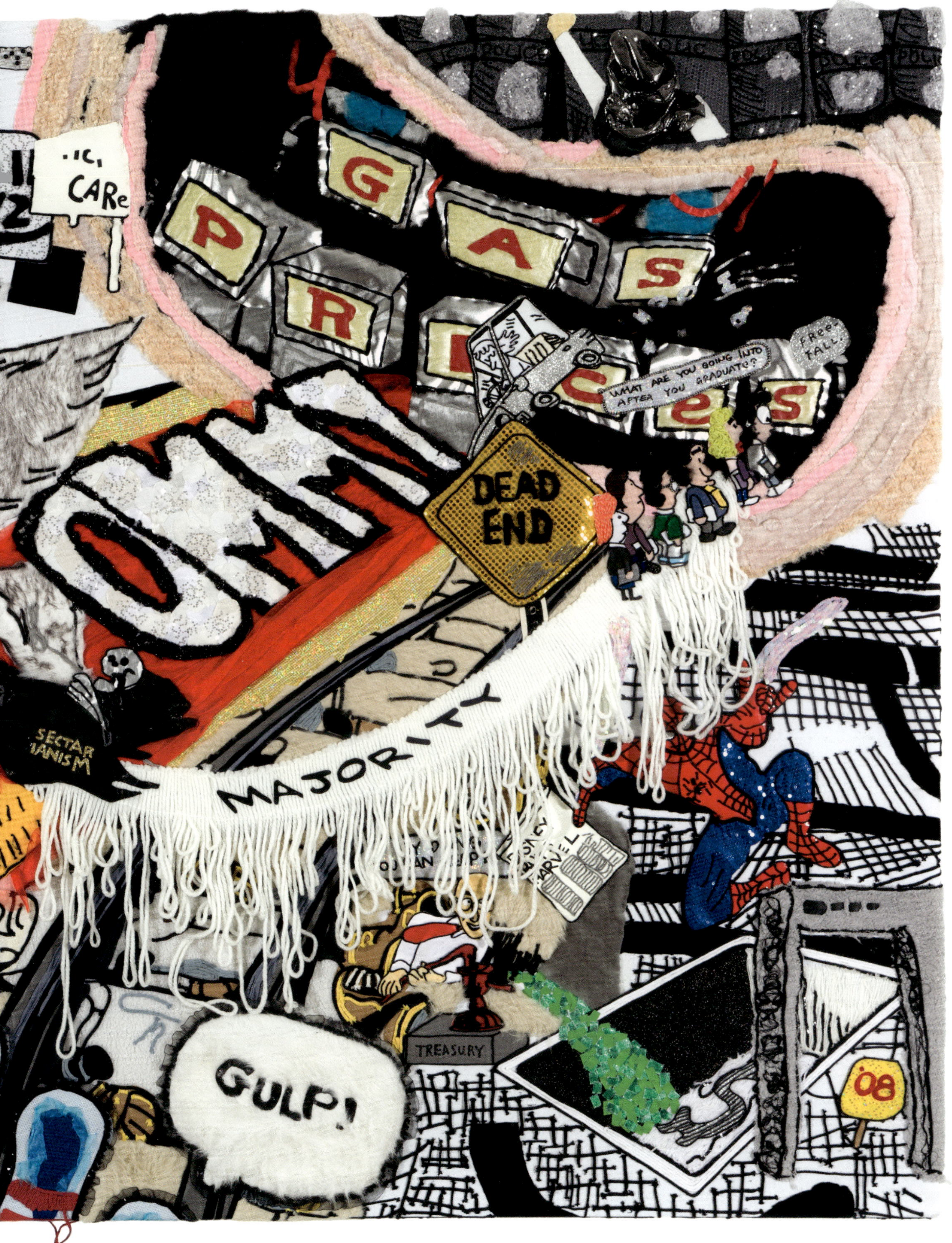
CARe
GAS PRICES
COMMI
SECTARIANISM
DEAD END
WHAT ARE YOU GOING INTO AFTER YOU GRADUATE?
FREE FALL
MAJORITY
MARVEL
TREASURY
GULP!
'08

"Spread C" is a general title for a series of soft sculptures. *Spread C-012* represents a panda attached to a dollar bill. These two elements, both coming from different American political cartoons, mock the paradoxical position of China in the world: a capitalist pet or a monster?

- Xu Zhen

蔓延C系列是蔓延的一个软体雕塑系列 。 蔓延系列以全球的政治漫画，插图，流行图像为线索， 拼接出一系列新的景观式的图景。蔓延C-012中的这只从钱中出来但是被捆绑的熊猫，源于两张美式风格的政治漫画，内容像是在调侃崛起中的中国给世界带来的双重矛盾，"资本的宠物或是怪兽"？

- 徐震

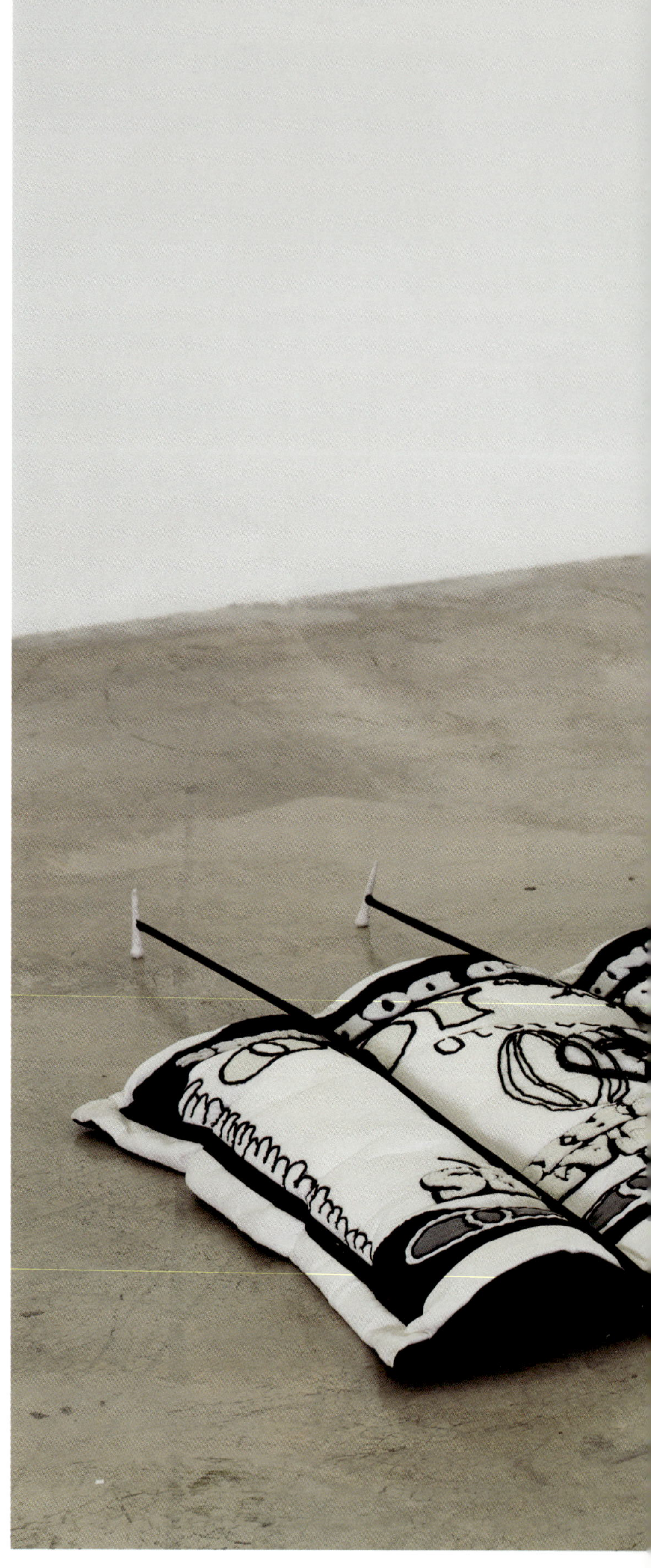

Xu Zhen, *Spread C-012*, 2010, wood, cellulose sponge, canvas and plaster board, 38 5/8 x 68 x 61 in. (98 x 173 x 155 cm), produced by MadeIn Company, acquired in 2011
徐震，《蔓延 C-012》，2010, 木头, 海绵填充物, 帆布, 石膏, 38 5/8 x 68 x 61 寸 (98 x 173 x 155 厘米)，没顶公司出品, 收藏于 2011

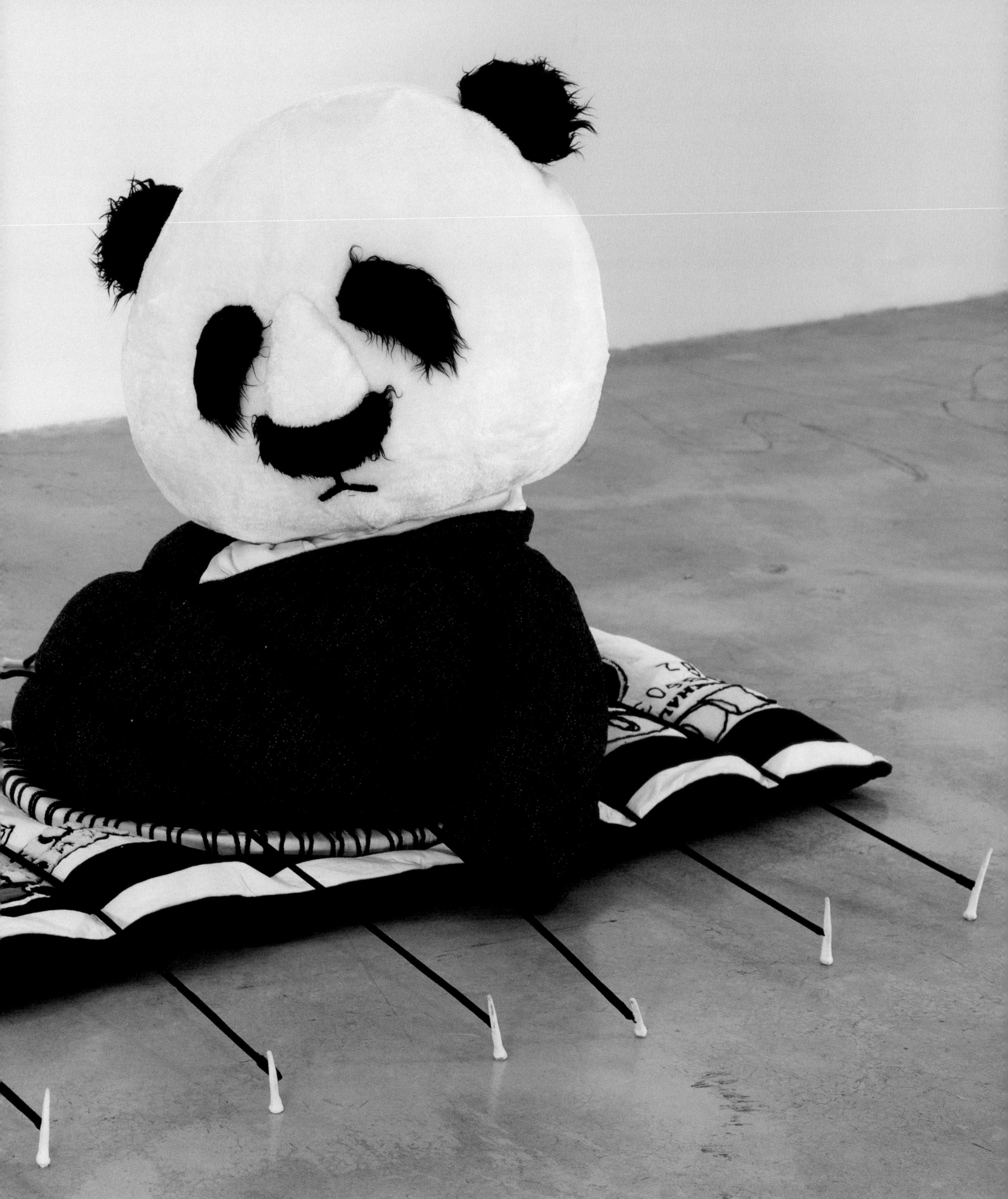

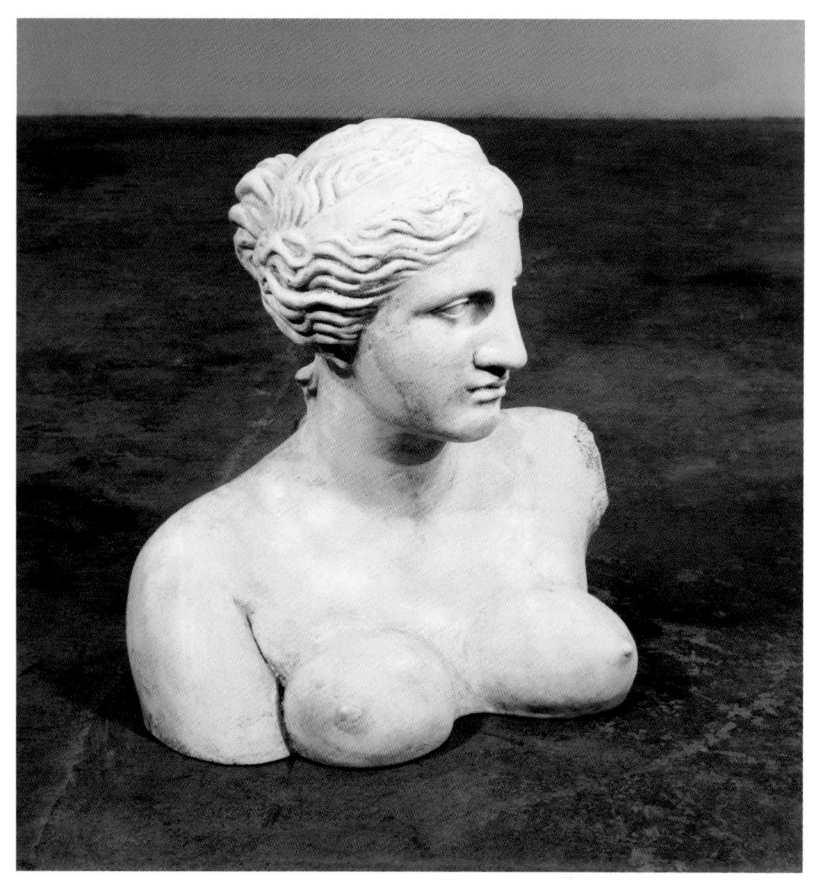

Xu Zhen, *"The people is a beast of muddy brain. It does not know its own force; it only knows absolute obedience"*, No. 1, installation, *marble*, 2010, digital fine art pigment print mounted on aluminum, 65 1/4 x 62 3/4 in. (165.5 x 159.5 cm), produced by MadeIn Company, acquired in 2011
徐震，《一只花花绿绿的巨兽——平民。它不知道自己的力量, 只知道绝对服从。》作品1，材料：大理石, 2010, 艺术微喷样裱铝扳, 65 1/4 x 62 3/4 in. (165.5 x 159.5 厘米), 没顶公司出品, 收藏于2011

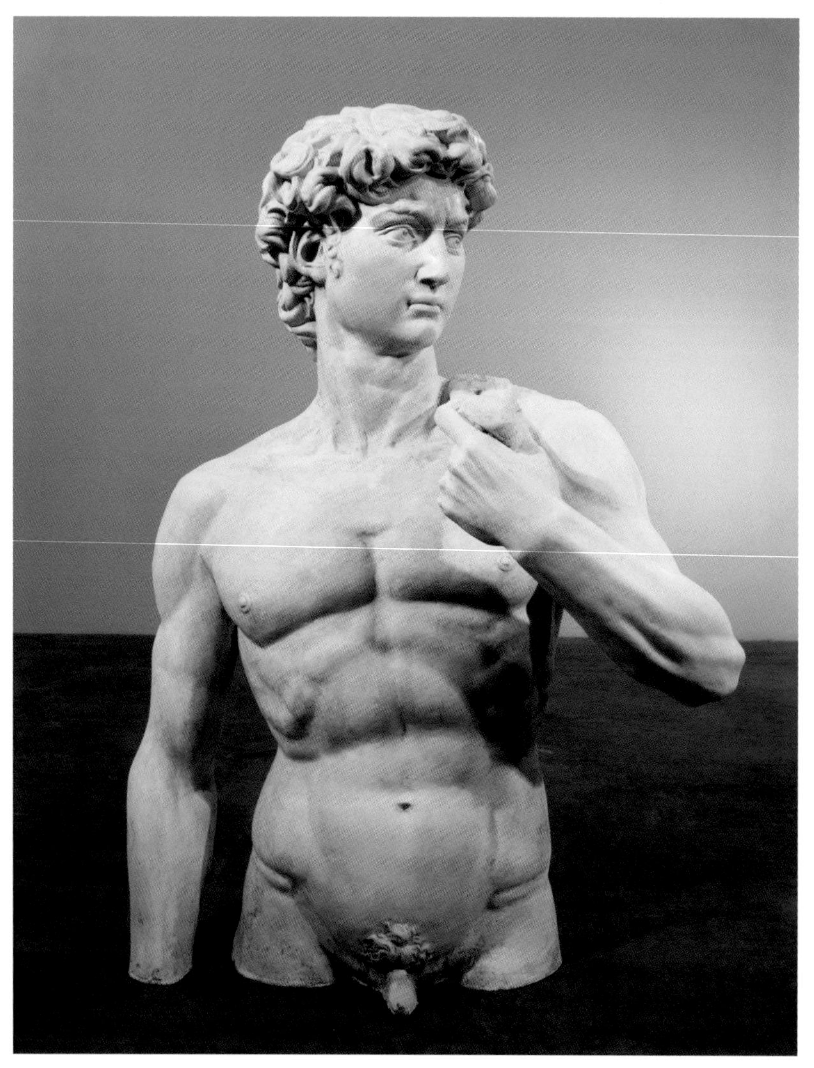

Xu Zhen, *"The people is a beast of muddy brain. It does not know its own force; it only knows absolute obedience"*, No. 3, installation, *marble*, 2010, digital fine art pigment print mounted on aluminum, 79 5/8 x 62 3/4 in. (202 x 159.5 cm), produced by MadeIn Company, acquired in 2011
徐震，《一只花花绿绿的巨兽——平民。它不知道自己的力量, 只知道绝对服从。》作品3，材料：大理石, 2010, 艺术微喷样裱铝扳, 79 5/8 x 62 3/4 in. (202 x 159.5 厘米), 没顶公司出品, 收藏于2011

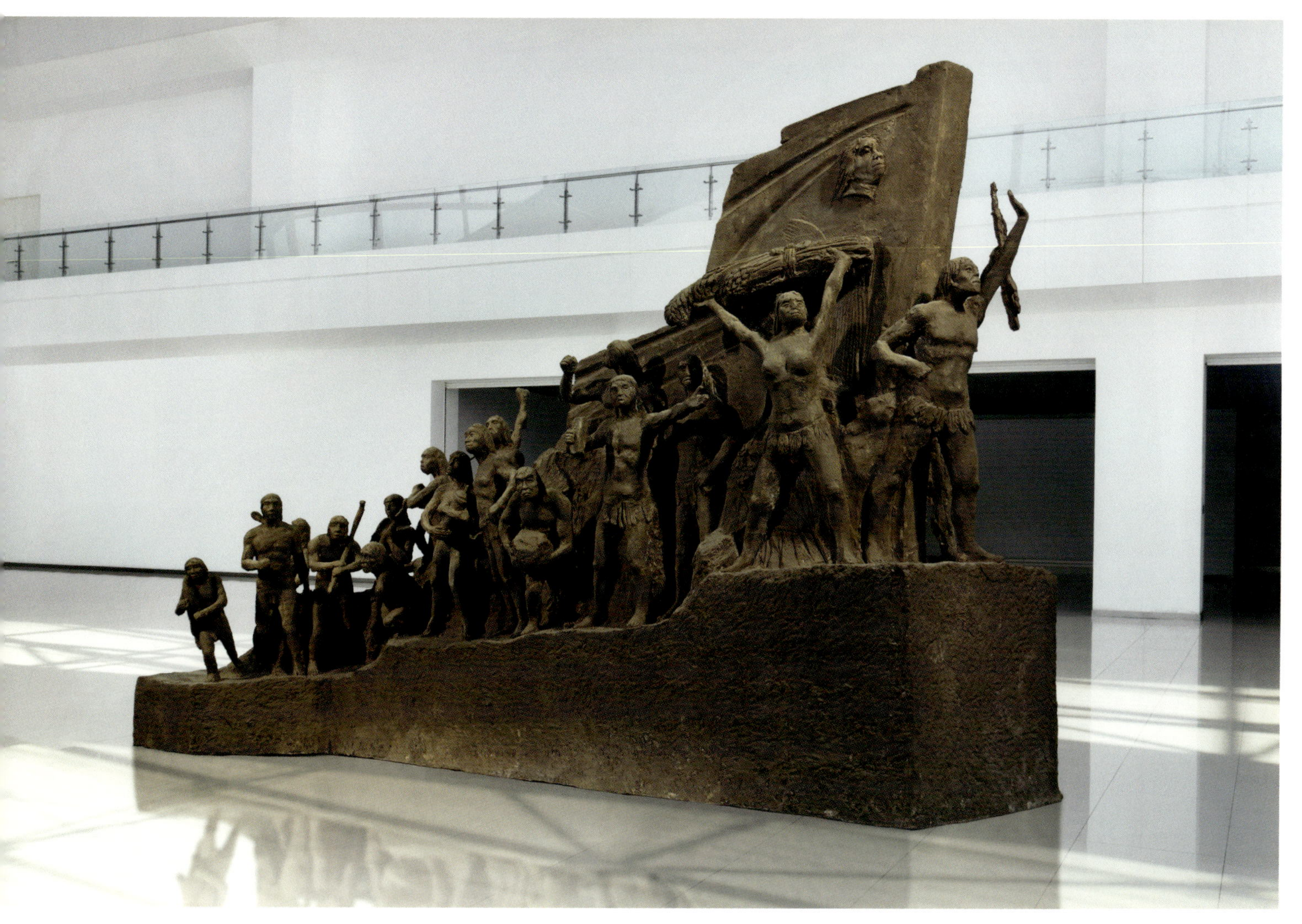

Artworks from the "True Image" series were first presented in the solo exhibition *Don't Hang Your Faith on the Wall*, and they consist of pictures of artworks that were destroyed after being photographed. "True Image" challenges artworks' existence in this period of media saturation, the image becomes the artwork itself. "True Image" is very rich in meaning, the image is more appealing than the subject in the photograph.

- Xu Zhen

"真相"系列的作品最早出现在个展"不要把信仰挂在墙上"中，这个系列都是以实体作品的摄影展现，最后原来的作品被销毁，所以这个系列作品不会称之为摄影，材料一般也都是原装置本身的材料。"真相"系列挑战了作品在媒体时代存在的另外一种可能，并且将图片的意义上升，成为了作品的主体，"真相"在内容上非常多样丰富，甚至比实体作品本身更具有表现的优势。

- 徐震

Xu Zhen, *"The struggle of man against power is the struggle of memory against forgetting"*, sculpture, resin, 2010, digital fine art pigment print mounted on aluminum, 62 5/8 x 89 1/4 in. (159 x 227 cm), produced by MadeIn Company, acquired in 2011
徐震，《人反抗权力的斗争，就是"记忆"反抗"遗忘"的斗争。》，材料：树脂，2010, 艺术微喷样裱铝扳，62 5/8 x 89 1/4 寸 (159 x 227 厘米)，没顶公司出品，收藏于2011

As one of the works from the "True Image" series, *The principal motor of action in this view is self-interest, guided by rationality, which translates structural and institutional conditions into payoffs and probabilities, and therefore incentives.*, consists of a photograph of a urine stain, cut and mounted upright. Such an image turned into a 'memorial' appears as rather absurd.

- Xu Zhen

作为真相系列的其中一个，"人类行为的主要动机是自利的，理性引导该行为，并将结构和制度条件转化为收益，可能性乃至动机"以尿的痕迹为拍摄对象，拍摄后用切割技术将它站立起来，这种图片成为"纪念碑"的形式看起来颇具荒诞。

- 徐震

Xu Zhen, *"The principal motor of action in this view is self-interest, guided by rationality, which translates structural and institutional conditions into payoffs and probabilities, and therefore incentives"*, material: water, proteins, glucose, mineral salt, 2012, digital fine art pigment print mounted on aluminum, Ed. 2/3, 225 x 88 3/4 x 47 in. (571 x 225 x 119 cm), produced by MadeIn Company, acquired in 2012

徐震，《人类行为的主要动机是自利的，理性引导该行为，并将结构和制度条件转化为收益，可能性乃至动机.》，材料：水，蛋白质，葡萄糖，无机盐，2012，艺术微喷样裱铝扳，版本 2/3，225 x 88 3/4 x 47 寸 (571 x 225 x 119 厘米)，没顶公司出品，收藏于 2012

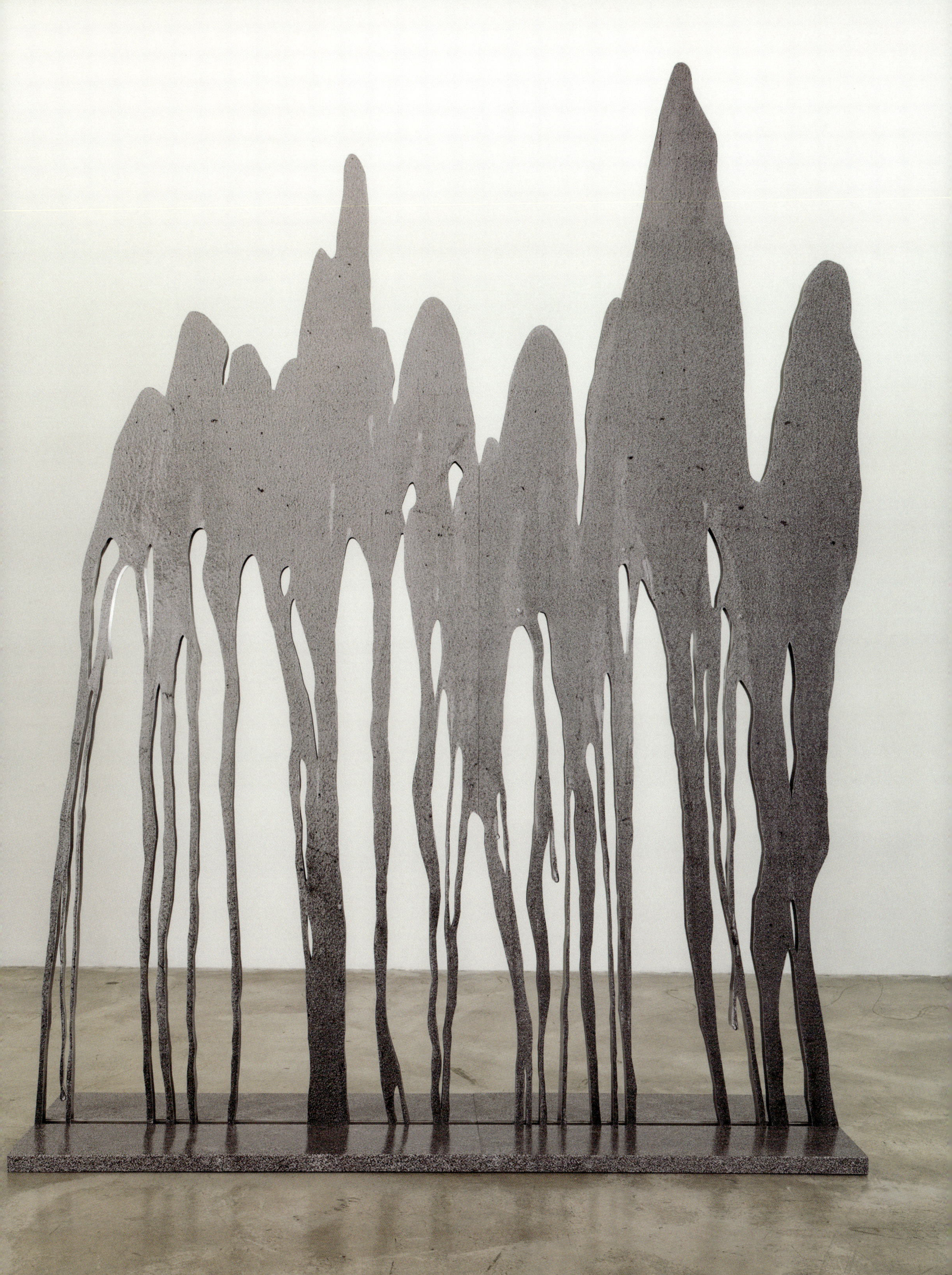

Beginning in 2011, foam sculptures were produced that play with notions of trophies or collectibles coveted by fetishists throughout the world, such as animal skins, antique sculptures, Asian and African sacred monuments, totems and so on. The particular softness and absorbent capacity of this medium reflect people's weakness and avidity. *Prey-Cervine Tiger 2* appropriates foam's natural color change: from a zebra to a tiger, prey and predator become one.

- Xu Zhen

2011年徐震开始以海绵为材料开展创作，利用海绵的材料特性雕塑出很多文明历史中恋物者的收藏品，如动物皮毛，全球古代雕塑，亚非拉大型建筑神迹等。这些海绵为材料的雕塑（包括神的系列等等）显示了它的柔软和可吸收性，更折射了大家在文明面前表现的那种软弱和饥渴。此作品利用海绵的天然颜色变化，突出了这种条纹花斑的迷惑性，或是虎皮，或是斑马，猎食和被猎食在拥有者面前是相同的。

- 徐震

Xu Zhen, *Prey - Cervine Tiger 2*, 2011, foam and spray paint, 1/2 x 70 3/4 x 7 3/4 in. (250 x 180 x 20 cm), produced by MadeIn Company, acquired in 2011

徐震，《猎物－鹿虎 2》，2011，海绵、喷漆，1/2 x 70 3/4 x 7 3/4 寸 (250 x 180 x 20 厘米)，没顶公司出品，收藏于2011

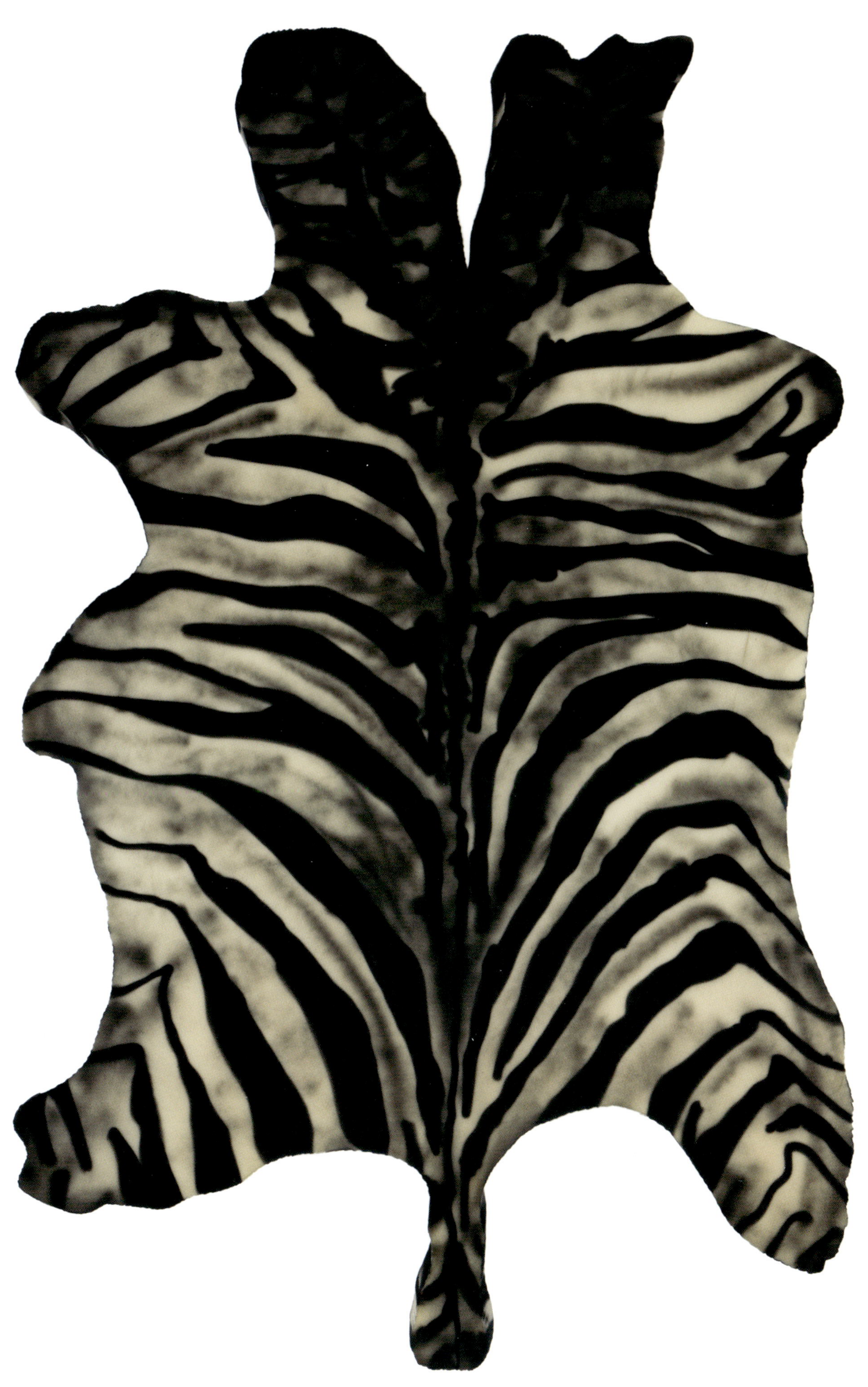

Yan Xing

鄢醒

Born in 1986, Chongqing, China
Lives and works in Beijing, China

一九八六年生於中國重慶
居住和工作於中國北京

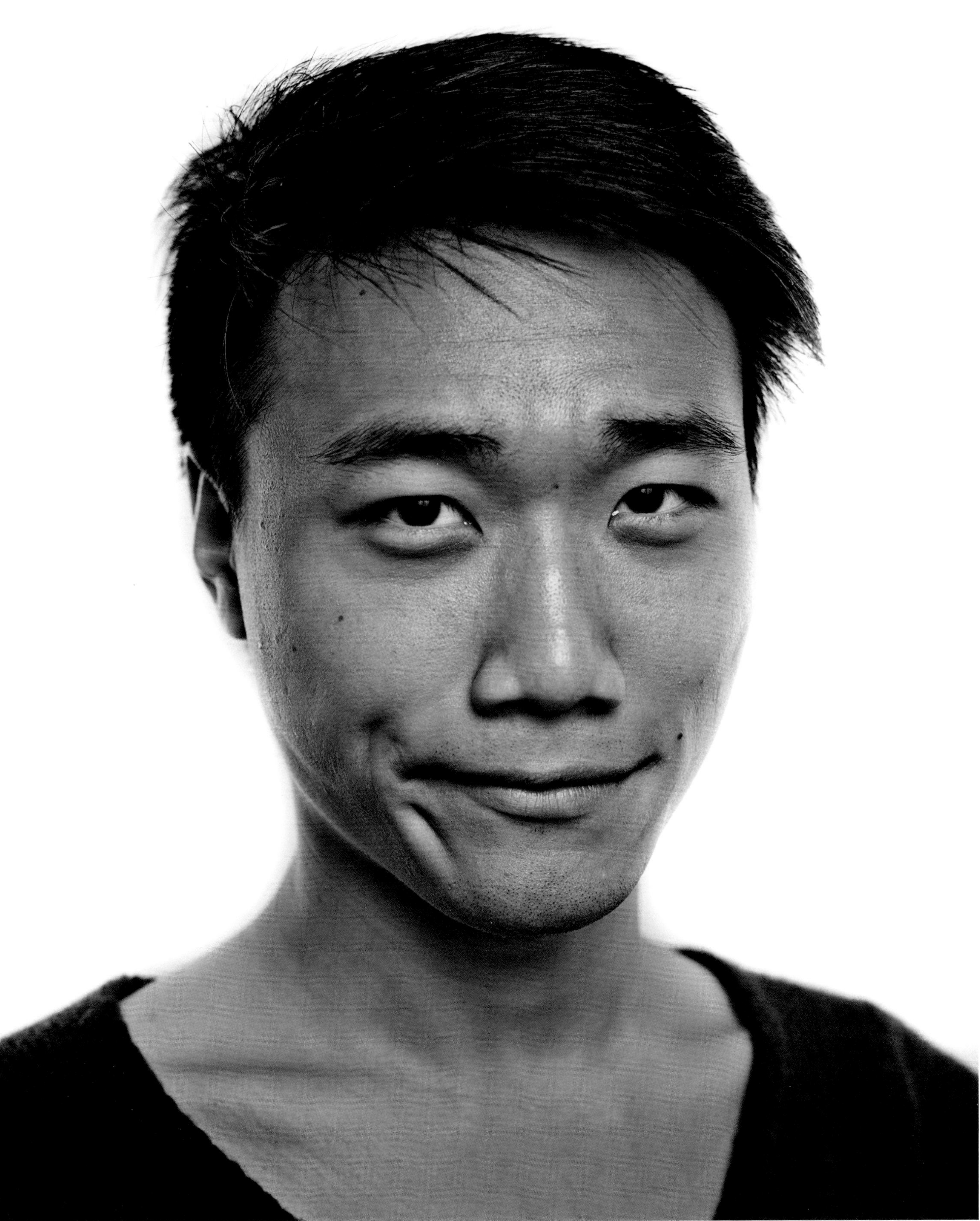

Realism (2011) is a multimedia piece that incorporates performance, sculpture, photography and installation. The work is also in itself a two hour long performance in which the actors and I move around a set of practical activities, such as calculating, portraying, exercising, occupying, negotiating and writing, as a defense for the "imagined reality." Through this live process, filled at once with divergence and repetition, opposition and unification, complexity and simplicity, unfolding and folding, separation and production, I try to explore more deeply the productive system of art history. In addition, it is the obstinate confidence I have as an artist in the persistence of "creating a reality with no difference," as well as the deranged bias I have towards "completing the necessary mistakes."

- Yan Xing

"现实主义"（2011）是一件包括了行为、雕塑、摄影、装置等多种媒介在内的作品。这件作品同时也是一次长达2小时的行为表演，我和演员们围绕着一系列的运算、描绘、演习、占领、谈判、书写等实践活动为一个"想象中的现实"辩护。我试图通过这一充满差异与重复、对立与统一、复杂与简单、展开与折叠、分化与生成的现场过程来深入地探讨艺术史的生成机制。这也是我作为艺术家对"创造一个毫无差别的现实"执着的笃定，也是我对"完成必须的错误"疯狂的偏执。

- 鄢醒

Yan Xing, *Realism*, 2011, fiberglass and clothes, sculpture: 136 x 65 3/4 x 41 in. (346 x 167 x 104 cm), overall: variable dimensions, acquired in 2013
鄢醒，《现实主义》，2011，玻璃纤维与衣服，雕塑：136 x 65 3/4 x 41 寸 (346 x 167 x 104 厘米)，整体：可变尺寸，收藏于2013

Yan Xing, *Realism*, 2011, black-and-white digital print, Ed. 2/3, 83 x 55 in. (210 x 140 cm), acquired in 2013
鄢醒，《现实主义》，2011，黑白数码印刷，版本 2/3，83 x 55 寸 (210 x 140 厘米)，收藏于2013

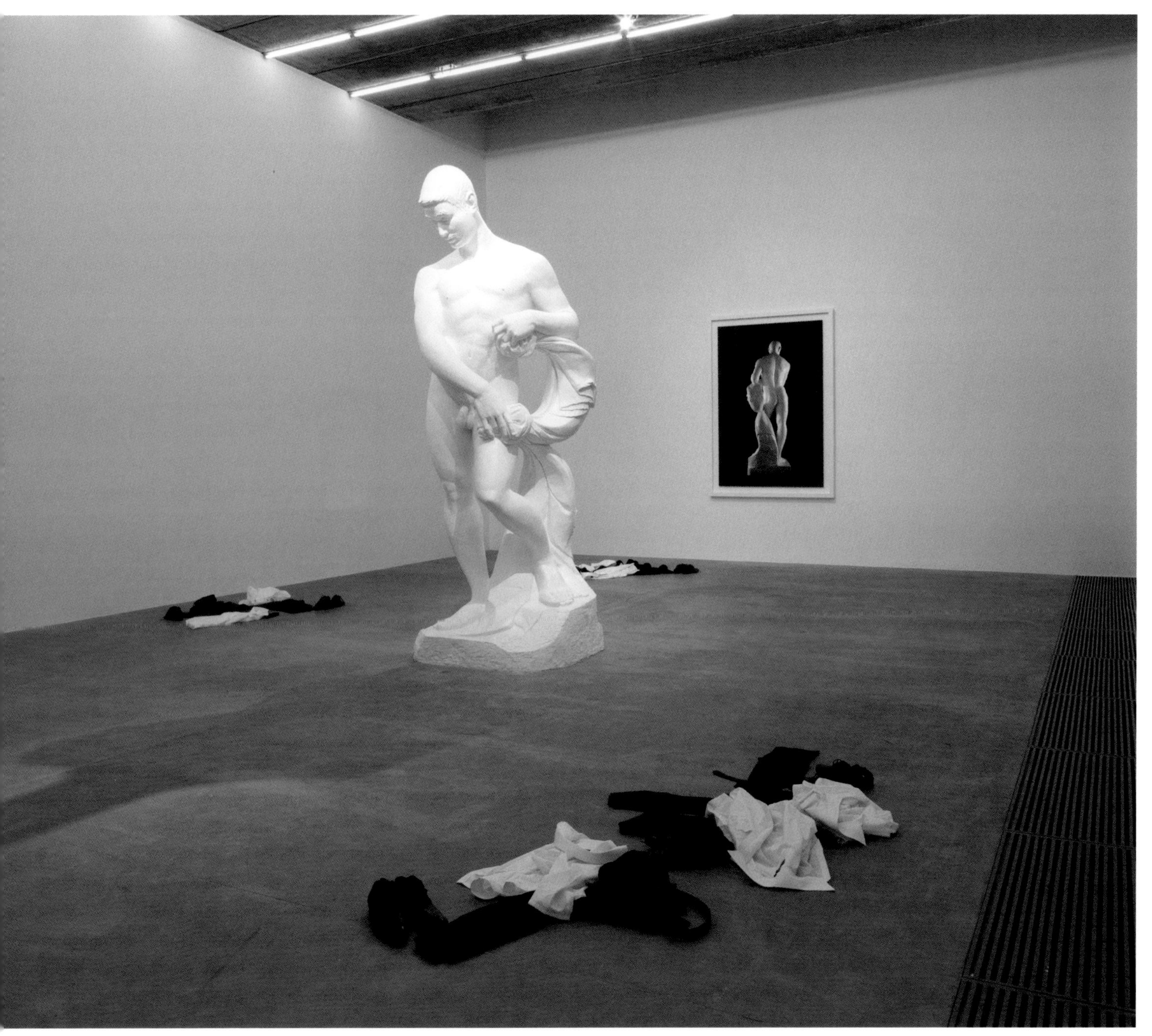

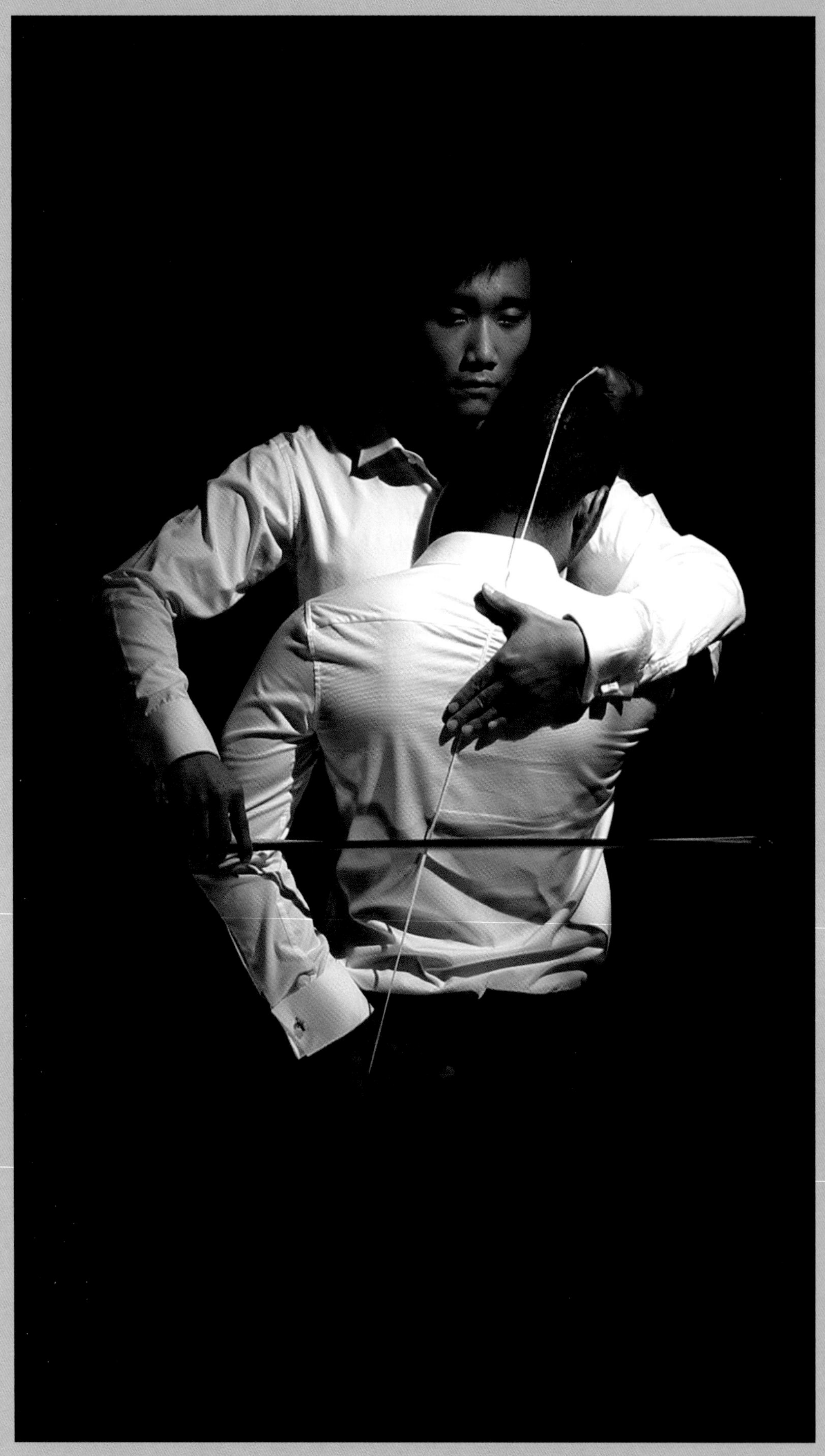

Yan Xing, *Kill (the) TV-Set*, 2012, two-channel video (black-and-white, silent), No. 1, duration: 2 hrs. 30 min., No. 2, duration: 3 hrs. 6 min., acquired in 2013

鄢醒，《谋杀电视机》，2012，双频录像装置，(黑白，无声)，1号，持续时间：2 小时 30分，2号，持续时间：3 小时 6 分，收藏于2013

This work encompasses two independent video installations. I appear in one video imitating the 1965 performance by Nam June Paik and Charlotte Moorman of John Cage's 1955 opus *26' 1. 1499" for a String Player* in a video performance. The other video features a Chinese bonsai with the English caption "Kill (the) TV-Set" incessantly flashing.

This work presents a discussion of the technical semantics of logic: how to define or describe the medium itself. Several processes of "deconstruction" appear herein: latter-day modernist artists employ new technology (or else their more primitive bodies) to interpret other artists' works; "new artists" either deride or pay tribute to their forerunners' creations, with old-fashioned discipline parading under the guise of standardized mechanical regimentation, while technological progression itself relentlessly chips away at the certitude of this medium. Our comprehension of technology is similar to this: we have the urge to occupy new areas, but at the same time we anticipate being occupied by these new areas. This serves as a parable of discipline and punishment.

- Yan Xing

作品由两个独立的录像装置组成。一个录像中将出现我模仿白南准（Nam June Paik）与中提琴家摩尔门（Charlotte Moorman）在1965年演奏约翰.凯奇（John Cage）1955年的作品"26' 1. 1499" for a string player"的行为录像。另一个录像中将出现一株中国盆景与不断闪烁的"Kill (the) TV-Set"（谋杀电视机）的英文字幕。

这件作品是一次关于技术语义的逻辑讨论——如何定义或描述媒介本身。这件作品中有几次"开方"的过程：现代主义后期的艺术家们用更新的技术（抑或是更原始的身体）演绎另一位艺术家的作品；"新的艺术家"挑衅或致敬着前辈们的创造；古老的规训技术呈现在机器自律的标准之下；技术自身的递进也在不断消解"媒介"的确定性。我们对于技术的理解是这样的——随时希望占领新的领域，又随时等待着被新的领域占领。这更像是一次关于"规训与惩罚"的寓言。

- 鄢醒

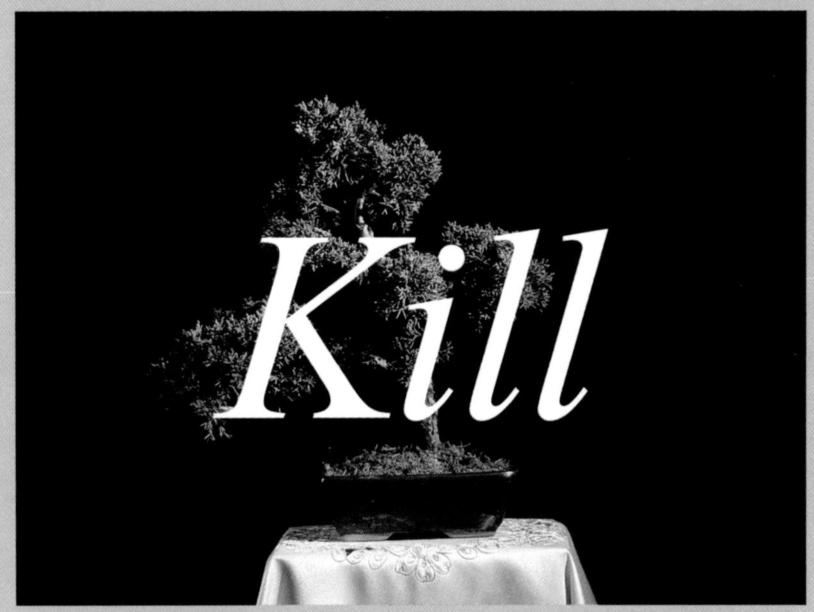

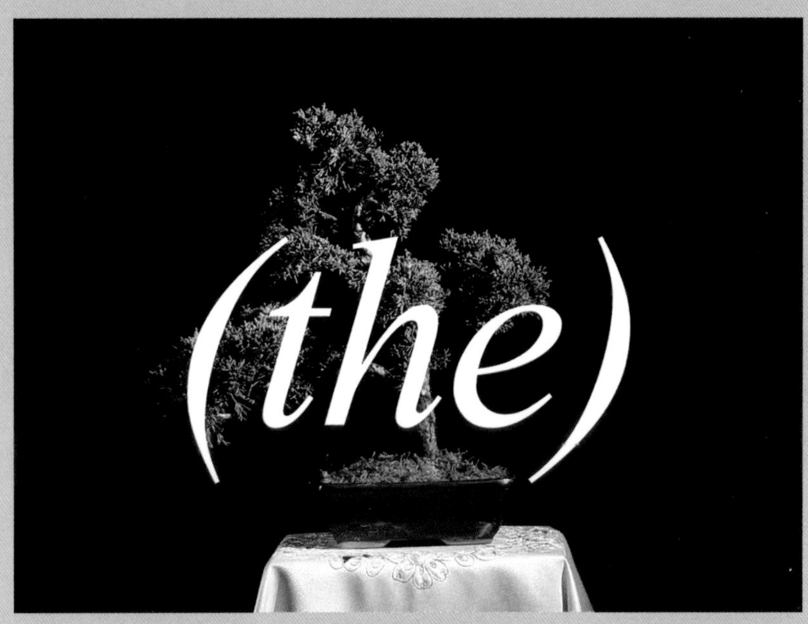

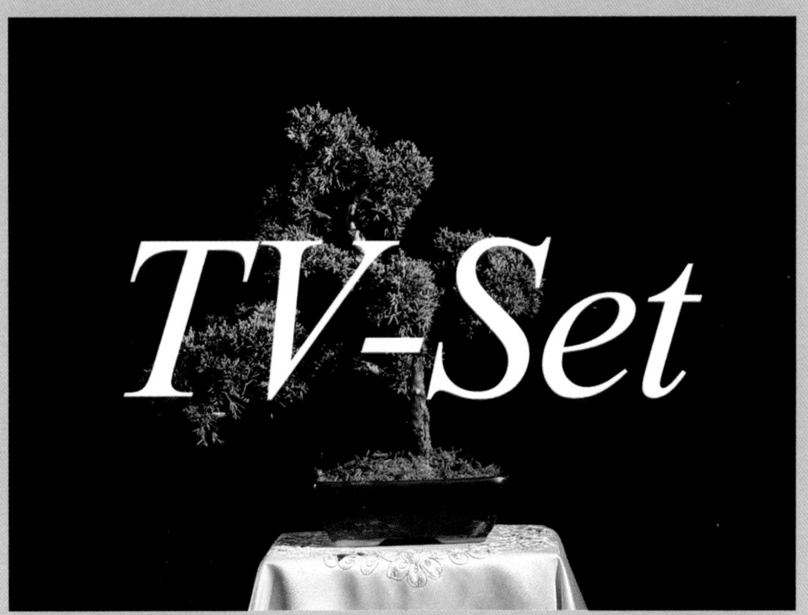

Zhang Enli 张恩利

Born in 1965, Jilin, China
Lives and works in Shanghai, China

一九六五年生於中国吉林
居住和工作於中国上海

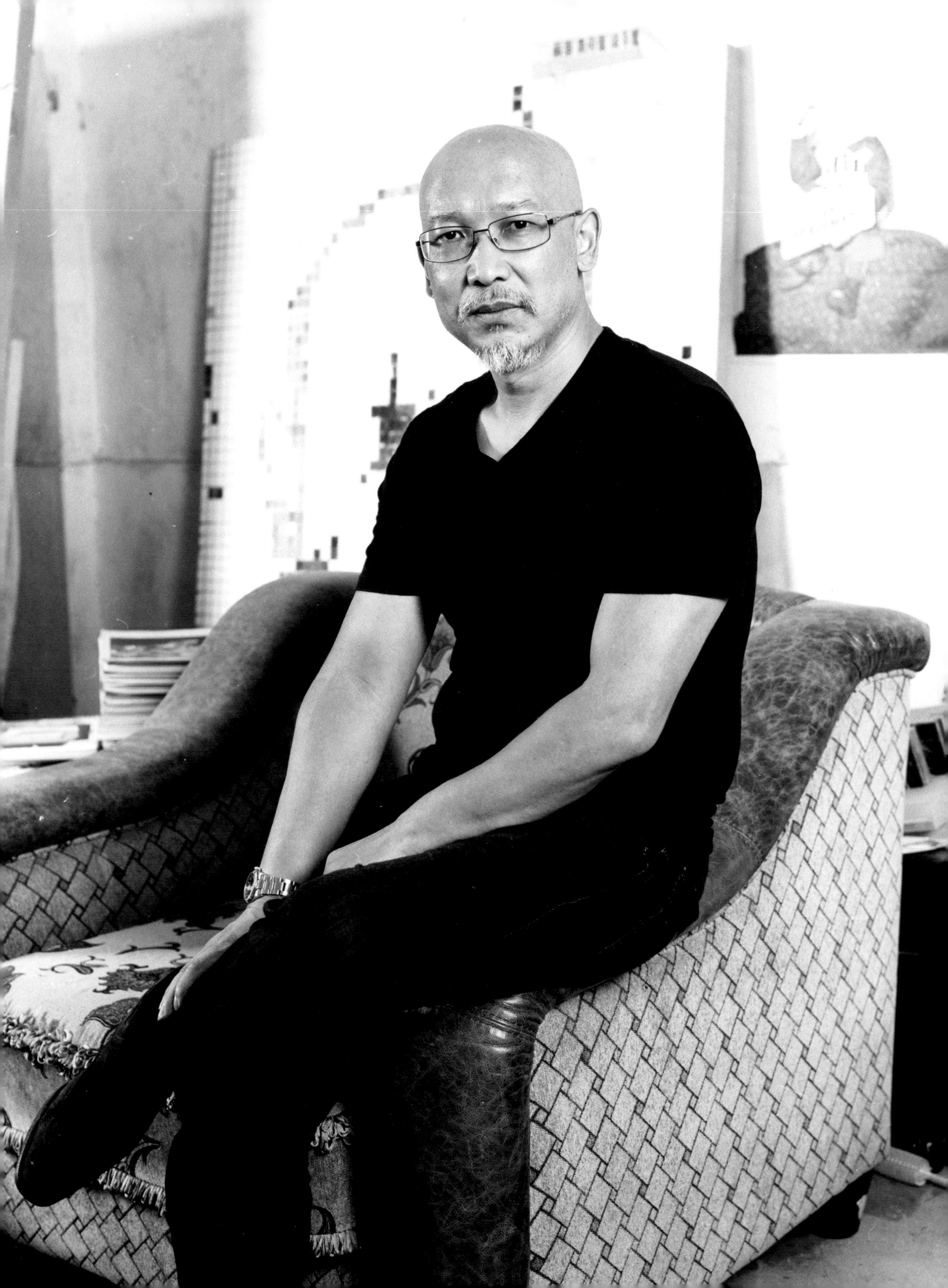

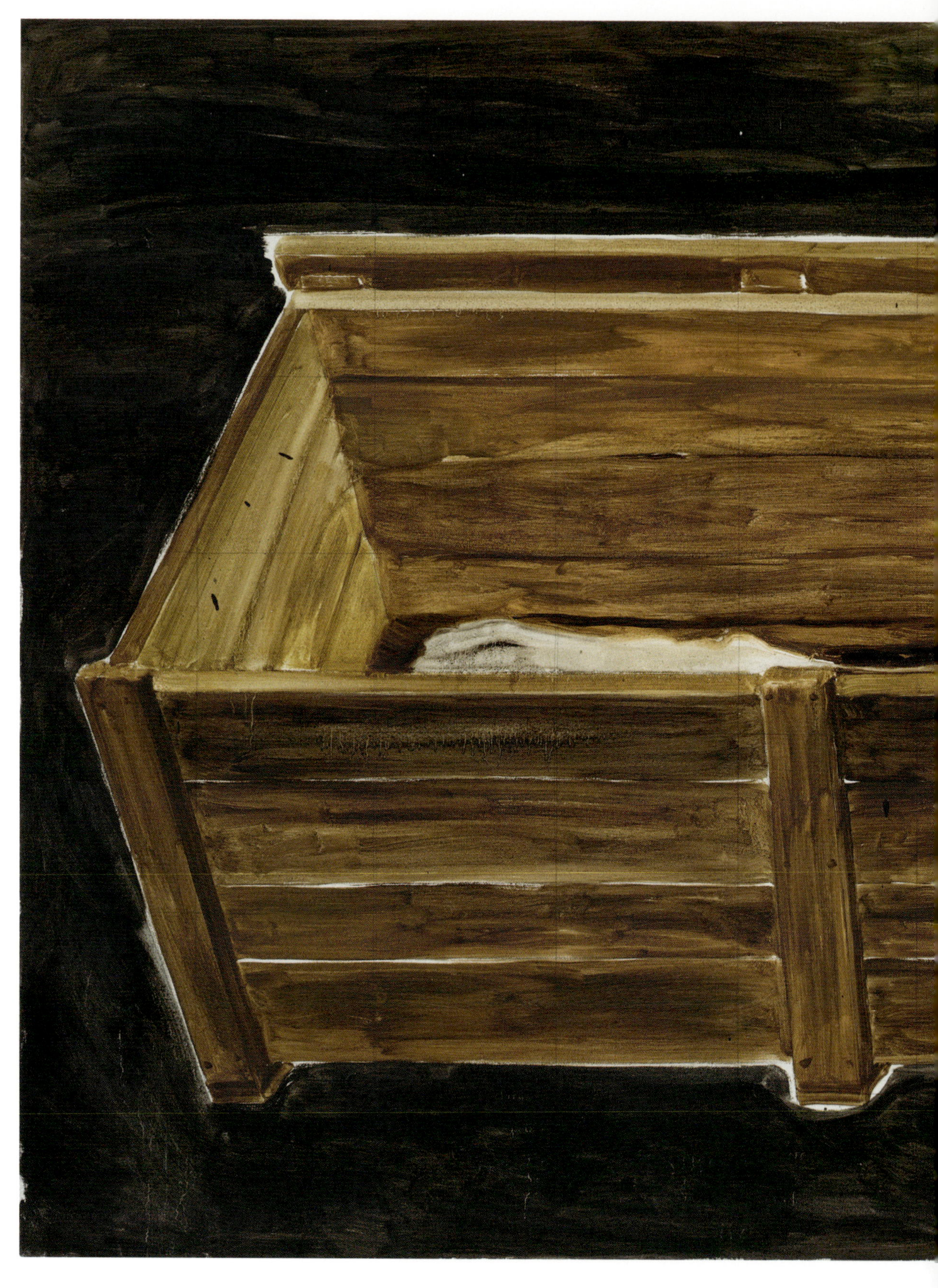

Zhang Enli, *Container 2*, 2006, oil on canvas, 54 3/8 x 93 1/4 in. (138 x 237 cm), acquired in 2007
张恩利，《容器 2》，布面油画，54 3/8 x 93 1/4 寸 (138 x 237 厘米)，收藏于 2007

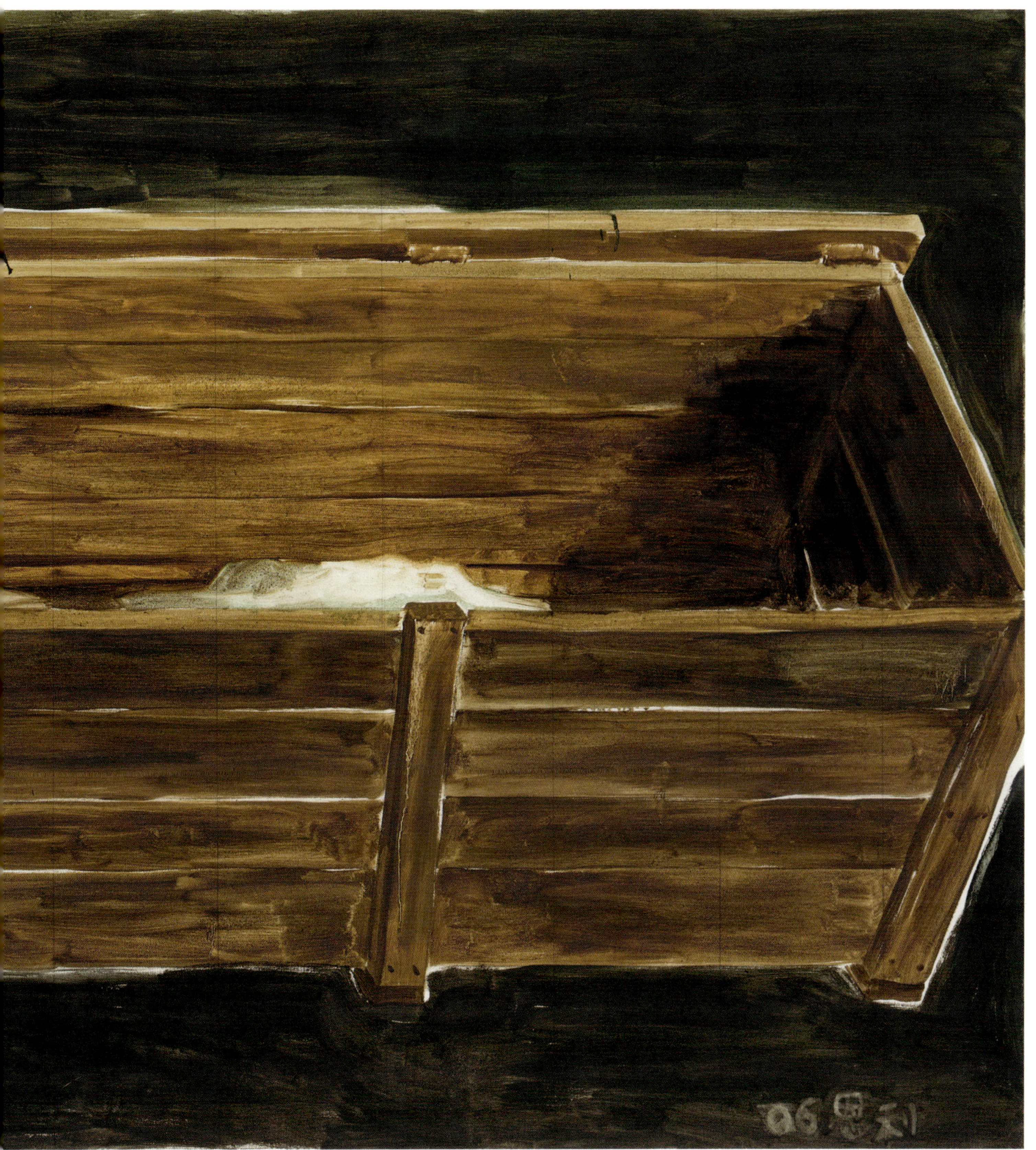

When the lid on a box is closed, will you think about what's inside?
Many years later, the box itself will carry a lot more meaning. We too are containers.

- Zhang Enli

当盒子盖上的时候，你会想里面是什么？ 多年以后，这个盒子的本身具有更多的意义，我们也是容器

- 张恩利

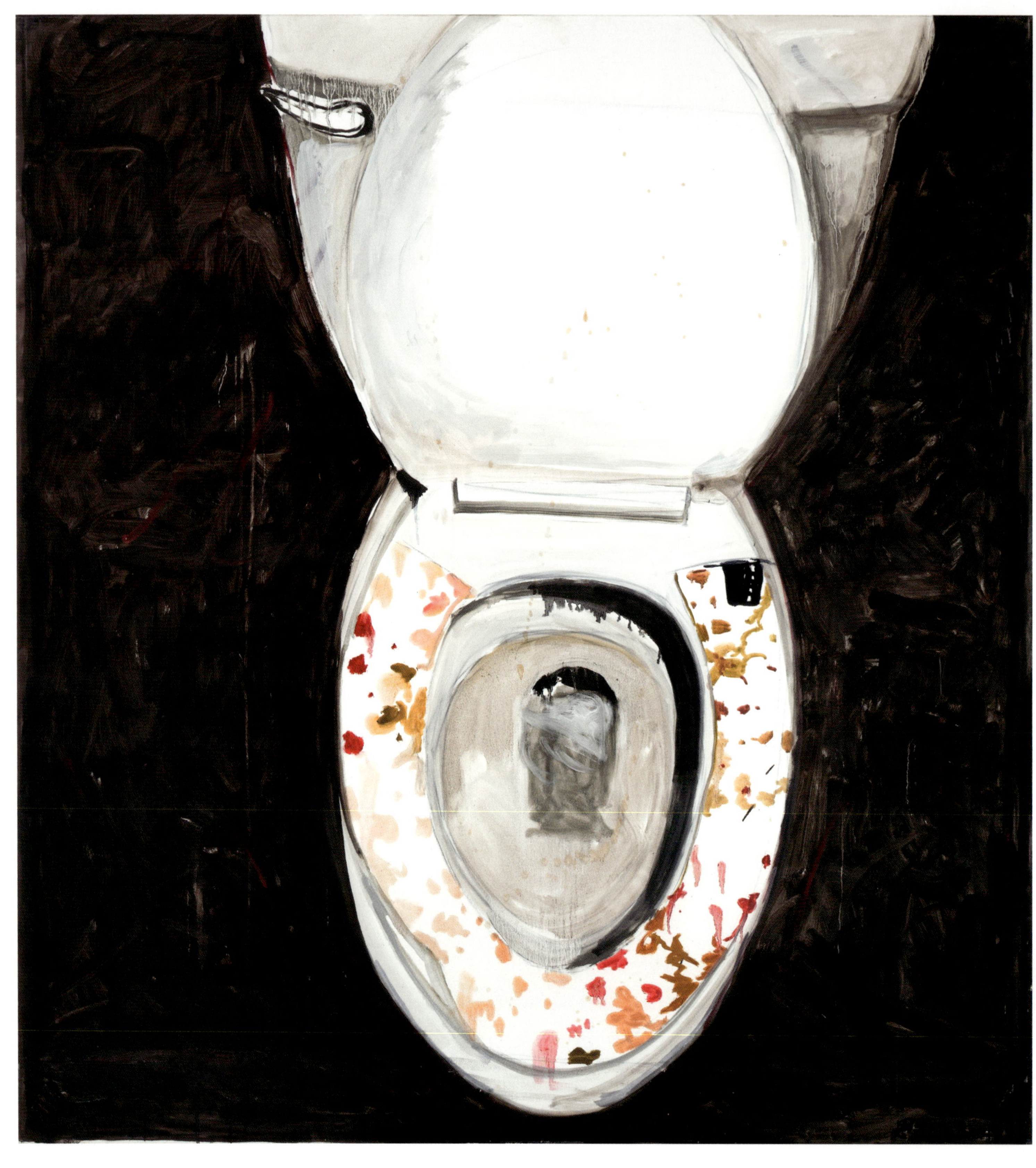

Zhang Enli, *Container 1 & 2*, 2003, oil on canvas, diptych, each: 50 3/8 x 44 7/8 in. (128 x 114 cm), acquired in 2006
张恩利，《容器1＆2》，2003，布面油画，二联作，每幅：50 3/8 x 44 7/8 寸 (128 x 114 厘米)，收藏于 2006

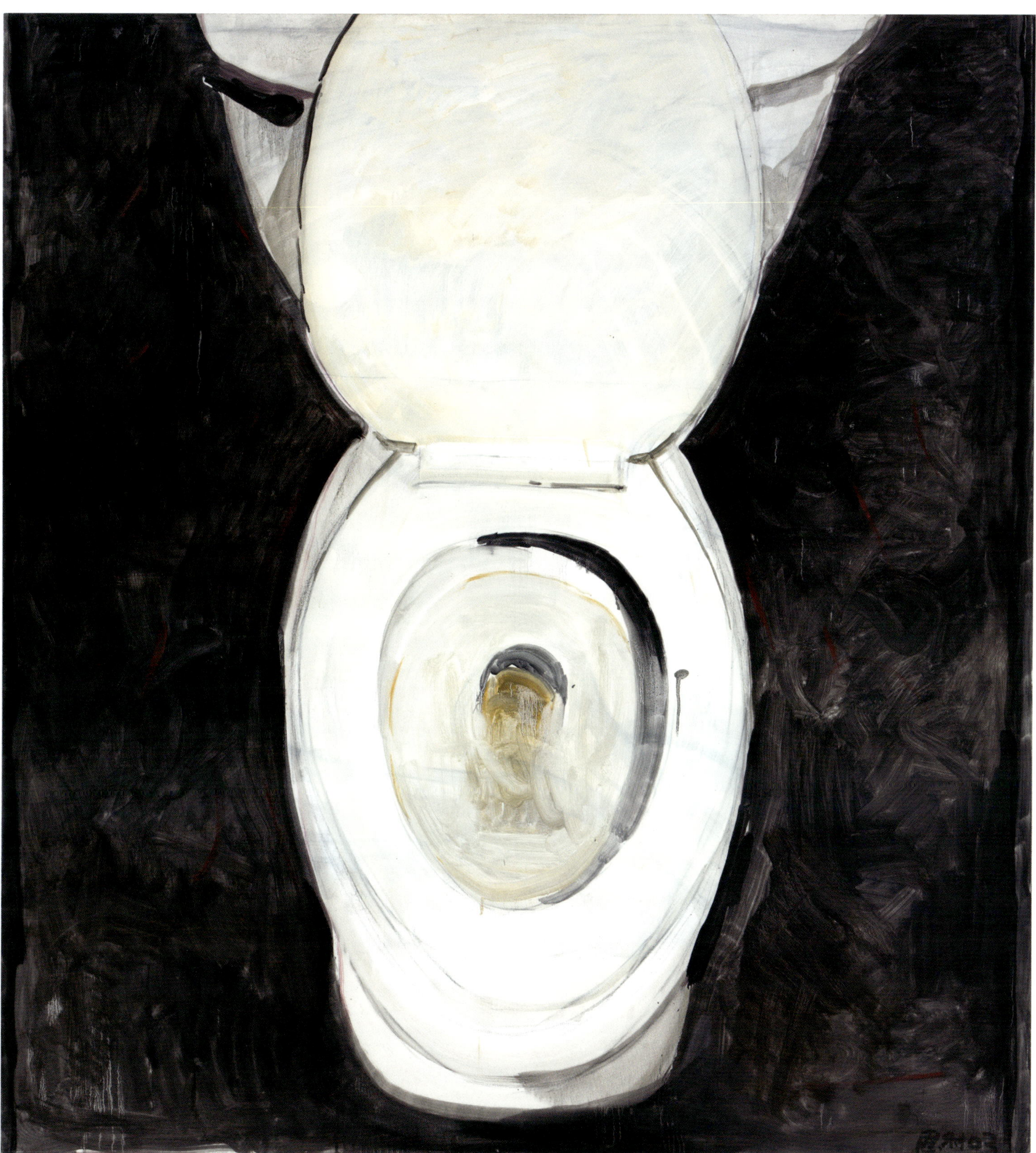

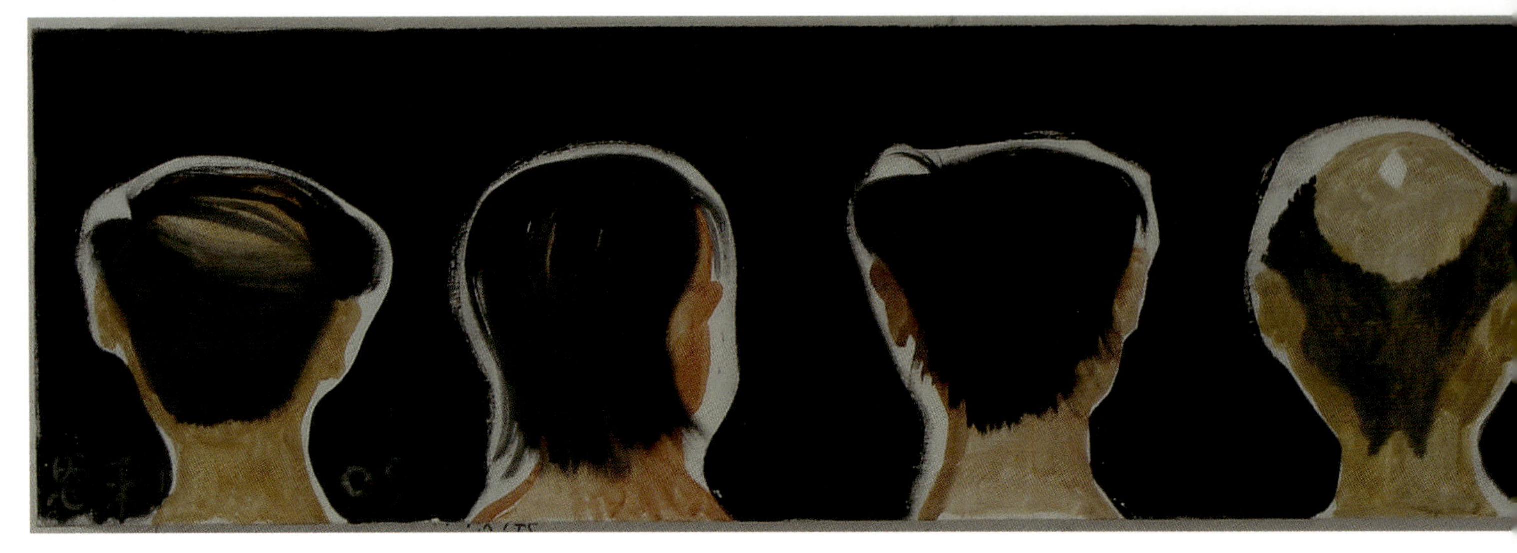

↑ Zhang Enli, *Hair 2*, oil on canvas, 15 3/4 x 97 5/8 in. (40 x 248 cm), acquired in 2006
张恩利，《头发 2》，布面油画，15 3/4 x 97 5/8 寸 (40 x 240 厘米)，收藏于 2006

→ Zhang Enli, *Hair 1*, 2005, acrylic on paper, 10 1/4 x 42 7/8 in. (26 x 109 cm), acquired in 2006
张恩利，《头发 1》，纸上丙烯，10 1/4 x 42 7/8 寸 (26 x 109 厘米)，收藏于 2006

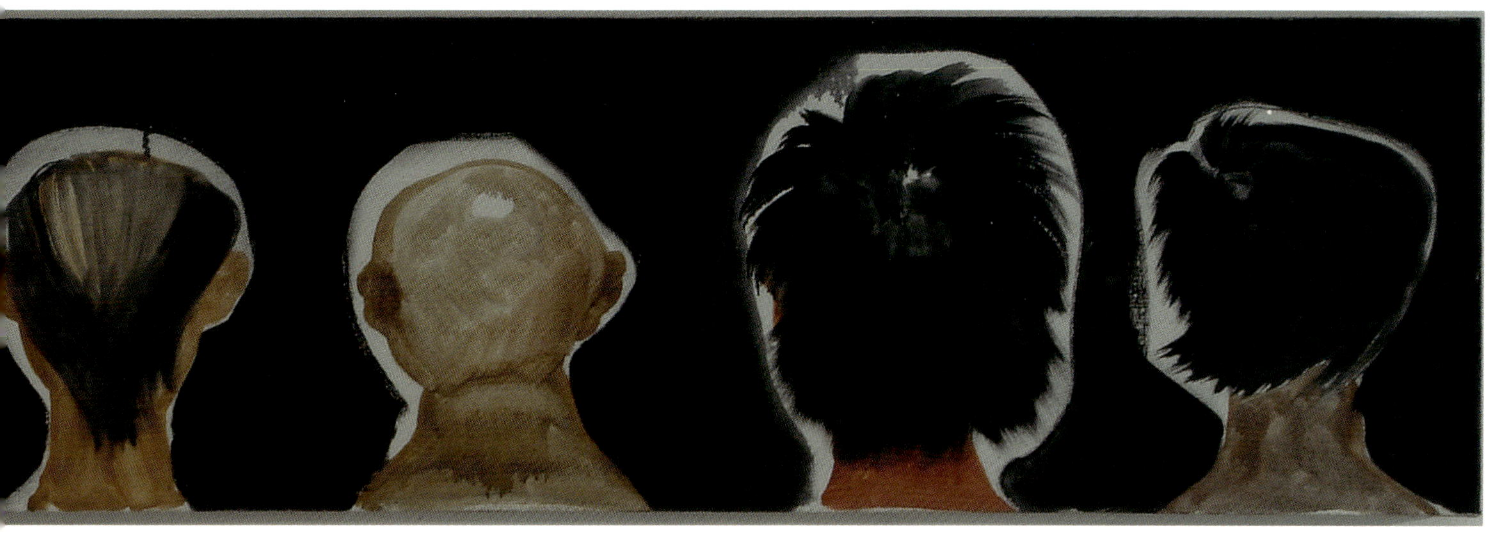

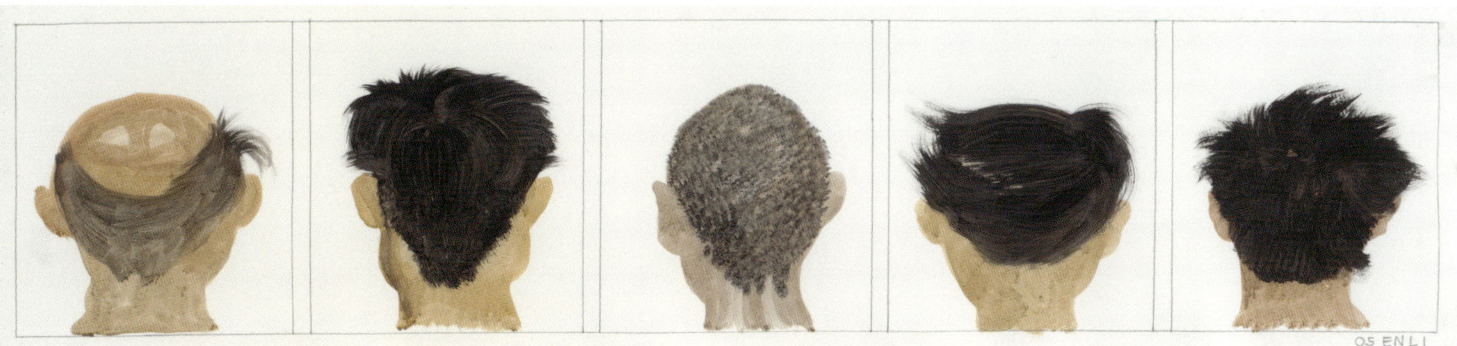
OS EN LI

Zhang Huan 张洹

Born in 1965, Henan, China
Lives and works in Shanghai, China
and New York, NY

一九六五年生於中国河南
居住和工作於中国上海和美国纽约

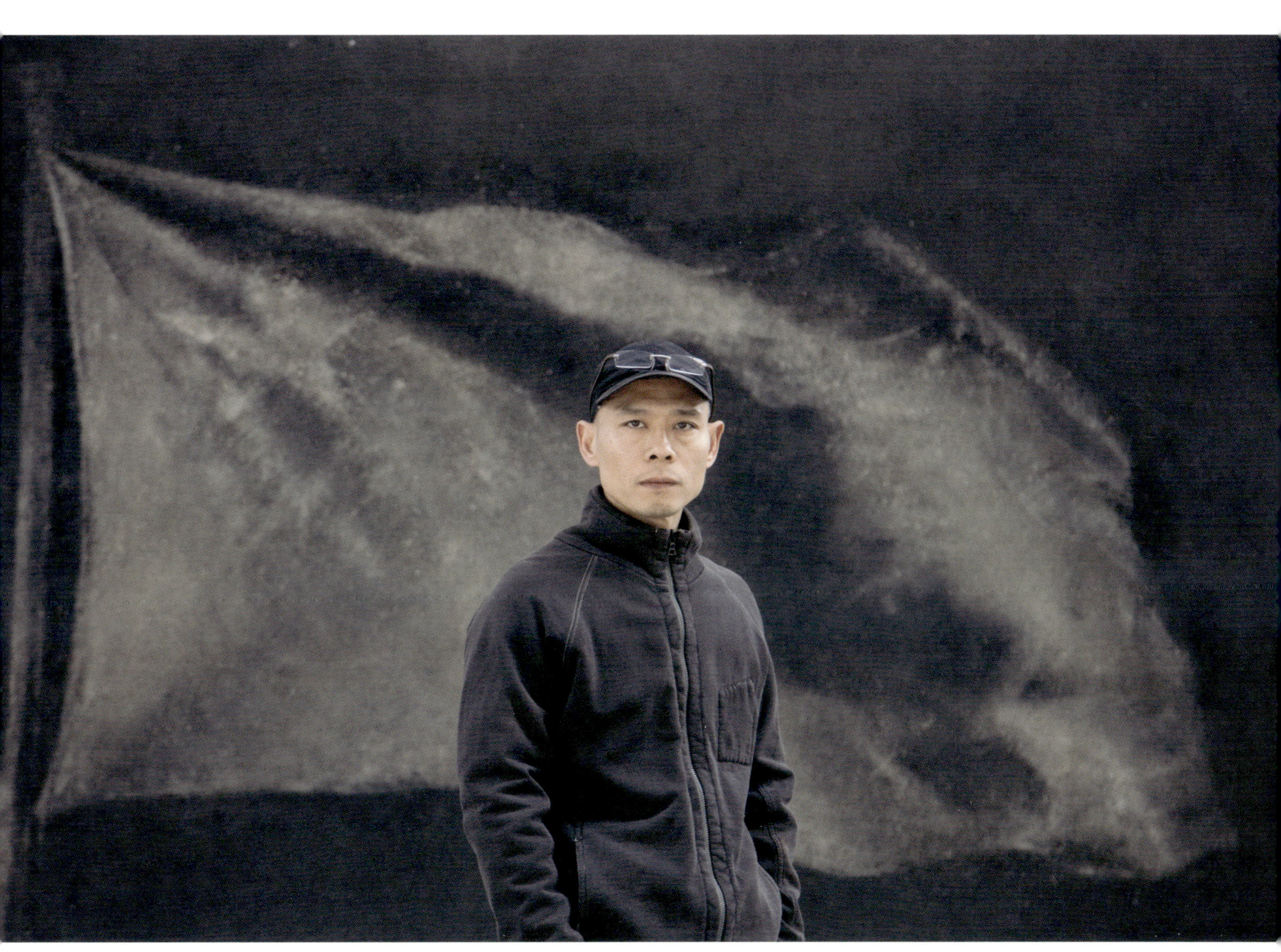

I moved to Beijing in 1991 and left the city in 1998. In those eight years, I moved thirteen times, because I either could not afford the rent or I was kicked out. I remember that I used to rent a room near Xinqiao at East Sishisan Tiao. It was actually the narrow corridor between two houses that was used to store coal. It was barely big enough for a twin-sized bed. Underneath my bed was the iron cover of a sewer. On rainy days, water from the sewer would flood the room. One night, a cat bumped the window and scared me. There are also exciting memories from that period, including the time I bought at an international book fair in Beijing a foreign book on Matisse that cost 800 yuan.

I wanted to move to a bigger place. A friend introduced me to the area in Beijing I later called the East Village. I found a place with high ceilings, suitable as a studio, and I rented it for 120 yuan per month. It was there that I created *65 kilograms*, a series of installations entitled *Angels*, and other "poor-artist" works. It was my first studio. At the time, most people in Beijing lived within the second and third rings of the city, and all the garbage from the city was dumped outside the third ring. The city was surrounded by mountains of garbage. My studio was two or three kilometers from the Kunlun Hotel at Liangmaqiao Bridge. There was a big garbage dump between the third and fourth rings, and my East Village was close to it. All my neighbors made their livings by picking up things from the garbage, making tofu, or selling vegetables. Five families lived on my courtyard, which was owned by a farmer who lived outside Beijing. To my left was a family—a couple with two kids—from Jiangxi Province. They lived by making tofu in a kitchen across from my studio. I ate all kinds of fresh tofu when I was there: tofu skin, tofu curd, firm tofu, and soft tofu. I became a tofu man, but soon tired of it. The garbage came from the city, and I found many three-dimensional objects there, such as old comforters, burned plastic things, broken toys, an old sofa, and a dead cat. I took them to my studio and created some of my most direct and honest works from these objects.

I created two works in 1994, *12 Square Meters* and *65 Kilograms*, to directly reflect our lives in the East Village. Twelve square meters is the area of

我从1991年到北京，直至1998年离开，住了有八年，一共搬了十三次家，不是因为交不起房租，就是被别人赶跑。我记得我曾经在东四十三条北新桥附近租了个房子，那其实是个两个房子间的夹道，本来是放煤球用的，小的勉强放得下一张单人床，床铺地下还有一个下水道的大铁盖，一到下雨天，污水就淤上来了。有些野猫半夜跑到我这里，以为是通的，结果一头撞到玻璃上，很恐怖。不过也有让人激动的事情，我在北京的一次国际书展上，买到了一本进口的贾柯梅蒂画册，花了800元人民币。

那时我很想找个大点儿的地方，经朋友介绍，看了后来被我命名叫"东村"的地方，觉得空间不错，屋顶很高，适合做工作室，就租下来了，120元一个月，我后来在这个空间作了65KG，天使装置系列，还有一屋子贫穷艺术类作品，那就算是东村的第一个工作室了。当时的北京以天安门广场为轴中心，向外分二环三环，每天这个城市消费的垃圾全部运到三环以外，所以这个城市被三环外的垃圾山给包围着。这个地方离亮马河饭店昆仑饭店大概有两三公里的地方，正好是三环到四环之间一个大垃圾场的地方，我的这个村庄就在垃圾场旁边，周围的邻居都是捡垃圾的，磨豆腐的，卖菜的。我的院子住着有五户外地人，房东是北京郊区的菜农，我的左边是江西来的磨豆腐的，两口子带着两个孩子，后来又生了一个，我的房子对面是他们的豆腐作坊，每天他们起的很早就开始工作，那段时期我吃到了各种各样的新鲜豆腐，豆腐皮，豆腐花，老豆腐，嫩豆腐，我完全变成了一个豆腐人，没多久就把我吃腻了。那里的垃圾场有很多很多从城市里扔出来的废物，我从这些废物里面找到了一些立体的东西，象破被子，烧焦的塑料制品，压扁的玩具，破旧的沙发，被汽车轧死的猫，我都把它们捡到了工作室，创作了一批直接而真实朴素的作品。

1994年我做了两件重要的作品，就是12平方米和65KG，这都是东村生活最直接的反映。12平方米是厕所的面积，这是大队的一个公共厕所，天天用。那一天午饭后我去了常用的一个厕所，刚下过雨，天刚放晴，可是这个厕所根本就没有可以落脚的地方，五六个粪池全都堆满了粪便，都溢出来了。我只好骑自行车到村里的另外一个厕所，那里相对干净些，可是我一进去，成千上万的苍蝇扑面而来，无奈只能蹲下来方便——这就是我的生活，谁也代替不了，你只能做你的生活。我一下子有了做12平方米的想法。第二天

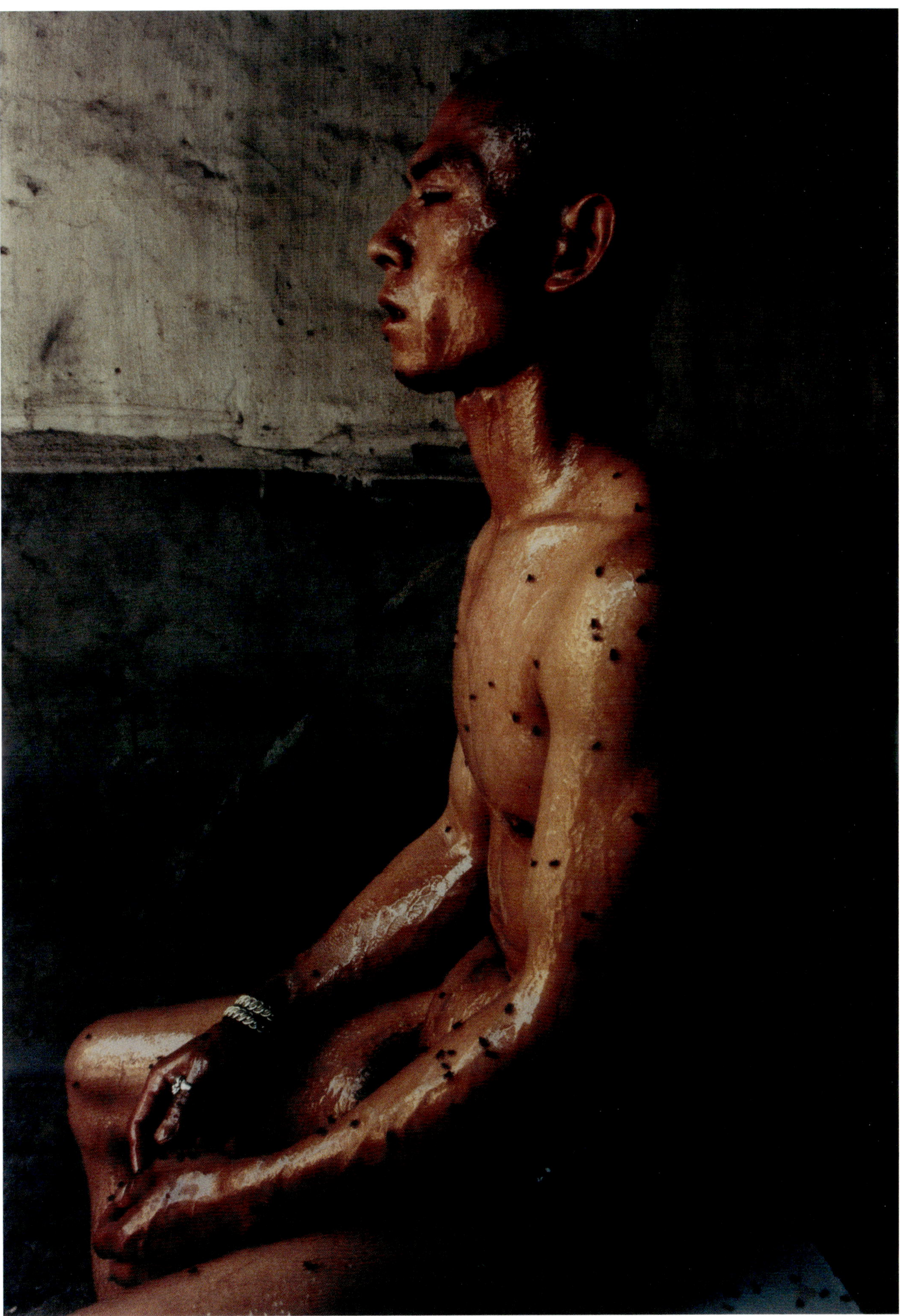

the public toilets that are used every day in China. One day after lunch, I went to the toilet as usual. The sun had just come out following a rainstorm, but there was no place to stand in the toilet for it was flooded. I had to bike to another public toilet in the village. It was relatively cleaner. When I stepped in, thousands of flies swarmed toward me and I still had to squat down. This was my life, and no one could experience it but me. I was determined to make artworks about my life and suddenly came up with the idea of *12 Square Meters*. The next day, I experimented with pieces of paper: on one side of the paper I put honey and on the other side fishy-smelling liquid. When I left the coated papers in the courtyard, flies swarmed to them. Several days later, I realized the performance. I invited photographers with still and video cameras to document the piece. I remember a video camera almost fell into the toilet during taping, which was unnerving since we had rented the expensive machine from a TV station. I sat upright and unsupported in the middle of the toilet for an hour. My body was covered with honey and fish juice, and before long, flies were all over my body, even my lips and eyes. It was uncomfortable. Some people walked in accidentally during the course of the performance. When they saw me, they were embarrassed and surprised. They wanted to leave but couldn't, because they had already begun to pee. They probably never would understand what they saw. In the course of the hour, I tried to forget myself and separate my mind from my flesh, but I was pulled back to reality again and again. Only after the performance did I understand what I experienced. An hour later, I walked out of the toilet and into a nearby pond that was polluted with garbage. I walked until water covered my head and hoards of flies struggled on the water to save their lives.

In the first half of 1998, I made *1/2*. Every morning in the market where I had breakfast, I could see rows and rows of ribs on sale at different stalls. When I saw the ribs, I saw myself. I imagined what the pigs looked like when they were alive. It was very pitiful. I was pitiful too. Half of a person is his body and the other half is his soul. This experience inspired a performance in which members of the audience were invited to write characters on my face and body. I asked them to write whatever they wanted. Some of the characters were about concepts, Buddhism, tolerance, and so on.

我就用两片纸板做实验，一片涂的是蜂蜜，一片涂的是取自鱼肚子里的腥液，放到院子里，结果苍蝇对他们都很感兴趣。几天后，我就实施了这个作品，请的有摄影师，录像师，我记得录像师在拍摄过程中差点连人带机器掉到粪池里，很惊险，因为那台租来的机器是电视台的，很贵。我端坐在厕所中间，一个小时，身上涂满了鱼液和蜂蜜，很快苍蝇就趴满了浑身上下，有些苍蝇趴在嘴唇眼睛耳朵这些部位，很不舒服。其间有人进来用厕，当他们突然发现我的时候，他们很尴尬，很惊讶，想出去但尿已经撒出来了，他们可能一辈子也不能理解眼前发生的事情。在这个过程中，我极力使自己忘记现实，让我的精神离开肉体，一次一次地被拉回现实，只有作品完成以后，我才知道我体验到了什么。一个小时之后，我走出了这个厕所，进入了一个厕所旁被污染过的充斥垃圾和粪便的水坑，直到水淹过我的头顶，水面上漂浮着无数只在逃生的苍蝇。

1998年上半年，我做了"1/2"。每天吃早点的菜市场，我都能看到整扇的猪排在小摊上贩卖，或者在自行车架子上挂着一扇猪排；看到这些猪排，我好像看到了我自己，我想象那些猪活着时候的样子，很可悲，我自己也很可悲。人的一半是身体，一半是灵魂。作品中的汉字是请在场的朋友写出他们想写的东西，象"观念"，"佛"，"卡夫卡"，"宽容"等等。

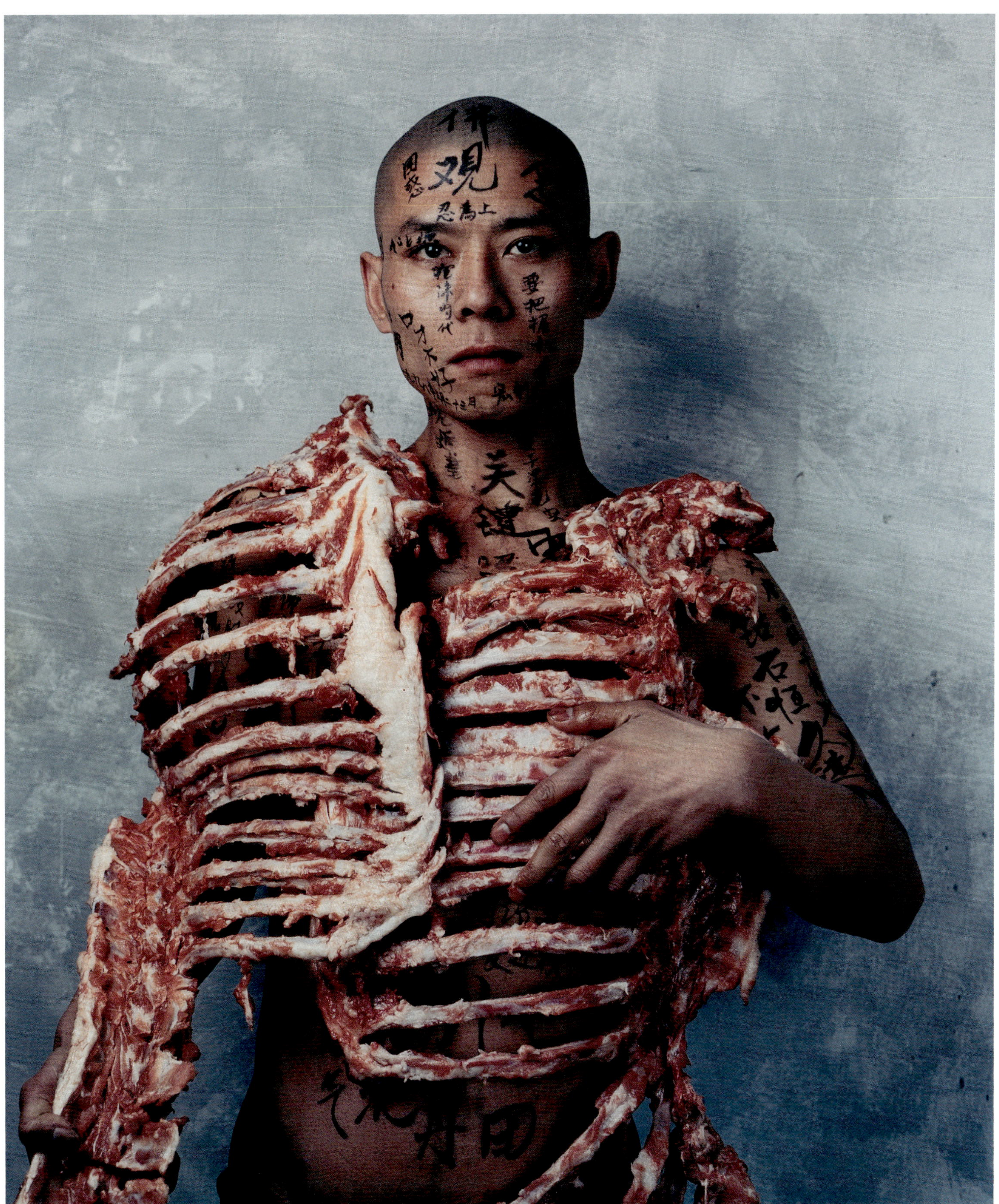

In the summer of 1997, I created *To Raise the Water Level in a Fishpond*. I invited more than forty immigrant workers in Beijing to participate. They came from all over the countryside and ranged in age from twenty to sixty. Some worked in moving companies and construction while others sold fish. I went to many shabby tents (their homes) in order to find them. At the time, I lived within walking distance from a fishpond. The immigrant workers didn't understand what I was doing but simply followed my instructions. When I saw them, they reminded me of my uncles and brothers from my childhood. The piece has three parts. First, we circled the pond with five to six meters between each person and faced the pond in silence. Next, we raised the water level of the pond. For the final part, we stood as a human wall to divide the fishpond in two. The boy on my back was the son of the fishpond owner and only five years old. Surprisingly, he did very well that day. I had created pieces related to mountains, so I wanted to make some related to water; this work fulfilled that desire. To my knowledge, it was the first time that an artist collaborated with immigrant workers.

- Zhang Huan

1997夏天，我还做了"为鱼塘增高水位"。我邀请了四十多位来自全国各地来北京打工的民工，有搬家公司的，有建筑工人，有卖鱼养鱼的；年龄从二十几岁到六十几岁。为了找这些民工，我走访了很多他们居住的简易棚子，这个鱼塘离我住的地方不远，我有时散步就能走到那儿。这些参与的民工并不理解我的本意，只是按照我的计划来实施这个作品。我看到他们的时候，他们就象我童年生活印象里的叔叔伯伯和兄弟。这个作品分三个部分。第一部分是把这个鱼塘围住，每个人面向水，间隔五六米，沉默看水；第二部分是增高水位：第三部分组成一排人墙将鱼塘一分为二。我身上背的小孩年仅五岁，是鱼塘主人的孩子，那一天他表现得很出色，有一种超乎年龄的早熟。我做过与大山有关的作品，还想做一个与水有关的作品，也算实现了内心的一个愿望。与民工合作作品，这在当时中国的艺术界还是第一次。接下来的一年，这件作品获邀在纽约展出引起了很大关注。

- 张洹

Zhang Huan, *To Add One Meter to an Anonymous Mountain*, 1995, C-print on Fuji archival paper, Ed. 1/15, 41 1/8 x 60 1/2 in. (104.5 x 153.7 cm), acquired in 1999
张洹，《为无名山增高一米》，1995, C-打印在富士档案纸, 版本 1/15, 41 1/8 x 60 1/2 寸 (104.5 x 153.7 厘米), 收藏于 1999

Zhang Huan, *To Raise The Water Level in a Fishpond (Close-up)*, 1997, C-print on Fuji archival paper, Ed. 14/15, 40 3/4 x 60 1/2 in. (102.9 x 153.7 cm), acquired in 1999
张洹，《为鱼塘增高水位》，1995, C-打印在富士档案纸, 版本 14/15, 40 3/4 x 60 1/2 寸 (102.9 x 153.7 厘米), 收藏于 1999

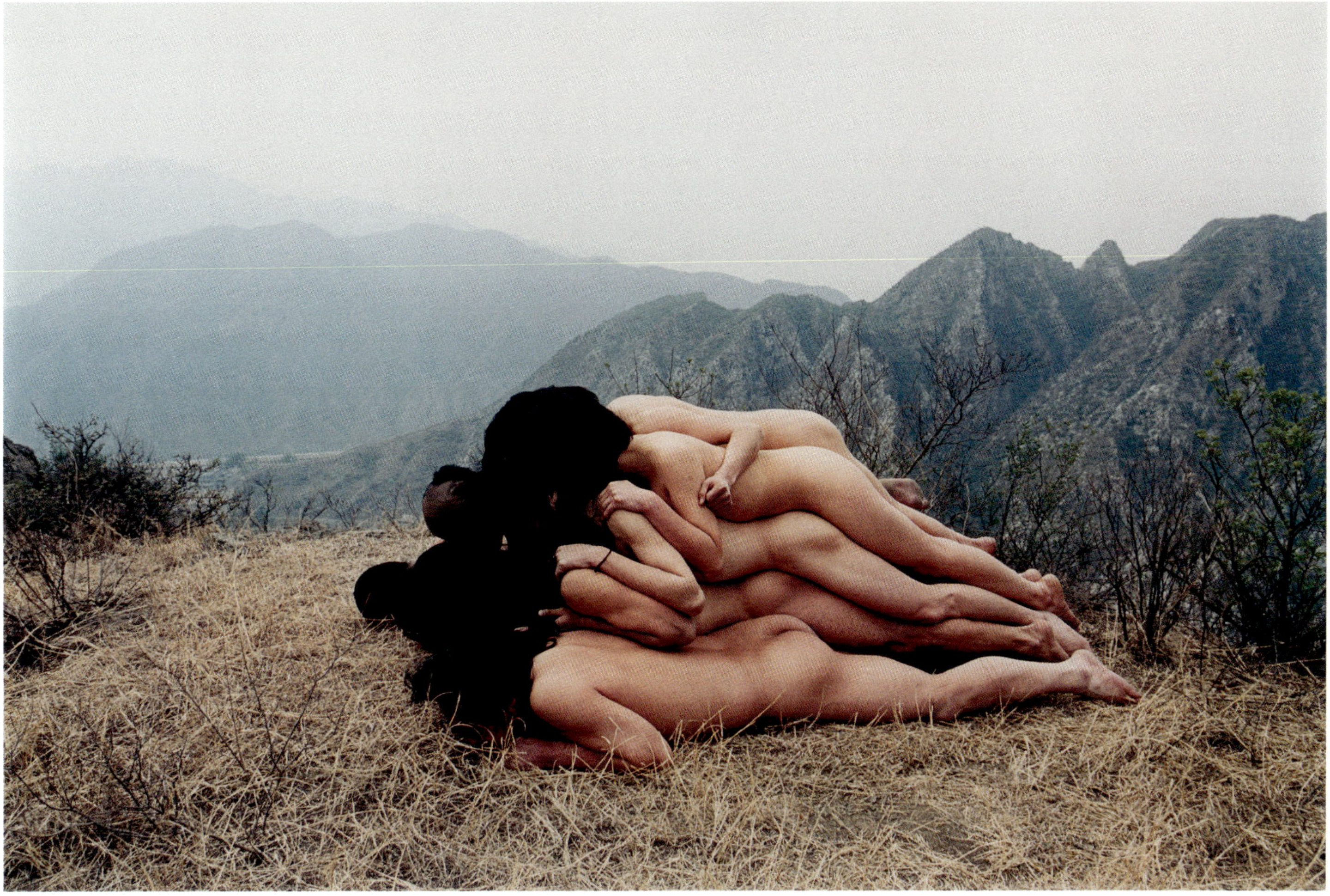

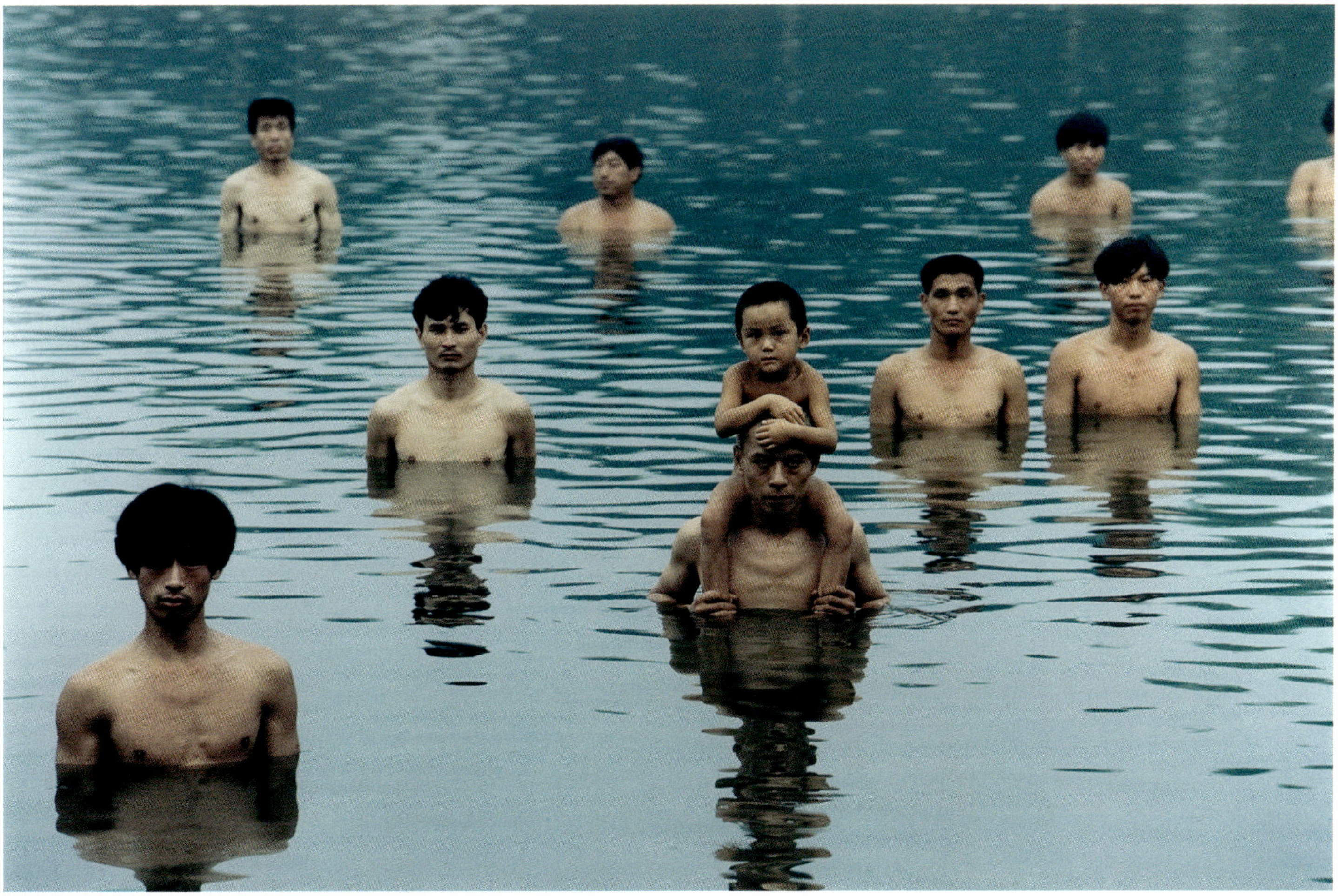

Zhang Huan, *Diary*, 2008, ash on linen, 63 x 59 1/8 in. (160 x 150 cm), acquired in 2008
张洹，《日记》，2008，灰在亚麻布上，63 x 59 1/8 寸 (160 x 150 厘米)，收藏于 2008

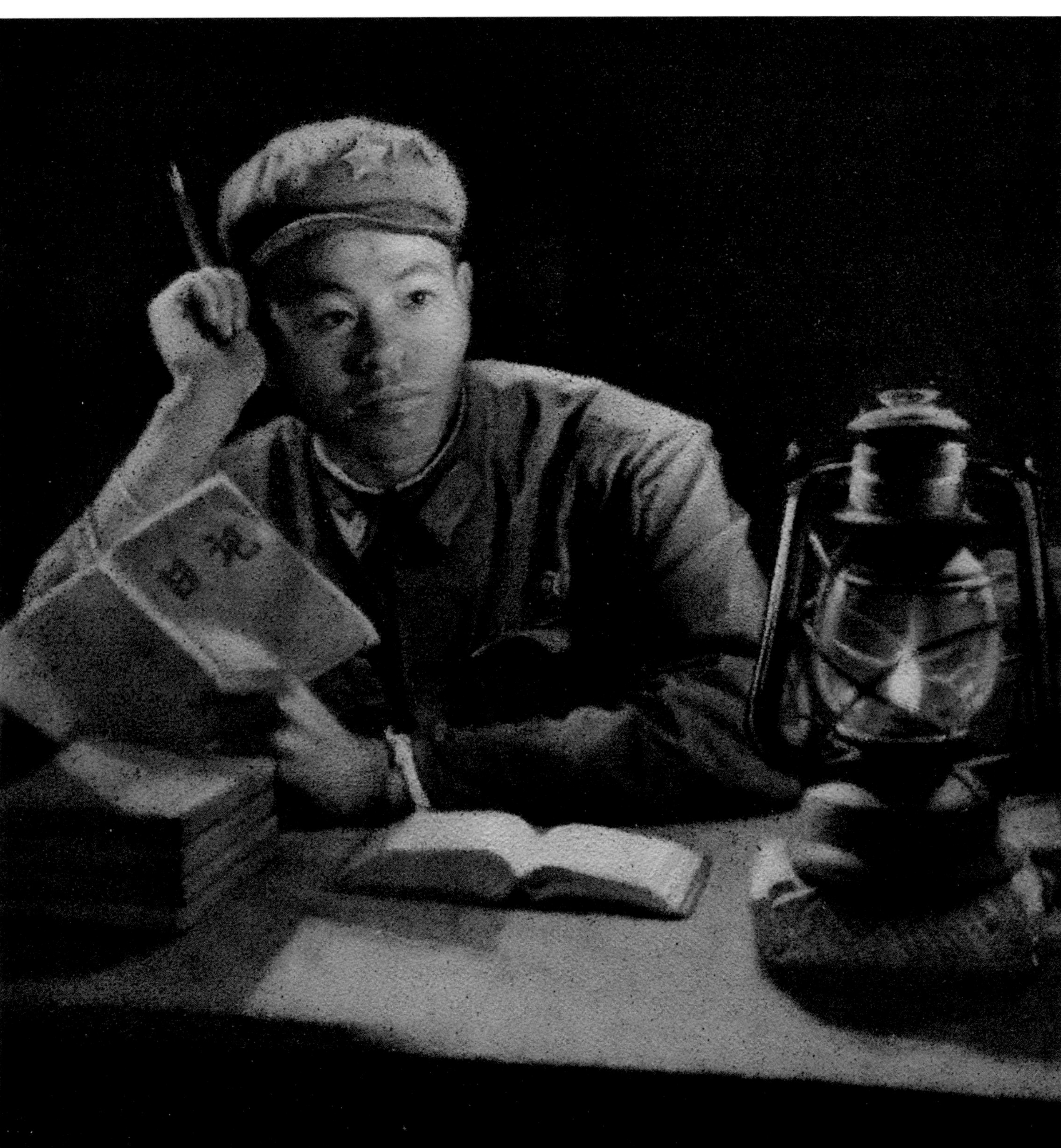

Zhao Yao

Born in 1981, Sichuan, China
Lives and works in Beijing, China

赵要

一九八一年生於中国四川
居住和工作於中国北京

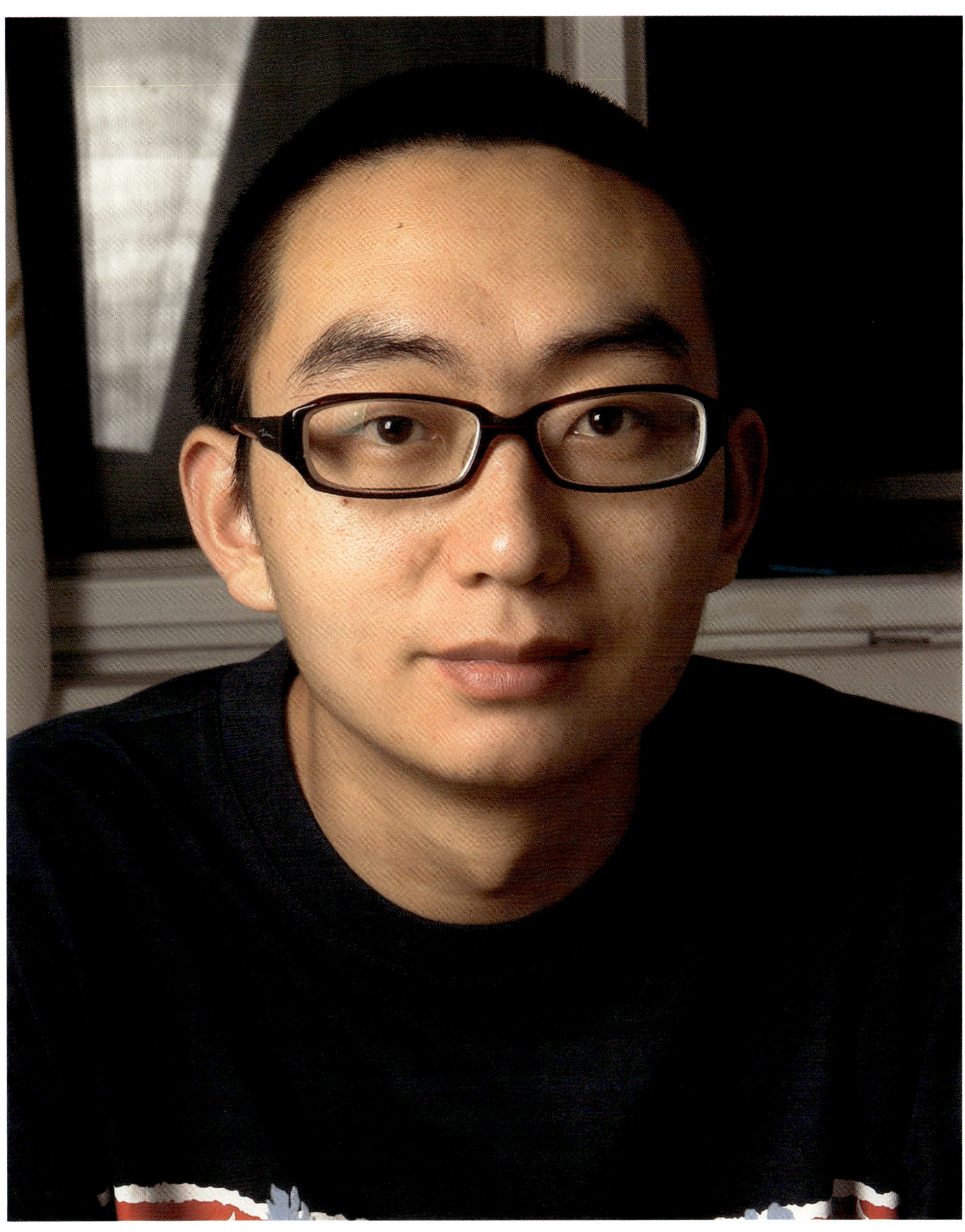

This is a long term project. Starting in the winter of 2008, over the course of one year I took Beijing's more than 900 public bus lines, being moved through the city in pursuit of the sun. With my camera I tried to catch the sun in the exact middle of the shot. Then I displayed these tens of thousands of pictures, playing eight frames per second. On the one hand to personally experience the sun as the relation between historical experiences and Beijing. On the other hand, the person and the camera are compressed and concentrated in a mobile point, which crosses through the interior of the material space of greater Beijing. It goes over fixed and planned lines from the center to the suburbs, from the suburbs to the center, and then again to another suburb. By repeating this, I have travelled to every corner of the city, and experienced all sorts of changes in the city of Beijing, as well as the sun's delicate relations with the city in time and space. The project was finished in November 2009.

Currently the whole process of creation is exhibited as if it were a TV series. This places the work in real life and can spark contemplations, foremost reflections about "the necessity of artistic creation".

- Zhao Yao

这是一个长期计划。从2008年的冬天开始，在一年的时间里，通过乘坐北京 900多条线路的公交车，在城市里被动的追逐太阳。用相机尽可能的抓拍下太阳在图像正中心的照片。然后把这几万张照片以每秒 8帧的速度播放展示。一方面体验太阳作为历史经验与北京的关系。另一方面，人和相机被压缩凝聚成一个移动的点，在大北京这个物理空间的内部穿行。以固定和规划化的线路从中心到郊外，从郊外再到中心再到另外一个郊外。如此反复，踏遍这个城市的各个角落，体验和感受北京城市的各种变化，以及太阳在一年四季里与这个城市在时间、空间上的各种微妙关系。整个计划于 2009年11月完成。

目前整个创作以一种"电视剧"的方式展开工作。使其成为放入现实生活并能启动思考的装置。并以 "艺术创作必要性 "的反思为核心。

- 赵要

Zhao Yao, *I Love Beijing 999*, 2009, single-channel video (color, silent), Ed. 1/6, duration: 41 min. 6 sec., acquired in 2012
赵要，《我爱北京999》，2009，单视频 (彩色，无声)，版本 1/6，持续时间: 41 分 6秒，收藏于 2012

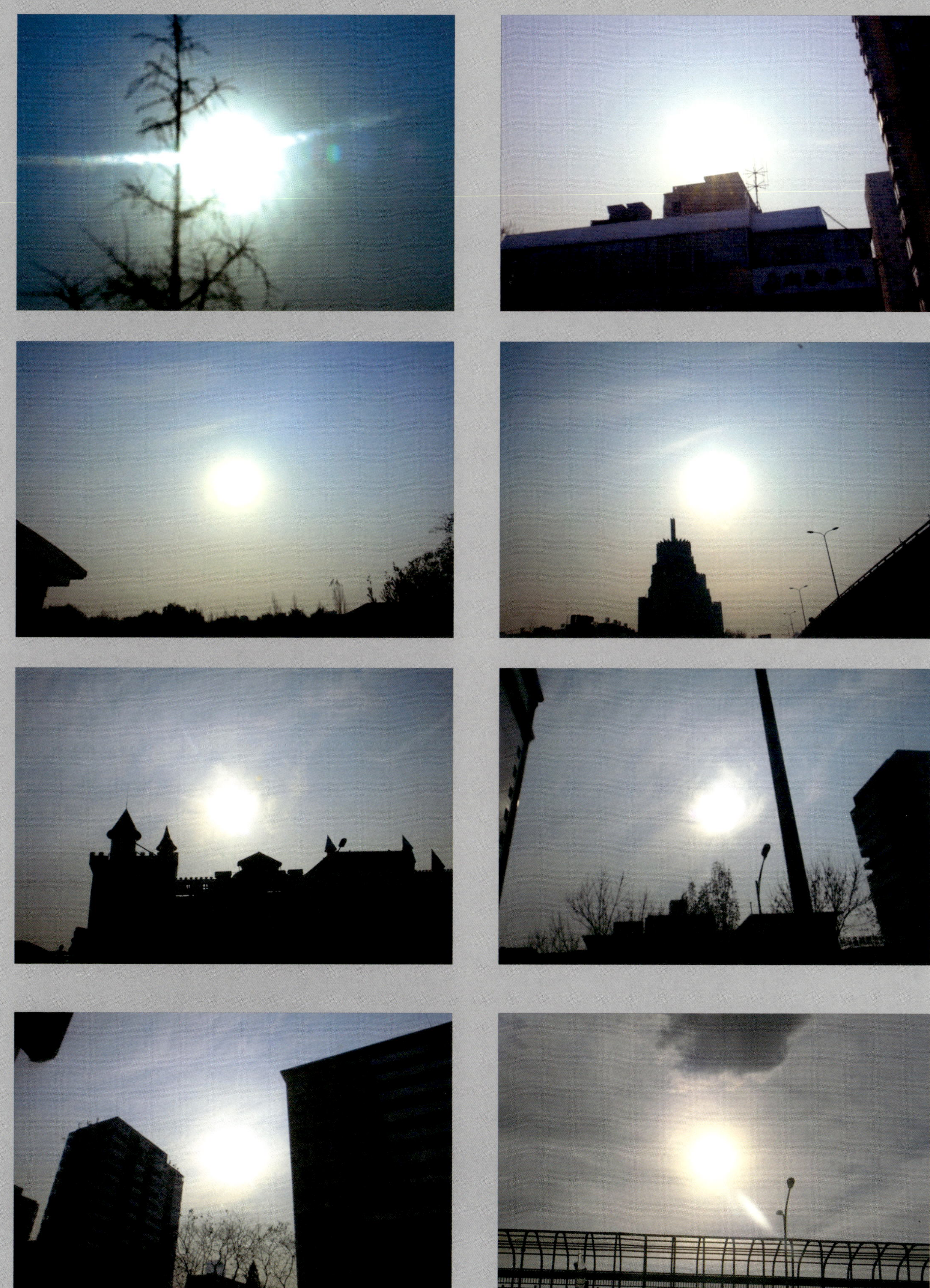

This is a group of paintings about painting. The shapes come from all sort of practice tests in a book called *1000 Intelligence Questions All Smart People Love*. In design they are very similar to existing abstract paintings, and through this method they directly bring out the recognition and memory of existing abstract paintings. These memories can enter the work as ready-made conceptual material, and thus generate the actual meaning of the work. What is used for the figures, colors, canvas and concept is all ready-made. These figures vary in form and shape. They are enlarged, thickened and placed on the ready-made textiles. From the ready-made textiles, one large part comes from geometric pattern cloth used in everyday urban life, while the other large part comes from traditionally manufactured, hand-knitted cloth from Wugong County in Shaanxi Province. Through combining these types of different abstract aesthetics into paintings, the series as a whole will gain a place within the system of paintings.

- Zhao Yao

这是一组关于绘画的绘画。这些图形来自《全世界聪明人都爱做的1000道智力题》一书里的各种测试。在图式上与现有的抽象绘画很相似，通过这个方式直接调动出对现有抽象绘画的认识和记忆。这些记忆作为一种现成的观念元素加入到作品中来，生成作品的现实意义。从图像，颜色、画布以及观念来说利用的都是现成的。这些图像各种各样并不固定，放大并且厚厚的平涂到各种现成的纺织布上。这些现成的织布包括两大部分，一部分来自城市日常生活的所见的各种抽象几何布料，另一部分来自陕西武功县传统方式生产的手织布。通过这几种现成抽象审美趣味的结合构成绘画，使其整个系列成为一种置入到绘画系统里的装置。

- 赵要

Zhao Yao, *A Painting of Thought I -962D*, 2011, acrylic on found fabric, 70 7/8 x 47 1/8 in. (180 x 120 cm), acquired in 2012
赵要，《很有想法的绘画I-962D》，2011，丙烯在现成的布上，70 7/8 x 47 1/8 寸 (180 x 120 厘米)，收藏于 2012

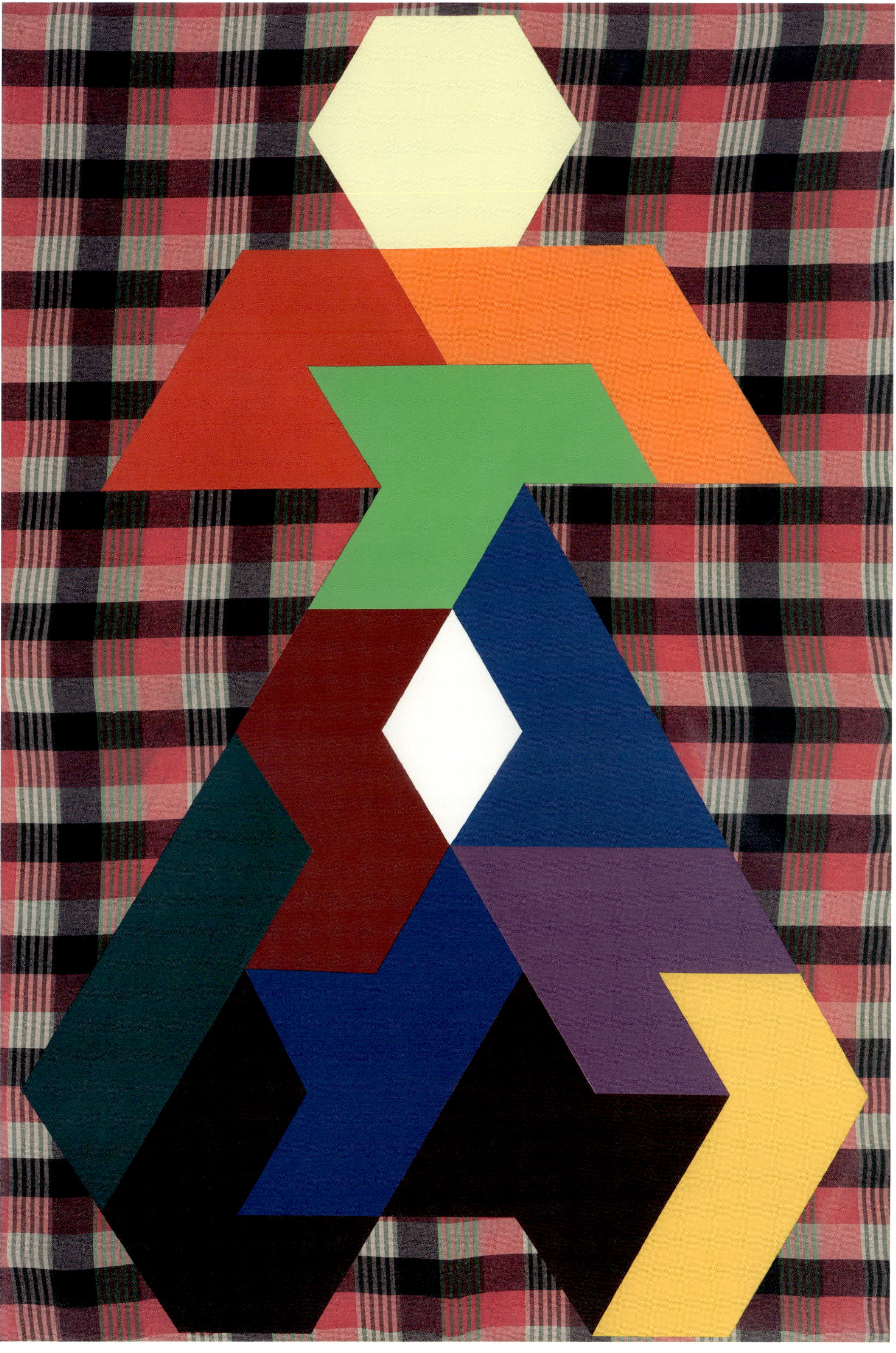

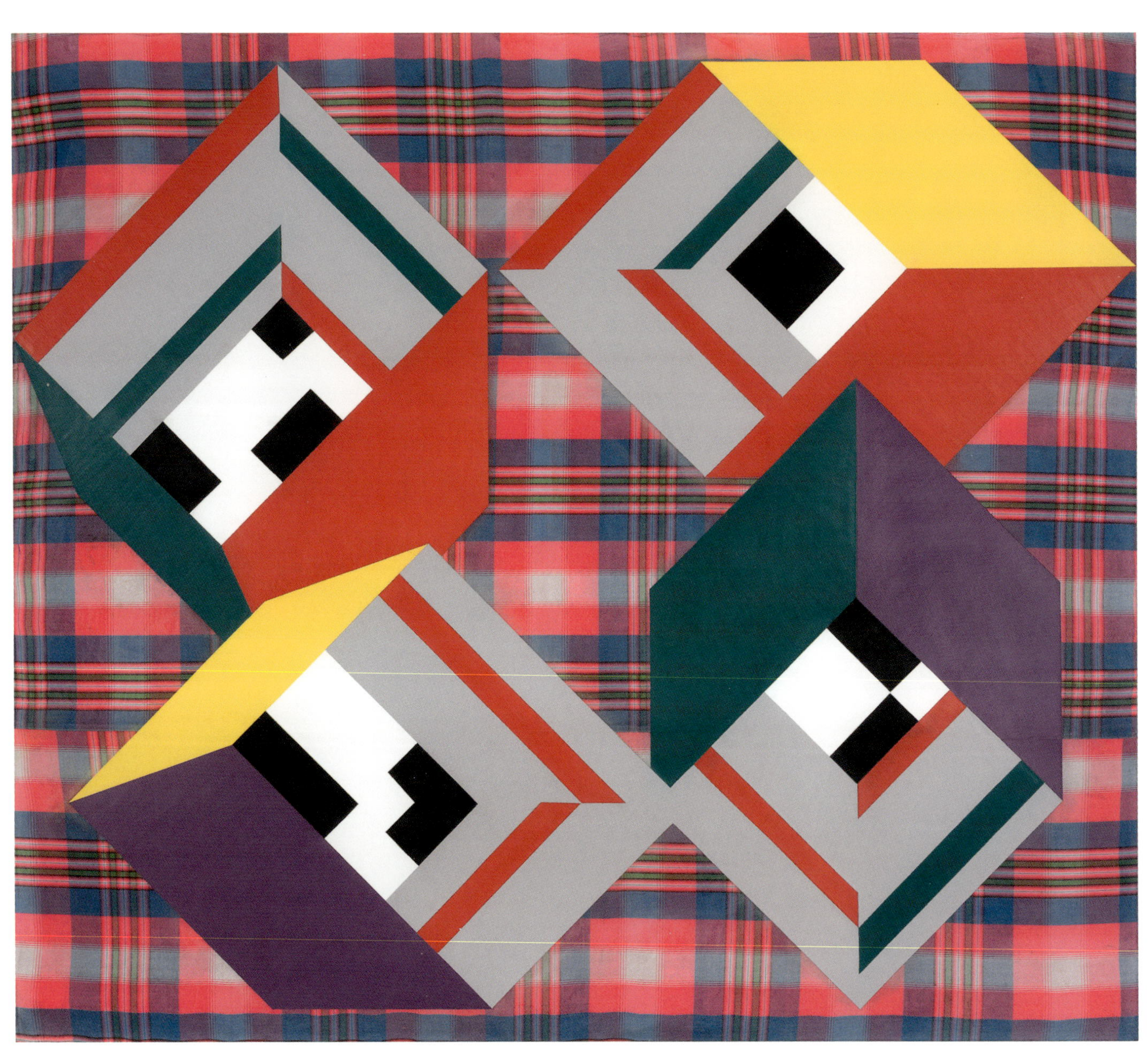

Zhao Yao, *A Painting of Thought III -69*, 2012, acrylic on found fabric, 70 3/4 x 78 3/4 in. (180 x 200 cm), acquired in 2012
赵要，《很有想法的绘画 III -69》，2012，丙烯在现成的布上，70 3/4 x 78 3/4 寸 (180 x 200 厘米)，收藏于 2012

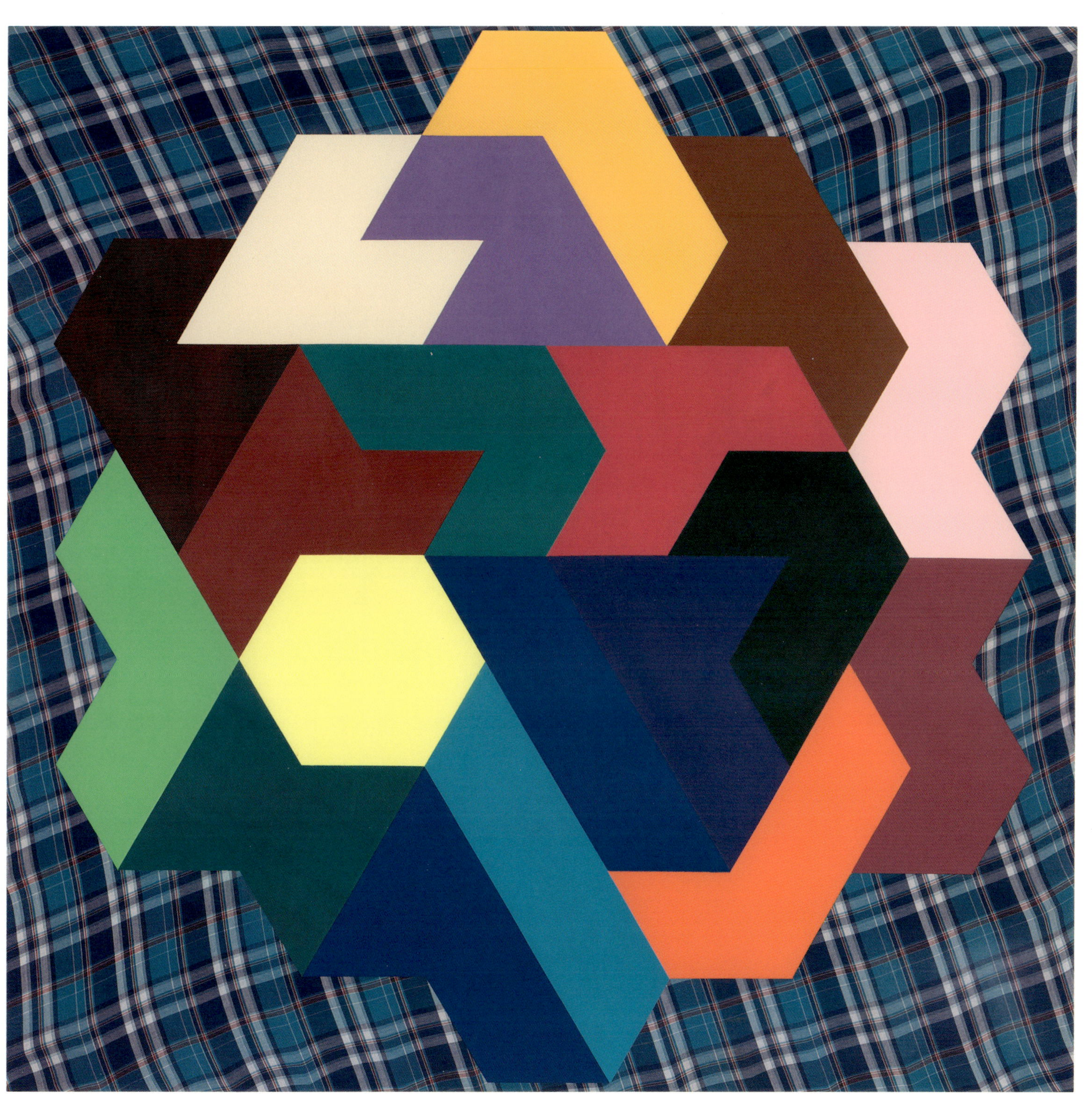

Zhao Yao, *A Painting of Thought III -162*, 2011, acrylic on found fabric, 47 1/4 x 47 1/4 in. (120 x 120 cm), acquired in 2012
赵要，《很有想法的绘画 III -162》，2011，丙烯在现成的布上，47 1/4 x 47 1/4 寸 (120 x 120 厘米)，收藏于 2012

Zhu Jinshi 朱金石

Born in 1954, Beijing, China
Lives and works in Beijing, China

一九五四年生於中國北京
居住和工作於中国北京

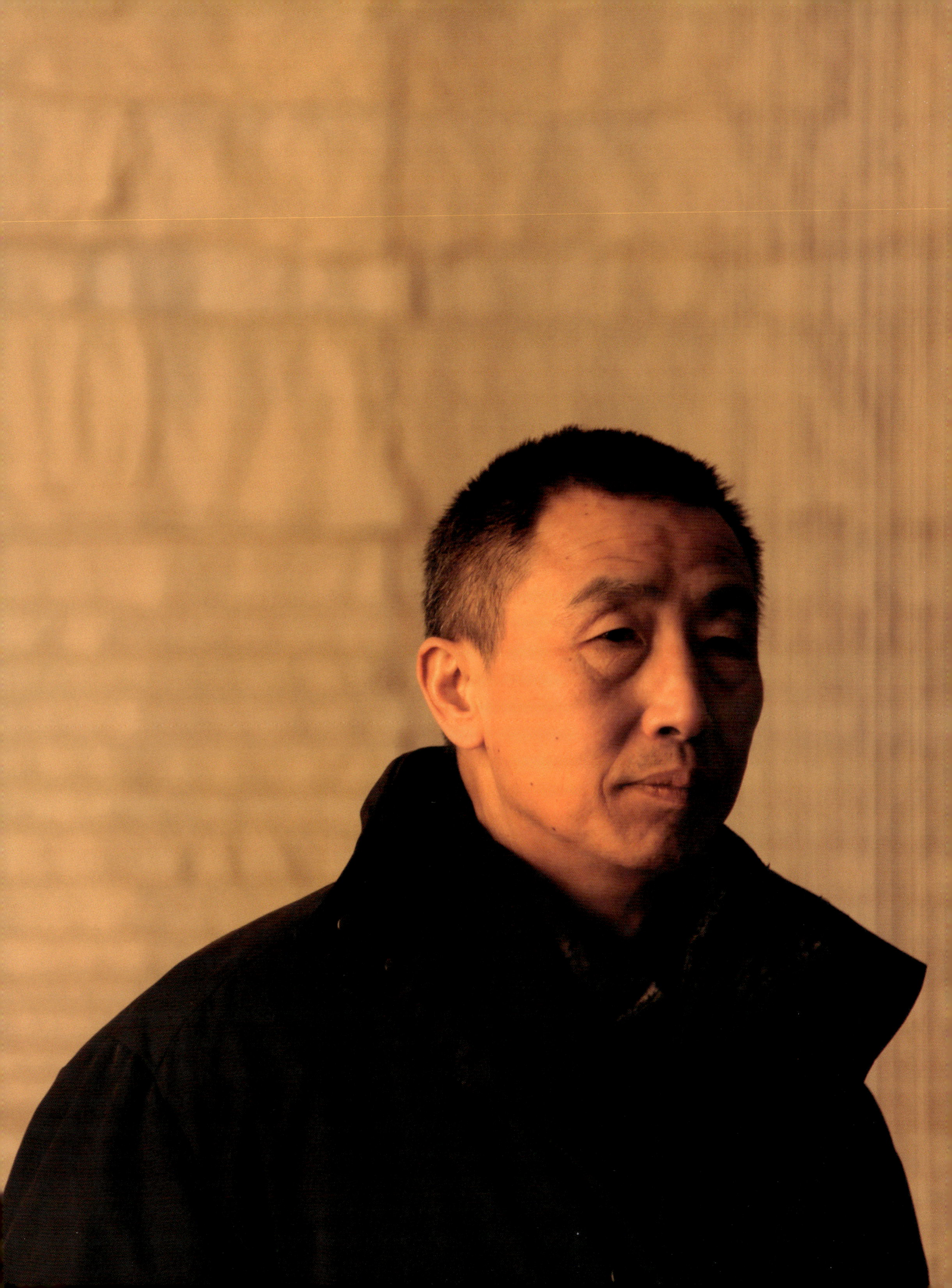

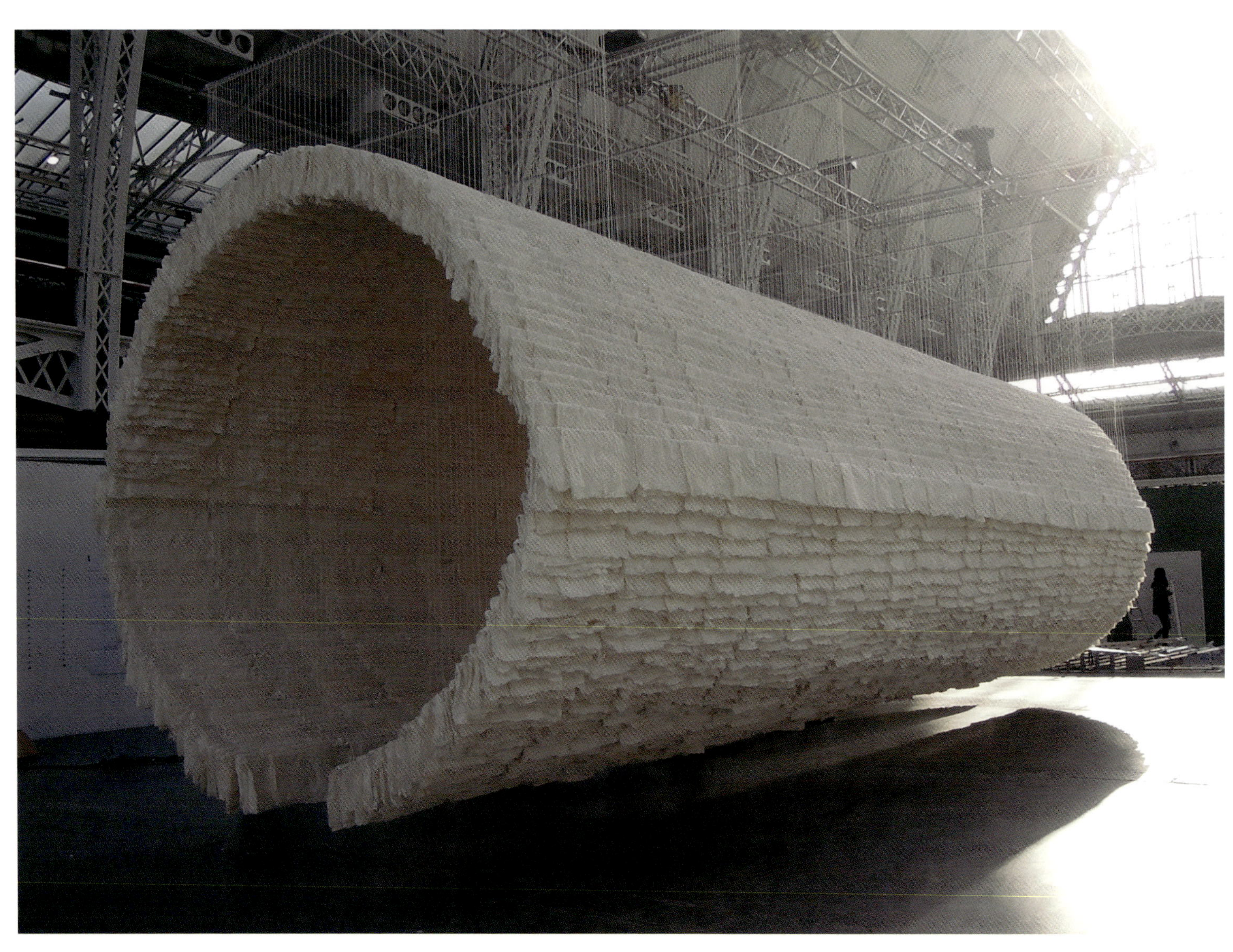

Zhu Jinshi, *Boat*, 2012, Xuan paper, bamboo and cotton thread, 590 x 137 x 165 in. (1500 x 350 x 420 cm), acquired in 2013
朱金石,《船》, 2012, 宣纸, 竹子和棉线, 590 x 137 x 165 寸 (1500 x 350 x 420 厘米), 收藏于 2013

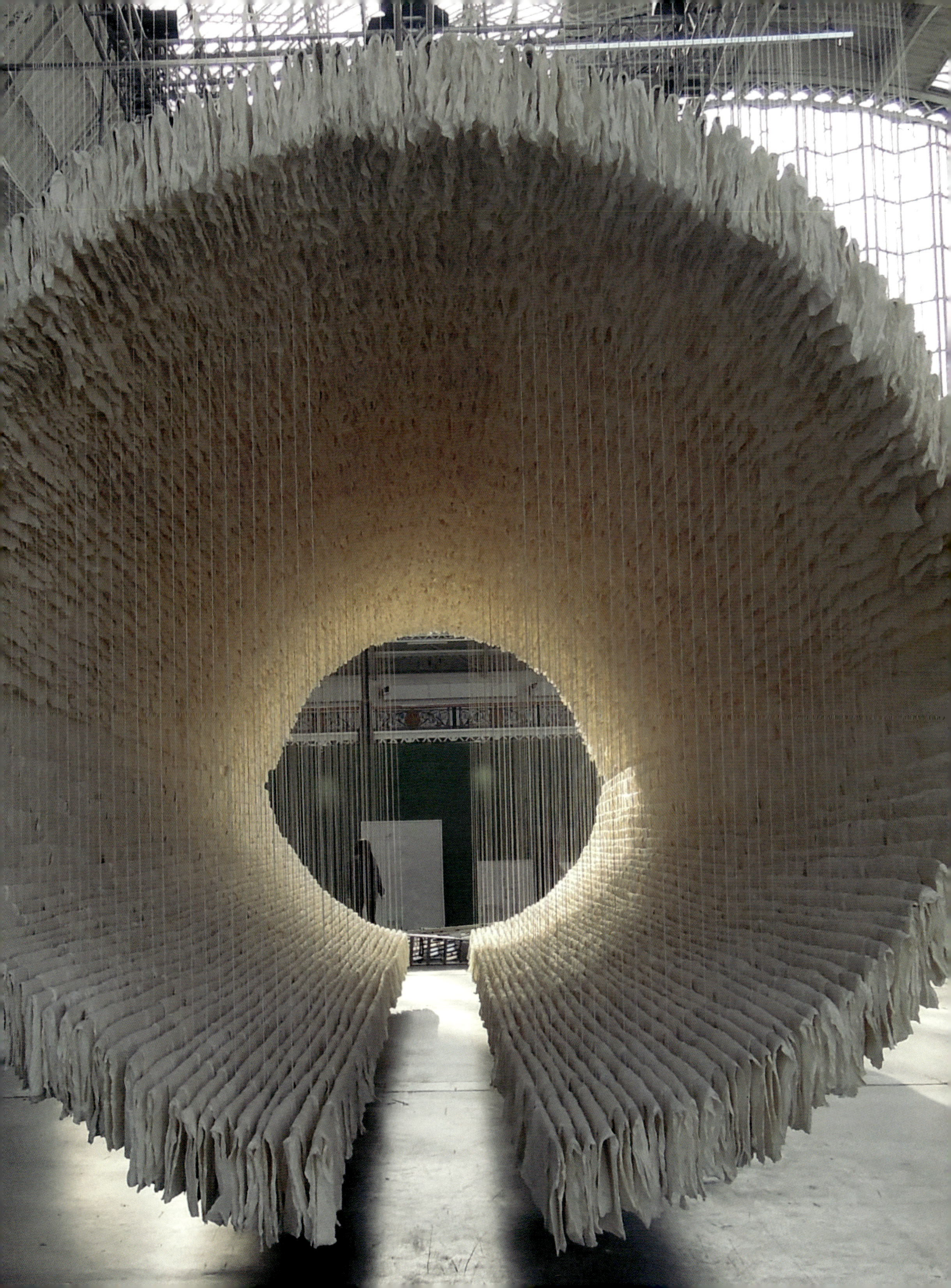

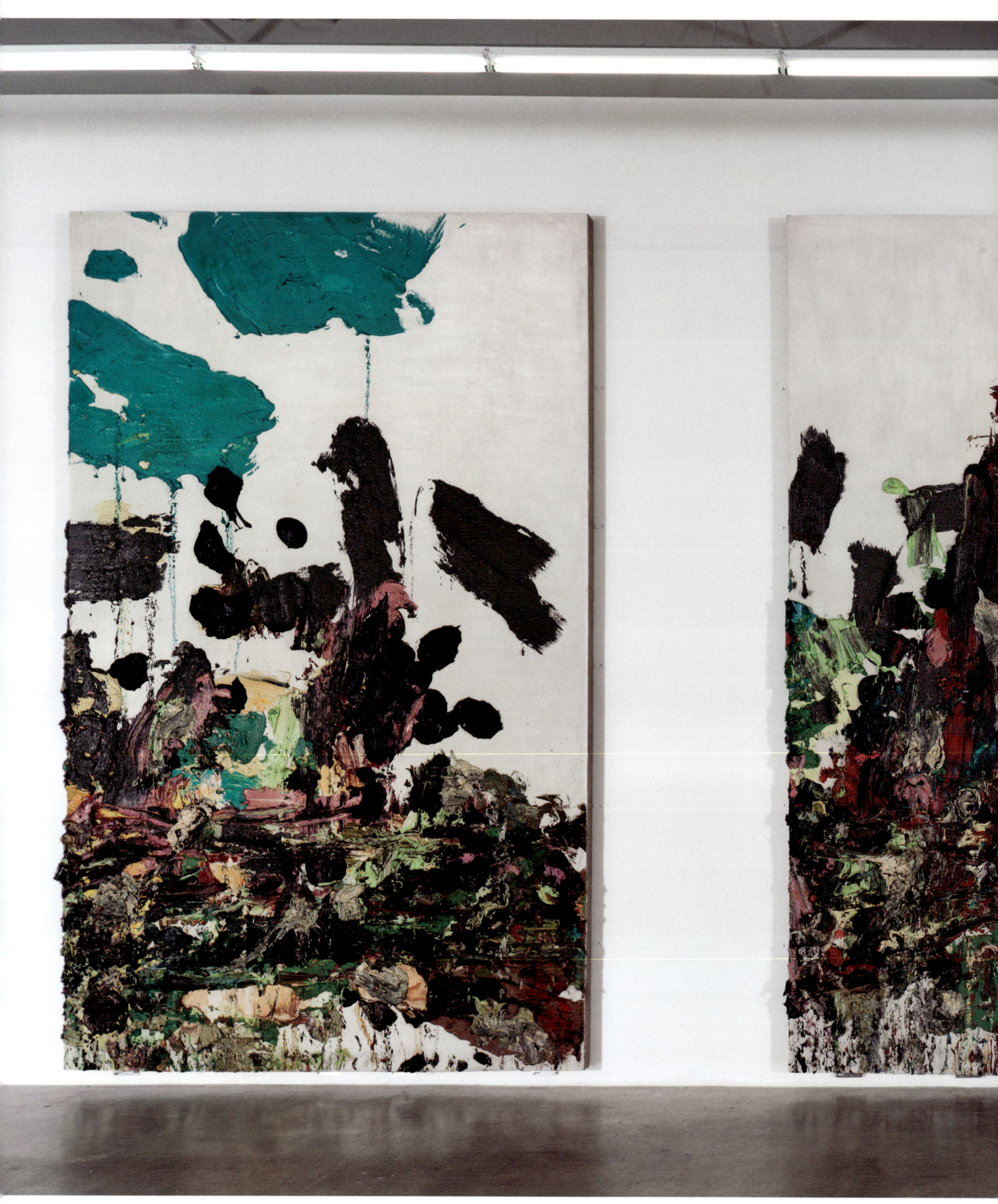

Zhu Jinshi, *Power and Kingdom*, 2007-2010, oil on canvas, triptych, each: 331 x 197 in. (840 x 500 cm), acquired in 2011
朱金石，《权力与江山》，2007-2010，布上油画，三联，每幅：331 x 197 寸 (840 x 500 厘米)，收藏于 2011

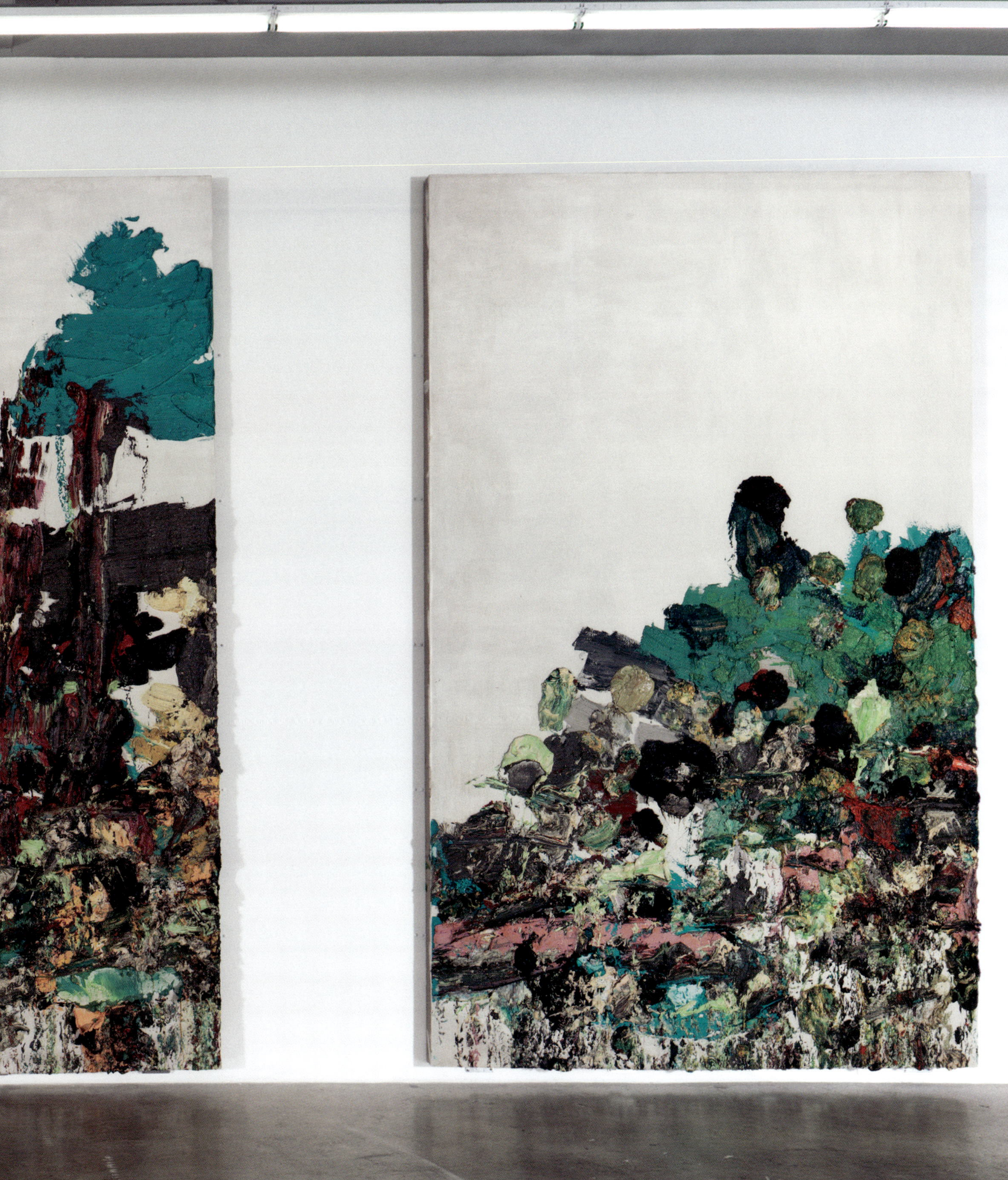

Philip Dodd: What state are you in when you finish a work?

Zhu Jinshi: After completing an artwork, I am content: I have a sense of comfort that needs no words. But completing an artwork does not mean the work is done. I feel like a chess player who replays a game in his mind after it is over. I ponder many of the details, much like a chess player reflects on each of his moves, on what he did right, did not. The details determine the quality and depth of the work; the final artwork is created by how the tools are used and manipulated, how the specific design of the picture frame is produced, why a different tonality of linen is chosen, and in the years of meditation expressed in each pigment application. Of course, the ultimate manifestation of all these decisions forever remains on the surface of the canvas, where I had to discard the conventionalised methods of oil painting in order to forge this new language.

Interestingly, even my knowledgeable artist friends take the view that the completion of my work is heavily reliant upon chance. I just laugh and offer no response to this. I find Pollock irritating; I prefer de Kooning, who in his greatest works controlled the balance of elements on the surface of the canvas to express the visual force of his inner self. To achieve what I want to achieve, an intense degree of expression, I can't let my assistants complete my work. I can't act like Jeff Koons and have other people complete my art—I just can't do that. I need the touch of my own hand; I need the touch of my hand to match my vision. Only when the capabilities of my hand and vision are at one, can the pulse of the work be shocked into a beating rhythm. Whether or not it begins to pulsate, isn't this the magic of painting? In any case, you asked about my state of mind when I complete an artwork: it is grounded in this complex idea. We are unable to know for certain when a work of art is complete. Instead, we believe a work of art to be continually becoming—and from this our state of mind is enriched.

Dodd: Is time important in your work? For example, after you complete a painting, the work typically requires a few years for the painted surface to completely air dry— an element beyond your control.

Zhu: In 1990, I painted a few works that are still not dry. I was mixing my own paints then, and my technique was probably not correct, but this accidental element created an effect; namely, that the works feel incomplete, and that their completion hinges on the influence of time, material and environment. There is

菲利浦‧多德：完成一件作品時，你是什麼狀態？

朱金石：完成一件作品之後產生愜意、舒展的感覺自不必言，但作品的完成並不意味工作的結束，這正像棋手對弈之後的複盤。事實上，我會琢磨很多細節，也正像棋手思考每一落子的得失。細節決定了作品的延深，從工具的使用與改變，從畫框特殊製作與不同亞麻布的底色效果，包括顏料在畫布上幾年之間產生的變化。當然，更具決定性的是對細節的關注會永遠保持在畫面上，當我幾乎拋棄了所謂的油畫的繪畫方式，就必然需要對新的語言進行具體的塑造。

有趣的是，即使是經驗豐富的藝術家朋友，他們都認爲我是依賴偶然性完成了作品，對此我總是笑而不語，我其實有些拒絕波洛克(Jackson Pollock)而喜歡德庫寧(Willem de Kooning)，後者在發揮偶然的極致時，同時又控制著畫面的平衡，由此產生視覺的動力。爲了達到這種要求，我無法讓助手替代我的工作，像傑夫‧昆斯(JeffKoons)那樣領著幾十人畫一幅畫我做不到，我需要自己的手感，需要這種手感與視覺默契的配合，只有它們的相通產生能量，心靈才會被震起博動，而這會不會就是繪畫的魔力？無論如何，你問的作品完成狀態也包括在於此，也就是說，我們無法真正確認一件作品結束，我們毋寧相信每一件作品永遠處於開始，而我們的狀態也由此充實起來。

多德：時間這個因素在你的作品中重要嗎？例如，創作完成後，你的作品通常需要幾年的時間，表層才會緩慢風乾——在這個過程中，時間是否是一種不可抗拒的因素？

朱：我在1990年畫的油畫到現在仍沒有乾透，當時我是自己做的油畫顏料，方法大概不對，但這無意中造成了一個現象，即作品的未完成感，而完成它依賴於時間、材料、環境對作品產生的影響，作品表層的變化也與剛剛完成它時明顯不同，有點飽經滄桑的感覺，表層產生的時間質感無疑加強了作品的視覺效果，但我關注的則更是另外一面，即時間賦予了繪畫新的生命，當這種由於顏色作為顏料的材料產生柔軟度，盡管在視覺上你無法看到；但時間卻看到了，看到了材料的呼吸，那麼，這個時候必然感染我，我注意到，這是一種保持著呼吸的繪畫，物質的呼吸帶給精神無限的想像力。有一次，我對Pearl說，千百年後繪畫還會再畫，就暗指這個意思。

多德：經過幾年的交往與觀察，Pearl發現你的繪畫藝術可分爲四個階段。一、上世紀八十年代初期，經典的中國抽象繪畫案例；二、九十年代

a distinct visual difference in the painted surface now and from when it was just completed, as if it has lived through many changes.

The time needed for the painted surface to dry undoubtedly helps to determine the work's visual effect, but what interests me, rather, is something else; namely, that the passage of time bestows upon the artwork new life, and the colour registers the painting material's degree of softness, even though on the surface you can't see it at any given moment. But time can see it; it can see the material breathing. I said to Pearl [Lam] once, "In a thousand years from now, a painting will still continue to paint."

Dodd: After several years of talking with you and looking at your work, Pearl Lam suggests that your work might be divided into four periods. The first is work from the early 1980s, classic abstract painting; the second, work from the early 1990s when the calligraphic brushstroke was a keystone of your paintings and you established your signature style of 'thick' painting; and the third, your painting from 2000 to 2010 with its deep ridges and troughs within the paint. The fourth period is the most recent work.

Do you consider the 1990s to be a 'transitional' period for your work?

Zhu: The questions you raise are all concerned with the development of my style over time, which is a particularly art historical way of thinking. This is not necessarily how artists think as they make work. You want to know if the period in the early 1990s was transitional for me in my painting practice? You see something in those works, but the language you use tells you nothing of the preparation to get there, nor the environment in which they were created. You approach the work as a Western art critic, using the formal language of a certain kind of art history. From the late 1980s to the early 1990s, China's practising artists rebelled against the collective approach to art that they had inherited, and it was at that moment that Chinese contemporary art entered the sphere of the international art world. At that time, just remember, painting was not just being called into question; it was 'the end of painting' according to contemporary art. Even today, you don't see critical art research into this period of Chinese painting. It is neglected. What's more, they have starkly divided painting and non-painting into two separate camps—'Chinese painting' and so-called 'contemporary Chinese art'. Despite its narrow and prejudiced field of vision, this way of thinking is still the bedrock of the prevailing theory in China today.

初期，在保持筆觸繪畫、書法繪畫的同時，開始凸顯個人風格，厚繪畫雛形已定；三、2000年之後，回歸繪畫，至2010年，厚繪畫盡顯鋒芒；第四階段即是當下的創作。

多德：在這裏，我好奇的是，九十年代是您的繪畫過渡期嗎？

朱：你連續提出的幾個問題都是對我的繪畫的形成形態的思考，換句話說，是一種藝術史的觀察角度。你其中問到，1990年代初是不是我的繪畫過渡期？你在這時似乎看到了什麼，但又毫不知情地準備與一個關鍵的時刻擦肩而過，而西方的批評，幾乎和你一樣，忽略了一個藝術史不可忽略的重大事件。

八十年代末至九十年代初，中國前衛藝術家在繪畫領域集體嬗變，由此開始，中國當代藝術以新的姿態進入到國際化的藝術系統，而反繪畫不僅是對繪畫的質疑，更是向藝術的當代主義靠攏，直到今天，仍未看到藝術批評研究這一時期的繪畫與反繪畫背後產生的影響力及破壞力，而是生硬的把繪畫藝術與非繪畫藝術分裂成兩大陣營，所謂當代藝術，在中國產生的偏見及狹窄視野，仍然有效地行使著單一的權力。

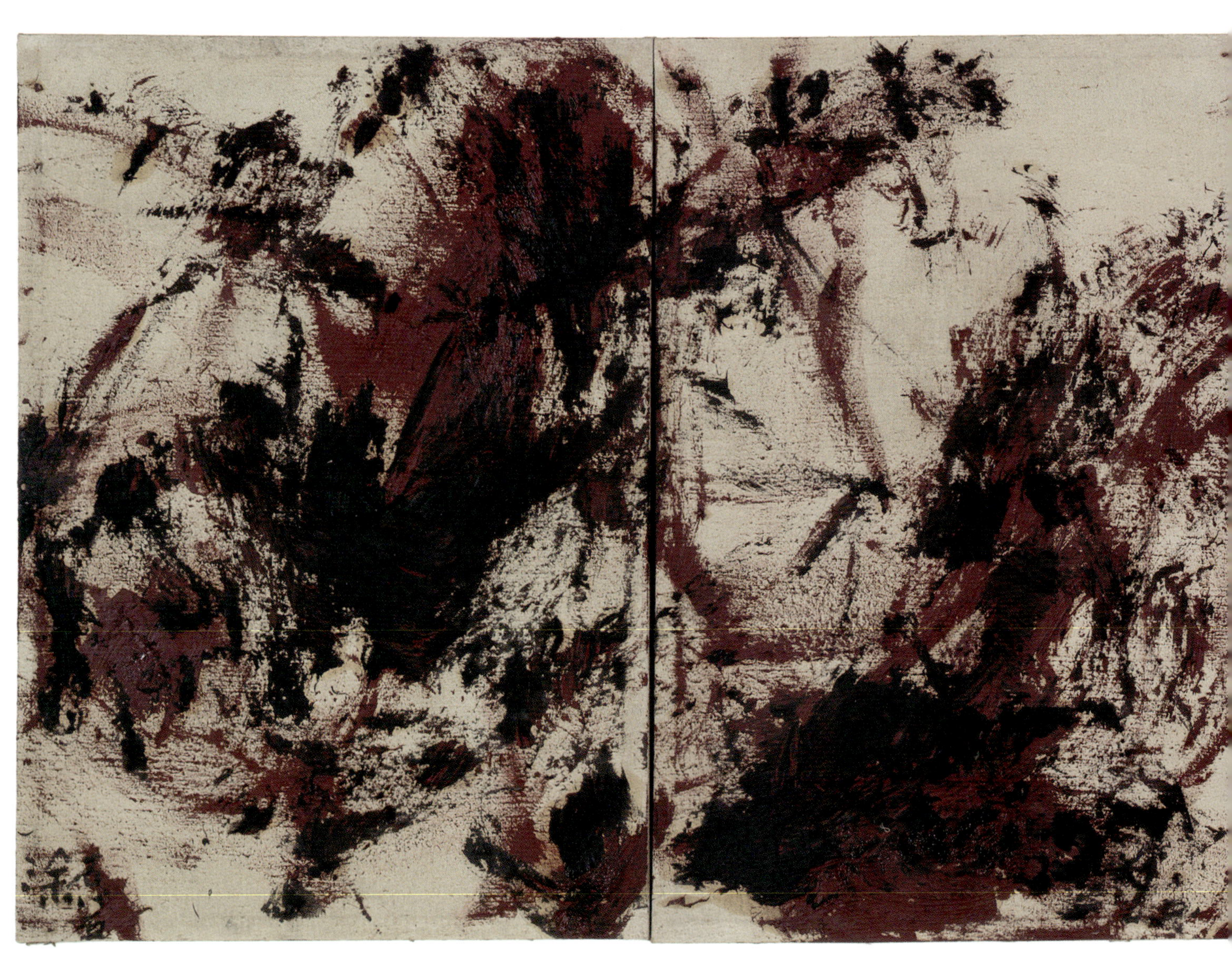

Zhu Jinshi, *Scribble 85*, 1985, oil on canvas, quadriptych, each: 39 x 110 in. (100 x 280 cm), acquired in 2011
朱金石，《涂鸦 85》，1985，布上油画，四联，每幅: 39 x 110 寸 (100 x 280 厘米)，收藏于 2011

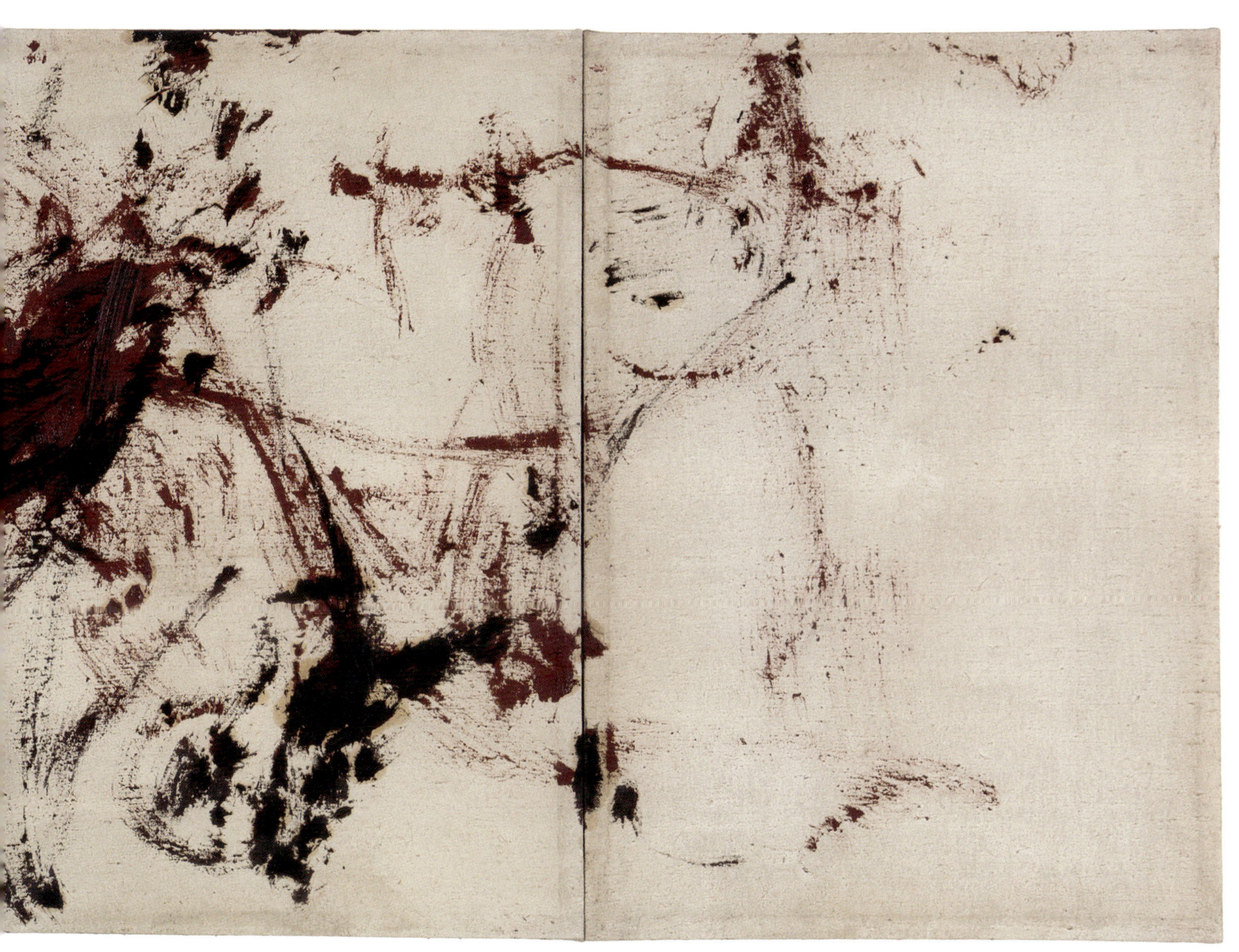

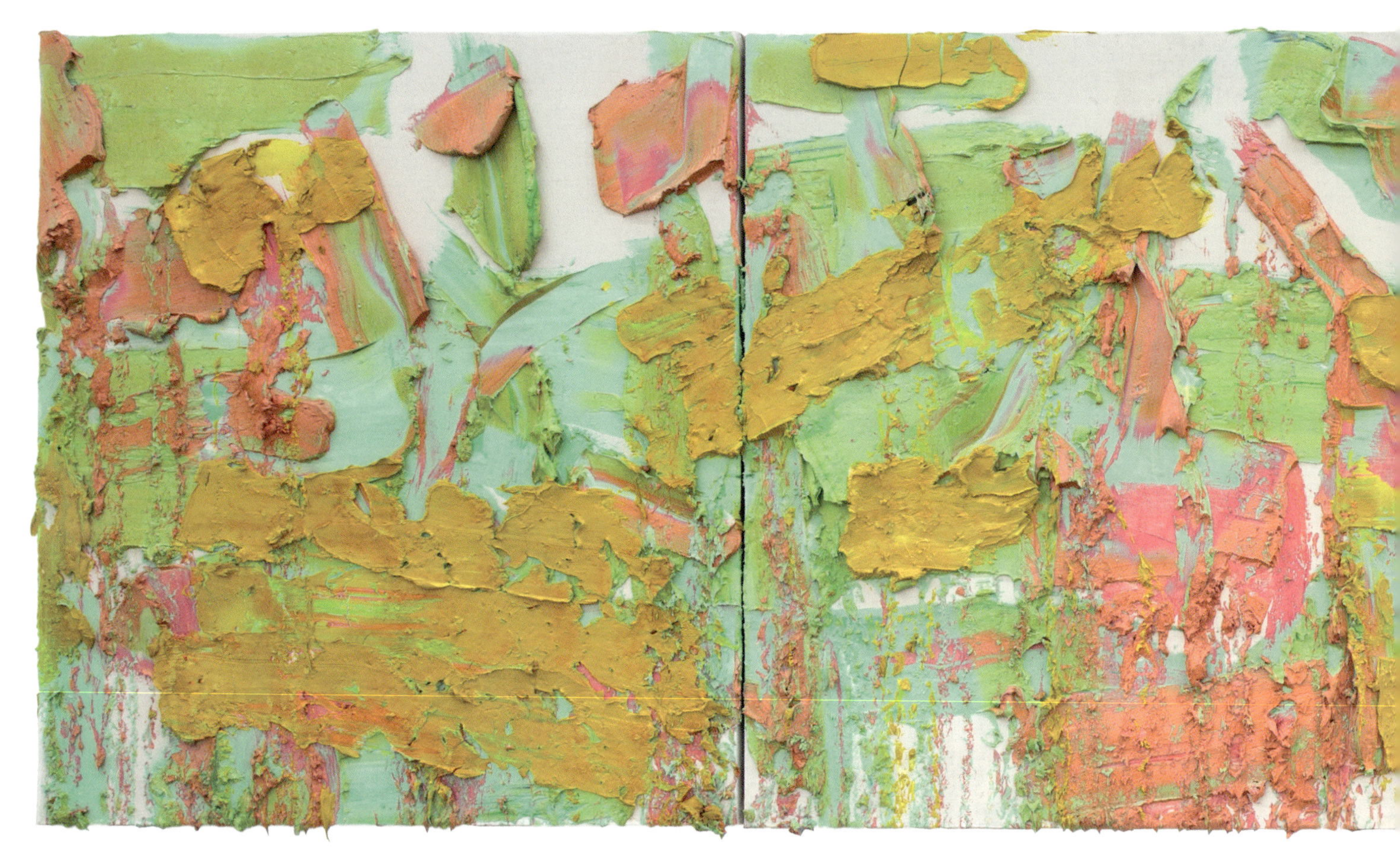

Zhu Jinshi, *Epoch Color*, 2010, oil on canvas, quadriptych, overall: 72 x 252 in. (183 x 640 cm), each: 72 x 63 in. (183 x 160 cm), acquired in 2011

朱金石，《大时代色彩》，2010，布上油画，四联，整体: 72 x 252 寸 (183 x 640 厘米)，每幅: 72 x 63 寸 (183 x 160 厘米)，收藏于 2011

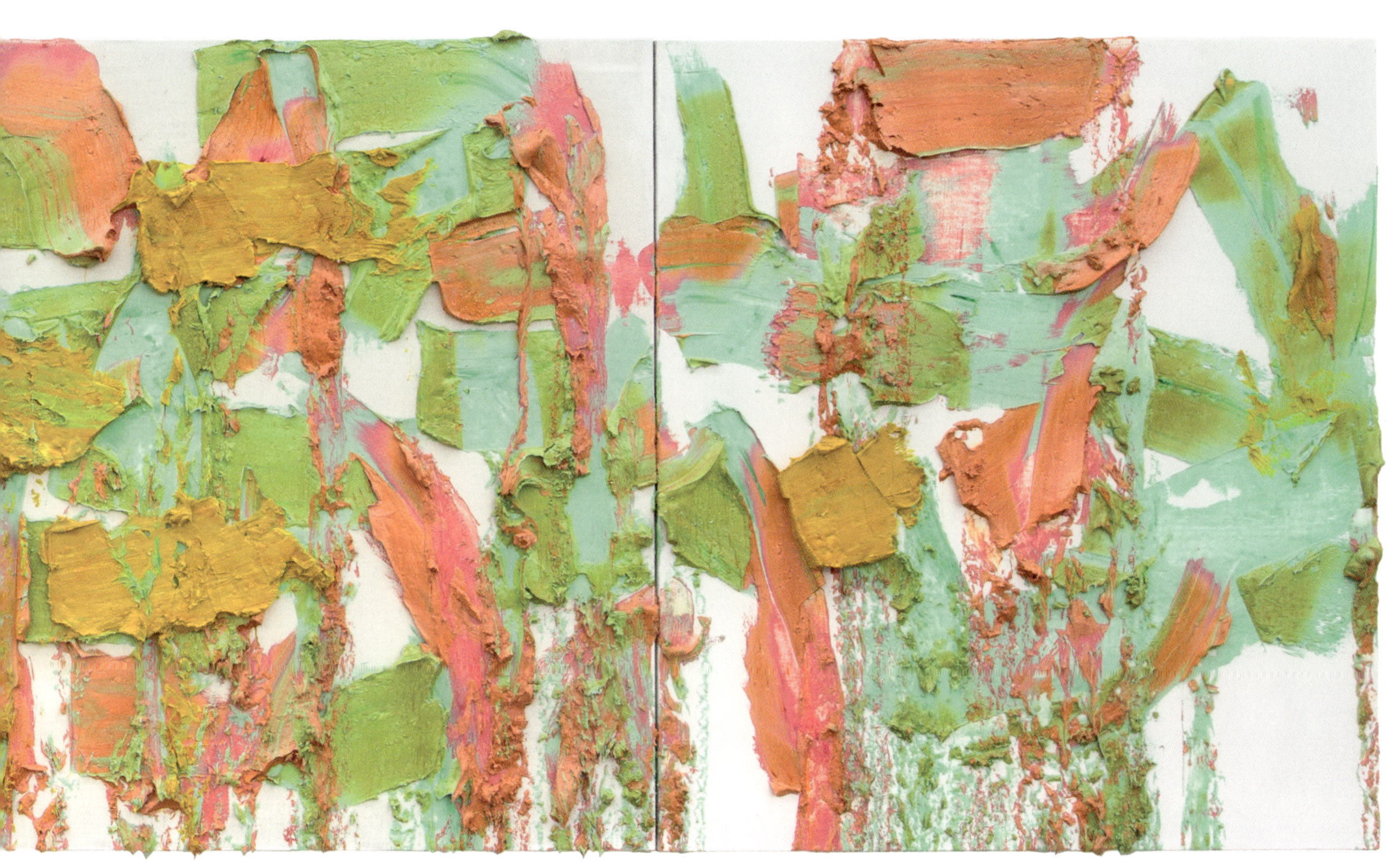

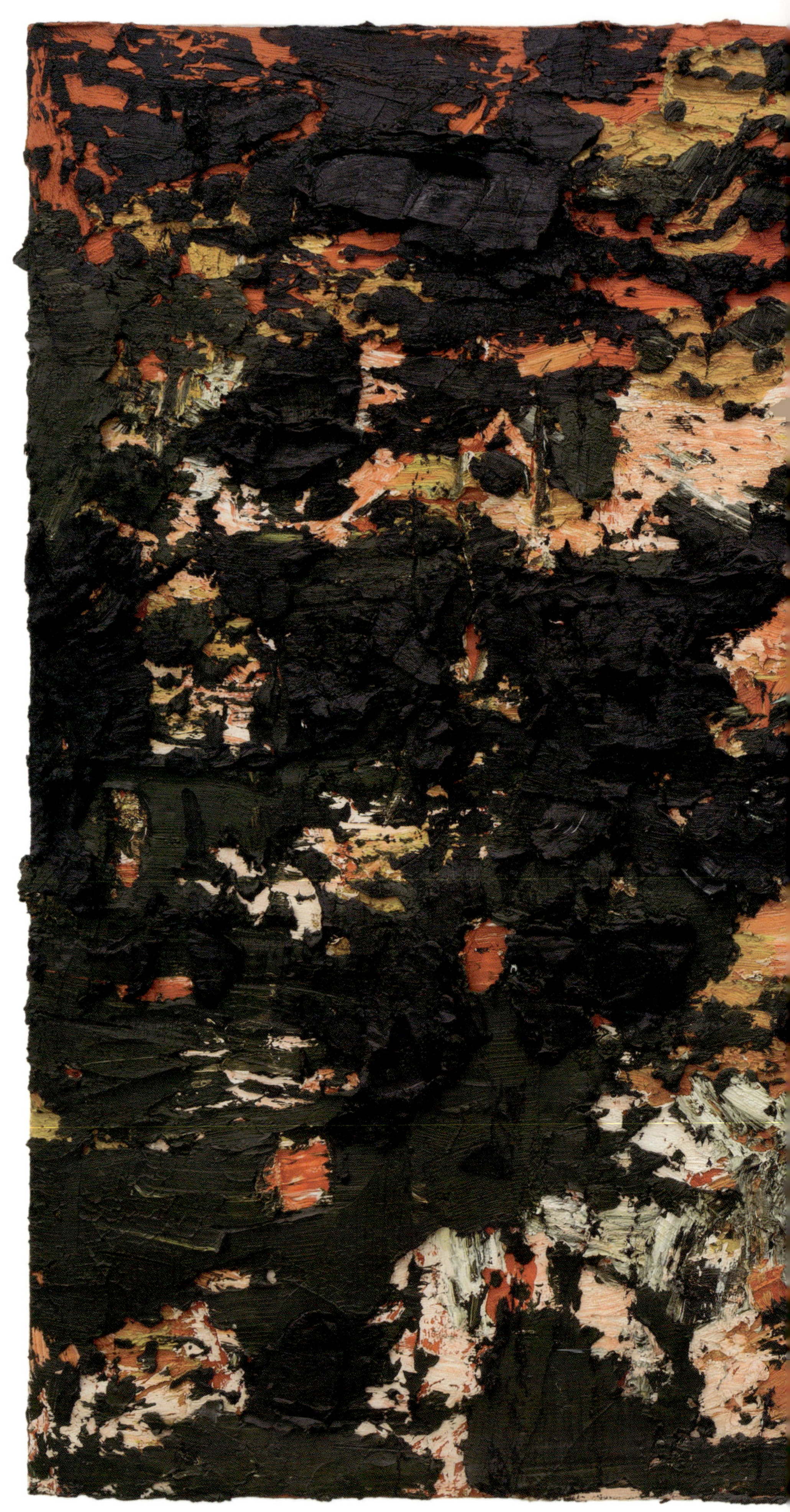

Zhu Jinshi, *Black and White Summer Palace - Black*, 2007, oil on canvas, 87 x 118 in. (220 x 300 cm), acquired in 2011
朱金石，《黑白颐和园－黑》，2007，布上油画，87 x 118 寸（220 x 300 厘米），收藏于 2011

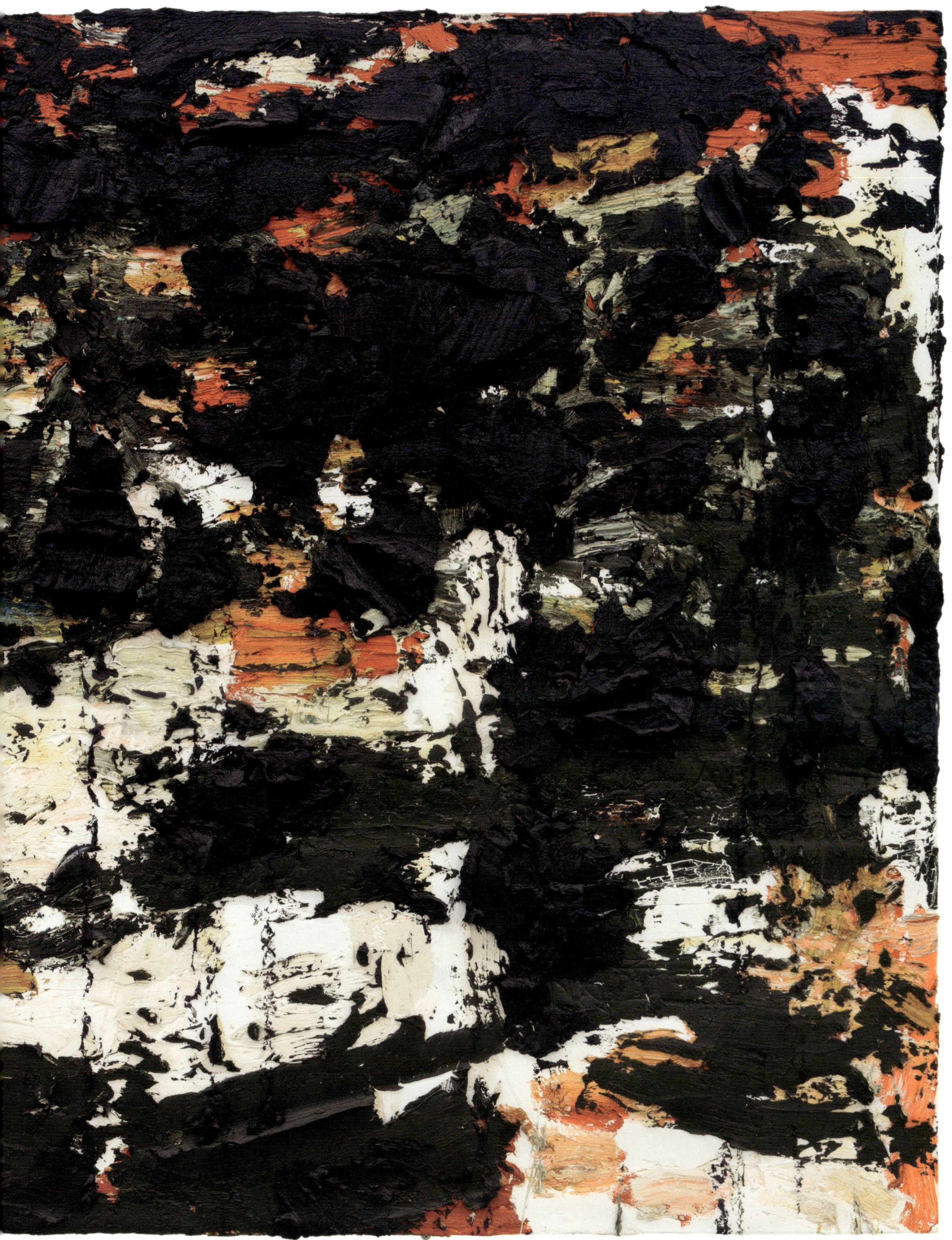

Ai Weiweiw 艾未未

Education 學歷
1978
Beijing Film Academy, Beijing, China
中国北京电影学院

Selected Solo Exhibitions 挑選个展
2013
Ai Weiwei – Disposition, collateral event of the 55th Venice Biennale, Zuecca Project Space, Giudecca and Chiesa Sant'Antonin, Venice, Italy
Ai Weiwei – Disposition，第55屆威尼斯双年展，Zuecca Project Space，威尼斯朱代卡岛与圣东安尼教堂，意大利威尼斯
Ai Weiwei – Resistance and Tradition, Centro Andaluz de Arte Contemporáneo, Seville, Spain
Weiwei – Resistance and Tradition，安达卢西亚当代艺术中心，西班牙塞维利亚
2012
Rebar – Lucerne, Galerie Urs Meile, Lucerne, Switzerland
Serpentine Gallery Pavilion 2012, Designed by Herzog & de Meuron and Ai Weiwei, London, England, UK
Rebar – Lucerne，麦勒画廊 北京-卢森，瑞士卢森 蛇形画廊临时展馆2012，由Herzog & de Meuron和艾未未设计，蛇形画廊，英国伦敦
De Pont 博物馆，荷兰蒂尔堡
Magasin 3，瑞典斯德哥尔摩
2011
Ai Weiwei in New York – Fotografien 1983-1993, Martin Gropius Bau, Berlin, Germany
Ai Weiwei in New York – Fotografien 1983–1993，Martin-Gropius-Bau博物馆，德国柏林
Ai Weiwei: Dropping the Urn, Victoria & Albert Museum, London, England, UK, Louisiana Museum of Modern Art, Humlebaek, Denmark
Ai Weiwei: Dropping the Urn，维多利亚和阿尔伯特博物馆, 英国伦敦 艾未未缺席／十二生肖兽首，台北市立美术馆，台湾台北 艾未未，路易斯安娜现代艺术博物馆，丹麦Humlebaek
Circle of Animals / Zodiac Heads, Somerset House, London, England, UK; Pulitzer Fountain, Grand Army Plaza at Central Park, New York, NY, USA; Los Angeles County Museum of Art, Los Angeles, USA; Taipei Fine Arts Museum, Taipei, Taiwan; Cleveland Museum of Art, Cleveland, Ohio, USA; Gallery of Ontario, Toronto, Canada; Pérez Art Museum Miami, Miami, FL, USA; Princeton University, Princeton, New Jersey, USA; The Crow Collection of Asian Art, Dallas, Texas, USA; Arken Museum of Modern Art, Skovvej, Denmark
十二生肖兽首，Somerset House，英国伦敦；中央公园Grand Army Plaza普里兹喷泉，美国纽约；洛杉矶郡艺术博物馆，美国洛杉矶
Ai Weiwei – Interlacing, Fotomuseum Winterthur, Switzerland; Kunsthaus Graz, Austria; Jeu de Paume, Paris, France; Kistefos-Museet, Jevnaker, Norway; Arthur M. Sackler Gallery, Smithsonian Institution, Washington D.C., USA; MIS – Museu da Imagem e do Som, São Paulo, Brasil
Ai Weiwei – Interlacing，温特图尔摄影博物馆，瑞士温特图尔，格拉兹美术馆，奥地利格拉兹
Ai Weiwei. Art / Architecture, Kunsthaus Bregenz, Bregenz, Austria
Ai Weiwei. Art / Architecture，布雷根茨美术馆，奥地利布雷根茨
2010
The Unilever Series: Ai Weiwei, Tate Modern, London, England, UK
Galerie Urs Meile, Lucerne, Switzerland
The Unilever Series: Ai Weiwei，泰特现代美术馆，英国伦敦 麦勒画廊 北京-卢森，瑞士卢森

Chen Wei 陳維

Education 學歷
2002
Zhejiang University of Media and Communication, Zhejiang, China
中国浙江传媒学院

Selected Solo Exhibitions 挑選个展
2012
MORE, Leo Xu Projects, Shanghai, China
《更多》Leo Xu Projects，中國上海
Rain In Some Areas, Galerie Rüdiger Schöttle, Munich, Germany
《局部有雨》，Rüdiger Schöttle畫廊，德國慕尼黑
2011
Tight Rope, Yokohama Creative City Center (YCC), Yokohama, Japan
《漠然之素》，創造都市中心，日本橫濱
The Augur's Game, Galleria Glance, Turin, Italy
《預言家的遊戲》，Glance畫廊，意大利都林
2010
Chen Wei: photography 2006-2009, Full Art, Seville, Spain
《陳維攝影2006-2009》，Full Art，西班牙塞維利亞
House of Recovery, Platform China, LISTE 15, Basel, Switzerland
《康復之屋，站臺中國》，LISTE 15，瑞士巴塞爾
2009
Chen Wei's Photography Works From 2007-2009, M97 Gallery, Shanghai, China
《陳維攝影作品2007 – 2009》，M97畫廊，中國上海
Everyday scenery and props, Gallery Exit, Hong Kong
《日常，佈景和道具》，安全口畫廊，中國香港
Partial Melancholy, Laboratory Art Beijing, Beijing, China
《局部的憂鬱》，北京藝術實驗室，中國北京
2008
The Fabulist's Path, Platform China Contemporary Art Institute, Beijing, China
《寓言家的小徑》，站臺中國當代藝術機構，中國北京

Selected Group Exhibitions 挑選群展
2013
Revel - Celebrating MoCA's 8 Years In Shanghai, Museum of Contemporary Art, Shanghai, China
《陶醉 ——上海當代藝術館8週年特別展》，上海當代藝術館，中國上海
Shanghai Surprise: Contemporary Art In Shanghai Since 2000, Chi K11 Art Space, Shanghai, China
《上海驚奇：一場關於上海當代藝術的群展》，Chi K11藝術空間，中國上海
ON/OFF: China's Young Artists in Concept and Practice, Ullens Center for Contemporary Art (UCCA), Beijing, China
《ON | OFF：中國年輕藝術家的觀念與實踐》，尤倫斯當代藝術中心，中國北京
2012
Daily of Concept: A Practice of Life, Shanghai Duolun Museum of Modern Art, Shanghai, China
《日常觀：一種生活實踐》，上海多倫現代藝術館，中國上海
CAFAM • Future, CAFA Art Museum, Beijing, China
《CAFAM· 未來》，中央美術學院美術館，中國北京
Things Beyond Our Control, Fredric Snitzer Gallery, Miami, FL, USA
《不可控之事物》，Fredric Snitzer畫廊，美國邁阿密
2011
The Other Wave: Contemporary Chinese Photography, Ben Brown Fine Arts, London, England, UK
《浪淘沙：當代中國攝影群展》，Ben Brown畫廊，英國倫敦
Smile, Hemuse Space, Beijing, China
《微笑》，禾木空間，中國北京

Chen Zhou 陳軸

Education 學歷
2009
BFA in Media Art, China Central Academy of Fine Arts, Beijing, China
北京中央美術學院數碼媒體藝術系學士學位

Selected Solo Exhibitions 挑選个展
2013
I'm not not not Chen Zhou, Magician Space, Beijing, China
《我不不不是陳軸》，魔金石空間，中國北京
2012
Hot Spots at SH Contemporary Art Fair with AIKE-DELLARCO,
Shanghai Exhibition Center, Shanghai, China
上海藝術博覽會國際當代藝術展聯合艾可畫廊之 '熱點板塊'，上
海展覽中心，中國上海
2009
Talk, Platform China Contemporary Art Institute, Beijing, China
《討論》，站台中國，中國北京

Selected Group Exhibitions 挑選群展
2013
I'm Not Involved in Aesthetic Progress: A Rethinking of Performance,
Star Gallery, Beijing, China
《我不在美學的進程里：再談行為》，星空間，中國北京
My Dear, You Shouldn't Believe in Fairytales, 2P Contemporary Art
Gallery, Hong Kong
《親愛的，你不該相信童話》，2P畫廊，中國香港
ON/OFF: China's Young Artists in Concept and Practice, Ullens
Center for Contemporary Art (UCCA), Beijing, China
《ON|OFF：中國年輕藝術家的觀念與實踐》，尤倫斯當代藝術中
心，中國北京
2012
Contemporary Visions on China, Yi&C, Taipei, Tawain
《中產階級拘謹的魅力：當代華人觀點》，易雅居當代空間館，台
灣台北
Dressing the Screen, Ullens Center for Contemporary Art (UCCA),
Beijing, China
《時· 光，中英時尚電影展》，尤倫斯當代藝術中心，中國北京
Unfinished Country: New Video from China, Contemporary Arts
Museum Houston (CAMH), Houston, TX, USA
《未完成的國度：來自中國的新錄像》，休斯頓當代美術館，美國
休斯頓
Until the End of the World, Tang Contemporary Art, Beijing, China
《直到世界盡頭》，唐人當代藝術中心，中國北京
*The 7th Shenzhen Sculpture Biennale - Accidental Message:
Art is Not a System, Not a World*, He Xiangning Museum, OCT
Contemporary Art Terminal (OCAT), Shenzhen, Guangdong, China
《第七屆深圳雕塑雙年展——偶然的信息：藝術不是一個體系，也
不是一個世界》，何香凝美術館　OCT當代藝術中心，中國深圳
Focus On Talents Project Finalists Exhibition, Today Art Museum,
Beijing, China
《關注未來藝術英才計劃入圍展》，今日美術館，中國北京
Chinese Young Artists Contemporary Art Exhibition, 18 Gallery,
Shanghai, China
《中國青年藝術家當代藝術展》，外灘18號畫廊，中國上海
Moving Image in China 1988-2011, Centro Per L'arte
Contemporanea Luigi Pecci, Prato, Italy
《中國影像藝術1988 – 2011》，路吉· 佩吉當代藝術中心，意大
利普拉托
2011
Video Art in China, MADATAC, Reina Sofia Museum, Madrid, Spain
《錄像藝術在中國》，MADATAC，索菲亞女王博物館，西班牙
馬德里
Little Movement, OCT Contemporary Art Terminal, Shenzhen,
Guangdong, China
《小運動——當代藝術中的自我實踐》，OCT當代藝術中心，中
國廣東深圳
Gallery Hotel Art Project, Gallery Hotel, Beijing, China
《瑞居藝術計劃》，瑞居酒店，中國北京

Fang Lu 方璐

Education 學歷
2007
MFA in New Genres, San Francisco Arts Institute, San Francisco, CA,
USA
美國舊金山藝術學院新類型系（錄像和行為）的碩士學位
2005
BFA in Graphic Design, School of Visual Art, New York, NY, USA
美國紐約視覺藝術學院平面設計學士學位

Selected Solo Exhibitions 挑選个展
2012
Amorous Acts, Arrow Factory, Beijing, China
《戀愛的人就是藝術家》，箭廠空間，中國北京
2011
Eclipse, Borges Libreria Contemporary Art Institute, Guangzhou,
Guangdong , China
《做食》（陳侗策展），博爾赫斯當代藝術機構，中國廣東廣州
Automatic Happening, A4 Cultural Arts Center, Chengdu, Sichuan,
China
《自動發生》（鮑棟策展），A4當代藝術中心，中國四川成都
2010
Unrecording, Space Station, Beijing China
《非記錄》（盧迎華策展），空間站，中國北京

Selected Group Exhibitions and Screenings 挑選群展和放映
2013
ON/OFF: China's Young Artists in Concept and Practice, Ullens
Center for Contemporary Art (UCCA), Beijing, China
《ON|OFF：中國年輕藝術家的觀念與實踐》，尤倫斯當代藝術中
心，中國北京
2012
Shuffling the Cards: 1st Round Chinese Contemporary Art Reloaded,
Hilger BROTKunsthalle, Vienna, Austria
《洗牌：中國當代藝術展第一圈》，Hilger BROTKunsthalle美術
館，奧地利維也納
Magic International Art Exhibition 2012, Shenzhen Bay Sports
Centre, Shenzhen, Guangdong, China
《魔力2012春蕾國際當代藝術展》，深圳體育中心，中國深圳
CAFAM· Future, CAFA Art Museum, Beijing, China
《CAFAM· 未來展》，中央美術學院美術館，中國北京
*The 7th Shenzhen Sculpture Biennale - Accidental Message:
Art is Not a System, Not a World*, He Xiangning Museum, OCT
Contemporary Art Terminal (OCAT), Shenzhen, Guangdong, China
《第七屆深圳雕塑雙年展——偶然的信息：藝術不是一個體系，也
不是一個世界》，何香凝美術館OCT當代藝術中心，中國深圳
JETLAG——FCAC Video Project, Sino-German Multimedia
Contemporary Art Exhibition Independent Project, Kunsthalle Faust,
Hanover, Germany
《時差——中德當代多美媒體藝術展獨立項目FCAC Video
Project》, Kunsthalle Faust, 德國漢諾威
2011
Chinese Artists of the New Generation, Museu do Oriente, Lisbon,
Portugal
《新生代中國藝術家》， 東方基金會博物館，葡萄牙里斯本
Video Art in China, MADATAC, Reina Sofia Museum, Madrid, Spain
《錄像藝術在中國——MADATAC》，索菲亞女王博物館，西班
牙馬德里
8+8 Contemporary International Video Art, 53 Museum, Guangzhou,
Guangdong, China
《8+8當代國際影像展》，53美術館，中國廣州
2010
Art Gwangju 2010, Emerging Asian Artists, KDJ Convention Center,
Gwangju, Korea
《2010藝術光州博覽會》，新亞洲藝術家單元，KDJ 會議中心，
韓國光州
Get It Louder, Sanlitun SOHO, Beijing, China
《大聲展》，三里屯SOHO, 中國北京

He Xiangyu 何翔宇

Education 學歷
2008
BFA in Painting, Shenyang Normal University, Shenyang, Liaoning, China
瀋陽師範大學油畫系學士學位

Selected Solo Exhibitions 挑選个展
2012
He Xiangyu, WHITE SPACE BEIJING, Beijing, China
《何翔宇》，空白空間，中國北京
A4 Young Artist Experimental Season 2nd Round Exhibition, A4 Contemporary Arts Center, Chengdu, Sichuan, China
《A4青年藝術家實驗季第二回展覽》，A4當代藝術中心，中國四川成都
Cola Project, 4A Centre for Contemporary Asian Art, Sydney, Australia
《可樂計劃》，A4當代亞洲藝術中心，澳大利亞悉尼
2011
The Death of Marat, Künstlerhaus Schloß Balmoral, Bad Ems, Germany
《馬拉之死》，Schloß Balmoral藝術空間，德國巴得伊姆斯
Man on the Chairs, WHITE SPACE BEIJING, Beijing, China
《椅子上的人》，空白空間，中國北京
Cola Project, LOFT Art Gallery, Paris, France
《可樂計劃》，Loft畫廊，法國巴黎
2010
Cola Project, WALL Art Museum, Beijing, China
《可樂計劃》，牆美術館，中國北京
2008
The Origin of Everything, RAAB art Gallery, Beijing, China
《一切的由來》，RAAB畫廊，中國北京
The Illusion of Dongba, Shenyang Normal University, Shenyang, Liaoning, China
《幻象東巴》，瀋陽師範大學，中國北京
2007
The City of Imagination, Jiudian Gallery, Beijing, China
《幻城》，九點畫廊，中國北京
My Universe, XYZ Art Gallery, Beijing, China
《我的世界》，XYZ畫廊，中國北京
2005
Thoughts Surging in the Heart, Shenyang Normal University, Shenyang, Liaoning, China
《心靈的激盪》，瀋陽師範大學，中國瀋陽

Selected Group Exhibitions 挑選群展
2013
FUCK OFF 2, Groninger Museum, Groningen, Netherlands
《FUCK OFF II》，格羅寧根美術館，荷蘭格羅寧根
Inter-Vision: A Contemporary Exhibition Across the Strait 2013, National Taiwan Museum of Fine Arts, Taichung City, Taiwan
《交互視象——2013海峽兩岸當代藝術展》，國立台灣美術館，台中，台灣
MEMO I, WHITE SPACE BEIJING, Beijing, China
《備忘錄I》，空白空間，中國北京
ON/OFF: China's Young Artists in Concept and Practice, Ullens Center for Contemporary Art (UCCA), Beijing, China
《ON|OFF：中國年輕藝術家的觀念與實踐》，尤倫斯當代藝術中心，中國北京
Get it louder, The Orange at Sanlitun Village, Beijing, China
《大聲展》，三里屯橙色大廳，中國北京
2012
Shanghai Sculpture Programme—Life Latitude, Shanghai Painting & Sculpture Institute Museum, Shanghai, China
《上海雕塑計劃——生活維度展》，上海油畫雕塑院美術館，中國上海

Hu Qingyan 胡慶雁

Education 學歷
2010
MFA in Sculpture, Central Academy of Fine Arts, Beijing, China
中央美術學院雕塑系碩士學位
2006
BFA in Sculpture, Guangzhou Academy of Fine Arts, Guangzhou, Guangdong, China
獲廣州美術學院雕塑系學士學位

Selected Solo Exhibitions 挑選个展
2013
Reincarnation in a New Guise, Galerie Urs Meile, Lucerne, Switzerland
《借屍還魂》，麥勒畫廊 北京－盧森，瑞士盧森
2011
REVEALING THE RUSE, Galerie Urs Meile, Beijing, China
《穿幫》，麥勒畫廊 北京－盧森，瑞士盧森

Selected Group Exhibitions 挑選群展
2013
Building Bridges – Zeitgenössische Kunst aus China, Wolfsberg, Ermatingen, Switzerland
《構建橋梁——中國當代藝術》，沃爾夫斯堡，瑞士厄馬廷根
(Middle), Not Vital Foundation, Ardez, Switzerland
《中》，Not Vital基金會，瑞士阿爾德茲
Colour Sculpture - Sui Jianguo and a Couple of His Students (2), Fujian Art Museum, Fuzhou, Fujian , China
《著色雕塑——隋建國與他的幾個學生（二）》，福建省美術館，中國福州
2012
Blind Spots – Group Exhibition of Young Artists, Gallery Yang, Beijing, China
《盲區——青年藝術家群展》，楊畫廊，中國北京
Starting – Youth Artists Introducing Plan by China Sculpture Institute, Today Art Museum/China Sculpture Institute, Beijing, China
《啓——中國雕塑學會青年推介計劃》，今日美術館，中國北京
2011
ENDLESS VARIATIONS, Redstar Gallery, Beijing, China
《龍生九子》，紅星畫廊，中國北京
Art Nova 100, Ditan Park, Beijing, China
《藝術100》，地壇公園，中國北京
EXTRACT – the 3rd Stall Keeper Show, C5Art, Beijing, China
《擺攤第三回：抽——青年藝術家匿名展》，西五藝術中心，中國北京
Optional Exercise, Li Space, Beijing, China
《自選動作》，荔空間，中國北京
2010
Get Moving, Li Space, Beijing, China
《動起來》，荔空間，中國北京
I CALL THE SHOTS OF MY YOUTH, Giant Cup Today National Art Students Annual Awards of Nomination 2010, Today Art Museum, Beijing, China
《我的青春我做主——2010巨人杯今日當代藝術院校大學生年度提名展》，今日美術院，中國北京
The Shape of Sculpture, Michael Schultz Gallery, Beijing, China
《雕塑的形狀》，秀瓷當代畫廊，中國北京
Little Step Forward: Contemporary Experimental Guest-Exhibition of Young Chinese Artists, Metal Warehouse, Creative Square of 798 Art Zone, Beijing, China
《向前一小步：當代青年試驗藝術邀請展》，798創意廣場藝術館金屬庫，中國北京
Sculpture - Artworks of Sui Jianguo and his Students, A4 Gallery, Chengdu, Sichuan, China
《雕塑——隋建國與他的幾個學生》，A4畫廊，中國四川成都
Space & Visual Energy, Zero Field Art Center, Beijing, China
《空間&形象能》，0藝術館，中國北京

Hu Xiangqian 胡向前

Education 學歷
2007
BFA in Painting, Guangzhou Academy of Fine Arts, Ghangzhou, Guangdong, China
廣州美術學院油畫系學士學位

Selected Solo Exhibitions 挑選个展
2013
A Looks Like B, Arrow Factory, Beijing, China
《A像B》，箭廠空間，中國北京
2012
Protagonist, Long March Space, Beijing, China
《主演》，長征空間，中國北京
2010
51 : No.7 Hu Xiangqian, Beijing, China
《51m2：7＃胡向前》，中國北京
Body as a Museum/Sweet and Sweat, 24hr Art, Northern Centre for Contemporary Art, Darwin, Australia
《身體美術館／甜蜜與汗水》，24hr Art，北領地當代藝術中心，澳大利亞達爾文
2009
Knee-Jerk Reaction, Observation Society, Guangzhou, Guangdong, China
《用膝蓋思考》，觀察社，中國廣東廣州

Selected Group Exhibitions 挑選群展
2013
Pessimism or Resistance?, Taikang Space, Beijing, China
《消極與抵抗？》泰康空間，中國北京
Sharjah Biennial 11: Re:emerge, Towards a New Cultural Cartography, Sharjah, UAE
《沙迦雙年展——重現新的文化製圖》，阿聯酋沙迦
ON/OFF: China's Young Artists in Concept and Practice, Ullens Center for Contemporary Art (UCCA), Beijing, China
《ON｜OFF：中國年輕藝術家的觀念與實踐》，尤倫斯當代藝術中心，中國北京
2012
Uninkable, Art-Ba-Ba Mobile Space, Shanghai, China
《墨不到》，Art-Ba-Ba流動空間，中國上海
Moving Image in China 1988-2011, Centro per l'Arte Contemporanea Luigi Pecci, Prato, Italy
《中國影像藝術1988-2011》，路吉‧佩吉當代藝術中心，意大利普拉托
2011
Moving Image in China 1988-2011, Minsheng Art Museum, Shanghai, China
《中國影像藝術1988-2011》，民生現代美術館，中國上海
Institution for the future, Asia Triennial Manchester 2011, Manchester, England, UK
《未來機構：2011曼徹斯特亞洲展》，英國曼徹斯特
Taking the stage over, Diagram for speed, 18 Gallery, Shanghai, China
《佔領舞台，速度圖》，外灘18號畫廊，中國上海
Image·History·Existence - Taikang Life 15th Anniversary Art Collection Exhibition, China Art Museum, Beijing, China
《圖像‧歷史‧存在——泰康15週年藝術收藏展》，中央美院美術館，中國北京
2010
Curated By Liu Wei - Wang Yuyang & Hu Xiangqian: Organisms, Ullens Center for Contemporary Art (UCCA), Beijing, China
《劉韡策劃——王郁洋＆胡向前：超有機》，尤倫斯當代藝術中心，中國北京
Great Performances, Pace Beijing, Beijing, China
《偉大的表演》，佩斯北京，中國北京
2009
Bourgeoisified Proletariat, Shanghai Songjiang Creative Studio, Shanghai, China
《資產階級化了的無產階級》，松江創意公房，中國上海

Huang Ran 黃然

Education 學歷
2007
MFA Fine Art, Goldsmiths College, University of London, London, England, UK
英國倫敦大學金匠學院純藝術碩士學位
2004
First Class Distinction BA (Hons) Fine Art, Birmingham Institute of Art and Design, University of Central England, Birmingham, England, UK
英國中部大學伯明翰藝術與設計學院純藝術一等榮譽學士學位

Selected Solo Exhibitions 挑選个展
2012
Disruptive Desires, Tranquility and the Loss of Lucidity, Long March Space, Beijing, China
《破壞性的欲望，鎮定劑，遺失的清晰》，長征空間，中國北京
2010
Blithe Tragedy (curated by Octavio Zaya), Space Station, Beijing, China
《愉悅悲劇》（Octavio Zaya策展），空間站，中國北京
Fake Action Truth, George Polke, London, England, UK; Nottingham, England, UK
《假動作逼真》，George Polke，英國倫敦
《假動作逼真》，Prussian Projekte，英國諾丁漢

Selected Group Exhibitions 挑選群展
2013
Current Films From Asia, Kino der Kunst, Munich, Germany
《亞洲流行影片》，Kino der Kunst，德國慕尼黑
ON/OFF: China's Young Artists in Concept and Practice, Ullens Center for Contemporary Art (UCCA), Beijing, China
《ON｜OFF：中國年輕藝術家的觀念與實踐》，尤倫斯當代藝術中心，中國北京
2012
Perspectives 180-Unfinished Country: New Video from China, Contemporary Art Museum Houston, Houston, TX, USA
《180種觀點——未竟之邦：中國新影像藝術，休斯頓當代藝術博物館，美國休斯頓》
Arcane of Patterns. Inceptive of Rhythm, an Order and Summon, Mindpirates Projektraum, Berlin, Germany
《圖案的神秘，節奏的開端，一個命令和召喚》，Mindpirates Projektraum，德國柏林
Videonale-Donetsk, IZOLYATSIA, Donetsk, Ukraine
《波昂錄像雙年展》，IZOLYATSIA文化項目平台，烏克蘭頓涅茨克
The Unseen: The 4th Guangzhou Triennial, Guangdong Museum of Art, Guangzhou, Guangdong, China
《看不見的：第四屆廣州三年展》，廣東美術館，中國廣東廣州
Youth Artist Experimental Season, A4 Contemporary Arts Center, Chengdu, Sichuan, China
《青年藝術家實驗季》，A4當代藝術中心，中國四川成都
Disruptive Desires, Sean Kelly Gallery, New York, NY
《破壞性欲望》，肖恩凱利畫廊，美國紐約
Exchigo-Tsumari Art Triennale 2013, Exchigo-Tsumari Satoyama Museum of Contemporary Art, KINARE, Tokamachi, Japan
《越後妻有大地三年展》，越後妻有里山現代美術館，日本新潟縣
Group exhibition, Eigen+Art Lab, Berlin, Germany
《群展》，Eigen + Art Lab，德國柏林
Moving Image in China 1988-2011, Centro per l'Arte Contemporanea Luigi Pecci, Prado, Italy
《中國影像藝術1988-2011》，Luigi Pecci 當代藝術中心，意大利普拉多
The 7th Shenzhen Sculpture Biennale - Accidental Message: Art is Not a System, Not a World, He Xiangning Museum OCT Contemporary Art Terminal (OCAT), Shenzhen, Guangdong, China
《第七屆深圳雕塑雙年展——偶然的信息：藝術不是一個體系，也不是一個世界》，何香凝美術館OCT當代藝術中心，中國廣東深圳

Huang Yong Ping 黃永砅

Education 學歷
1982
BA, China Academy of Fine Arts, Hangzhou, Zhejiang, China
浙江杭州中國美術學院學士學位

Selected Solo Exhibitions 挑選个展
2013
Huang Yong Ping : Amoy/Xiamen, Musée d'art contemporain de Lyon, France
《黃永砅：Amoy/廈門》，里昂當代藝術博物館，法國里昂
Abbotabad 2012, Marseille-Provence 2013, Hôtel de Gallifet, Aix-en-Provence, France
Abbotabad 2012，Gallifet酒店，法國普羅旺斯地區艾克斯
2012
Circus, Gladstone Gallery, New York, NY, USA
《馬戲團》，各萊斯頓畫廊，美國紐約
Bugarach, Kamel Mennour, Paris, France
《Bugarach》，Kamel Mennour畫廊，法國巴黎
Fantastic 2012, Lille 3000, Musée de l'Hospice Comtesse, Lille, France
《非凡里爾 2012》，里爾3000，Hospice Comtesse博物館，法國里爾
2011
Huang Yong Ping, Nottingham Contemporary, Nottingham, England, UK
《黃永砅》，諾丁漢當代藝術中心，英國諾丁漢
2010
Wu Zei, Musée Océanographique de Monaco, Monte Carlo, Monaco
《烏賊》，摩納哥海洋學博物館，摩納哥蒙特卡洛
2009
Arche 2009, Chapelle des Petits Augustins, Ecole Nationale Supérieure des Beaux-Arts, Paris, France
《方舟 2009》，Chapelle des Petits Augustins，法國巴黎
Caverne 2009, Kamel Mennour, Paris, France
《岩洞2009》，Karnel Mennour畫廊，法國巴黎
Tower Snake, Barbara Gladstone Gallery, New York, NY, USA
《蛇塔》，芭芭拉格萊斯頓畫廊，美國紐約
2008
Frolic, The Curve at Barbican Art Gallery, London, England, UK
《歡樂》，巴比肯藝術畫廊，英國倫敦
Ping Pong, Astrup Fearnley Museum of Modern Art, Oslo, Norway
《乒乓》，阿斯特魯普費恩現代藝術博物館，挪威奧斯陸
Ping Pong, Kunsthallen Brandts, Odense, Denmark
《乒乓》，Kunsthallen Brandts，丹麥歐登塞
House of Oracles, Ullens Center for Contemporary Art (UCCA), Beijing, China
《神諭之屋》，尤倫斯當代藝術中心，中國北京
2007
Huang Yong Ping: From C to P, Barbara Gladstone Gallery, New York, NY, USA
《黃永砅：從C到P》，格萊斯頓畫廊，美國紐約
2006
Pantheon, Centre International d'art et du Paysage de l'ile de Vassiviere, l'ile de Vassiviere, France
《萬神殿》，國際美術品中心，法國l'ile de Vassiviere
Les Mains de Bouddha, Galerie Anne de Villepoix, Paris, France
《Les Mains de Bouddha》，Anne de Villepoix 畫廊，法國巴黎
2005
House of Oracles: A Huang Yong Ping Retrospective, Walker Art Center, Minneapolis, MN, USA; Massachusetts Museum of Contemporary Art, North Adams, MA, USA; Vancouver Art Gallery, Vancouver, British Columbia, Canada
《神諭之屋：黃永砅回顧展》，沃克藝術中心，美國明尼阿波利斯（2006年於美國馬賽諸塞州當代藝術博物館、2007年於加拿大溫哥華美術館展出）
2004
Un Cane Italiano, Espace Beaumont, Luxembourg, France
《Un Cane Italiano》，Espace Beaumont，法國盧森堡

Lan Zhenghui 藍正輝

Education 學歷
1987
Sichuan Fine Arts Institute, Chongqing, China
四川美術學院

Selected Solo Exhibitions 挑選个展
2013
Vigorous Splash: Stroke of Heavy Ink: Lan Zhenghui Solo Exhibition, Sanshang Art, Hangzhou, Zhejiang, China
《恣意的潑筆——藍正輝個展》，三尚當代藝術，中國浙江杭州
2011
Ink Painting Dream: Lan Zhenghui Solo Exhibition, Pearl Lam Galleries, Shanghai, China
《水墨夢想——藍正輝個展》，對比窗藝廊，中國上海
2010
The Great Ink: My Road of Abstraction, 789 Art Zone, Beijing, China
《水墨金剛：我的抽象之路》，789藝術區，中國北京
2009
Lan Zhenghui: Mighty Rain, O House Gallery, Jakarta, Indonesia
《狂雨——藍正輝印尼個展》，歐豪斯畫廊，印尼雅加達
2006
Heavy Ink Painting by Lan Zhenghui, National Art Museum of China, Beijing, China
《體量水墨——藍正輝個展》，中國美術館，中國北京
2004
Lan Zhenghui Contemporary Ink Painting Special Exhibition, 1000 Years Celebration of Jingdezhen, Jingdezhen, Jiangxi, China
《藍正輝水墨特展》，景德鎮1000年慶典，中國江西景德鎮
2003
Stride: Ink Art Performance, IS Gallery, Toronto, Ontario, Canada
《一跨》水墨行為表演，IS畫廊，加拿大多倫多
Running Ink: Lan Zhenghui Solo Exhibition, Guangdong Museum of Art, Guangzhou, Guangdong, China
《水墨疾走——藍正輝個展》，廣東美術館，中國廣東廣州

Selected Group Exhibitions 挑選群展
2013
Beyond Black and White: Chinese Contemporary Abstract Ink, Pearl Lam Galleries, Shanghai, China
《黑白至上：中國當代抽象水墨》，對比窗藝廊，中國上海
The Logics of Ink: 25 Expressions from 25 Artists, Esse Space, Beijing, China
《水墨的邏輯——25位藝術家的25種表達》，現實空間，中國北京
2012
Art Stage Singapore 2012, Pearl Lam Galleries, Marina Bay Sands Convention and Exhibition Center, Singapore
《藝術登陸新加坡2012博覽會》，對比窗藝廊，浜海灣金沙會展中心，新加坡
Natural Mind: 2012 Italy, China Art Biennale, Milan, Italy
《自然之心——2012意大利》，中國藝術雙年展，意大利
2010
Toronto Art Fair, Toronto, Canada
《多倫多藝術博覽會》，加拿大多倫多
Art Dubai 2010, Dubai, UAE
《2010迪拜藝術博覽會》，阿聯酋迪拜
China Vision, Beijing 3 Art Gallery, Beijing, China
《中國視野》，在3畫廊，中國北京
2009
Ink Painting, Calligraphy: The Third Abstraction, Pearl Lam Galleries, Shanghai, China
《水墨，書法——第三種抽象》對比窗藝廊，中國上海
Meditation from the East, Baden-Württemberg, Germany
《來自東方的冥想》德國巴登符藤堡州
Ink Painting Today—2009 Shanghai New Ink Art Exhibition, Shanghai Duolun Museum of Modern Art, Shanghai, China
《水墨當下——2009上海新水墨大展》，上海多倫美術館，中國上海

Li Ming 李明

Education 學歷
2008
BFA in New Media, China Academy of Fine Arts, Hangzhou, Zhejiang, China
浙江杭州中國美術學院新媒體系學士學位

Selected Solo Exhibitions 挑選个展
2009
XX, Platform China Contemporary Art Institute, Beijing, China
《XX》，展台中國當代藝術機構，中國北京
There Is No Reason For You To See, Closed Gallery, Beijing, China
《我不需要任何理由讓你們看見》，亮亮畫廊，中國北京
2008
Diary, BizArt, Shanghai, China
《日記》，比翼藝術中心，中國上海

Selected Group Exhibitions 挑選群展
2013
ON/OFF: China's Young Artists in Concept and Practice, Ullens Center for Contemporary Art (UCCA), Beijing, China
《ON|OFF：中國年輕藝術家的觀念與實踐》，尤倫斯當代藝術中心，中國北京
2012
Fictional Recoveries, Pearl Lam Galleries, Shanghai, China
《虛構的復得》，對比窗藝廊，中國上海
SH Contemporary 2012, ifagallery, Shanghai, China
《2012上海藝術博覽會國際當代藝術展》，藝法畫廊，中國上海
Unfinished Country: New Video from China, Contemporary Arts Museum Houston (CAMH), Houston, TX, USA
《未完成的國度：來自中國的新錄像》，休斯頓當代美術館，美國得克薩西州休斯頓
An Exhibition in "Listen", South Gate of 798, FM98.5, Beijing, China
《傳說展》，798藝術區南門，調頻FM 98.5，中國北京
CAFAM • Future, CAFA Art Museum, Beijing, China
《CAFAM · 未來展》，中央美術學院美術館，中國北京
THE GIRL, XI WANG ART MUSEUM, Beijing, China
《有個姑娘》，睎望藝術館，中國北京
Standing on the Shoulders of Little Clowns, curated by MadeIn Company, GUEST project, Ullens Center for Contemporary Art (UCCA), Beijing, China
《站在小丑的肩膀上》（沒頂公司策展，Guest項目合作），尤倫斯當代藝術中心，中國北京
Someone singing like calling your name: A Saamlung Karaoke Lounge, MusicBox Karaoke, Hong Kong
《Someone singing like calling your name:A Saamlung Karaoke Lounge》，MusicBox Karaoke，香港
Mist/Return Journey/If There is no Prophecy/Within 3 Meters/ Whether Future Effects on Present?/God's Thoughts/Details After one Second/Everyday, 18 Gallery, Shanghai, China
《霧水／歸途／如果沒有預言／三米之內／未來是否會影響現在／上帝的沈思／一秒鐘以後／每一天》，外灘十八號畫廊，中國上海
2011
Impossible Universe: Now Here, Parer Place Urban Screens, QUT Brisbane, Australia
《不可能的宇宙：現在這裡》，Parer Place Urban Screens，QUT布里斯本，澳大利亞
The Knife's Edge: Video Recently Seen In Beijing, Fremantle Arts Centre, Fremantle, Australia
《刀鋒：最近在北京看過的視頻》，費里曼特爾藝術中心，澳大利亞費里曼特爾
In a perfect world..., Meulensteen Gallery, New York, NY, USA
《完美世界...》，Meulensteen画廊，美国纽约
House of Bees, in LISTE 16—The Young Art Fair in Basel, Platform China, Beijing, China
《蜂窩》，LISTE 16——巴塞爾青年藝術博覽會，站台中國，中國北京

Li Ran 李然

Education 學歷
2009
BFA in Oil Painting, Sichuan Fine Arts Institute, Chongqing, China
四川美術學院油畫系學士學位

Selected Solo Exhibitions 挑選个展
2013
Another "The Other Story", Discoveries sector at Art Basel Hong Kong with AIKE-DELLARCO, Hong Kong
《另一個"他者的故事"》，發現單元——香港藝術巴塞爾與上海艾可畫廊，中國香港
2012
I Want To Talk To You, But Not to All Of You, Goethe-Institut Open Space, Shanghai, China
《我想和你談談，但不是你們》，歌德學院開放空間，中國上海
Pretty Knowledge, AIKE-DELLARCO, Shanghai, China
《漂亮的知識》，艾可畫廊，中國上海
Mont Sainte-Victoire, Magician Space, Beijing, China
《聖克維多爾山》，魔金石空間，中國北京

Selected Group Exhibitions 挑選群展
2013
FORMER WEST: Notes from Berlin, basis voor actuele kunst (BAK), Utrecht, Netherlands
《前西：來自柏林的筆記》，BAK藝術中心，荷蘭烏德勒支
Standing in the Shadow, Ota Fine Arts, Tokyo, Japan
《坐落於陰暗處》，大田畫廊，日本東京
Off Course: A Narration Between Italy and Greater China, Fondazione Querini Stampalia, Venice, Italy
《不確定的過程中——意大利與中國之間的一段敘述》，斯坦普利亞基金會，意大利威尼斯
FORMER WEST: Documents, Constellations, Prospects, Haus der Kulturen der Welt (HKW), Berlin, Germany
《前西：文獻、星群、前景》，世界藝術文化宮（HKW），德國柏林
The Experimental Practices from the Oil Painting Department of Sichuan Fine Arts Institute, Suzhou Art Museum, Suzhou, China
《來自四川美術學院油畫系20年的實驗與踐與》，蘇州美術館，中國江蘇蘇州
I'm Not Involved In Aesthetic Progress: A Rethinking of Performance, Star Gallery Beijing, China
《我不在美學的進程里：再談行為》，星空間，中國北京
Alternatives to Ritual: A Case Study of Shenzhen OCT Contemporary Art Terminal, OCT Contemporary Art Terminal (OCAT), Shenzhen, Jiangsu, China
《慣例下的狂歡——以OCT當代藝術中心為案例》，OCT當代藝術中心（OCAT），中國深圳
ON/OFF: China's Young Artists in Concept and Practice, Ullens Center for Contemporary Art (UCCA), Beijing, China
《ON|OFF：中國年輕藝術家的觀念與實踐》，尤倫斯當代藝術中心，中國北京
2012
The Discreet Charm of Bourgeoisie - Contemporary Visions on China, Yi&C, Taipei, Taiwan
《中產階級拘謹的魅力：當代華人觀點》，易雅居當代空間館，台灣台北
FOCUS ASIA: Beyond Geography, Art Toronto 2012, Metro Toronto Convention Centre, Toronto, Ontario, Canada
《關注亞洲——地理之外》，藝術多倫多，加拿大多倫多
Unfinished Country: New Video from China, Contemporary Arts Museum Houston (CAMH), Houston, TX, USA
《未完成的國度：來自中國的新錄像》，休斯頓當代美術館（CAMH），美國得克薩斯州休斯頓
ROUNDTABLE, The 9th Gwangju Biennale 2012, Gwangju, Korea
《圓桌》，2012年第九屆光州雙年展，韓國光州
CAFAM • Future, CAFA Art Museum, Beijing, China
《CAFAM · 未來展》，中央美術學院美術館，中國北京

Li Shurui 李姝睿

Education 學歷
2004
BFA, Sichuan Fine Arts Institute, Chongqing, China
四川美術學院油畫系學士學位

Selected Solo Exhibitions 挑選个展
2012
Li Shurui - The Shelter (El refúgio), Galería SCQ, Santiago de Compostela, Spain
《李姝睿——庇護所》，SCQ畫廊，西班牙聖地亞哥德孔波斯特
The Shelter: All Fears Come from the Unknown Shimmering at the Edge of the World, WHITE SPACE BEIJING, Beijing, China
《批護所：所有的恐懼來自於世界變邊際未知的閃爍》，空白空間畫廊，中國北京
2010
LSR - Solo Exhibition of Li Shurui, Connoisseur Art Gallery, Hong Kong
《LSR——李姝睿個展》，Connoisseur Art Gallery，香港
2008
Li Shurui, Gallery A Story, Busan, South Korea
《李姝睿個展》，A STORY畫廊，韓國釜山
Lights, Connoisseur Art Gallery, Hong Kong
《光》，Connoisseur Art Gallery，香港

Selected Group Exhibitions 挑選群展
2013
MEMO I, WHITE SPACE BEIJING, Beijing, China
《備忘錄I》，空白空間，中國北京
ON/OFF: China's Young Artists in Concept and Practice, Ullens Center for Contemporary Art (UCCA), Beijing, China
《ON|OFF：中國年輕藝術家的觀念與實踐》，尤倫斯當代藝術中心，中國北京
2012
Painting Lesson II—Negative and Positive Style, Gallery Yang, Beijing, China
《繪畫課II——消極與積極的風格》，楊畫廊，中國北京
Negative Space, WHITE SPACE BEIJING, Beijing, China
《負空間》，空白空間，中國北京
Cohere & Unroll, Space Station, Beijing, China
《敷 · 衍》，空間站，中國北京
2011
Cui Jie, Li Shurui, Zhang Jungang & Li Jie, Leo Xu Projects, Shanghai, China
《崔潔、李姝睿、張君鋼 & 李潔》，Leo Xu Projects，中國上海
FAT ART 2011, Today Museum, Beijing, China
《FAT ART 2011》，今日美術館，中國北京
Visual Structure, A4 Gallery, Chengdu, Sichuan, China
《視覺的結構》，A4藝術中心，中國四川成都
2010
Future Visions: The APT Global Art Collection, Artist Pension Trust, Li Space Gallery, Beijing, China
《未來視野——APT國際藝術收藏》，APT藝術家未來信托基金，荔空間，中國北京
2009
Santa's Workshop Shanghai, James Cohan Gallery, Shanghai, China
《聖誕工坊》，James Cohan畫廊，中國上海
It Ain't Fair, Deitch Projects, Art Basel Miami Beach, Miami, FL, USA
《這不公平》，Deitch Project，巴塞爾邁阿密海灘博覽會，美國佛羅里達州邁阿密
2008
Surfacing, Shanghai Gallery of Art, Shanghai, China
《浮現》，滬申畫廊，中國上海
Delirious Beijing, PKM Gallery, Beijing, China
《瘋狂北京》，PKM畫廊，中國北京
2007
On the Yellow Sea, Gallery A Story, Busan, Korea
《在黃色的海洋上》，A Story畫廊，韓國釜山

Li Songsong 李松松

Education 學歷
1996
BFA in Oil Painting, Central Academy of Fine Arts, Beijing, China
北京中央美術學院油畫系學士學位

Selected Solo Exhibitions 挑選个展
2013
Li Songsong: We Have Betrayed the Revolution, Pace London, London, England, UK
《李松松——我們曾背叛了革命》，佩斯畫廊，英國倫敦
2012
Li Songsong, Pace Beijing, Beijing, China
《李松松》，佩斯北京，中國北京
2011
Li Songsong, Pace New York, New York, NY, USA
《李松松》，佩斯紐約，美國紐約
2009
Li Songsong: Abstract, Pace Beijing, Beijing, China
《李松松：抽象》，佩斯北京，中國北京
2006
Li Songsong: Hypnogenesis, Galerie Urs Meile, Beijing, China; Lucerne, Switzerland
《李松松：催眠》，麥勒畫廊，中國北京，瑞士盧塞恩
2004
Li Songsong: 2001–2004, China Art Archives & Warehouse, Beijing, China
《李松松2001-2004》，中國藝術文件倉庫，中國北京
Li Songsong, Galerie 99, Aschaffenburg, Germany
《李松松》，99畫廊，德國阿莎芬堡

Selected Group Exhibitions 挑選群展
2013
FUCK OFF 2, Groninger Museum, Groningen, Netherlands
《FUCK OFF II》，格羅寧根美術館，荷蘭格羅寧根
Real Life Stories, Bergen Art Museum, Bergen, Norway
《一種生存實在屬性的敘事》，卑爾根美術館，挪威卑爾根
The Collectors Show 2013: Weight of History, Singapore Art Museum, Singapore
《2013年收藏家展：歷史的重量》，新加坡藝術博物館，新加坡
2011 - 2012
Beijing Voice 2011: Leaving Realism Behind, Pace Beijing, Beijing, China
《北京之聲：現實主義之後》，佩斯北京，中國佩斯
2010
Roundtrip: Beijing –New York NOW, Selections From The Domus Collection, Ullens Center for Contemporary Art (UCCA), Beijing, China
《往返：北京——紐約現在，多姆斯收藏精選》，尤倫斯當代藝術中心，中國北京
2009
Red Storm, Rijksmuseum Twenthe, Enschede, Netherlands
《紅色風暴》，敦特國立美術館，荷蘭恩斯赫德
2008
Christian Dior & Chinese Artists, Ullens Center for Contemporary Art (UCCA), Beijing, China
《迪奧與中國藝術家》，尤倫斯當代藝術中心，中國北京
The Revolution Continues: New Art From China, Saatchi Gallery, London, England, UK
《革命在繼續：來自中國的新藝術》，薩奇畫廊，英國倫敦
Mahjong: Contemporary Chinese Art from the Sigg Collection, The University of California, Berkeley Art Museum, Berkeley, CA, USA Encounters, Pace Beijing, Beijing, China
《麻將——希克收藏的中國當代藝術展》，伯克利美術博物館，美國加利福尼亞
Half-Life of a Dream: Contemporary Chinese Art from the Logan Collection, San Francisco Museum of Modern Art, San Francisco, CA, USA
《夢的半衰期：來自羅根收藏的當代中國藝術》，舊金山現代美術館美國舊金山

Li Zhanyang　李占洋

Education　學歷
1994
BFA, Sculpture, Lu Xun Academy of Fine Arts, Shenyang, Liaoning, China
瀋陽魯迅美術學院雕塑系學士學位
1999
MFA, Central Academy of Fine Arts, Beijing, China
北京中央美術學院碩士學位

Selected Solo Exhibitions　挑選个展
2012
The Nightmare, Galerie Urs Meile, Beijing, China
《噩夢》麥勒畫廊，北京－盧森，中國北京
2010
Chinese Patients, White Box Museum of Art, Beijing, China
《中國病人》，白盒子藝術館，中國北京
2009
Libido, Galerie Urs Meile, Lucerne, Switzerland
《性· 情》，麥勒畫廊，北京－盧森，中國北京
2008
'Rent' – Rent Collection Yard, Galerie Urs Meile, Beijing, China
《租——收租院》，麥勒畫廊，北京－盧森，中國北京
2007
The Naked Human Body, Zhu Qizhan Art Museum, Shanghai, China
《裸露的人生》，朱屺瞻美，中國上海
2006
Scenes, Galerie Urs Meile, Lucerne, Switzerland
《場景》，麥勒畫廊，北京－盧森，中國北京
2003
Life Myriad, China Art Archives & Warehouse (CAAW), Beijing, China
《人間萬象》，藝術文件倉庫（CAAW），中國北京

Selected Group Exhibitions　挑選群展
2013
Voice of the Unseen: Chinese Independent Art Since 1979, collateral event of the 55th Venice Biennale, Venice, Italy
《未曾呈現的聲音：1979至今中國獨立藝術展》，第55屆威尼斯雙年展平行展，意大利威尼斯
2012
Magnanimity - Collection of Atypical Works by 21 Chinese Artists, White Box Museum of Art, Beijing, China
《依於仁，游於藝——21位中國藝術家代表作品展》白盒子藝術館，中國北京
National Exhibition of Artistic Works in Celebration of 85th Anniversary of the Chinese People's Liberation Army (PLA), i.e. the 12th Exhibition of Artistic Works of the Whole Army, National Art Museum of China (NAMOC), Beijing, China
《紀念中國人民解放軍85週年全國美術作品展暨第十二屆全軍美術作品展》，中國美術館，中共北京
2nd Western China International Art Biennale, TianYe Art Museum, Yinchuan, China
《第二屆中國西部國際藝術雙年展》，銀川文化藝術中心，中國寧夏銀川
Disenchantment of Chinese Imagination –The 1st Project of the 4th Guangzhou Triennial, Guangdong Museum of Art, Guangzhou, Guangdong, China
《去魅中國想像——第四屆廣州三年展項目展第一回》，廣東美術館，中國廣東廣州
2011
Start From the Horizon – Chinese Contemporary Art Since 1978, Sishang Art Museum, Beijing, China
《清晰的地平線——1978年以來的中國當代雕塑》寺上美術館，中國北京
2nd Chongqing Young Artist Biennale, Chongqing Art Museum, Chongqing, China
《第二屆重慶青年藝術家雙年展》，重慶美術館，中國重慶
Enlightenment – Datong 1st International Sculpture Biennale, Datong Art Museum, Datong, Shanxi, China
《開悟——大同國際雕塑雙年展》，大同美術館，中國山西大同

Liu Chuang　劉窗

Education　學歷
2001
MFA, Hubei Institute of Fine Arts, Wuhan, Hubei, China
湖北武漢湖北美術學院碩士學位

Selected Solo Exhibitions　挑選个展
2012
Liu Chuang: Works #16-21, Leo Xu Projects, Shanghai, China
《劉窗：第16-21＃作品展》，Leo Xu Projects，中國上海
2010
51m2: No.13 Liu Chuang, Taikang Space, Beijing, China
《51m2：13＃劉窗》，康泰空間，中國北京

Selected Group Exhibitions　挑選群展
2013
ON/OFF: China's Young Artists in Concept and Practice, Ullens Center for Contemporary Art (UCCA), Beijing, China
《ON｜OFF：中國年輕藝術家的觀念與實踐》，尤倫斯當代藝術中心，中國北京
2012
Until the End of The World, Tang Contemporary Art Beijing, Beijing, China
《直到世界盡頭》，唐人當代藝術中心，中國北京
La Chambre Claire, Taikang Space, Beijing, China
《明室》，泰康空間，中國北京
Boy: A Contemporary Portrait, Leo Xu Projects, Shanghai, China
《男孩：當代肖像》，Leo Xu Projects，中國上海
2011
51m2: 16 Emerging Chinese Artists, Taikang space, Beijing, China
《51m2：16位年輕藝術家》泰康空間，中國北京
Image-History-Existence, Taikang Art Collection, National Art Museum Of China, Beijing, China
《圖像－歷史－存在》，康泰收藏展，中國美術館，中國北京
Super-Organism CAFAM Biennale 2011, CAFA Art Museum, Beijing, China
《2011超有機 CAFAM 雙年展》，中央美術學院美術館，中國北京
Moving Image in China 1988-2011, Minsheng Art Museum, Shanghai, China
《中國影像藝術1988-2011》，民生現代美術館，中國上海
Video Wednesdays I, Gallery Espace, Lalit Kala Akadem, New Delhi, India
《Video Wednesdays I》，Gallery Escape，Lalit Kala Akademi，印度新德里
2010
China Power Station, Pinacoteca Giovanni e Marella Agnelli, Turin, Italy
《中國發電站》，Pinacoteca Giovanni e Marella Agnelli，意大利都林
Studies & Theory, Kwadrat, Berlin, Germany
《研究與理論》，Kwadrat，德國柏林
Trailer, Boers-Li Gallery, Beijing, China
《線索》，博而勵畫廊，中國北京
2009
The Generational: Younger Than Jesus, New Museum of Contemporary Art, New York, NY, USA
《世代：比耶穌年輕》，當代新美術館，美國紐約
Permanent Migrant, Inheritance – Shenzhen, Shenzhen, Guangdong, China
《永久移民》，傳承項目空間，中國廣東深圳
Just Around the Corner, Arrow Factory, Beijing, China
《就在拐角》，箭廠空間，中國北京
2008
Forever Young, Anne+ art project, Paris, France
《永葆青春》，Anne＋Art Project，法國巴黎
Insomnia, BizArt Art Center, Shanghai, China
《失眠攝影展》，比翼藝術空間，中國上海
Poznan Mediations International Biennale Of Contemporary art, Poznan, Poland
《調解》，波茲南當代藝術國際雙年展，波蘭波茲南

Liu Wei 劉韡

Education 學歷
1996
China Academy of Fine Arts, Hangzhou, Huangdong, China
浙江杭州中国美术学院
1989
Central Academy of Fine Arts, Beijing, China
北京中央美術学院

Selected Solo Exhibitions 挑選个展
2013
Lehmann Maupin, New York, NY, USA
《劉韡》，樂曼慕品畫廊，美國紐約
2012
Liu Wei: Foreign, Galerie Almine Rech, Paris, France
《劉韡個展：Foreign》，Almine Rech 畫廊，法國巴黎
Liu Wei, Long March Space, Beijing, China
《劉偉》，長征空間，中國北京
2011
Liu Wei: Trilogy, Minsheng Art Museum, Shanghai, China
《劉韡：三部曲新書發佈會》，Galleria Illy，Flos & Moroso主辦，英國倫敦
Myriad Beings, Today Art Museum, Beijing, China
《萬物》，今日美術館，中國北京
2010
Diversion Era: Liu Wei, CAN Foundation, Seoul, South Korea
《轉換的時代：劉偉》，CAN 基金會，韓國首爾
2009
The Forgotten Experience, Galerie Hussenot, Paris, France
《被遺忘的經驗》，Hussenot 畫廊，法國巴黎
Yes, That's All!, Beors-Li Gallery, Beijing, China
《對，這就是全部》，博而勵畫廊，中國北京
2007
The Outcast, Boers-Li Gallery, Beijing, China
《徘徊者》，博而勵畫廊，中國北京
Love It, Bite It, China Art Archives and Warehouse in association with Boers-Li Gallery, Beijing, China
《愛它，咬它》，藝術文獻倉庫與博而勵畫廊合作，中國北京
2006
Property of L. W., Beijing Commune, Beijing, China
《劉韡專有》，北京公社，中國北京
Purple Air, Grace Li Gallery, Zurich, Switzerland
《紫氣》，Grace Li 畫廊，瑞士蘇黎世
Love It, Bite It, BizArt, Shanghai, China
《愛它，咬它》，比翼藝術中心，中國上海
2005
Liu Wei, Courtyard Gallery, Beijing, China
《劉韡個展》，四合苑藝術空間，中國北京

Selected Group Exhibitions 挑選群展
2013
Shamans and Dissent, West Heavens- Artist Dispatch Project Exhibition, Hanart Square, Hong Kong
《巫士與意見》，西天中土——藝術家特派展，漢雅軒畫廊，香港
EXPO 1: New York, MoMA PS1, Long Island City, NY, USA
《EXPO 1: 紐約》，MoMA PS1，紐約長島
Every Day Matters, Faurschou Foundation, Copenhagen, Denmark
《日常瑣事》，林冠藝術基金會，丹麥哥本哈根
Sharjah Biennial 11: Re:emerge, Towards a New Cultural Cartography, Sharjah, UAE
《沙迦雙年展——重現新的文化製圖》，阿聯酋沙迦

Qiu Zhijie 邱志傑

Education 學歷
1992
BFA, Printmaking Department, China National Academy of Fine Arts, Hangzhou, Huangdong, China
浙江杭州中國美術學院版畫系學士學位

Selected Solo Exhibitions 挑選个展
2013
Bird Eye View, Hanart TZ Gallery, Hong Kong
《鳥瞰》，漢雅軒畫廊，香港
The Universe of Naming, Spring Workshop, Hong Kong
《命名世界》，Spring Workshop，香港
The Unicorn and the Dragon, Foundation Querini Stampalia, Venice, Italy
《獨角獸和龍》，Foundation Querini Stampalia，意大利威尼斯
2012
Bi-Cities Exhibitions of Chinese new painting: Qiu Zhijie-Tathagata, Tian Ren He Yi Art Center, Hangzhou, Huangdong, China
《雙城記‧ 中國新繪畫系列個展：邱志傑——如來》，天仁合藝藝術中心，中國杭州
Blueprints, Witte de With, Rotterdam, Netherlands
《藍圖》，With De Witte 藝術中心，荷蘭鹿特丹
2011
Qiu Zhijie: DEJA VU, Hanart TZ Gallery, Hong Kong
《邱志傑：似曾相識》，漢雅軒畫廊，香港
Energy, Times Square, Hong Kong
《能量》，時代廣場，香港
Cell, Pace Beijing, Beijing, China
《細胞》，佩斯北京，中國北京
2009
Mochou: Recent Works by Qiu Zhijie, Chambers Fine Art, New York, NY, USA
《莫愁：邱志傑近作》，前波畫廊，美國紐約
A Suicidology of The Nanjing Yangtze River Bridge 4 - Twilight of the idols, The House of World Cultures, Berlin, Germany
《南京長江大橋自殺現象干預計劃之四：偶像的黃昏》，世界文化宮，德國柏林
A Suicidology of The Nanjing Yangtze River Bridge 3 - Breaking through the ice, Ullens Center for Contemporary Art (UCCA), Beijing, China
《南京長江大橋自殺現象干預計劃之三：破冰》，尤倫斯當代藝術中心，中國北京
2008
A Suicidology of The Nanjing Yangtze River Bridge 1 - Ataraxic of Zhuang Zi, Shanghai Zendai Museum of Modern Art, Shanghai, China
《南京長江大橋自殺現象干預計劃之一：庄子的鎮靜劑》，正大現代藝術館，中國上海
A Suicidology of The Nanjing Yangtze River Bridge 2 -The Bridge, Nanjing, Under the Heaven, The Singapore Tyler Print Institute, Singapore
《南京長江大橋自殺現象干預計劃之二：大橋，南京，天下》泰勒版畫院，新加坡
Mochou, Chambers Fine Art, Beijing, China
《莫愁》，前波畫廊，中國北京
The Bridge, Nanjing, Under the Heaven, Hanart Gallery, Hong Kong
《大橋，南京，天下》，漢雅軒畫廊，香港
Nanjing: A bridge, A City, Guanxiang Art Center, Taipei, Taiwan
《南京：一座橋和一座城市，觀想藝術中心，台灣台北
2007
The Shape of Time, Chambers Fine Art, New York, NY, USA
《時間的形狀》，前波畫廊，美國紐約
Cryptogram: Qiu Zhijie in Untersberg, Hanart Gallery, Hong Kong
《密碼》，漢雅軒畫廊，香港
Archeology of Memory, Long March Space, Beijing, China
《記憶考古》，長征空間，中國北京

Shang Yixin 尚一心

Education 學歷
2007
MFA in Oil Painting, China Academy of Arts, Beijing, China
北京中國美術學院油畫系碩士學位
1999
Graduated from the Affiliated School of China Academy of Arts,
Beijing, China
北京中央美術學院附屬中等美術學校

Selected Solo Exhibitions 挑選个展
2007
Cancels?Restarts?, Red Bridge Gallery, Shanghai, China
《註銷？重啓？》紅橋畫廊，中國上海

Selected Group Exhibitions 挑選群展
2013
ON/OFF: China's Young Artists in Concept and Practice, Ullens
Center for Contemporary Art (UCCA), Beijing, China
《ON|OFF：中國年輕藝術家的觀念與實踐》，尤倫斯當代藝術中
心，中國北京
2011
Nothing White, J Gallery, Shanghai, China
《白相》，J畫廊，中國上海
Paint Beyond the Frame, FEIZI Gallery, Shanghai, China
《沒有邊框的繪畫》，FEIZI 畫廊，中國上海
Echo: Mind-in-Hands, PIFO New Art Gallery, Beijing, China
《圖畫手工》，偏鋒新藝術空間，中國北京
Micro Life, Soka Art Center, Beijing, China
《微生活》，索卡藝術中心，中國北京
Painting Lesson I: Illusion or Delusion, Gallery Yang, Beijing, China
《繪畫課I：錯覺與幻象》，楊畫廊，中國北京
2010
Optical via invisibility, In-Shine Gallery, Beijing, China
《視而不見》，印象空間，中國北京
Hands On No.3 - Obsessive Compulsive Disorder, DDMWareHouse,
Shanghai, China
《手感3——強迫症》，東大名創庫，中國上海
Invisible Wings, Times Art Museum, Beijing, China
《隱形的翅膀》，時代美術館，中國北京
The Youths Upstairs, Times Art Museum, Beijing, China
《樓上的青年》，時代美術館，中國北京
Free Terminology Contemporary Art Exhibition, A4 Gallery, Chengdu,
Sichuan, China
《自由的術語——當代藝術展》，A4畫廊，中國成都
2009
Points & Crosses- Exhibition of Contemporary Painting in China,
2010 Arts Centre, Shanghai, China
《時空的經緯——中國當代藝術邀請展》，上海2010藝術中心，
Blank3: Making life, Medium Art Centre, Beijing, China
《空白展3：製造生活》，中間美術館，中國北京

Wang Guangle 王光樂

Education 學歷
2000
BFA in Oil Painting, Central Academy of Fine Arts, Beijing, China
北京中央美術學院油畫系學士學位

Selected Solo Exhibitions 挑選个展
2012
Wang Guangle, Pace New York, NY, USA
《王光樂》，佩斯畫廊，美國紐約
2011
Wang Guangle, Beijing Commune, Beijing, China
《王光樂》，北京公社，中國北京
2009
Wang Guangle, Beijing Commune, Beijing, China
《王光樂》，北京公社，中國北京
2007
Coffin Paint, aye gallery, Beijing, China
《壽漆》，aye畫廊，中國北京
2005
Waterstone, Onemoon gallery, Beijing, China
《漢語》，一月當代畫廊，中國北京

Selected Group Exhibitions 挑選群展
2013
ON/OFF: China's Young Artists in Concept and Practice, Ullens
Center for Contemporary Art (UCCA), Beijing, China
《ON|OFF：中國年輕藝術家的觀念與實踐》，尤倫斯當代藝術中
心，中國北京
Nothing White, Gland Space, Beijing, China
《白相》，Gland空間，中國北京
2012
Spin: The First Decade of the New Century, Today Art Museum,
Beijing, China
《自旋：新世紀的十年》，今日美術館，中國北京
Re: Painting, Platform China, Beijing, China
《再繪畫》，站台中國，中國北京
CAFAM • Future, CAFA Art Museum, Beijing, China
《CAFAM· 未來展》，中央美術學院美術館，中國北京
Water Stains on The Wall-The Carrier of Formation, Zhejiang Art
Museum, Hangzhou, Zhejiang, China
《屋漏痕——形式的承載》，浙江美術館，中國浙江杭州
Face, Minsheng Art Museum, Shanghai, China
《開放的肖像》，民生現代美術館，中國上海
2011
Beijing Voice 2011: Leaving Realism Behind, Pace Beijing, Beijing,
China
《北京之聲：現實主義之後》，佩斯北京，中國北京
Chinese Abstract Slow Art, Singer Laren Museum, Laren,
Netherlands
《中國抽象慢藝術》，辛格美術館，荷蘭拉倫
Dissociation: 2011 Art Changsha, Hunan Provincial Museum,
Changsha, China
《解離：2011藝術長沙》湖南省博物館，中國湖南長沙
Fly Through the Troposphere - Memo of The New Generation
Painting, Iberia Center for Contemporary Art, Beijing, China
《飛越對流層：新一代繪畫備忘錄》，伊比利亞當代藝術中心，中
國北京
Panting Lesson I: Illusion or Delusion, Gallery Yang, Beijing, China
《繪畫課I：錯覺與幻象》，楊畫廊，中國北京
Extract: The 3rd Stall Keeper Show, C5 Art, Beijing, China
《擺攤第三回：抽——青年藝術家匿名展》，西五藝術中心，中
國北京
Decade of the Rabbit, White Rabbit Art Museum, Sydney, Australia
《十年白兔》，白兔美術館，澳大利亞悉尼

Wang Xingwei 王興偉

Education 學歷
1990
BFA, Shenyang Normal University, Shenyang, Liaoning, China
遼寧瀋陽師範學院學士學位

Selected Solo Exhibitions 挑選个展
2013
Wang Xingwei, Ullens Center for Contemporary Art (UCCA), Beijing, China
《王興偉》，尤倫斯當代藝術中心（UCCA），中國北京
Wang Xingwei (Sketches), 01100001 Gallery, Beijing, China
《王興偉（草圖）》，01100001畫廊，中國北京
2011
Wang Xingwei, Galerie Urs Meile, Beijing, China; Lucerne, Switzerland
《王興偉》麥勒畫廊 北京－盧森,中國北京
2008
Wang Xingwei – one-man show, Galerie Urs Meile, Beijing, China
《王興偉——個人展》，麥勒畫廊 北京－盧森,中國北京
2007
Wang Xingwei – Large Rowboat, Galerie Urs Meile, Beijing, China; Lucerne, Switzerland
《王興偉——大划船》，麥勒畫廊 北京－盧森,中國北京
《王興偉——大划船》，麥勒畫廊 北京－盧森, 瑞士盧森
2004
Interlinked Dreams, Galerie Urs Meile, Lucerne, Switzerland
《交織的夢》，麥勒畫廊 北京－盧森, 瑞士盧森
2003
Fostered Art, ShanghArt Gallery, Shanghai, China
《過繼》，上海香閣納畫廊，中國上海
2001
Still Paint – Wang Xingwei & Chen Danqing, China Art Archives & Warehouse (CAAW), Beijing, China
《還在畫畫——王興偉和陳丹青》，藝術文件倉庫（CAAW），中國北京

Selected Group Exhibitions 挑選群展
2013
Duchamp and/or/in China, Ullens Center for Contemporary Art (UCCA), Beijing, China
《杜尚與／或／在中國》，尤倫斯當代藝術中心（UCCA），中國北京
2012
Go Figure! Contemporary Chinese Portraiture, National Portrait Gallery, Canberra; Sherman Contemporary Art Foundation, Sydney, Australia
《象想！中國當代肖像展》，國立肖像美術館，堪培拉；舍曼當代藝術基金會，澳大利亞悉尼
CAPITAL. Merchants in Venice and Amsterdam, Swiss National Museum, Zurich, Switzerland
《CAPITAL——商人在威尼斯和阿姆斯特丹》，瑞士國家博物館，瑞士蘇黎世
The 7th Shenzhen Sculpture Biennale - Accidental Message: Art is Not a System, Not a World, He Xiangning Museum OCT Contemporary Art Terminal (OCAT), Shenzhen, Guangdong, China
《第七屆深圳雕塑雙年展——偶然的信息：藝術不是一個體系，也不是一個世界》，何香凝美術館　OCT當代藝術中心，中國廣東深圳
Face, Minsheng Art Museum, Shanghai, China
《開放的肖像》，民生現代美術館，中國上海
2011
Picture•History•Existence – Taikang Life Art Collection 15th Anniversary Exhibition of Taikang Life Insurance Stock Co., Ltd, National Art Museum of China (NAMOC), Beijing, China
《圖像· 歷史· 存在——泰康人壽保險股份有限公司成立15週年藝術品收藏展》，中國美術館，中國北京

Xie Molin 谢墨凛

Education 學歷
2007
MFA, Edinburgh College of Art, Edinburgh, Scotland
英国爱丁堡美术学院绘画专业
2003
BA, Central Academy of Fine Arts, Beijing, China
中国中央美术学院壁画系

Selected Solo Exhibitions 挑選个展
2012
Xie Molin, Beijing Commune, Beijing, China
《谢墨凛》, 北京公社, 北京, 中国
2011
XYZ, Space Station Gallery, Beijing, China
"XYZ", 空间站画廊, 北京, 中国群展

Selected Group Exhibitions 挑選群展
2013
ON/OFF: China's Young Artists in Concept and Practice, Ullens Center for Contemporary Art (UCCA), Beijing, China
《ON|OFF：中國年輕藝術家的觀念與實踐》，尤倫斯當代藝術中心，中國北京
2011
Beijing Voice 2011: Leaving Realism Behind, Pace Beijing, Beijing, China
《现实主义之后》,佩斯北京,北京,中国
First Issue: SH Contemporary Special Projects 2011, Shanghai, China
《首届展览》项目,上海当代国际博览会,上海,中国
Nothing White, J Gallery, Shanghai, China
《白相》,J画廊,上海,中国
Breaking Away – An Abstract Art exhibition, Boers-Li Gallery, Beijing, China
《决绝》,Boers-Li画廊,北京,中国
2010
The 5th A+A, PIFO Gallery, Beijing, China
《A+A》第五回展,偏锋新艺术空间,北京,中国
2009
BLANK: Making Life, Inside-Out Art Museum, Beijing, China
《制造生活-2009空白展》,中间艺术馆,北京,中国
In the Making- 2009 BCA Market Summer, Beijing Center for the Arts, Beijing, China
《全手工-夏季艺术市集》,天安时间当代艺术中心,北京,中国
2007
Joint Exhibition of Drawings, Edinburgh College of Art, Edinburgh, Scotland
《纸上作品联展》,爱丁堡艺术学院与查尔斯王子绘画学校，爱丁堡/伦敦,英国
On the Rock lighthouse: ECA M.F.A. Student Group Show, Edinburgh College of Art, Edinburgh, Scotland
《在石头上》爱丁堡艺术学院研究生Lighthouse展
Royal Scottish Academy Student Exhibition (Hope Scottish Trust Award for an Outstanding Postgraduate Student Work), Royal Scottish Academy, Edinburgh, Scotland
《苏格兰皇家学院学生作品展》（获"Hope Scottish Trust"奖）
Seawhite material prize: ECA January exhibition, Edinburgh College of Art, Edinburgh, Scotland
《爱丁堡艺术学院一月展》（获"Sea White Material奖）

Xu Zhen 徐震

Education 學歷
1996
Shanghai School of Arts and Crafts, Shanghai, China
上海市工藝美術學校

Selected Solo Exhibitions 挑選个展
2013
Light Source, Tian Ren He Yi Art Center, Hangzhou, Zhejiang, China
《光源》，天仁合藝術中心，中國杭州
Movement field, Long March Space, Beijing, China
《運動場》，長征空間，中國北京
Offsite, Vancouver Artgallery, Vancouver, British Columbia, Canada
《平靜》，溫哥華美術館，加拿大不列顛哥倫比亞
2012
Movement – Madeln Company, Madeln Company Exhibition Space, Shanghai, China
《運動——沒頂公司》，沒頂公司展廳，中國上海
Sleeping Life Away – Madeln Company Solo Exhibition, Galerie Nathalie Obadia, Paris, France
《醉生夢死——沒頂公司個展》，Galerie Nathalie Obadia，法國巴黎
2011
Action of Consciousness, ShanghART Gallery, Shanghai, China
《意識行動》，香格納畫廊，中國上海
Physique of Consciousness, Long March Space, Beijing, China; Kunsthalle Bern, Bern, Switzerland
《意識形狀》，長征空間，中國北京
《意識形狀》，伯爾尼美術館，瑞士伯爾尼
2010
Don't Hang Your Faith on the Wall, Long March Space, Beijing, China
《不要把信仰掛在牆上》，長征空間，中國北京
Seeing One's Own Eyes, IKON Gallery, Birmingham, England, UK
《看見自己的眼睛》，IKON美術館，英國伯明翰
Spread - by Madeln at ShanghART Beijing Solo Exhibition, ShanghART Beijing, Beijing, China
《蔓延到北京——沒頂北京個展》，香格納畫廊，中國北京
2009
Metal language, ShanghART Gallery, Shanghai, China
《金屬的語言》，香格納畫廊，中國北京
Madeln – Seeing One's Own Eyes - europalia. china, S.M.A.K, Ghent, Belgium
《沒頂——看見自己的眼睛 – europalia china》，S.M.A.K，比利時根特
Lonely Miracle: Middle East Contemporary Art, James Cohan Gallery, New York, NY, USA
《孤獨的奇蹟：中東當代藝術展》，James Cohan畫廊，美國紐約
Seeing One's Own Eyes - Middle East Contemporary Art, ShanghART Gallery & H-Space, Shanghai, China
《看見自己的眼睛——中東當代藝術展》，香格納畫廊＆H空間，中國上海

Selected Group Exhibitions 挑選群展
2013
China China, PinchukArtCenter, Kyiv, Ukraine
《中國中國》，平丘克藝術中心，烏克蘭基輔
Green Box: Remapping - The Space of Media Reality, Tianhong Mei Heyuan Arts Center, Hangzhou, Zhejiang, China
《綠盒子：重繪形貌——媒體現實的空間》，天鴻美和院文化藝術發展中心，中國浙江杭州

Yan Xing 鄢醒

Education 學歷
2009
BFA in Oil Painting, Sichuan Fine Arts Institute, Chongqing, China
四川美術學院油畫系學士學位

Selected Solo Exhibitions 挑選个展
2013
Recent Works, Galerie Urs Meile, Beijing, China
《近作》，麥勒畫廊 北京 – 盧森，中國北京
2012
Yan Xing, Chinese Arts Centre, Manchester, England, UK
《鄢醒》，華人藝術中心，英國曼徹斯特
2011
REALISM, Galerie Urs Meile, Beijing, China
《現實主義》，麥勒畫廊 北京 – 盧森，中國北京

Selected Group Exhibitions 挑選群展
2013
Art Unlimited - Art Basel, Messe Basel, Messeplatz, Basel, Switzerland
《無限意想》，巴塞爾藝術博覽會，瑞士巴塞爾
Future Generation Art Prize@Venice 2013, collateral event of the 55th Venice Biennale, Palazzo Contarini Polignac, Venice, Italy
《2013威尼斯未來世代藝術獎》，第55屆威尼斯雙年展平行展，Contarini Polignac宮殿，意大利威尼斯
China China, PinchukArtCentre, Kiev, Ukraine
《中國中國》，平丘克藝術中心，烏克蘭基輔
The Experimental Practices from the Oil Painting Department of Sichuan Fine Arts Institute, Suzhou Art Museum, Suzhou, Jiangsu, China
《來自四川美術學院油畫系20年的實驗與實踐》蘇州美術館，中國江蘇蘇州
ON/OFF: China's Young Artists in Concept and Practice, Ullens Center for Contemporary Art (UCCA), Beijing, China
《ON|OFF：中國年輕藝術家的觀念與實踐》，尤倫斯當代藝術中心，中國北京
2012
Art Kabinett at Art Basel Miami Beach, Miami Beach Convention Center, Miami, FL, USA
《藝術私房》，邁阿密海灘巴塞爾藝術展，邁阿密海灘會議中心，美國佛羅里達邁阿密
Perspectives 180-Unfinished Country: New Video from China, Zilkha Gallery, Contemporary Arts Museum Houston (CAMH), Houston, TX, USA
《未完成的國度：來自中國的新錄像》，休斯頓當代美術館，美國得克薩斯州休斯頓
Future Generation Art Prize - Finalists Exhibition, PinchukArtCentre, Kiev, Ukraine
《未來世代藝術獎入圍展》，平丘克藝術中心，烏克蘭基輔
CAFAM • Future, CAFA Art Museum, Beijing, China
《CAFAM · 未來展》，中央美術學院美術館，中國北京
Exhibition of Young Artist Experimental Season 2nd Round, A4 Contemporary Arts Center, Chengdu, Sichuan, China
《青年藝術家實驗季第二回展覽》，A4當代藝術中心，中國四川成都
The III Moscow International Biennale for Young Art, Central House of Artists (CHA), Moscow, Russia
《第三屆莫斯科青年藝術雙年展》，中央藝術之家，俄羅斯莫斯科
The Seventh Shenzhen Sculpture Biennale, He Xiangning Museum OCT Contemporary Art Terminal (OCAT), Shenzhen, Guangdong, China
《第七屆深圳雕塑雙年展 》，何香凝美術館　OCT當代藝術中心，中國廣東深圳
Focus on Talents Project - Finalists Exhibition, Today Art Museum, Beijing, China
《關注未來藝術英才計劃》入圍展，今日美術館，中國北京
The Untouchables, Saamlung Gallery, Hong Kong
《不可觸摸》，Saamlung畫廊，香港

Zhang Enli 張恩利

Education 學歷
1989
Arts & Design Institute of Wuxi Technical University, Jiangsu, China
江蘇無錫輕工業大學藝術學院

Selected Solo Exhibitions 挑選个展
2013
Landscape, Museo d'Arte contemporanea di Villa Croce, Genova, Italy
《風景》，Villa Croce當代藝術博物館，意大利熱那亞
Space Painting, Institute of Contemporary Arts, London, England, UK
《空間繪畫》，現代藝術機構，英國倫敦
2012
Hauser & Wirth, Zurich, Switzerland
《表皮》，Hauser & With，瑞士蘇黎世
2011
Zhang Enli, Hauser & Wirth, New York, NY
《張恩利個展》，Hauser & With，美國紐約
Zhang Enli, China Art Museum, Shanghai, China
《張恩利個展》，民生現代美術館，中國上海
2010
Zhang Enli, Minsheng Art Museum, Shanghai, China
《張恩利個展》，民生現代美術館，中國上海
Zhang Enli, Hauser & Wirth London, London, England, UK
《張恩利個展》，Hauser & With，英國倫敦
2009
Zhang Enli, Kunsthalle Bern, Berne, Switzerland; Ikon Gallery, Birmingham, England, UK
《張恩利個展》，IKON美術館，英國伯明翰
2008
Zhang Enli, ShanghART H-Space, Shanghai, China
《張恩利個展》，香格納H空間，中國上海
2007
Zhang Enli, Hauser & Wirth Zürich, Zurich, Switzerland
《張恩利個展》，Hauser & With，瑞士蘇黎世
2004
Human, Too Human, BizArt, Shanghai, China
《個性的，太人性的》，比翼藝術中心，中國上海
2000
Dancing, ShanghART F-Space, Shanghai, China
《舞蹈》，香格納畫廊主空間，中國上海

Selected Group Exhibitions 挑選群展
2013
Metropolis: Reflections on the Modern City, Birmingham Museum and Art Gallery, Birmingham, England, UK
《大都市：現代城市的思考》，伯明翰美術館，英國伯明翰
O'Clock. time design, design time, CAFA Art Museum, Beijing, China
《時鐘，時間設計，設計時間》，中央美術學院，中國北京
2012
Kochi-Muziris Biennale 2012, Kochi, India
《Kochi – Muziris印度雙年展》，印度柯枝
Place of Residence, ShanghART, Shanghai, China
《居住地》，香格納畫廊，中國上海

Zhang Huan 張洹

Education 學歷
1993
MFA, Central Academy of Fine Arts, Beijing, China
北京中央美術學院碩士學位
1988
BA, He Nan University, Kai Feng, Henan , China
河南開封河南大學學士學位

Selected Solo Exhibitions 挑選个展
2013
Looking East, Facing West: The World of Zhang Huan, Frederik Meijer Gardens & Sculpture Park, Grand Rapids Charter Township, MI, USA
《看東方，看西方：張洹的世界》，Frederik Meijer園林雕塑公園，美國密西根
Zhang Huan: Soul and Matter, Palazzo Vecchio and Forte di Belvedere, Florence, Italy
《張洹：靈魂與物質》，韋奇奧宮和貝爾韋代雷城堡，意大利佛羅薩倫
2012
Zhang Huan: Ash Paintings and Memory Doors, Art Gallery of Ontario, Toronto, Canada
《張洹：香灰畫和記憶們》，安大略美術館，加拿大多倫多
Zhang Huan: The Mountain is Still a Mountain, White Cube, London, England, UK
《張洹：看山還是山》，白立方，英國倫敦
Zhang Huan: Jin Hui Dui, Gallery 100, Taipei, Taiwan
《張洹》錦灰堆》，百藝畫廊，台灣台北
2011
Zhang Huan: Q Confucius, Rockbund Art Museum, Shanghai, China
《張洹：問孔子》，上海外灘美術館，中國上海
Zhang Huan: 49 Days, Blum & Poe, Los Angeles, CA, USA
《張洹：49天》Blum & Poe畫廊，美國洛杉磯
Zhang Huan: East Wind, West Wind, Espace Louis Vuittion Macao, Macao
《張洹：西風再渡》，澳門路易威登藝術空間，澳門
Zhang Huan: Aura of Disappearance, Edouard Malingue Gallery, in Cooperation with The Pace Gallery, Hong Kong
《張洹：消失的氛圍》馬凌畫廊，和佩斯畫廊合作，香港
Zhang Huan: Ash Banquet, ProjectB Gallery, Milan, Italy
《張洹：灰宴》，ProjectB畫廊，意大利米蘭
2010
Zhang Huan: Dawn of Time, China Art Museum, Shanghai, China
《張洹：創世紀》，中國美術館，中國上海
Amituofo: A Solo Exhibition by Zhang Huan, Museum of Contemporary Art Taipei, Taipei, Taiwan
《阿彌陀佛：張洹個人展》，台北當代藝術館，台灣台北
Zhang Huan: Ashman, PAC Museum, Milan, Italy
《張洹：香灰俠》，PAC美術館，意大利米蘭
Zhang Huan: Free Tiger Returns to Mountains, Pace Beijing, Beijing, China
《張洹：放虎歸山》，佩斯北京，中國北京
Zhang Huan: Hope Tunnel, Ullens Center for Contemporary Art (UCCA), Beijing, China
《張洹：希望隧道》，尤倫斯當代藝術中心，中國北京
Zhang Huan, Hakgojae Gallery, Seoul, Korea
《張洹》，學古齋畫廊，韓國首爾
2009
Semele Opera (Director & Set Designer), Theatre Royal de La Monnaie I de Munt, Brussels, Belgium; Poly Theatre, Beijing, China (2010); Four Seasons Centre for the Performing Arts, Toronto, Canada (2012)
《歌劇塞美麗（導演及舞台設計）》馬內皇家歌劇院，比利時布魯塞爾；北京保利劇院（2010）；加拿大多倫多四季表演中心（2012）
Neither Coming Nor Going, PaceWildenstein, New York, NY, USA
《不來也不去》，佩斯畫廊，美國紐約

ZHAO YAO 趙要

Education 學歷
2004
BFA, Sichuan Fine Arts Institute, Chongqing, China
四川美術學院學士學位

Selected Solo Exhibitions 挑選个展
2013
Spirit Above All, Pace London gallery, London, England, UK
《精神高於一切》，佩斯倫敦，英國倫敦
2012
Zhao Yao: You Can't See Me, You Can't See Me, Beijing Commune, Beijing, China
《趙要：你看不見我，你看不見我》，北京公社，中國北京
2011
Zhao Yao: I am Your Night, Beijing Commune, Beijing, China
《趙要：我是你的黑夜》，北京公社，中國北京
2009
52m2: 3# Zhao Yao, Taikang Space, Beijing, China
《52m2：＃3趙要》，泰康空間，中國北京

Selected Group Exhibitions 挑選群展
2013
ON/OFF: China's Young Artists in Concept and Practice, Ullens Center for Contemporary Art (UCCA), Beijing, China
《ON|OFF：中國年輕藝術家的觀念與實踐》，尤倫斯當代藝術中心，中國北京
China China, PinchukArtCenter, Kyiv, Ukraine
《中國中國》，平丘克藝術中心，烏克蘭基輔
2012
Global Groove 1973/2012, Edythe and Eli Broad Art Museum, Lansing, MI, USA
《全球槽1973/2012》，Eli and Edythe Broad Art Museum，美國密西根
2011
The Knife's Edge: Video Recently Seen In Beijing, Fremantle Arts Centre, Fremantle, Australia
《刀鋒：最近在北京看過的視頻》，費里曼特爾藝術中心，澳大利亞費里曼特爾
51m2: 16 Emerging Chinese Artists, Taikang Space, Beijing, China
《51平方：16微年輕藝術家》，泰康空間，中國北京
2010
Seven Young Artists, Beijing Commune, Beijing, China
《七個年輕藝術家》，北京公社，中國北京
No Soul for Sale – A Festival of Independents, Tate Modern Museum, London, England, UK
《靈魂不可出賣》，泰特現代美術館，英國倫敦
Move on Asia: The End of Video Art, Alternative Space LOOP, Seoul, Korea; Para/Site Art Space, Hong Kong
《移動的亞洲影像展》，LOOP藝術中心，韓國首爾；Para／Site藝術空間，中國香港
DISCOVERIES 2010: Re-value, ShContemporary10, Shanghai Exhibition Center, Shanghai, China
《發現2010：價值重構》，上海當代藝術博覽會，上海展覽中心，中國上海
ReFlection of Minds-MoCA Shanghai Envisage III, Museum Of Contemporary Art, Shanghai, China
《心境──上海當代藝術館文獻展III》，上海當代藝術館，中國上海
2010 Get It Louder: Sharism, Sanlitun SOHO, Beijing, China
《2010大聲展：分享主義》，三里屯SOHO，中國北京
Media Landscape-Zone East, Korean Cultural Centre, London, England, UK
《媒體風貌──東部地帶》，韓國文化中心，英國倫敦
Conception as Enzyme, A4 Contemporary Arts Center, Chengdu, Sichuan, China
《概念之酶》，A4藝術中心，中國成都

Zhu Jinshi 朱金石

Education 學歷
1977
Central Academy of Fine Arts, Beijing, China
中國北京中央美术学院
1994
Architecture Department lectureship at Berlin Technical University, Berlin, Germany
任柏林TU大學建築系講師

Selected Solo Exhibitions 挑選个展
2013
Art Emperor, Pearl Lam Galleries, Hong Kong, China
《香港藝術門：【朱金石：厚繪畫】個展》，對比窗藝廊，中國香港
Zhu Jinshi: The Reality of Paint, Pearl Lam Galleries, Hong Kong, China
《厚绘画》，對比窗藝廊，中國香港
Boat, Pearl Lam Galleries at Art13, London, England, UK
《船》，對比窗藝廊在Art13，英國伦敦，英国
2012
Boat, Pearl Lam Galleries Special Project Space, Shanghai, China
《船》，對比窗藝廊，中國上海
Zhu Jinshi, Blum & Poe, Los Angeles, CA, USA
《朱金石個展》，Blum & Poe，美國洛杉磯
2010
New Abstract, Gallery 604, Busan, South Korea
《新抽象》，604畫廊，韓國釜山
Shinsegae Gallery, Busan, South Korea
《Hongje畫廊／Shinsegae畫廊》，韓國首爾
2009
Social Chromatology, Joy Art Space, Beijing, China
《社會色彩學》，卓越藝術空間，中國北京
2008
Power and Jiangshan, Arario Gallery, Beijing, China
《權利與江山》，阿拉里裡奧畫廊，中國北京
2007
Four Tables, Courtyard Gallery, Beijing, China
《四張桌子》，四合院畫廊，中國北京
2006
Plane Pattern, Tongzhou Private Art Center, Beijing, China
《平面方式》，通州私人藝術中心，中國北京
2002
On the Road, Prague City Museum, Prague, Czech Republic
《在路上》，布拉格市立美術館，捷克

Selected Group Exhibitions 挑選群展
2012
Alone Together, Rubell Family Collection, Miami, FL
《一起孤單》，盧貝爾家族收藏博物館，美國邁阿密
Chinese Contemporary Abstract, 1980s Until Present: MINDMAP, Pearl Lam Galleries, Hong Kong
《中國現代抽象，1980至今：MINDMAP》，對比窗藝廊，中國香港
Pearl Lam Galleries at Art Stage Singapore, Marina Bay Sands, Singapore
《藝術登陸新加坡2012博覽會》，對比窗藝廊，浜海灣金沙會展中心，新加坡
2011
ArtHK 2011, Pearl Lam Fine Art, Hong Kong
《香港藝博會2011》，對比窗藝廊，中國香港
China International Gallery Exposition 2011 (CIGE), Pearl Lam Galleries, Beijing, China
《中國國際畫廊展2011（CIGE）》，對比窗藝廊，中國北京
Wu Ming, Form is Formless: Chinese Contemporary Abstract Art, Pearl Lam Galleries, Shanghai, China

THIS EXHIBITION WOULD NOT BE POSSIBLE WITHOUT THE FOLLOWING
本次展览之所以成功有赖以下各位

Aike-Dellarco, Shanghai and Torino
Beijing Commune, Beijing
Boers-Li Gallery, Beijing
Bonhams, New York
Gladstone Gallery, Brussels and New York
Hauser & Wirth, London and Zurich
Pearl Lam Galleries, Hong Kong and Shanghai
Long March Space, Beijing
Lehmann Maupin, Hong Kong and New York
Galerie Urs Meile, Beijing and Lucerne
Pace Gallery, Beijing, London and New York
Phillips de Pury & Company, New York
Platform China, Beijing
Max Protetch Gallery, New York
Sotheby's, New York
White Space, Beijing

SPECIAL THANKS TO ALL OF THE ARTISTS IN THE EXHIBITION AND
特别鸣谢此展览中的所有艺术家和以下各位

Lorenz Helbling
Hu Junjun
Pearl Lam
Rachel Lehmann
Leng Lin
Lu Jie
Lu Jingjing
Luluc Huang
Urs Miele
Karin Seiz
Natalie Sun
Tian Yuan
Philip Tinari
David Tung
Nina Wang
Zhang Di
Xiaoming Zhang
Judy Yi Zhou